GARY LEISER is the author of many scholarly articles and several books on medieval Islamic topics. These include *Questions and Answers for Physicians: A Medieval Arabic Study Manual* (2004), the translation of M. F. Köprülü's iconic *Early Mystics in Turkish Literature* (with Robert Dankoff, 2006), and *Turkish Language, Literature, and History: Travelers' Tales, Sultans, and Scholars since the Eighth Century* (edited with Bill Hickman, 2015). He holds a Ph.D. in Middle Eastern History from the University of Pennsylvania.

"Gary Leiser's book is based on an exhaustive examination and interrogation of primary texts and secondary studies. His lively coverage of prostitution and sex in the Near East is both broad and probing. He ranges across a very long period that encompassed several profound political shifts and cultural transformations. His impressive command of the specialized vocabulary requisite to accurate translations is apparent throughout. There is nothing comparable in the field at present, and the sheer scope of this book means it is unlikely to be superseded any time soon. The research on which it is based is thoroughly comprehensive, while its zesty style of presentation persuasively supports the author's objectives: his use of illustrative anecdotes is a highly successful means of capturing and holding the reader's attention."

Carl F. Petry, Professor of Middle East Studies and Professor of Teaching Excellence, Northwestern University, author of *The Criminal Underworld in a Medieval Islamic Society* and editor of *The Cambridge History of Egypt Volume One: Islamic Egypt, 640–1517*

PROSTITUTION IN THE EASTERN MEDITERRANEAN WORLD

THE ECONOMICS OF SEX IN THE LATE ANTIQUE AND MEDIEVAL MIDDLE EAST

Gary Leiser

I.B. TAURIS
LONDON · NEW YORK

Published in 2017 by
I.B.Tauris & Co. Ltd
London • New York
www.ibtauris.com

ISBN: 978 1 78453 652 7
eISBN: 978 1 78672 086 3
ePDF: 978 1 78673 086 2

A full CIP record for this book is available from the British Library
A full CIP record is available from the Library of Congress
Library of Congress Catalog Card Number: available

Text designed and typeset by Tetragon, London
Printed and bound by CPI Group (UK) Ltd, Croydon, CR0 4YY

MIX
Paper from responsible sources
FSC® C013604

In recollection of a unique constellation of scholars and teachers of Middle Eastern history and culture at the University of Pennsylvania in the early 1970s: Schuyler Cammann, Noel Coulson, Shelomo Goitein, Albert Hourani, Halil İnalcık, George Makdisi, and Thomas Naff.

Contents

List of Illustrations

Maps (courtesy Beca Lafore)

Figures

Preface

No book has been written on the history of prostitution in Southwest Asia, the modern Middle East, in the Middle Ages. The present work, although confined to the lands of the Eastern Mediterranean world, therefore represents the first word on this subject. It will not be the last. It is meant, above all, to establish a rough framework for further research, answer some basic questions, and provoke others. Indeed, much of the material presented here has implications that warrant further investigation.

Until fairly recently, scholars in the West and the Middle East have not deemed sexuality to be an appropriate field of research in our place and time. On the whole, they have approached this subject tepidly, and chiefly with regard to the early modern and modern eras, for which the sources are easier to identify. In fact, in the West the subject of sexuality in the Middle East had long been, at most, marginalized for the titillation of a select group—scholars and clergy trained in the classical languages. While reading Edward Gibbons' *History of the Decline and Fall of the Roman Empire*, it is amusing to see how he switches from English to Latin when the topic of sex arises. W. K. Lowther Clarke toned down the language on sexual temptations in his English translation from Greek of the *Lausiac History of Palladius*, which he published in 1918. This Greek account of the lives of the saints in the Eastern Mediterranean was fine for the monks (saints!)

in the desert who read the original, but it was not fitting for the modern gentle Christian reader. Even in the mid-twentieth century, the renowned Arabist and Islamist Giorgio Levi Della Vida changed from English to Latin when he came to earthy passages while translating Arabic papyri dating from between the eighth and fourteenth centuries. Again, this language would not have bothered contemporary readers. It may seem strange to us today, given our greater openness to sexual matters, that sex, which is, of course, one of the most powerful forces of human behavior, has been largely absent from the study of Southwest Asia in the Middle Ages. The present work should help to introduce this part of life more broadly into scholarly discussions.

It has two underlying themes: first, the remarkable continuity, in general, in the practice of prostitution in the transition from Christian to Muslim rule; and second, the necessity of prostitution as an institutionalized service industry which took various forms at different times and places in our region. In this latter respect, its role in social and economic history was both widespread and multifaceted. Its place in society could be subtle or omnipresent. And its significance to women and men could be inconsequential or a matter of life and death. Thus prostitution cannot be described, much less explained, simplistically by the hoary assertion that "it is the world's oldest profession," which is an admission of ignorance, or such claims as "it was the worst form of exploitation of women in the Middle Ages," which is an ideological assertion in some quarters and based on preconceived ideas. Both statements, which seem to constitute the "conventional wisdom" on this topic, reflect a static and one-dimensional view of prostitution.

As for the major conclusions of this study, I would especially like to emphasize here the following: 1) within both the Christian and Muslim communities, prostitution was never illegal; 2) prostitution was a state enterprise in medieval Egypt; 3) prostitution had a symbiotic relationship with many trades and was well integrated into commercial life; 4) there was a significant influx of European prostitutes into Syria and Egypt during the Crusades; 5) there is strong evidence, more so for Muslims, that pious religious endowments profited from the sex trade; and 6) the practice of prostitution at caravan staging points and in the major ports of the Indies,

China, and Europe was an incentive to international trade. Altogether, prostitution had a far more complex and positive role in social and economic history than has heretofore been appreciated.

The word "prostitution" would seem to need no definition. We all know what it is. Yet, because it has so many nuances and permutations, not to mention different legal and traditional meanings in different cultures, modern scholars have sometimes struggled, in voluminous fashion, to define the term comprehensively. We need not be so demanding here, mainly because our sources rarely give us the kind of refinements of the subject that we would like. Consequently, for the purpose of this study, it suffices to define prostitution as "the frequent and indiscriminate sale by women of their sexual favors to men."

Even with this simple definition, there are a number of difficulties in attempting to write an objective account of this business. One is that most of the terminology associated with prostitution is morally charged. This is true of our medieval sources as well as modern discussions, and can easily result in a skewed analysis. We have no term in English for prostitute which has the neutral resonance of, say, "rug merchant." Instead, this word and its many synonyms are loaded with negative baggage, which can be a distraction and obscure what is going on apart from the sale of sex. The need for a term or expression which elicits the least visceral reaction in this respect led me to the use of "public woman" for one who sells her sexual favors. This somewhat muted expression is not a solution to the search for linguistic neutrality, but it is a start.

Another, more serious, problem is that the women who are the subject of this book do not speak for themselves; and presumably the great majority of them were illiterate and could not speak for themselves. All our sources were written by men, who, for the most part, took little interest in their profession or condition. We know nothing of the personal experiences of these women or what they thought of their trade or about men. It would be foolish, however, to assume that all prostitutes saw their business in the same light, or that of modern moralists and ideologues, or that their views of it never changed over the course of their lives. We simply do not know. The sources, then, are what they are. We cannot change them; but we should keep in mind that the women concerned have no voice. It might be helpful to remember that men who engaged in various trades that were despised, such as butchers and tanners, also do not speak for themselves in the sources.

Even while acknowledging that our sources were composed by men, we are faced with the difficulty of actually finding them. One reason that modern historians have not investigated this subject is that no treatises on it have come down to us from the medieval period. We are not even sure that any were written, although we know the titles of a few lost works that are suggestive in this respect. This is evidence, of course, that contemporary writers did not believe our subject worthy of special attention. In any case, few references to prostitution have survived, and they are usually very short. Moreover, they are scattered over a wide array of works. We may come across the mention of prostitution, often unexpectedly, in texts on almost any subject: religious, legal, medical, geographical, historical, commercial, or literary. Then, from this hodgepodge of material, we must try to create a coherent narrative.

Given the vast literary output of medieval writers, even for our narrow region and period, I certainly make no claim to have examined all the existing works that might include a reference to our subject. This would be a challenge even for a Methuselah, although the creation of databases derived from scanned medieval texts should, in theory, make systematic keyword searches of potential sources less daunting. Nevertheless, the material that I have gleaned over many years and from a fairly broad spectrum of the literary heritage suffices, I believe, to provide a general outline (albeit an uneven one) of the trade for our place and time. The gaps in the outline, resulting from the nature of the sources, are sometimes frequent. In these cases, I have on occasion resorted to speculation, but I hope this speculation is at least reasonable, if unverifiable.

In order to ensure consistency, I have mostly used the system of the *International Journal of Middle Eastern Studies* for the transliteration of Arabic and Ottoman Turkish. I have, however, made an attempt to remove the diacritical marks in names such as Istanbul, Ibn Battuta, and so on, as these are so widely known in the English-speaking world.

It is with pleasure that I express my gratitude to a group of senior scholars for reading and commenting on individual chapters of this study. They saved me from a number of errors and oversights while raising stimulating questions, all to the benefit of the final text. Speros Vryonis, Jr., Fred Donner, Carole Hillenbrand, and Scott Redford read Chapters 1, 2, 4, and 5 respectively. Thomas Naff read the entire work. Robert Hillenbrand answered a number of questions on Islamic art. Furthermore, I received helpful feedback from the twenty-six women and two men at St. Mary's College in Moraga, California who took my course on this subject and allowed me to present my findings to an interested audience for the first time. I also owe a debt of thanks to Cornel Metternich and Patricia Leiser for providing assistance on the finer points of German and French, and to Walter Denny for several of the photographs. The interlibrary loan staff of the Vacaville Public Library, Town Square, in Vacaville, California performed yeomen's service in locating many obscure books and thus greatly facilitated the progress of my research. Finally, the polished text owes much to my sharp-eyed and meticulous copy editor, Sarah Terry. No institution or foundation provided financial or other support for the preparation of this work. It was done in complete freedom.

ONE

Public Women in the Eastern Mediterranean World in Late Antiquity

POLITICAL AND SOCIAL CONTEXT

At the end of the third century CE, the Roman Empire was at the height of its territorial expansion. It stretched from Britain in the West to the Caucasus Mountains in the East, and from the Danube in the North to the Sahara Desert in the South. Yet this enormous state, which incorporated the entire Mediterranean basin, or most of the "known world," faced a series of crises that ultimately led to its collapse.

Among these crises were decades of military anarchy and barbarian invasions. In order to suppress the anarchy and provide a more effective means of defending the Empire against invasions, chiefly by the Germanic peoples in Europe, Diocletian (r. 284–305) divided the Empire into four political sections, two in the West and two in the East. Furthermore, he divided rule between two emperors, one for the West and one for the East. Diocletian chose Maximian as his co-emperor (r. 286–305). He was to be responsible for the West, and had his headquarters in Milan or Trier. Diocletian was to be responsible for the East, and had his headquarters in Nicomedia (modern Izmit in Turkey) at the easternmost shore of the Sea of Marmara.

After Diocletian and Maximian resigned in 305, however, this arrangement led to a power struggle and war among those vying to be emperor. Eventually Constantine I, whose father Constantius had briefly succeeded Diocletian, emerged as sole emperor (r. 324–37). The division between West and East did not resume until some 60 years after his death. Recognizing that the strength and wealth of the Empire lay in the East, with its rich ports, fertile hinterland, and perhaps somewhat greater safety from barbarian incursions, Constantine moved the capital from Rome to the town of Byzantium on the European side of the southern entrance to the Bosphorus. The new capital was not far from Nicomedia, where Constantine had been educated at Diocletian's court. Byzantium took the name Constantinople in his honor, and its dedication in 330 is generally taken as the starting point of Byzantine history.

The Roman Empire lingered as a unified state, in theory, until the death of Theodosius I in 395, when the division between West and East became permanent. The shift in power and resources from Rome to Constantinople made the West impossible to defend. It sank into anarchy and was ravaged by invaders. Rome lost its political importance. In 476 the last emperor in the West was deposed by the Goths under Odoacer. This date traditionally marks the end of the West Roman Empire.

At the time of Theodosius (r. 379–95), the western limit of the East Roman Empire (or Byzantium, as it is now called) was a rough line running south from modern Montenegro, through the Strait of Otranto, and across the Mediterranean to Libya. In the east the frontier extended south from the Caucasus Mountains through the Syrian Desert to the Red Sea. The Danube and Black Sea in the north and Egypt in the south rounded out the borders of the empire.

During the fourth and fifth centuries, as the West gradually slipped away, Byzantium had to face a number of barbarian invasions of the Balkans. On the Syrian (or eastern) front, however, Theodosius concluded a peace treaty with Persia which resulted in comparative tranquility for more than a hundred years. Indeed, Byzantium not only managed to survive and thrive but also to evolve into a distinct civilization of its own. Although its administration was organized along Roman lines and Latin was the language of government, the army and the laws, its cultural orientation—civic institutions, customs, and education—were Greek. Hellenism permeated the Eastern Mediterranean world, and Greek was the lingua franca.

By the early sixth century Byzantium had become strong enough to try to assert itself in the Western Mediterranean. Fueled by the wealth of the east, Justinian I (r. 527–65) attempted to recover all the lost provinces of the West Roman Empire. His ambition was realized at great price and only in part, regaining him North Africa, Italy, the islands of the Western Mediterranean, and southeastern Spain. Preoccupied with expensive campaigns in the west, Justinian and his successors had difficulty defending the frontiers to the north and east. The greatest threat came from a resurgent Persia, the only state that could compete with Byzantium as a world power. A protracted struggle began in 572. It was interrupted by peace in 591, but renewed in 611 when the Persians overwhelmed Byzantine defenses in Mesopotamia. The major cities of Syria fell in rapid succession: Antioch, Apamea, and Emesa (Ḥums in modern Syria) in 611, and Damascus in 613. Jerusalem was sacked in 614. In the same year Chalcedon, on the Bosphorus opposite Constantinople itself, was taken. Egypt was completely overrun by 621.[1] The Byzantine Empire seemed to be on the verge of destruction, but after a long and desperate conflict it was saved by Heraclius (r. 610–41), an emperor who was both a military and organizational genius. After several campaigns, he shattered the might of Persia in 627 near modern Mosul.

This long struggle drained both empires of enormous wealth and manpower. It also wreaked havoc with life in the major cities around the Eastern Mediterranean and much of the countryside. In the course of it, neither Byzantium nor Persia were concerned—assuming they even noticed—with a series of events that were taking place in two remote and obscure towns of Arabia, namely Mecca and Yathrib (later called Medina). These events would eventually culminate in the rise of a new religion, Islam, inspired by the Prophet Muhammad, which would change the fate of Byzantium and Persia. A few years after the death of Muhammad in 632, Arab armies, the strike force of the new community of believers, streamed out of Arabia and quickly overwhelmed Syria, Egypt, and Persia. Damascus fell in 635, Jerusalem in 637 or 638, and Alexandria in 642. The Arabs also managed to temporarily overrun Anatolia, and between 674 and 678 even besieged Constantinople. This great prize eluded them, however, and the frontier between Byzantium and the Umayyad caliphate, which was established in Damascus, receded and was more or less stabilized along the Taurus Mountains north of Syria. The Arab conquests permanently deprived Byzantium of its southern provinces and ended its status as the most powerful state in the world.

The backdrop to the emergence of Byzantium and its early history was the growth of Christianity and the Christological controversies that followed. A growing difference between the West and East Roman Empires had been their general religious orientation. The West had strong pagan traditions, while the East gradually became imbued with Christianity. It was in a province of the East Roman Empire that the religion originated. Constantine was the first emperor to adopt Christianity. He was also the first to legalize it. Nevertheless, it remained the religion of a small minority for some time. It was Theodosius I who, in 380, made Christianity the official religion of the Empire and proscribed all Graeco-Roman cults. By the early fifth century it was, at least nominally, the religion of most of the population. And in Byzantium it was on its way to becoming a single religious culture as well as faith.

This is not to say, however, that there was dogmatic conformity among Christians. Arguments over the nature of Christ were widespread. Dogmatic differences and local political interests eventually contributed to the emergence of the sees of Alexandria and Antioch, in addition to Constantinople, as the major regional centers of ecclesiastical authority within the Empire. Their views of Christ could not be reconciled with those of Constantinople, despite many councils or synods. Successive emperors then resorted to persecution. As a result, Alexandria and Antioch—that is, Egypt and Syria—welcomed the Arabs as liberators.[2]

PUBLIC WOMEN IN AN URBAN SETTING[3]

Our information on prostitution in the Eastern Mediterranean world within the aforesaid political and social context of Late Antiquity is fragmentary.

Our most important sources are a few Byzantine chronicles, early Christian writings (especially the lives of the saints), Roman/Byzantine law, and archeology. Using these and a few other sources, let us now examine what is known about public women between the fourth and seventh centuries. We will travel from place to place around the Eastern Mediterranean, from Alexandria to Constantinople.

Alexandria

When the new capital was dedicated at Constantinople (formerly the town of Byzantium) in 330, the port of Alexandria was already the greatest city of the East Roman Empire. Indeed, it was the rival of Rome as the greatest city of the world. Alexandria itself had long been the capital of the Roman province of Egypt and was the most important intellectual and cultural center of the East. Its population, mostly Greek but with large Jewish and Egyptian communities, was probably at least several hundred thousand. Its location at the crux of Africa and Southwest Asia, with direct access to the Mediterranean and indirect access to the Red Sea, brought it enormous wealth. In a long speech delivered to the people of Alexandria, probably during the reign of Trajan (r. 98–117), the Greek orator Dio Chrysostom, "the Golden-Mouthed" (ca. 40–ca. 120), who was from Prusa (modern Bursa in Turkey, near Nicomedia), praised the great city in the course of denouncing the shortcomings and vices of its populace, stating:

> not only have you a monopoly of the shipping of the entire Mediterranean by reason of the beauty of your harbors, the magnitude of your fleet, and the abundance and the marketing of the products of every land, but also the outer waters that lie beyond are in your grasp, both the Red Sea and the Indian Ocean, whose name was rarely heard in the former days. The result is that the trade, not merely of islands, ports, and a few straits and isthmuses, but of practically the whole world is yours. For Alexandria is situated, as it were, at the crossroads of the whole world, of even the most remote nations

> thereof, as if it were a market serving a single city, a market which brings together into one place all manner of men, displaying them to one another and, as far as possible, making them a kindred people.[4]

The rich and teeming maritime metropolis of Alexandria was thus a world market for a vast array of goods and services. Among the businesspeople who sought to take advantage of its numerous attractions and opportunities were many women who sold their sexual services to male clients. Given the large pool of prospective customers—administrative officials, sailors, soldiers, merchants, farmers from the countryside, and others—public women must have been common and their trade fully incorporated into the rhythm of life. In Late Antiquity there may even have been an association of prostitutes with a chosen leader.[5] In the event, Alexandria, like all major cities of the time, was notorious for its pleasures, among which female comfort was prominent. Dio Chrysostom himself accused the entire population of acting "like women of low repute, who, however wanton they may be at home, should behave with decorum when they go abroad, and yet it is especially in the streets that they are most guilty of misconduct."[6]

Alexandria's most important center of entertainment was its circus, where various spectacles were held. It included a racecourse or hippodrome and, by extension, a theater. The former was given over above all to chariot and horse racing, and the latter to raucous diversions that were often a mixture of burlesque and vaudeville: performances by actors, mimes, dancers, singers, musicians, acrobats, and the like. The presence of a circus and theater, along with public baths, was what helped define urban life.[7] As we will see later in other contexts, wherever large numbers of men gathered, there too public women conducted their business. Dio Chrysostom states that Alexandria was "mad over music and horse-races" and behaved "in a manner entirely unworthy of itself."[8] He adds that entertainers, usually a euphemism for public women, plied their trade "in what is practically the centre of the civilized world and in the most populous city of all."[9] In his old age, in another discourse apparently delivered in Rome, Dio denounced the presence of brothel-keepers in the cities of the Empire in general and excoriated them for prostituting women who had been captured in war or purchased in the market. He claimed that brothels were set up everywhere in the cities, "at the doors of the houses of magistrates and in market-places, near government buildings and temples, in the midst of all that is holiest."[10] Presumably he included Alexandria and the other major cities of the East in his criticism.

It seems that public women either conducted their business in brothels in the employ of others, sometimes as slaves, or were "private contractors." In addition, their services were taxed, at least from the time of Caligula (r. 37–41).[11] Evidence pertaining directly to Alexandria is lacking, but a price list for passes to leave Egypt by way of a Red Sea port, surviving from the year 90, indicates that a ship's captain or skilled laborer had to pay 8 drachmas (silver coins), certain ratings 10, sailors and the ship's carpenter 5, common-law wives of soldiers 20, and prostitutes 108.[12] Sarah Pomeroy[13] and, following her, Thomas McGinn,[14] believe the high amount imposed on prostitutes reflected their ability to pay. It seems more likely, however, that this high fee was meant to discourage an important source of state revenue from leaving the country. One wonders if the same fee was charged to both free and slave women. "Common-law wives" of soldiers may also have been a euphemism for camp follower/prostitute; hence the relatively high fee charged to them as well. Several second-century CE Egyptian ostraca (inscribed potsherds) from Elephantine, which was on an island off Aswan in Upper Egypt, show government authorities dealing directly with public women, who were apparently independent, and granting them permission to sell their services in certain cities on certain days and giving them tax receipts.[15] Clearly these women were itinerant. Elephantine was a military- and customs-post with Nubia, and the method of taxation no doubt depended on the women's mobility or independence. Second-century papyri from Oxyrhynchus, also in Upper Egypt, show that farmed taxes were probably levied on brothels as units in its market.[16]

Only one Byzantine chronicle referring to prostitution in Alexandria (albeit obliquely) in our period has come to light. This is the work of St. Theophanes the Confessor, who was born around 760 in Constantinople and died in 818 on the island of Samothrace. He was a member of the Byzantine aristocracy, but embraced the religious life. Theophanes says that in the year 389–90, when Theodosius was emperor, Theophilus, the bishop of Alexandria, applied to the emperor and then "cleansed the pagan temple [of Sarapis] in Alexandria and turned it into a church and also made public the secret rites of the pagans, including their phalli and other things even more lewd and more profane."[17] The implication, of course, is that prostitution—or fornication, at the very least—was practiced there. However, because Theophilus was a zealous Christian who viewed pagans in the worst possible light, we should perhaps accept his accusations with some skepticism. A rare specific reference to public women in Alexandria comes from a fourth-century papyrus describing a court case in which a mother claimed compensation for the loss of income resulting from the murder of her daughter, whom she had turned over to a procurer so they could earn a living.[18]

The richest sources by far for the presence of prostitution in Alexandria and other cities in the Eastern Mediterranean world in Late Antiquity are the lives of saints. These saints included both men and women. Numerous male saints "ministered" to public women and tried to convince them to abandon their profession,[19] while many female saints—beginning with Mary Magdalene, the second most important woman in the Gospels—had been, so it seems, former prostitutes. As many modern writers have pointed out, the early Christian stories about public woman *cum* saint (the origin perhaps of the topos of the hooker with the heart of gold) usually had a moral and were meant to be edifying for the faithful. For a Christian, prostitution was the measure of extremity for a woman's sinfulness. (We must distinguish here between a sin and a crime, which were not necessarily the same thing.) This made the conversion of a prostitute, the forgiveness of her transgression, and her salvation especially awesome.[20] Given the propagandistic nature of these stories, their historicity may in many cases be doubtful. Nevertheless, they are useful in describing the presence and setting of contemporary prostitution.

The two most important compendia of the lives of saints which include references to Alexandria are Palladius' *Lausiac History* and John Moschos' *The Spiritual Meadow*, both in Greek. Palladius was born in Galatia (the center of modern Turkey) in 364. Around 386 he entered the monastic life, and in 388 went to Alexandria and spent the next ten years or so in the monasteries of Egypt. Then he returned to Asia Minor and through the influence of the renowned John Chrysostom, the bishop of Constantinople (whom we will meet again shortly), became bishop of Helenopolis on the southern coast of the present-day Gulf of Izmit on the Sea of Marmara. Embroiled in controversies surrounding Chrysostom, he was briefly exiled to Egypt in 404–5. He eventually returned to Asia Minor and in 412 was appointed to the See of Aspona, which was southeast of modern Ankara. Around 420 he wrote the *Lausiac History*, which he dedicated to Lausus, the chamberlain at the court of Theodosius II. He probably died during the following decade.

The *Lausiac History* is a collection of short biographies of ascetics, men and women, based on what Palladius saw and heard during the breadth of his experience. Many of the memories were old, and Palladius was not a little credulous. Still, he does provide some insight into his time and place; and his preoccupation with sexuality—a major theme in the writings of the early Church Fathers—in the lives of his subjects is not without interest. He provides an especially pertinent account of one of his neighbors in Egypt, an Alexandrian named Heron, who became disillusioned with the monastic life. He was "attacked by pride" and insulted the Fathers. Finally,

> driven as it were by fire, he could not remain in his cell, but went off to Alexandria, by (divine) dispensation, and, as the saying goes, "knocked out one nail with another." [...] For he frequented the theater and circuses and enjoyed the diversions of the taverns. And thus, eating and drinking immoderately he fell into a mire of concupiscence. And when he was resolving to sin he met an actress and had converse with her.[21]

As a result, a carbuncle developed on his genitals—perhaps a reference to venereal syphilis—which then rotted and fell off. He realized his mistake, confessed, and subsequently returned to the Fathers.

As for John Moschos, the author of *The Spiritual Meadow*, he was born during the reign of Justinian I (527–65), apparently in Damascus, and died no earlier than 619. Like Palladius he renounced the world and embraced the religious life. His home monastery was near Bethlehem. At the beginning of the reign of Tiberius II (578–82), he went to Egypt to collect the lore of those elders who were the guardians of the monastic tradition. He remained in that country for more than ten years. Afterward he traveled to Palestine, Syria, Cilicia, and back to Egypt sometimes as a refugee from the Persians. Eventually he fled to Rome, where he finished his book and died.

With respect to Alexandria, Moschos tells us that a certain Abba (Father) Theonas and Abba Theodore related to him the story of a young woman from that city, whose wealthy parents had died during the time of the Greek Patriarch Paul of the Egyptian Church (r. 537–42). One day when she went into the garden that her parents had left her, she discovered a man who was trying to hang himself because he was deeply in debt. She saved his life by spending her entire fortune to pay his debts. Then, having no one to look after her and being in great need, she turned to prostitution. Eventually, however, she repented and became a Christian.[22]

Later Moschos tells another story, which may associate public women with the public baths. He says that one Abba Peter told him that once, when he and his father were at the residence of a certain Abba Macarius, some people came to them from the eighteenth milestone from Alexandria. They were accompanied by a "consecrated virgin/widow" ([*sic*]—she is also described as a nun) who was possessed by a demon, which in early Christian literature was often a euphemism for sexual desire.[23] Macarius was asked to cure her. He made the sign of the cross and reproached the demon, but the demon refused to come out of her, saying:

> She was my instrument. I taught her to go often to the baths, shamelessly and unblushingly adorned. I shot and wounded many with her [looks]—and her with theirs, ensnaring not only worldlings, but clerics too, and I titillated them [inciting them] to shameful intercourse with her. By [their] assent to shameful thoughts and by what they saw with their eyes at night (for I made it all visible to them) I trapped them into ejaculation.[24]

Unsuccessful, Macarius sent her on to another father.

Another genre of literature related to early Christian monasticism consists of collections of the *Sayings of the Fathers* or, in Latin, *Apophthegmata Patrum*. These "sayings" are primarily anecdotes, moralistic stories, and words of wisdom from the monks in the deserts of Egypt, Palestine, and Syria. They date from the fourth to the sixth centuries and were recorded in various languages. One collection of sayings, which has several references to public women, is the *Alphabetical Collection* in Greek. It took its final form at the end of the sixth century.[25]

There is little historical or geographical context for the references to prostitutes in the sayings, but they at least have the merit of providing the setting for public women that was familiar to contemporaries. First we have, according to the Greek alphabet, an incident in the life of a certain Abba Ephrem. One day, while on the road in Egypt or Syria, a prostitute approached him and tried to cajole him into having shameful intercourse or to anger him, for no one had seen him angry before. He told her to follow him and, when they had reached a crowded place, instructed her to do the deed there. She could not do it in front of a crowd, however, and was shamed.[26] Second, we have John the Dwarf, who was born around 339 and spent his life in the Egyptian desert. He states that there was in a city (Alexandria?) a courtesan who had many lovers. "One of the governors" approached her and said that if she promised to be good he would marry her. She agreed; and later when some of her former lovers sought her out, she shut her doors to them.[27] Third, John relates the story of a young girl whose parents had died and left her a house. She turned it into an inn for the Fathers of Scetis, a monastic center in the desert west of the Delta. For a long time she gave them hospitality, but eventually her resources were exhausted. At that point some wicked men convinced her to turn to prostitution. John went to see her, and succeeded in getting her to repent and go into the desert with him, where she died.[28] Fourth, we have an anecdote about the monk Pambo. He was born around 303 and later joined a monastic community in Nitria, just north of Scetis. He became one of the great masters of the desert and died around 373. It seems that Athanasius, the Patriarch of Alexandria (r. 328–73), invited him to come to Alexandria from the desert. No sooner did he do so than he saw an "actress" and began to weep. He explained that his tears were for the loss of this woman and because she was more concerned to please wicked men than he was to please God.[29] Fifth, we have a story about one Abba Serapion. One day, while passing through a village in Egypt, he saw a public woman who stayed in her own cell. He told her that he wanted to spend the night with her. She replied, "Very well, *abba*," and got ready and prepared the bed. When he returned, he asked her if the bed was ready. She said, "Yes, *abba*," and he entered her room and closed the door. He then told her that he had to pray. By the time he had finished, he was begging God to convert and save her. The women then realized that he had in fact come not to make love but to save her soul; and he took her to a monastery of virgins.[30] Finally, a certain Abba Timothy reported that there was a woman who committed fornication in Egypt and then gave her earnings, which were increasing, away in alms. So Timothy went to see her and gave her the word of God. She repented and entered a monastery.[31]

The most noteworthy example of an itinerant public woman in Alexandria was none other than Theodora, the future wife of Justinian and Empress of the Byzantine Empire, and saint in the Orthodox Church. We will have more to say about her when we discuss prostitution in Constantinople. For now it suffices to say that she was born around 497 in Cyprus, Syria, or the region of Paphlagonia in Northern Anatolia. She was brought up in the theater in Constantinople, where she began to sell her sexual services at an early age. An attractive girl, she was introduced to Hecebolus, a man from Tyre, and as a young woman accompanied him as his lover when he was appointed governor of the Pentapolis, the five Greek cities of Cyrenaica (present-day northeastern Libya). Hecebolus eventually threw her out, however, and, finding herself abandoned, Theodora returned to her former profession in order to support herself. She went first to Alexandria and then worked her way from city to city around the Eastern Mediterranean, returning to Constantinople around 522.[32]

Another itinerant public woman who conducted business in Alexandria—and was a possible contemporary of Theodora—was Mary of Egypt. She became the patron saint of penitents in the Orthodox, Catholic, and even Anglican churches. The chief source for her life is the biography composed by St. Sophronius, who was the Patriarch of Jerusalem (r. 634–8) when the Arabs conquered it. Sophronius states that he learned her story from an account provided by St. Zosimas, who was born in the second half of the fifth century and became an elder in a monastery in Palestine. Zosimas had encountered Mary naked in the desert. She was then an old woman, and she related her life to him. She said that her native land was Egypt. When she was 12 she left her parents and went to Alexandria. There she lost her virginity and, with unquenchable desire, turned to prostitution. Sometimes she provided her services without pay. She supplemented her income by begging and spinning flax. One day, after 17 years in this life, she saw a large group of Libyans and Egyptians hastening toward the sea. She asked where they were going, and was told that they were pilgrims traveling by ship to Jerusalem for the feast of the Exaltation of the Cross. She decided to accompany them, for the festival would provide many potential clients. She had no money for passage, but said to one of them, "I will go and get into one of the ships that are going and they will take me even if they do not want to. I have a body that will serve as both food and fare for me."[33] The pilgrims were happy to have her. Thus she worked her way to Jerusalem. As she said to Zosimas:

> What tongue can say, what ear can hear what happened on that ship and during that voyage, for I compelled into sin even those who were unwilling. There was no kind of perverted and unspeakable lust that I did not perform with them.[34]

Upon reaching Jerusalem, she went about selling her services to local citizens and those who were there as pilgrims. While searching for young men on the day of the Exaltation of the Cross, she saw a large crowd surge toward the Church of the Holy Sepulcher and followed it. She tried to enter the Church, again in pursuit of customers, but was prevented from doing so by a mysterious force. She came to realize a divine presence in the force and that it was her "unclean" life that had prevented her from passing through the doors. This realization then led to her repentance, salvation, and sainthood. Her death date is given variously as 421 [*sic*], 522, or 530.[35]

In the sixth or seventh century, a certain Dionysius Exiguus translated into Latin from an anonymous Greek work the life of St. Thais, a former courtesan from Egypt (no doubt Alexandria). Little is reported about her, and it is not clear when she was supposed to have lived. Her historicity is, in fact, dubious. According to Dionysius' source, she was such a great beauty that "many for her sake sold all that they had and reduced themselves to utter poverty; quarrels arose among her lovers and often the doorstep of this girl's house was soaked in the blood of young men."[36] Learning of this, a monk named Paphnutius put on secular clothes and went to visit her. He handed her a piece of silver as the price of committing sin. She accepted it and said, "Let us go inside." He went in and sat down on the bed, which was draped with precious covers. Then he said to her, "If there is a more private chamber, let us go in there." She replied, "There is one, but if it is people you are afraid of, no one ever enters this room; except, of course, for God, for there is no place that is hidden from the eyes of divinity." Paphnutius, surprised by her knowledge of God, then remarked that her way of life threatened her soul. She then agreed to a humiliating penance, for which she was later made a saint.[37] There is some ambiguity in this tale; it could easily suggest that the monk's intention of visiting her was sexual rather than altruistic.

Finally, with respect to Alexandria, we should mention Leontius of Neapolis (modern Limassol in Cyprus), who wrote several hagiographical works including a biography of St. John the Almsgiver, the Patriarch of Alexandria (r. 606–16). Leontius, who was bishop of Neapolis, was probably born at the beginning of the seventh century and died perhaps during the reign of Constans II (641–68). He may have known St. John, a fellow Cypriot. In his biography, which may post-date the Arab conquest of Alexandria in 642, he recounts the story of a certain Vitalios, a monk from a monastery in Gaza who went to Alexandria, where he behaved in a manner somewhat reminiscent of Paphnutius. His life was, however, much more scandalous in the eyes of ordinary people, although it was meritorious to God. He made a list of all the public women in Alexandria and then visited them one by one. He supposedly paid each of them *not* to have sex with him while he passed the night chanting hymns, praying for her soul, and making prostrations. In the morning he demanded that each woman promise to say nothing about what had happened. Presumably he feared that these women would not admit him if the truth of his behavior were told. Consequently, his visits were of course misinterpreted, and he was accused of entering brothels to engage in intercourse. When word of this reached St. John, he told the slanderers to desist, and Vitalios continued his salutary work. Indeed, public women often flocked to his cell to attend his liturgy. Many abandoned their profession, married, or became nuns.[38]

Jerusalem

Moving north from Alexandria around the Mediterranean coast, the next city to appear in our sources concerning prostitution is Jerusalem. In the fourth century it was perhaps a large provincial town, rather than a city. It could not compare in size with Alexandria. It was neither a port nor a major commercial hub, but it did have important religious sites that attracted pilgrims, both Jewish and Christian. We know little about the composition of the city at that time. Constantine had barred Jews from the city, although they could visit the western wall of the Temple; and once a year they were allowed to go into the site of the Temple. Even if they gradually returned, their presence must have been small. Indeed, by then Jews were a small minority in all of Palestine.[39] Thus most of the population must have been Christian.

In any case, Jerusalem, like other urban centers, had a reputation for vice. It had, in fact, been denounced metaphorically as a whore in the strongest terms as early as Ezekiel 16. As Christianity spread and more and more people wished to visit the sites of Christ's life and death, the question arose whether there was merit in a pilgrimage to the Holy Land. In a letter to a certain Kensior, St. Gregory (ca. 330–95) of Nyssa in Cappadocia (central Turkey), one of the great early Church Fathers, argued against it because pilgrims would inevitably encounter such temptations as public women. As we have seen, Mary of Egypt was a later example. Gregory asserted that:

> since, in the regions of the East, the hostelries, the wayside inns, and many cities, show licentiousness and indifference with regard to vice, how can it be that one passes through the smoke without his eyes being inflamed? [...] If grace were more abundant in Jerusalem's holy places than elsewhere, then sin would not haunt the inhabitants of the region as it does, for there is no kind of vice to which they are not addicted: fornication, adultery, theft, idolatry, witchcraft, jealousy, and murder; such crimes are so common that nowhere else is there such a readiness to kill in cold blood, moved by their greediness and avidity, not unlike wild beasts wallowing in the blood of some of their kind![40]

In his *Lausiac History*, written in the early fifth century, Palladius says he knew a virgin in Jerusalem who became a prostitute. She had worn sackcloth for six years and shut herself up in a cell, foregoing all pleasures in life. Eventually, however, she could not tolerate this "because of her excessive arrogance." Therefore, "She opened the window and admitted the man who waited on her and sinned with him."[41]

Later, in the seventh century, John Moschos tells us in his *Spiritual Meadow* that he had heard from one Abba Theodore about a certain recluse on the Mount of Olives who was tormented by the demon of sexual desire. The demon agreed to leave him if he would cease venerating an icon of the Virgin carrying her son. The recluse explained what had happened to Theodore, who comforted him, saying, "It were better for you to leave no brothel in town [Jerusalem] unentered than to diminish reverence from our Lord Jesus Christ and from his Mother."[42]

John also relates that a certain Abba John, an anchorite, heard one Abba Stephan the Moabite say that when he was in the community of St. Theodosius (outside Bethlehem), two brothers were there who swore never to part from each other. One was eventually overcome with desire and wanted to go back to the world. So he went to Jerusalem, and the other brother went with him:

> The afflicted brother went into the house of fornication whilst the other brother stood outside. Taking up dust from the ground he threw

> it on his own head, reproaching himself. When the brother who had gone into the brothel came out again, having done the deed, the other brother said to him: "My brother, what have you gained by this sin, and what have you lost by it?"

But he decided to remain in the world and continued his riotous living in Jerusalem until he repented and withdrew, late in life, to a cave near the Jordan.[43]

John reports too that one Abba Polychronios told him that in the monastery of Penthoucia, which was apparently near Jerusalem, was a brother who left the community and went to Jericho to satisfy his desires. There he entered a den of fornication. No sooner did he enter then he was afflicted with leprosy. He immediately returned to the monastery, giving thanks to God for turning him away from lust. Suffering from leprosy was thus better than making love.[44]

As we will see shortly when discussing Antioch, some public women, knowing very well of the struggle of ascetics with "the demon," sought them out as customers, although the women couldn't have received much for their services. This sense of taking the initiative may be reflected in the story that Abba John, a priest of the Monastery of the Eunuchs near the Jordan, heard from an anchorite named Abba Sisinius. As the latter related, "One day I was in my cave near the holy Jordan [...] a Saracen woman came that way and entered my cave. She sat herself down before me and took off her clothes." He spoke to her in Hebrew[45] and asked why she played the harlot, and she said it was because she was hungry. She said she was a Christian. He demanded that she give up harlotry and come to him each day and he would feed her.[46]

Before moving north from Palestine, we should mention that a brothel from the early Byzantine period has been discovered at Scythopolis (Beth'shan, west of the Jordan and south of Lake Tiberias). This city had been an important Roman center, and reached its height in the sixth century before falling to the Arabs. The brothel, a fairly large structure reminiscent of similar institutions in Pompeii, seems to have been closely associated with the public baths. Excavations have also turned up evidence of prostitution associated with the baths in the port of Ascalon on the southern coast of Palestine dating from between the fourth and sixth centuries.[47] Further up the coast, the maritime city of Caesarea had a circus and theater. In the third and fourth centuries it was both an important commercial and cosmopolitan city—home to famous rabbis, the great library of the early Christian scholar and theologian Origen (184/5–254/5), and the early Church historian Eusebius (ca. 260–339), whom we will meet shortly. It is highly likely that Caesarea too had a significant number of public women.

Tyre

Further north, the next port where we have definite literary evidence for the presence of prostitution is Tyre. The site of an ancient Phoenician harbor, it had long been one of the most famous (perhaps *the* most famous) commercial cities on the Eastern Mediterranean littoral. It was a fairly large city in the fifth century, and attracted merchants from around the Mediterranean. In the third century it was the capital of the province of Syria Phoenice, which included Damascus, Emesa, and Palmyra, and was well known for the production of purple dye and glass. In the early fifth century Theodosius II (r. 408–50) made it the capital of Phoenicia Prima or Maritima, which included all of the central part of the Eastern Mediterranean coast. Like Caesarea it had both a circus and theater.

In his *Spiritual Meadow*, John Moschos gives a brief account of another Moschos, a merchant from Tyre. John learned of him from a father at the community of the Cave of St. Sabas (439–532) in Palestine. When this father was in Tyre, he met the aforesaid merchant, who told him the following story:

> When I was engaged in commerce, late one evening I went to bathe. On the way I came across a woman standing in the shadows (apparently near the bath). I went up and greeted her; she agreed to follow me. I was so diabolically delighted that I did not bathe but went

> straight to dinner. I did my best to persuade her, but she would not consent to taste [a morsel]. Finally, we got up to go to bed and, as I began to embrace her, she let out a tremendous cry and broke into tears, saying: "What a woeful wretch I am!" I was trembling as I asked her what was the matter. She wept even more and said: "My husband is a merchant and he has been shipwrecked. He lost both his own property and others'. Now he is in prison because of the others' losses. I am at my wits' end what to do and how to get bread for him. I decided, in great shame, to sell my body; it was to get bread."[48]

The merchant then does not touch her for fear of the judgment of God, and pays her husband's debts. Years later he finds himself in prison in Constantinople. When he is brought before the emperor, who should he see standing next to him but the very same woman. She then asks the emperor to save him because he had respected her body.[49]

In his biography of St. John the Almsgiver—who, as mentioned, was the Patriarch of Alexandria (r. 606–16)—Leontius of Neapolis, who was his late contemporary, says John read the life of a father which contained a story about the hazards of judging one's neighbor. It seems that two monks were on an errand in Tyre. As one of them passed through a square, a harlot called out to him, "Save me, father, as Christ saved the harlot." He asked her to follow him. He took her by the hand and they went through the city openly. Thus a rumor spread that the abbot had taken her as his wife. As the monk was taking her to a convent, the woman found a baby who had been left exposed on the ground. She took it with the intention of raising it. A year later, some people from Tyre went to the country where the abbot and woman were staying and, seeing her with the child, said, "You have certainly got a fine chick by the abbot." They then spread it abroad in Tyre that she and the abbot had a son. Years later the abbot, the nun, and the boy returned to Tyre. There the abbot fell fatally ill. On his deathbed, he called for a censer full of hot coals and then poured the coals on his robe. The coals did not, however, singe his robe, thus proving his purity and the falsehood of the rumors. After he died, several other public women followed the nun to the convent.[50]

Damascus

Damascus was an ancient oasis city and crossroads of many caravan routes. These routes connected it with Petra and Arabia to the south, with branches of the Silk Road to China to the east, and with Palmyra to the northeast. It prospered under the Romans, who upgraded its status to a *colonia* in the third century. Through the nearby ports of Tyre, Sidon, or Berytus (Beirut), which had a circus and theater, it satisfied much of the Roman demand for Oriental goods. In the early fifth century, Theodosius II detached it from the administration of Tyre and placed it in the province of to Phoenicia Libanesia, the capital of which was Emesa, north of Damascus. The size of its population is unclear, but it was a fairly large city in the fourth century and, as a significant trade center, its inhabitants were a mixture of Christians, Jews, Greeks, Arabs, and others. Under Theodosius I its Temple of Jupiter was converted to a church dedicated to St. John the Baptist. On this site was later built the famous Umayyad Mosque.

As for prostitution, our only source is the aforesaid Eusebius, the historian of the early Church who died in the first half of the fourth century. In his history, he says that during the reign of Maximian (r. 286–305), when persecutions of Christians had increased,

> an army officer—called *dux* by the Romans—at Damascus in Phoenicia arranged for some disreputable women to be removed by force from the city square, and threatened to torture them. In this way he compelled them to sign a statement to the effect that they had once been Christians and were aware of breaches of the law by Christians, who in their very churches were guilty of immoral practices and everything else he wished the women to say in defamation of the Faith.[51]

It seems, therefore, that public women sold their services in the commercial heart of the city.

Palmyra

As mentioned, caravan routes radiated from Damascus in all directions. Immediately to the south they led to the cities of Bostra (Buṣrā in Syria) and Gerasa (Jerash in Jordan). Both had circuses and theaters, but we have no literary records regarding prostitution. To the northeast a route led to the renowned oasis of Palmyra, about which we are somewhat better informed. This caravan hub in the middle of the Syrian Desert was the capital of a short-lived empire established by Zenobia, who was apparently a native of the region and was one of the most enigmatic women of the time. Aurelian overthrew her empire and captured her in 272–3. Near the agora, or marketplace, was found a stone, dated 137 CE, on which there is a long inscription in Greek and Palmyrene listing taxes on various goods and services. Among the latter are taxes on prostitution, which are listed like any other business transaction. The tax collector was to take one *denarius* (a silver coin) from prostitutes who received one *denarius* or more for their services, eight *asses* (bronze coins; 10 *asses* = 1 *denarius*) from women who received eight *asses* for their services, and six *asses* from women who received six *asses* for their services.[52] In other words, there was a daily tax that was equal to what a woman charged for her services to one customer. We will see a similar tax rate in effect centuries later in Egypt. The differences in taxation suggest, of course, that there was either a ranking of public women or of the nature of services they provided.

Emesa

Due west of Palmyra and north of Damascus was the city of Emesa. Located on the Orontes River and near the gap in the Lebanon range between the Mediterranean and the Syrian Desert, it was an ancient city and an important trading center in the early Byzantine period.

Our seventh-century historian Leontius of Neapolis wrote a biography of St. Symeon Salos (The Fool) who lived the latter part of his life in this city. Symeon, who feigned madness in order to convert pagans, Jews, sinners, prostitutes, and others, lived in the sixth century. According to Leontius, he frequently brought public women to lawful marriage through jesting or made others chaste with money and then directed them to the monastic life.[53] Indeed, he did not hesitate to cavort with prostitutes, but such scandalous behavior was attributed to madness. Inwardly he was pure. As Leontius states,

> often he skipped and danced, holding hands with one dancing-girl on this side and another on that, and he associated with them and played with them in the middle of the whole circus, so that the disreputable women threw their hands into his lap, fondled him, poked him, and pinched him. But the monk, like pure gold, was not defiled by them at all.[54]

In one especially shocking instance, Symeon was seen being carried through the streets of Emesa by one prostitute while another whipped him.[55] Derek Krueger, the author of a recent translation and study of Leontius' biography of Symeon, sees the life of the saint as a literary fiction.[56] Nevertheless, for our purposes it is noteworthy that the author makes the commercial center of Emesa a setting for public women.[57]

Dura-Europos

East of Palmyra, across the Syrian Desert, and on the west bank of the middle Euphrates was the ancient town of Dura-Europos. It was founded by the Seleucids around 300 BCE as a military colony. Given its location on the frontier with Persia, it often changed hands. Rome took it in 116 CE. Later it was linked to the rise and decline of Palmyra, but Rome ultimately retained control. It was abandoned after a Persian siege in 256–7. In the later history of the town, Greek survived as the official language, but texts in many languages have been found there, including Latin, Aramaic, Hebrew, and Middle Persian. It clearly had a mixed population. In addition to having a Roman garrison, it was at the site of an important crossing of the Euphrates and a staging point for caravans.

Excavations in Dura-Europos in the 1930s revealed inscriptions that seem to shed light on large-scale itinerant prostitution in late Roman Syria. The inscriptions were found in a house in the northern section of the agora and very close to the Roman army camp. They date to the time of the Persian siege. According to the inscriptions, a group of 33 women and 14 men, who were "entertainers" or "performers," had come to Dura from the city of Zeugma further up the Euphrates. Like Dura, Zeugma, which means "junction," was at an important crossing of the river. The group was under management and remained in Dura for nine months. During that time, several small groups, also from Zeugma, joined them. None of these groups originated from Zeugma. Rather, they were part of a trade in entertainment that emanated from Syria. Dura was one of many stops. Most—if not all—members were slaves and of Syrian stock. As entertainers they no doubt sold sexual favors and served the needs of the garrison.[58] Roman soldiers, it should be stated, were forbidden to marry during their twenty-year enlistment.

There is no reason to believe that this kind of itinerant prostitution did not continue into the Byzantine period. This may be reflected, in fact, in the story of the saints Theophilus and Mary, who arrived in Amida (Diyarbakır in Turkey) in 530. This city is on the west bank of the Tigris and some distance north of Dura-Europos. As the story goes, Theophilus appeared in the streets of Amida as a mime and Mary, his assistant, seemed to be a prostitute. In other words, they were traveling entertainers.[59]

Edessa

A very short distance from Zeugma, east of the Euphrates, was Edessa (Urfa in Turkey). It was an ancient center on the geographical divide between Anatolia and Mesopotamia, and thus came under the sway of various states and cultures. The Romans first made it a protectorate in the first century BCE and eventually a colony. In the Byzantine period Justin I (r. 518–27) rebuilt it. The city then took the name Justinopolis. It was an Armenian city, and Christianity soon arrived. A Christian council was held there as early as 197. In fact, Edessa became the most important bishopric in Syria. It is not surprising, therefore, that this city often appears in the early Christian literature of the lives of the saints.

One woman associated with Edessa, and of interest to us, was Mary, the niece of Abraham of Qidun. Her story, of doubtful historicity, is found in the life of her uncle, a fourth-century hermit and holy man. The earliest account of his life, by an unknown author, is found in a Syriac manuscript from the fifth century, Syriac being the primary literary language of Edessa. As the story goes, at the age of seven Mary was orphaned and went to live with her uncle Abraham in Qidun, which was near Edessa. After living a pure life for twenty years, she was assaulted by a man who was supposedly a monk. Afterward, she cast off her monastic garments and established herself in a tavern. Two years later, Abraham learned where she had gone and, disguised as a soldier, went to the tavern. He asked the tavern keeper for her so he could enjoy her. When he saw her elegantly dressed as a prostitute, he controlled his emotions while weeping inwardly. As they sat drinking, she drew close and started to embrace him and kiss his neck. In the midst of this she noticed "the smell of asceticism"[60] from his body. She recalled her early life and choked with grief. Mary then invited him to her bedroom so they could sleep together. Upon entering the room, Abraham saw a large bed and sat down on it next to her. She asked him to take off his shoes and close the door. Instead of taking off his shoes, he grasped her firmly as if to kiss her, took off his helmet, and revealed his identity. Awestruck with fear and terror, she repented. He then took her back to her former home and enclosed her in part of it. She spent the rest of her life as a penitent.[61]

A much more credible reference to public women with respect to Edessa is found in Procopius' (ca. 500–ca. 556) history of the wars of Justinian. Born in Caesarea in Palestine, Procopius went on to become the leading Byzantine historian of the sixth century. The first two books of the wars of Justinian concern his wars with Persia. According to the author, in 540 the Persian emperor Chosroes (Khusraw I, r. 531–79) captured and sacked the great city of Antioch. Afterward he decided to sell off all the captives. When the people of Edessa learned of this, they made a great effort to raise sufficient funds to redeem them. As Procopius states,

> there was not a person who did not bring ransom for the captives and deposit it in the sanctuary according to the measure of his possessions. And there were some who even exceeded their proportionate amount in so doing. For the harlots took off all the adornment which they wore on their persons, and threw it down there. [...] So there was collected an exceedingly great amount of gold and silver and money in other forms...[62]

This indicates, of course, that some prostitutes could become wealthy and that they decked themselves in finery.

Amida

In the same work, Procopius also tells us of the presence of public women in Amida. His report is in addition to the aforesaid story of Theophilus and Mary. Amida was not far to the east of Edessa, and its history was much the same. In the first century BCE, it came under Roman and subsequently Byzantine control. Amida was also an Armenian town and quickly became Christian. Because of its location on the northern edge of Mesopotamia, it suffered, like Edessa, from Persian attacks. Procopius relates that in 502 the Persian ruler Cabades (Kubādh I, r. 488–96, 499–531) invaded the lands of the Armenians. He reached Amida and laid siege to it. Initially unsuccessful, Cabades was about to break off the attack when

> the besieged, as though they had no thought of their danger, began laughingly from the fortifications to jeer at the barbarians. Besides this some courtesans shamelessly drew up their clothing and displayed to Cabades, who was standing close by, those parts of a woman's body which it is not proper that men should see uncovered.[63]

If their display were intended to be an act of psychological warfare, it backfired. Cabades was incited to renew the siege, and the city fell in 503.

Antioch

Returning to the Mediterranean coast, we come next to Antioch. As we have seen, Antioch was the seat of one of the four great patriarchates of the Christian world. The followers of Christ were first called "Christians" in Antioch, and the Gospel of Matthew was probably written there. Pompey annexed it in 65 BCE and it became the capital of the province of Syria. Afterward, it grew to become one of the greatest cities of the Roman and then Byzantine empires. Before most of the city was destroyed by an earthquake in 526, its Greek-speaking population may have been 250,000, including a large Jewish community. Located on the Orontes a few kilometers from the sea, it was on the edge of a well-watered and fertile plain. It was also the terminus of the main commercial road from Asia to the Mediterranean. Its harbor of Seleucia at the mouth of the Orontes attracted merchants from throughout the Mediterranean world. Like Alexandria, its status as a center of civil, military, and ecclesiastical administration added to its wealth.[64]

In the fourth century the glories and pleasures of Antioch were described in detail and with great pride by its native son Libanius. Born in 314 to a wealthy Antiochene family, he received an excellent education and became a renowned Greek rhetorician and man of letters. Despite his adherence to paganism, he enjoyed the favor of Theodosius I and knew many of the leading personalities of his time. On the occasion of the Olympic Games held in Antioch in 360,[65] he delivered a long oration in praise of the city. In this speech he touted the natural beauty of its setting, its temperate climate, its fertile lands and abundant products, and the admirable character of its people. He gave special attention to the plan of Antioch, its institutions, public buildings, and places of pleasure, including the hippodrome, theater, and baths. Moreover, Antioch was the metropolis of Asia, drawing people from throughout the world. If one sat in the marketplace, "he will sample every city, there will be so many people from each place with whom he can talk."[66] Speaking of its harbor at Seleucia, he says:

> Wherefore all ships put to sea from all parts of the world, carrying goods from everywhere, from Libya, from Europe, from Asia, from

> the islands and the coasts and the best of what is best everywhere is brought there since the quickness of selling draws hither the wits of merchants, and because of this we enjoy the fruits of the whole earth.[67]

Some two centuries later, after the great earthquake, Procopius describes Alamoundaras, the "king of the Saracens," telling the Persian ruler Cabades that Antioch was "in wealth and size and population the first of all the cities of the Eastern Roman Empire."[68] Alamoundaras (al-Mundhir III, r. 503–54) was the king of the Arab Lakhmid dynasty. A client of Persia, he ruled from al-Ḥīra, which was southeast of present-day Najaf in Iraq. His argument helped convince Cabades to invade Syria again.[69]

While Libanius reveled in Antioch's beauty and wealth, one of his students, who became no less famous than Libanius himself, saw it in starkly different terms. This was St. John Chrysostom, the second "Golden-Mouthed," whom we mentioned earlier in passing. He was born in Antioch around 347 and Libanius was his first teacher. He learned the skills of rhetoric from the master, but unlike him became a fervent Christian. He was ordained deacon at Antioch in 381 and priest in 386. His powers as a preacher brought him wide acclaim, and he eventually became bishop of Constantinople in 398. In his numerous and lengthy sermons, Chrysostom frequently and passionately—one is tempted to say with relish—denounced the luxuries and pleasures of this world. For him Antioch was a cesspool of vice and corruption.

In John's homilies on the Gospel of Matthew, for example, he bemoans the activities in the theater. It is a place of whoredom where women play the harlot both figuratively and literally.[70] Furthermore, he often scolds virgins and other respectable women in the city for wearing jewelry, makeup, and fine clothes, for this makes them indistinguishable from public women. Dressing in this fashion attracted the gaze of men who feasted their eyes. As he asserts,

> But dost thou, when thou appearest, turn towards thee the eyes of them at the market-place? Well then; for this very reason, thou shouldest not wear gold, that thou mayest not become a common

> gazing stock, and open the mouths of many accusers. For none of those whose eyes are toward thee admireth thee, but they jeer at thee, as fond of dress, as boastful, as a carnal woman.[71]

In his homilies on the Epistles of St. Paul to Timothy, delivered at Antioch, John returns to the theme of female vanity. In the course of telling women how they should *not* dress, he provides a detailed, if not stereotypical, description of how prostitutes behaved in his hometown. Women should clothe themselves with

> such attire as covers them completely, and decently, not with superfluous ornaments, for the one is becoming, the other is not. [...] Imitate not therefore the courtesans. For by such a dress they allure their many lovers; and hence many have incurred a disgraceful suspicion, and, instead of gaining any advantage from their ornaments, have injured many [by jealousy or temptation]. [...] "What can I do," thou sayest, "if another suspects me?" But thou givest the occasion by thy dress, thy looks, thy gestures. It is for this reason that Paul discourses much of dress, and much of modesty. And if he would remove those things which are only the indications of wealth, as gold, and pearls, and costly array; how much more those things which imply studied ornament, as painting, colouring the eyes, a mincing gait, the affected voice, a languishing and wanton look; the exquisite care in putting on the cloak and bodice, the nicely-wrought girdle, and the closely-fitted shoes? For he glances at all these things, in speaking of *modest apparel* and *shamefacedness*. For such things are shameless and indecent.[72]

John, who clearly paid *very* close attention to what women wore, goes on to warn that even simple dress could be sexy.

> For when a very dark coloured robe is drawn closely around the breast with the girdle (as dancers on the stage are attired), with such nicety that it may neither spread into breadth nor shrink into scantiness, but be between both; and when the bosom is set off with many folds,

> is not this more alluring than any silken robes? And when the shoe, shining through its blackness, ends in a sharp point, and imitates the elegance of painting, so that even the breadth of the sole is scarce visible—or when, though you do not indeed paint the face, you spend much time and pains on washing it, and spread a veil across the forehead, whiter than the face itself—and above that put on a hood, of which the blackness may set off the white by contrast—is there not in all this the vanity of dress? What can one say to the perpetual rolling of the eyes? To the putting on of the stomacher [the front of the bodice] so artfully as sometimes to conceal, sometimes to disclose, the fastening? For this too they sometimes expose, so as to shew the exquisiteness of the cincture, winding the hood entirely round the head.[73]

It seems that once a woman stepped into the street she could attract male attention no matter how she dressed. Among other things, this suggests that it was easy for public women to advertise their availability.

John's characterization of Antioch as a center of wickedness and shameless women is symbolized by the life of St. Pelagia, another holy harlot. Indeed, John may even refer to her in one of his sermons (Homily 67 on Matthew). If so, she would have lived in the late fourth century. Her life was recorded in Greek by Jacob, the deacon of a certain Bishop Nonnos. The latter, while on his way to Antioch from Egypt, brought about Pelagia's conversion. One day, while Jacob and several bishops, including Nonnos, were sitting outside an inn a few kilometers from Antioch, a rich prostitute, the leader of a troupe of actors, suddenly passed by them.

> This prostitute then appeared before our eyes, sitting prominently on a riding donkey adorned with little bells and caparisoned; in front of her was a great throng of her servants and she herself was decked out with gold ornaments, pearls, and all sorts of precious stones, resplendent in luxurious and expensive clothes. On her hands and feet she wore armbands, silks, and anklets decorated with all sorts of pearls, while around her neck were necklaces and strings of pendants

> and pearls. Her beauty stunned those who beheld her, captivating them in their desire for her. Young boys and girls accompanied her in haughty fashion, holding her lascivious feet; they too were adorned with golden girdles and had jewelry strung around their necks.[74]

As the woman passed before the men, the scent of her perfumes and reek of her cosmetics overwhelmed them. The bishops were

> amazed at her and her clothes, as well as the splendor of her cortege, and the fact that she went by with her head uncovered, with a scarf thrown around her shoulders in a shameless fashion, as though she were a man...[75]

Nonnos then asks his brothers if they lust after her in their hearts. He himself implicitly confesses to doing so. Consequently, he decides to convert her and, of course, succeeds. Afterward, she eventually makes a list of all of her accumulated wealth: gold, silver, jewelry, and expensive clothes. All of this is given to the needy. She becomes a penitent and, by example, leads many of her fellow public women to Christ.[76]

Of somewhat better historicity is a reference in Theophanes' chronicle written in the early ninth century. He records that in the year 632–3, when Julian was emperor, "[a] certain Thalassios, notorious for his licentiousness and profligacy, a man who had procured his own daughter for prostitution, was honored by the emperor as an examiner of entrails and lived close to the palace in Antioch."[77] He was killed when his house collapsed, but his wife and members of his household, who were Christians, were unharmed. Altogether, there is no doubt that the services of public women were easily obtained in Byzantine Antioch.

Tarsus

A short distance west of Antioch and near the coast was Tarsus (modern Tarsus in Turkey), another city with a long past. Pompey annexed it to the province of Cilicia around 67 BCE and it became the capital of that province. Tarsus was the birthplace, of course, of St. Paul. Nevertheless, like other cities it had a reputation for sinful pleasures. In the second century, Dio Chrysostom reproached the citizens of Tarsus for base behavior, just as he had denounced the people of Alexandria. For example, he chided them on the one hand for allowing their women to dress in a shockingly immodest manner in the street, and on the other for "snorting," a term that covered a range of despicable acts and could indicate the presence of a brothel.[78]

John Moschos, in his compilation of the lives of the early Church Fathers completed at the beginning of the seventh century, later makes two references associating some public women with Tarsus. The first is in the brief story of Mary the Harlot. According to Moschos, two fathers had set out from the town of Aegion for Tarsus. Aegion was not far to the east. En route they came to an inn, where they rested. Staying at the inn were three young men, who had a harlot named Mary with them. They were on their way to Aegion, no doubt from Tarsus. One of the fathers then began to read the Gospel, and this led Mary to abandon her profession and convert. Eventually she was placed in a monastery.[79] Immediately following this story is an account of the conversion of Babylas the actor and of Cometa and Nicosa, his "concubines." Babylas and his female companions worked in Tarsus. He led a disorderly life worthy of the "demons." One day he went to church and, hearing the Gospel, he repented and changed his evil ways. He then turned his possessions over to his companions, who said, "We have shared with you in the experience of sin and in the destruction of our own souls,"[80] and they asked to follow him. Afterward Babylas shut himself in one of the towers of the walls of the city, and Cometa and Nicosa did the same nearby. We seem to have here, in both instances, evidence of managed itinerant prostitution reminiscent of that at Dura-Europos.

Sykeon

Moving west from Tarsus across Anatolia toward Constantinople, the only reference to public women that I have encountered in this region in the

Byzantine period is from the obscure village of Sykeon. We know, however, that prostitution was fairly widespread in Anatolia in Antiquity. The great geographer Strabo, who was born in Amaseia (Amasya in modern Turkey) in Northern Anatolia near the Black Sea around 64 BCE and died after 21 CE, mentions it several times. In a well-known reference to Comana, which was east of Amaseia, he says it was a populous city and a notable emporium for Armenia. During the "exoduses" of the goddess, which occurred twice a year, people gathered from everywhere for the festival. He goes on to say,

> there is a multitude of women who make gain from their persons, most of whom are dedicated to the goddess, for in a way the city is a lesser Corinth, for there too, on account of the multitude of courtesans, who were sacred to Aphrodite, outsiders resorted in great numbers and kept holiday. And the merchants and soldiers who went there squandered all their money, so that the following proverb arose in reference to them: "Not for every man is the voyage to Corinth."[81]

We appear to have here a case of sacred prostitutes or, more likely, prostitutes who gathered in Comana to take advantage of the festival.[82] In any case, they fleeced an eager clientele. Later, while describing the village of Carura in Southwestern Anatolia, Strabo says it had inns and hot springs. "Moreover, it is said that once, when a brothel-keeper had taken lodging in the inns along with a large number of women, an earthquake took place by night, and that he, together with all the women, disappeared from sight."[83] Again, this is evidence of continuity in itinerant prostitution and the association of this trade with inns and baths. Strabo also says the people of the city of Alabanda, which was not far from Carura, lived in luxury and debauchery and that there were many girls who played the harp.[84] These girls were perhaps performers in the theater.

Returning to Sykeon, it was the birthplace of St. Theodore of Sykeon. His life was recorded by the abbot George, who was a novice in the monastery of Sykeon when Theodore died in 613. Sykeon has been located with some certainty near the city of Beypazarı, about 100 kilometers west of Ankara.[85] Theodore was a contemporary of St. John the Almsgiver, the

Patriarch of Alexandria. His biography provides a rare glimpse of life in Byzantine Anatolia just before the Arab invasion. According to George, the public highway or imperial post ran through Sykeon and

> on the road stood an inn kept by a very beautiful girl, Mary, and her mother, Elpidia, and a sister Despoinia. And these women lived in the inn and followed the profession of courtesans.[86]
>
> At that time when Justinian of pious memory was Emperor [r. 527–65] certain imperial decrees were being dispatched from the capital, and thus it chanced that a certain well-known man, Cosmas by name, who had become popular in the Hippodrome in the corps of those who performed acrobatic feats on camels, was appointed to carry out the Emperor's orders.
>
> On this man's journey to the East he stayed for some time in the inn, and seeing Mary and how fair she was, he desired her and took her to his bed.[87]

As a result of this union, Mary gave birth to a son and named him Theodore, meaning "gift of God." Abandoned by his father, who may not have been aware of his birth, Theodore grew up to be the bishop of the nearby city of Anastasiopolis and became a saint. His mother, aunt, and grandmother gave up prostitution. His mother married a leading citizen of Ankara and his grandmother entered a convent. After a life in which Theodore performed many miracles, he died in 613.[88] He is one of the few saints whose mother was a public woman, and his biographer attaches no stigma to this. In fact, it makes his rise to a saintly life all the more extraordinary.

Constantinople

At last we come to Constantinople, the capital of the Byzantine Empire. After its inauguration as the new seat of government in 330, it began to expand rapidly. Located at a point commanding the southern entrance to the Bosphorus, the great waterway between the Mediterranean and the Black Sea, the city was provided with immense scope for commercial enterprise and political action over a vast region. The location alone would have sufficed to make it a global emporium. When trade was combined with the attributes of an imperial capital—the court, government, headquarters of the army and navy—plus a university and the seat of an increasingly powerful patriarchate, the creation of one of the greatest cities in history inevitably followed. We cannot overemphasize the fact that Constantinople continuously drew people from great distances. Apart from traders, they included petitioners, litigants, scholars, foreign officials, and even pilgrims who came to see a growing collection of Christian relics. Furthermore, its great circus, theater, and numerous baths gave it a reputation as a pleasure dome. Writing in the sixth century, Procopius claimed the people of the city took delight in devoting themselves to shameful and base pursuits. They turned to religion during the time of plague, but afterward reverted to their old ways.[89] By the time of the Arab conquests, Constantinople had surpassed Alexandria as the greatest city in Europe and the Middle East. Not surprisingly, it provided the greatest prospects for public women.

Prostitution was associated with Constantinople from the beginning. Even the mother of Constantine herself, Helena (later St. Helena) had reputedly worked at an inn as a maid, which was a euphemism for a public woman. It is possible that she met Constantine's father, Constantius, at her place of work, which was probably near Nicomedia. Constantius had been an army officer before becoming emperor.[90] Perhaps their story paralleled in certain respects that of Mary and her uncle Abraham of Qidun, which also occurred in the fourth century. In any case, prostitution quickly took hold in Constantinople. It was so profitable that Constantine (who, like Theodore, was made a saint) decided to tax it. This levy was included in his *collatio lustralis,* a tax in gold and silver imposed throughout the empire every five years on traders in the widest sense.[91] The emperor supposedly also tried to contain this profession by confining it to a single large brothel whose entrance was marked by a statue of Aphrodite. It was located, significantly, in the Zeugma ("Junction") quarter on the Golden Horn.[92] As McGinn has suggested, however, this was probably an attempt by later writers to make Constantine more Christian than he was. Otherwise there was no justification for such containment unless it was meant to facilitate tax collection.[93]

Theodosius I, who as mentioned above made Christianity the state religion, was apparently the first emperor to try to improve the lot of public women, which again indicates that they were commonplace. According to John Malalas (ca. 491–ca. 578), the first Byzantine world chronicler, early in his reign (379–95) Theodosius

> pulled down the three temples in Constantinople on what was formerly known as the Acropolis. [...] The Temple of Aphrodite he made into a carriage-house for the praetorian prefect, and he built lodging-houses close by and gave orders that penniless prostitutes could stay there free of charge.[94]

Later, when Theodosius II published a codification of Roman law between 429 and 438, it included a provision depriving fathers and mothers of their legal right to force their daughters or slaves into prostitution.[95] Again, this code was in force, theoretically, throughout the empire. The tax on prostitution, however, was maintained. It was abolished by Anastasius in 498, apparently as a result of growing religious pressure on the state to refrain from profiting from the wages of public women.

A few years after the Theodosian Code was promulgated, St. Daniel the Stylite arrived in Constantinople. His life sheds additional light on prostitutes in the great metropolis. He was born in 409 in a village near Samosata on the upper Euphrates (Samsat in Turkey). He spent his youth in a monastery nearby. During a visit to Antioch he met the renowned ascetic St. Simeon the Stylite, who spent his life on a stone pillar (Greek *stylos* = pillar) close to that city. Inspired by Simeon, and having received his blessing, Daniel decided to follow his path. In 451 he went to Constantinople. Some time later he mounted a pillar at Anaplus (Rumeli Hisarı), which was a few kilometers up the European side of the Bosphorus. Eventually Emperor Leo I (r. 457–74) erected for him several pillars with a platform on top. Daniel's reputation for sanctity spread, and many people came to hear him preach or seek cures for illnesses.

According to his biographer, who appears to have been a young disciple, Daniel's fame and growing influence aroused the envy of certain elements of Constantinople. At that time there was a certain harlot in the city, named Basiane. She had come to Constantinople from the east to seek her fortune and had become infamous for entrapping "those who hunted after women of her sort." Therefore those who were envious of Daniel made her a proposition: if she would seduce him and ruin his reputation, they would pay her a hundred gold pieces. "The shameless woman agreed and went up to the holy man with much parade and took with her a crowd of young men and prostitutes and simulated illness and remained in the suburb opposite the Saint's enclosure."[96] Daniel, however, was unmoved. Failing in her purpose, Basiane nevertheless told her supporters that she had, in fact, seduced him. As a ploy to get their money, she claimed that the saint had become enamored of her and invited her up to his pillar, but she refused to mount it. Then, fearing that she might be killed, she fled to the city. As a result of her allegations, the rumor spread that the saint had been compromised. Later, however, God made her feel guilty; she admitted publicly that she had lied, and provided the names and ranks of the men who had supported her.[97] This affair strengthened, of course, the esteem for Daniel, and he died happily on his pillar in 493. Daniel had played a role in the controversy over the doctrine (which he had opposed) that Christ did not have two distinct natures but one. His biographer describes the supporters of Basiane as "heretics." Consequently, this incident may also be meant to show how low his adversaries would stoop in order to smear him. It symbolizes as well how renowned public women could be used to effect certain political or religious goals.

A number of former prostitutes, like Constantine's mother, seem to have married well and to have risen to positions of power. The most famous of them was, of course, the Empress Theodora. We encountered her above during her career as a courtesan in Cyrenaica and Egypt. In his *Secret History*, Procopius, who knew her well, goes into great detail on her scandalous life before she met the future emperor Justinian. He says she had an attractive face and good figure, but she was short and somewhat pallid, also stating: "Her glance was invariably fierce and intensely hard."[98]

Theodora was born a few years after St. Daniel passed away. Her father was a keeper of circus animals in Constantinople and died when she and her two sisters were quite young. No doubt in order to survive, their mother put each of them on the stage as soon as she seemed old enough for this profession. The eldest, Comito, quickly became one of the most popular harlots of the day. As Procopius states,

> Theodora, who came next, clad in a little tunic with long sleeves, the usual dress of a slave girl, used to assist her in various ways, following her about and invariably carrying on her shoulders the bench on which her sister habitually sat at public meetings. For the time being Theodora was still too undeveloped to be capable of sharing a man's bed or having intercourse like a woman; but she acted as a sort of male prostitute to satisfy customers of the lowest type, and slaves at that, who when accompanying their owners to the theatre seized their opportunity to divert themselves in this revolting manner; and for some considerable time she remained in a brothel, given up to this unnatural bodily commerce. But as soon as she was old enough and fully developed, she joined the women on the stage and promptly became a courtesan, of the type our ancestors called "the dregs of the army." For she was not a flautist or harpist; she was not even qualified to join the corps of dancers; but she merely sold her attractions to anyone who came along, putting her whole body at his disposal.[99]

Later she joined the actors on stage and sometimes stripped naked and danced. She even went to dinner parties, sometimes at the homes of distinguished citizens, and indulged in group sex. She frequently became pregnant, but "by using pretty well all the tricks of the trade she was able to induce immediate abortion." In order to advertise herself, she would sometimes walk into the crowd at the theater while wearing only a girdle about her private parts. Then,

> with this minimum covering she would spread herself out and lie face upwards on the floor. Servants on whom this task had been imposed

> would sprinkle barley grains over her private parts, and geese trained for the purpose used to pick them off one by one with their bills and swallow them.[100]

Procopius goes on to describe some of her performances on stage, which were live sex shows. Her behavior must have made her famous—or rather, notorious—throughout Constantinople. She certainly came to the attention of men of the highest rank. As we have seen, she left the theater to become the mistress of the governor of the Pentapolis in Cyrenaica. Subsequently abandoned by him, she worked her way around the Eastern Mediterranean and returned to Constantinople. Soon after she arrived, she met none other than Justinian, the heir to the throne, and became his mistress. He appointed her to the rank of patrician, which brought her great influence and wealth. Justinian wished to marry her, but Roman law barred a man ranked as senator from marrying a courtesan. Justinian therefore persuaded Justin I, his uncle, to change the law. Theodora then became his wife and, when Justinian succeeded his uncle in 527, she ascended the imperial throne as empress.[101]

Despite being her severest critic, Procopius gives Theodora credit for trying to curb the practice of prostitution in the capital once she became empress. He says that she rounded up more than 500 public women who sold their services in the middle of the forum for a shilling ([*sic*]—per the translator, that is, small change) a time, just enough to survive. They were then sent to the mainland opposite the city, perhaps to modern Galata across the Golden Horn or to the Asian shore, and confined to the convent known as Repentance. However, this attempt to force them to change their ways was a failure. From time to time some of them leapt from the walls and either killed themselves or escaped.[102]

The Byzantine chronicler John Malalas reports that Theodora also tried to stop the abuses of brothel-keepers. They used to travel about looking for poor men with daughters and, for a few gold coins (*nomismata*), take the girls as though under contract. Then they prostituted the girls, dressing them for the part. Theodora ordered that all such brothel-keepers be arrested and be brought in with their girls. She then bought out their "contracts" and freed the girls, giving them a set of clothes and one *nomisma* each.[103]

We should mention here that one of Theodora's closest associates, if not her friend, Antonina (the wife of Belisarius, who was Justinian's famous general and commander-in-chief), had also been a public woman. Our source of information is again Procopius. He relates that her father and grandfather had been charioteers who raced in Byzantium—that is, Constantinople—and Thessalonica to the west. Her mother was an actress who sold her sexual services. Antonina grew up to live the same kind of life and gave birth to a number of children. Under unclear circumstances, she met, charmed, and, with due ceremony, married Belisarius, who was well aware of her previous life but found it no obstacle to marriage or his career.[104] Again, this is evidence that courtesans were ubiquitous, could move in the highest circles of the state, and were accepted seemingly without reservation. Marriage, especially in the upper classes, was the ultimate test of social acceptability.

THE ARMY

Before describing Justinian's legal reforms which improved the lot of prostitutes in the Empire, and which may have been introduced with the prodding of Theodora, a few words are in order about public women and the army. The defense or expansion of the Empire depended in large measure on a well-trained standing army that included garrisons at strategic locations. As we have seen above and will see again repeatedly in later chapters, prostitutes flocked to wherever there were large groups of men. Soldiers—and, it goes without saying, sailors—provided an excellent market for their services. As we have learned with respect to Dura-Europos, some of these women traveled from garrison to garrison. Others must have been local women who set up shop close to the military camps, and still others traveled with the army when it went on the march.[105] This may be what Procopius means when he refers to prostitutes as "the dregs of the army." Our sources, however, shed little light on this, probably because it was such a common feature of military life that it was not considered worth mentioning, or prostitutes were simply included collectively among "camp followers."

One Byzantine source that is worthy of note in this respect is the *Tactica* of Leo VI (r. 886–912). Although compiled at the beginning of the tenth century, it was a summary of many military treatises from Antiquity and was intended to be a handbook for officers. Its rare references to women are only in the context of "fornication," which can be interpreted to include (if not strictly to mean) the services of public women. Officers were to guard against fornication because it undermined discipline. It therefore must have been omnipresent. According to the *Tactica*, "Self-control is a valued possession for the general and for the army, just as fornication is adverse and destructive, especially when it occurs with captive women."[106] Furthermore, "Above everything else you must drive fornication out of the army, for this introduces the greatest evils, as we have learned from both ancient and recent histories."[107] As we will see later in the chapters on Egypt and Syria, prostitutes accompanied the Crusader armies, and Christian religious officials attributed defeats at the hands of Muslims to fornication committed by the soldiers of God.

There is a curious reference to the important role of a public woman as a courier during a military coup d'état in Byzantium. In 919, when the commander of the Byzantine fleet, Romanus Lecapenus, overthrew the regency of Zoe, the fourth wife of Leo VI, and married his daughter to Leo's young son Constantine VII, Zoe's commander-in-chief Leo Phocas rebelled. Romanus then sent letters in the name of the emperor to Leo's troops in order to spread disaffection in their ranks. The documents were in the care of a cleric named Michael and a prostitute named Anna. Those of Anna reached their destination and resulted in wholesale desertions.[108] Perhaps Anna's profession made it easy for her to move among troops.

PROSTITUTION, ROMAN LAW, AND CHRISTIAN TOLERANCE

Among the major accomplishments of Emperor Justinian was his codification of Roman law. The results of this project, which was a condensation and harmonization of the whole of Roman law, appeared in several stages between 529 and 533. Earlier codes were repealed (their provisions were deleted or altered), while recent laws, including those issued by Justinian (*novellae*), were included. Justinian's codification was in Latin, so its use in the Greek-speaking Byzantine Empire may have been limited until it was translated. In any case, it was, theoretically, in effect throughout the Empire.

The code, especially the *novellae*, has much to say about prostitution.[109] Most importantly, prostitutes had legal status, although their work was considered to be dishonorable. A prostitute was defined as a woman who lived unchastely and earned money by openly selling her sexual favors in such places as houses of ill-fame or taverns, which included inns. "Openly" meant she sold her favors indiscriminately and frequently. If a woman accepted money for intercourse with only one or two men, she would not be considered to have openly prostituted herself.[110] Thus, if a woman were in dire straits and were compelled to sell her favors a few times, this would not suffice to declare her a prostitute. A woman who openly prostituted herself was not allowed to testify as a witness.[111] Prostitutes wore distinctive dress, but it was not described.[112]

Whereas a woman could sell her sexual favors as a legitimate business transaction, procuring was subject to punishment. A procurer was one who profited by the prostitution of slaves or free women. If he did this in addition to another business—such as innkeeper, stable-keeper, or bath-keeper—where he provided women to strangers, it too would still be considered procuring.[113] In like manner, a procuress was a woman who prostituted women for money. Included in this category were women who operated taverns and kept women there who sold themselves.[114] A procurer had no right of accusation in court.[115] If a man purchased a female slave on condition of not prostituting her and then did so, she was entitled to her freedom.[116]

It should be mentioned here that unlike prostitution, adultery was for women (and men) a serious crime. For a woman it was defined as intercourse between a married woman and any man other than her husband. For a man the definition was much narrower. He could have sex with a wide range of women without incurring the penalties for adultery. These women included slaves, prostitutes, and actresses. In order to avoid the punishment for adultery, a woman might, in fact, claim she was a prostitute.[117] Roman law, however, took this ruse into account.[118] Later, as we will see in the next chapter, Islamic law paralleled many of these provisions of Roman law.

We have seen above how, according to John Malalas, Theodora attempted to end the abuses of brothel-keepers. Her efforts may have been carried out in concert with Justinian's *novellae* in which he attempted to curtail the abuses of organized prostitution. In the preamble to an important section concerning prostitution, the emperor states that the calling of procurer was so odious that there were many legal enactments against it including his own—which suggests, of course, that they were ineffective. He adds that he was well aware that certain men traveled through the provinces and other places and promised young girls clothes in order to deceive them. After taking possession of these girls, these men brought them to Constantinople, placed them in their houses, and profited by prostituting them. Moreover, the girls were compelled to sign contracts in which they agreed to continue in this business as long as those who possessed them required.[119]

Justinian goes on to lament that those who organized this kind of prostitution carried out their evil actions

> in almost all this Imperial City, as well as in the countries beyond the seas; and (what is worse) houses of this kind exist in close proximity to holy places and religious establishments; and at the present time this wickedness is so prevalent that any persons who wish to withdraw these unhappy girls from the life that they are leading, and legally marry them, are not permitted to do so.
>
> Some of these wretches are so unprincipled as to deliver over to corruption girls who have not yet reached their tenth year, and in order to ransom these unhappy beings for the purpose of contracting lawful marriage, great sums of money are exacted. Ten thousand means of effecting their ruin exist which are not susceptible of being described in words; and the resulting evil is so great, and the cruelty so widespread that, while it was first confined to the most remote parts of the Capital, it now not only extends over the city itself but also over all its suburbs.[120]

The emperor, therefore, forbade anyone from leading young women astray and keeping them in houses to be prostituted by promising them clothing, food, and ornaments. All contracts binding these women to such people were null and void. Those who imposed these contracts were to be expelled from Constantinople as pestiferous persons for reducing free women to slavery by requiring them to lead a licentious life. Furthermore, if anyone forced a girl into prostitution and, without giving her sufficient food, kept the wages of her work, he was to be arrested by the chief magistrate (*praetor*) and condemned to death. If anyone knowingly rented a house to a procurer, he was to pay a fine of 100 pounds of gold (which may indicate that such houses were quite profitable). In short, pandering was absolutely forbidden.[121]

In order to avoid the prohibition on contracting women for prostitution, recruiters then resorted to extracting oaths from women to the same effect. Justinian forbade this as well and imposed a penalty of ten pounds of gold on anyone who did so. This sum was to be given to the unfortunate woman. If the governor of a province himself were guilty of extracting such oaths, the fine was to be collected by a military magistrate or metropolitan bishop.[122] It seems, therefore, that even some high-ranking state officials may have found prostitution to be a lucrative investment.

With respect to prostitution, Justinian's codification remained the law of the land, at least on the books, until the fall of Byzantium in 1453.[123] But over the centuries, the realities of daily life, changing political and social circumstances, and distance from the capital, made its enforcement problematic. Still, it must have limited some abuses from time to time in the business of prostitution. The business itself continued, legally recognized, as a common feature of urban life. Writing much later, the Muslim theologian ʿAbd al-Jabbār ibn Aḥmad (d. 415/1025), who lived in Baghdad and then in Rayy, asserts—perhaps based on reports of merchants—that the cities of Byzantium had many markets for prostitutes. These women had their own shops and sat in their doorways, uncovered and conspicuous.[124] Michael Psellus (1018–ca.1078/96), the greatest Byzantine man of letters in the eleventh century, corroborates, and sheds additional light on, the magnitude of this business around the same time. He says that Emperor Michael

IV (r. 1034–41) desired forgiveness of his sins. One way to achieve this was to save lost souls. So he decided to save public women in Constantinople en masse.

> Scattered all over the city was a vast multitude of harlots, and without attempting to turn them away from their trade by argument—that class of women is deaf anyway to all advice that would save them—without even trying to curb their activities by force, lest he earn the reputation of violence, he built in the Queen of Cities a place of refuge to house them, an edifice of enormous size and very great beauty. Then, in the stentorian notes of the public herald, he issued a proclamation: all women who trafficked in their beauty, provided they were willing to renounce their trade and live in luxury, were to find sanctuary in this building: they were to change their own clothes for the habit of nuns, and all fear of poverty would be banished from their lives forever, "for all things, unsown, without labour of hands, would spring forth for their use (Homer, *Odyssey*, ix, 108–9)." Thereupon a great swarm of prostitutes descended upon this refuge, relying on the emperor's edict and changed both their garments and their manner of life, a youthful band enrolled in the service of God, as soldiers of virtue.[125]

As for the Church, its attitude toward public women was rather ambivalent, tolerating their profession as a social necessity while being opposed to lewd conduct in the widest sense. In the literature of the Church, like that of Roman writers, prostitution was a despised profession. For the Romans this view was compounded by the fact that, for them, most prostitutes were slaves and not fit for the company of respectable people under any circumstances.[126] The Church, however, saw prostitutes as weak or strayed women who could be saved in spite of themselves. As we have seen, this notion is found repeatedly in the lives of the saints. It certainly contributed to a more sympathetic view of their lot and attempts by the Byzantine authorities to improve their working conditions. Furthermore, the prostitution of slaves seems to have declined significantly with the rise of Byzantium and the spread of Christianity.

The Church's ambivalence toward prostitution was epitomized by (and indeed can be traced to) St. Augustine (354–430). A rake before his conversion, he subsequently found sexual intercourse to be offensive and became the champion of celibacy. For Augustine nothing was more sordid than prostitution. Yet, in his view, if it were eliminated from society, everything would be polluted by lust. Therefore prostitution had to be tolerated as a social necessity. Augustine argued that prostitution guaranteed the established patterns of sexual relationships.[127] In other words, prostitution held society together. Later theologians and canonists accepted Augustine's view. Some of them, in fact, held that this institution was necessary for the public good.[128] The chief objects of Church punishment were not the public women but those who exploited their services: pimps, procurers, and brothel-keepers.[129]

CONCLUSION

Despite the uneven quality of our sources and their many gaps in time and place, a number of general conclusions can be reached about the nature of prostitution in the Eastern Mediterranean world in Late Antiquity, from the reign of Constantine I to the Arab conquests. Above all, it was a common urban service industry. It was found in all the large towns and cities, especially the ports. It was a legitimate profession for a woman and was frequently taxed like other trades. Taxation confirmed its institutionalization and legitimacy. Procuring was sometimes subject to punishment, but public women were entitled to sell their services and retain their earnings. Apart from taxation, the state only intervened occasionally to curb certain abuses in the business. The Church frowned on prostitution, but ultimately tolerated it. Prostitution was the grist of edifying religious tales of redemption and was a social necessity that helped maintain and preserve conventional sexual relationships—it protected respectable women.

Prostitutes were both slaves and free women from various religious, ethnic, and social backgrounds. In Late Antiquity there may have been more free women than slaves, but this is difficult to determine. Some worked in brothels, while others worked in other establishments or on the street. Some worked under contract while others were independent businesswomen. Many were itinerant, either in groups or alone. Public women were drawn to wherever a large number of men assembled—a classic example of supply meeting a continuous demand. In addition to all commercial hubs, profitable places of business included fairs, festivals, places of pilgrimage, and army garrisons—and many of these were outside urban areas. Some women certainly accompanied or followed the army while it was on the march. In urban areas, prostitutes sold their services in town squares, agoras (marketplaces), forums (public meeting places), theaters, circuses, taverns, inns, and public baths. Taverns, inns, and some baths, or hot springs, were also found along the major commercial highways. Some public women in the cities may even have periodically gone into the countryside in search of customers. The number of prostitutes in the cities must have been large and their prices low so that their services were affordable to most men. Their customers included government officials, merchants, pilgrims, soldiers, sailors, clergy, and slaves. Prostitutes were a common and unremarkable feature of life, and most people were indifferent to them.

The chief motivation to become a public woman was, as in any job, to earn a living—in some cases specifically to escape poverty or to provide for one's family. Others turned to the business because they were cajoled or intimidated, were raped, or saw it as a means of upward mobility. It was one of the few professions open to an independent businesswoman, one who decided to work outside the family or kin group. Prostitution could take a woman to the highest levels of male power and society. It was not a bar to marriage. Actresses, mimes, dancers, and musicians often doubled as prostitutes. Public women did not cover their faces, which they accented with cosmetics, and wore clothing, including shoes, that distinguished them from other women. Indeed, their clothing was suggestive and elegant and was complemented with jewelry and perfume. All this was part of their marketing, and made these women easy to find. Furthermore, both their gait and speech could be used to entice clients. They were certainly skilled in seducing young men.

Finally, the information that we have on prostitution during this period is almost completely detached from the vicissitudes of social and political life in the Byzantine Empire, including religious controversy. Yet it must have been affected by such turmoil as the Nika Riot in the reign of Justinian, which fed off the mobs in the circuses, not to mention the disruptions resulting from plagues, earthquakes, foreign invasions and other disasters.[130] Then again, the lack of such contexts might be taken as evidence of its ubiquity and that it was too ordinary to mention. Moreover, given the nature of prostitution, it was a profession that could thrive, of course, in times of both economic decline and prosperity. In the seventh century most of the eastern and southern regions of Byzantium underwent a profound and permanent political change after they fell to Arab armies and came under Muslim control. In the following chapters we will explore the extent to which the aforesaid features of prostitution were commonplace, and new ones appeared, within a new political and religious ethos, until the late Middle Ages.

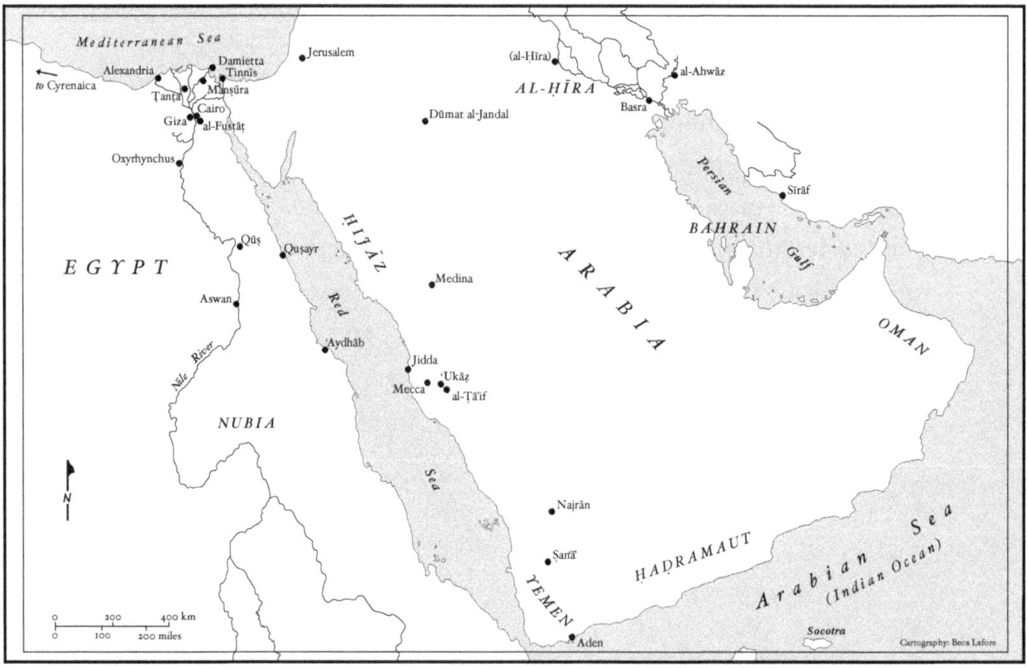

MAP 1 *Egypt and Arabia in the Middle Ages*

TWO

Public Women in Medieval Arabia

POLITICAL AND SOCIAL CONTEXT

Although Arabia, with its contrasting desolate and luxuriant landscapes, was on the periphery of the Byzantine and Persian empires, it was intimately connected, politically and economically, to those realms in the centuries before Islam. The population of the peninsula, which may not have been much more than that of the city of Alexandria at its height, was mostly settled. The remainder was nomadic or seminomadic. Most of the settled population lived in South Arabia, whose high mountains captured monsoon rains and produced abundant groundwater. Here agriculture flourished and fairly large and powerful polities or states arose. Elsewhere, Arabia was uninhabited or chiefly characterized by widely scattered oasis towns and modest agricultural settlements. Writing in the mid-second century CE, Ptolemy (d. 168) listed 151 settlements in the entire peninsula. He described only six as cities, all in South Arabia. The rest were villages, towns, and market centers.[1]

Both Byzantium and Persia had long cultivated political ties with various groups and entities in Arabia. This was largely because of the importance of local or transit trade through the peninsula and because it was the launching point for long-distance trade with India and the Far East. Byzantine influence generally spread south along the west coast of Arabia and that of

Persia along the eastern and southern coasts. By the seventh century, Persia had outmaneuvered Byzantium. It controlled Bahrain and Oman and sent forces to Yemen to help the tribal confederation of Ḥimyar expel Christian colonists from Ethiopia, an erstwhile ally of Byzantium in the struggle for South Arabia. As a result, Persia controlled all the major Arabian ports.[2] Meanwhile, in the opposite direction, on the northern fringe of Arabia, Byzantium and Persia had established client states in their respective spheres of influence in the west and east. The client state for Byzantium was that of the Ghassānids, centered on Jābiya near Lake Tiberias in Syria, and for Persia that of the Lakhmids, centered on al-Ḥīra in Southern Iraq. Both states were tribal confederations. Furthermore, both were Christian, although the Lakhmids were Nestorians, considered heretics by Christian adherents of the Council of Chalcedon. Their namesake—Nestorius, the Patriarch of Constantinople (r. 428–31)—had advanced the belief that the human and divine natures of Jesus were separate. In any case, al-Ḥīra, the greater metropolis, was a major center of the spread of Christianity to Arabia. Furthermore, to the extent that the Ghassānids and Lakhmids attempted to emulate their master's culture, they also transmitted or filtered to some degree various aspects of that culture to Arabia.[3]

On the eve of Islam the majority of the people in Arabia were pagans, Jews, or Christians. Pagans worshipped an assortment of divinities and made pilgrimages during certain annual holy months to a number of shrines and sanctuaries scattered about the peninsula. Elements of a large and ancient Jewish community were found in the northern oases, especially Yathrib (later called Medina) and South Arabia.[4] Competing with Jews for the allegiance of the pagans was a smaller Christian community. Christians were strong in Eastern Arabia and had footholds in South Arabia where they received political and military support from time to time from Ethiopia. Byzantium also provided them with assistance, although it was somewhat more ephemeral. Beginning in the fifth century, the main Christian center in South Arabia was the city of Najrān (in Northern Yemen). Around 520 the Judaizing king of Ḥimyar captured the city and subjected its Christian population to severe persecution. This provoked an invasion from Ethiopia and Byzantium. As a city of Christian martyrs, Najrān then grew into a great place of pilgrimage for Christians in Arabia. It later suffered from the Persian invasion of 570, but was not eclipsed until the rise of Islam.[5]

The religious mixture in Arabia was combined with considerable ethnic diversity in the major trading centers, especially the ports. As mentioned, the Persians controlled the ports of Eastern Arabia and frequently those of South Arabia as well. Greek and other merchants from the Mediterranean region also made their way to South Arabia. At the end of the first century, Strabo describes merchants from Alexandria who traveled down the Red Sea to South Arabia and on to India.[6] The anonymous Greek work the *Periplus of the Erythraean Sea*, which apparently dates to the same period, describes Muza (modern-day Mocha) as bustling with commercial activity. Countless ship owners, charterers, and sailors were found there.[7] Traders from Ethiopia, other parts of Africa, and even India also conducted business at the ports and inland markets of the peninsula. Moreover, it is not impossible that some Chinese reached Arabia.[8]

OPPORTUNITIES FOR PUBLIC WOMEN, AND THEIR EXPLOITATION, UP TO THE TIME OF MUHAMMAD

We have seen in the previous chapter that public women in the Eastern Mediterranean world sold their services mainly in places where large numbers of men gathered. The only significant exceptions were taverns and inns at staging posts, which were usually a day's march apart, along commercial routes where the traffic could be light but steady. There is no reason to doubt that these conditions also pertained to Arabia. Thus, public women there would have been drawn or brought to the ports, inland cities and large market towns, periodic fairs, and pilgrimage sites in addition to taverns and inns along trade routes.

We have very few literary sources on this matter, but they support this assumption. One of these sources is al-Ṭabarī (d. 310/923), the great Muslim historian and commentator on the Qur'an. He says that the Persian ruler Kisrā (Khusraw) Anūshirwān (r. 531–79) ordered one of his cavalry commanders Basak (?), son of Māhbūdh, to build the fortress of al-Mushaqqar, which was located in the region of Ḥajar in Eastern Arabia or Bahrain. He began construction, but was then told that the workmen would not remain there unless they were provided with womenfolk: "So he brought for them whores from the regions of the Sawād and al-Ahwāz."[9] Sawād was then the Arabic word for Iraq, especially Lower Iraq, near the head of the Persian Gulf. Al-Ahwāz was a town about 200 kilometers north of the Gulf and connected to it by river. The implication is that Basak imported prostitutes for the workers and that these women were brought from gulf ports.

Muḥammad ibn Ḥabīb (d. 245/860), who describes the customs and history of pre-Islamic and early Islamic Arabia, mentions the business of prostitution in Dūmat al-Jandal, which was an oasis and major market in Northern Arabia on the direct route between Bostra in Syria and Yathrib (Medina) and between al-Ḥīra in the east and Yathrib. He states that many slaves lived there in tents (*buyūt sha'r*) and that their owners compelled the young women among them to work as prostitutes (*fa-kānū yukrihūna fatayātahum 'alā 'l-bighā'*).[10] The same practice occurred more or less contemporaneously hundreds of kilometers to the south in Mecca, another market town and seat of the pre-Islamic Kaaba shrine and the god Hubal. The polymath Ibn Qutayba (d. 279/889), the geographer Ibn Rusta (fl. late fourth/early tenth century), and others say that 'Abd Allāh ibn Jud'ān, a notable member of Muhammad's Quraysh tribe and who lived at the end of the sixth century, was a notorious slave trader in Mecca. He hired out slave girls as prostitutes (*yusā'īna*) and sold their children.[11] In his great *al-Fihrist* (Index) of books, Ibn al-Nadīm ((d. 385/995) records that al-Haytham ibn 'Adī—one of the pupils of al-Wāqidī (d. 207/822), the great authority from Mecca on early Islamic history—wrote a work called "The Names of the Prostitutes of the Quraysh during the Pre-Islamic Period and the Names of those to Whom They Gave Birth."[12] Unfortunately, it has not survived.

Some towns had a quarter set aside for prostitutes. This was the case in al-Ṭā'if, an agricultural town south of Mecca and source of much of its fruit. We learn that the town had such a quarter in the well-known story concerning the controversy over the paternity of Ziyād ibn Abīhi whom

Muʿāwiya, the first Umayyad caliph (r. 41–60/661–80), declared to be his half-brother in 44/664–5. According to the version of the story told by the historian al-Masʿūdī (d. 346/956), one Abū Maryam al-Salūlī, the proprietor of a tavern (*khammār*) in al-Ṭā'if during the time before Islam, testified that he had brought together Abū Sufyān, Muʿāwiya's father, and Sumayya, the mother of Ziyād, for the purpose of fornication (*zinā'*). At that time Sumayya was one of those who "possessed the banners" (*dhawāt al-rāyāt*) in the town, meaning that they were prostitutes who indicated their availability by hanging banners from their place of work. This might suggest that local authorities taxed them, but we have no record of such a procedure. In any case, Sumayya was a slave of the physician al-Ḥārith ibn Kalada (d. 13/634–5) and paid him a share of her earnings. She carried on her business where the prostitutes (*baghāyā*) were installed in al-Ṭā'if, outside the residential area in the place called the "quarter of the prostitutes" (*ḥārat al-baghāyā*), which seems to indicate that brothels were "zoned."[13] She had been married to ʿUbayd, a Greek (*Rūmī*) slave in the household of al-Ḥārith.[14] Al-Masʿūdī goes on to say that Abū Miryam declared that Abū Sufyān had come to him in al-Ṭā'if while he was a tavern keeper in the Jāhiliyya (the time before Islam) and said, "Bring me a prostitute." Abū Miryam carried out his wish but could only find Sumayya, the slave girl of al-Ḥārith. Abū Sufyān asked the tavern keeper about her cleanliness, but he said he was in no position to judge. Abū Miryam brought him the woman and locked the door of the tavern. Shortly thereafter, Abū Sufyān came out, wiped his brow, and said, "I've never made love to a woman like that before Abū Miryam, despite her flaccid breasts and odor."[15] Muʿāwiya clearly felt no embarrassment at claiming Ziyād as a relative from such a union.[16]

In addition to showing that some towns had a special quarter for prostitutes, this story clearly reveals that taverns could serve as their place of business and that tavern keepers could act as procurers. Furthermore, some passages from pre-Islamic Arabic poetry, the renowned *Muʿallaqāt* ("Suspended Odes") are highly suggestive of the prostitution of singing girls in taverns or at wine-drinking parties. In the *muʿallaqa* of the poet al-Aʿshā (ca. 570–625; educated in al-Ḥīra) we read, concerning a visit to a tavern,

> 'Twas as though the harp waked the lute's responsive note,
> when the loose-robed chantress touched it, singing shrill
> with quavering throat
> Here and there, among the party, damsels fair superbly glide;
> each her long white skirt lets trail and swings a wineskin at her
> side.[17]

The poet Ṭarafa, whose birth and death dates are unknown, describes a drinking party in his *muʿallaqa*, saying:

> A singing-wench comes to us in her striped gown and saffron robe,
> Wide the opening of her collar, delicate her skin
> to my companions' fingers, tender her nakedness.
> When we say "let's hear from you," she advances to us
> Chanting fluently, her glance languid, in effortless song.[18]

The taverns could be located, of course, at caravan staging posts as well as in cities and towns. Those between Yathrib (Medina) and Mecca, for example, were convenient and well traveled.[19]

Located between al-Ṭā'if and Mecca, and a short distance from both, was ʿUkāẓ, the site of the most famous and most important of the annual fairs of the Arabs before Islam. Near it were the fairs of Majanna and Dhū 'l-Majāz. The medieval philologist al-Marzūqī (d. 421/1030) lists some 16 such fairs that flourished around the periphery of Arabia, mainly in the west, before Islam.[20] Most, if not all, were held during certain sacred months when fighting was forbidden. A few were held in conjunction with local pilgrimages. ʿUkāẓ, for example, was held just before the pilgrimage to ʿArafa (or ʿArafāt) and Minā outside Mecca.[21] These fairs were, above all, temporary markets for the exchange of all kinds of goods, including slaves. In addition they were accompanied by cultural events, such as poetry readings. The combination of trade, cultural exhibitions, and perhaps pilgrimage resulted in a great festival that must have attracted people from great distances. Among them, of course, were a large number of men, many of whom were traveling without female companionship. This provided opportunities for public women, who set up shop at the fairs.

In his study of pre-Islamic and Islamic fairs, Sa'īd al-Afghānī records the story of one Mu'āwiya ibn 'Amr ibn al-Sharīd (the Vagabond!) who went to the 'Ukāẓ fair and, while walking through the market, encountered a beautiful woman named Asmā' al-Muriyya. He thought she was a prostitute (*baghīy*) and summoned her, but he was mistaken.[22] The same writer tells us the tale of a certain Ibn Salīṭ, who also went to 'Ukāẓ. There a woman from the Banū Khath'am caught sight of him and he, in turn, admired her. She proved amiable toward him and he made love to her. She later gave birth to a daughter whom she named Jāriyat ("the girl of") ibn Salīṭ. One day Ibn Salīṭ again found himself in 'Ukāẓ. The woman to whom he had made love, her mother, and aunt approached him and solicited him. As soon as the woman saw him she recognized him and said to her mother, "This is [the father of] Jāriya [the girl]." Her mother replied, "Like a *jāriya* [in this case a play on words, meaning "slave girl"], let the harlot commit fornication in secret or openly [*bi-mithli jāriya fa-litazni al-zāniya sirran aw 'alāniyyatan*]."[23] The meaning of this is unclear. Perhaps her mother was saying that the possibility of having a child by a customer should not deter her from her trade. We have already mentioned above that slave girls were prostituted at Dūmat al-Jandal, which also was the site of a fair.

Irfan Shahîd has likened these fairs to the festival of Classical Greece, the *panēgyris*.[24] It is worth noting that these festivals, which were religio-commercial affairs, continued in Byzantium and passed on to post-Byzantine (or Ottoman) life in the Balkans and Anatolia. Speros Vryonis, Jr. cites Libanius, the fourth-century orator whom we met in Antioch in the previous chapter, as saying, "When *panēgyreis* are about to take place desire comes to men, when they are occurring there is pleasure, and when they have ceased there is remembrance."[25] In short, the *panēgyris* was a place to purchase the services of a pretty girl. This seems to have been the case well into Ottoman times. The renowned seventeenth-century Ottoman traveler Evliya Chelebi (d. ca. 1687) corroborates this in his description of the great *panēgyris* that he attended in 1665 in the city of Fohşan, which was located on both sides of the Kovel (?) River dividing Wallachia from

Moldavia. He reports that the fair teemed with people who seemed to come from the ends of the earth. Countless booths and shops were set up and concerts of various instruments summoned "prostitutes (*fâhişe*) by the thousands."[26] Later, in 1670, he describes another huge *panēgyris* that he witnessed at the meadow and plain of Doyran in the district of Strumitza in Macedonia in which "The jostling crowds are like a rabble army, and the market is brisk for forty days and forty nights. Even women openly sell their secret wares."[27] The pre-Islamic fairs in Arabia must have had the same carnival-like atmosphere and must have drawn public women from many towns and cities. Some of these women may have been itinerant, going from fair to fair, either independently or under the management of their owners.

As mentioned, there were many pilgrimage sites and shrines scattered about Arabia in the time before Islam. The association of some of them with fairs raises the question of the extent to which prostitutes served pilgrims. Like Mary of Egypt who followed Christian pilgrims to Jerusalem, there must have been many public women who sought out the pilgrims in Arabia, no matter if they were in or out of a state of ritual purity. Moreover, even if a pilgrimage site was not associated with a fair and was only a local center of trade, as was the case with Mecca, this would not preclude the need for a "service industry" in the widest sense for visitors.

SACRED PROSTITUTION?

We can take this one step further and ask if sacred prostitution was practiced at these holy sites. Before trying to answer this question, however, a definition of this practice is in order. In a recent study, Stephanie Budin has provided a comprehensive and workable definition of such prostitution. She says, "Sacred prostitution is the sale of a person's body for sexual purposes where some portion (if not all) of the money or goods received for this transaction belongs to a deity."[28] She goes on to divide sacred prostitution into three types, as recorded in Classical sources: 1) a once-in-a lifetime prostitution and/or sale of virginity in honor of a goddess; 2) women who are professional prostitutes owned by a deity or a deity's sanctuary; and 3) a temporary version in which women are either prostitutes for a limited period before being married, or only prostitute themselves during certain rituals.[29]

In 1903, in his classic work *Kinship and Marriage in Early Arabia*, W. Robertson Smith stated, “In Arabia [...] unrestricted prostitution of married and unmarried women was practised at the temples, and defended on the analogy of the licence allowed to herself by the unmarried mother-goddess.”[30] But Smith was, in fact, referring to certain alleged practices in Syria in Late Antiquity, not Arabia, for which he provides no evidence of sacred prostitution.

Some two decades later, Maurice Gaudefroy-Demombynes, in a long study of the Muslim pilgrimage to Mecca, proposed the existence of a form of sacred prostitution in pre-Islamic Mecca based on what may be an early source. In the late fourth/tenth century Abū ’l-Walīd al-Azraqī composed the book *Akhbār Makka*, which was a collection of various materials concerning the history of Mecca. Some of his information goes back to pre-Islamic times. Al-Azraqī was actually a descendant of a child born to the Greek slave ‘Ubayd and Sumayya, the mother of Ziyād ibn Abīhi, mentioned above.[31] He records several traditions according to which pilgrims drank sacred wine at the moment of desacralization marked by the completion of the circumambulations of the Kaaba. At that point, no longer in a state of ritual purity, they could also engage in sexual relations. Gaudefroy-Demombynes proposed that just as this wine was sacred so too were sexual relations that followed the circumambulations; and he was tempted to see a rite of sacred prostitution in ritual, or simply solemn, sexual relations that followed desacralization.[32] But this is simply speculation. There is no reason to believe that there was anything sacred about having sex with a public woman or any other woman after completing the pilgrimage rituals. Moreover, prostitution under such circumstances would not meet Budin’s definition of sacred because nothing accrued to a deity nor was there a limitation on the period of the practice.

Gaudefroy-Demombynes returned to this subject later in a mammoth volume on Muhammad. This time he mentioned it in the context of two gods who were worshipped in Mecca before Islam.[33] He cites al-Ṭabarī,[34] but the most basic form of the story of these gods is found in *Kitāb al-Aṣnām*

(Book of Idols),[35] an important work on Arab paganism by Hishām al-Kalbī (d. 204/819 or 206/821). On the authority of ʿAbd Allāh ibn al-ʿAbbās (or Ibn al-ʿAbbās, d. 68/686–8), perhaps the greatest scholar of the first generation of Muslims, Hishām relates that Isāf ibn Yaʿlā and Nāʾila bint Zayd, who were from the ancient Arab tribe of Jurhum, were passionately in love. They went to Mecca on the pilgrimage and, finding themselves alone inside the Kaaba, had intercourse there (*fajara bihā*). As a result they were immediately turned into two stones, which were erected on the spot. They were subsequently worshipped by the tribes of Khuzāʿa, Quraysh, and all pilgrims.[36] Gaudefroy-Demombynes interpreted this story as a souvenir of ancient Arab sacred prostitution. But again this is guesswork, if not a fantasy, and it does not meet our definition of such a practice, even if pilgrims made offerings to the stones.[37] Indeed, it would be more reasonable to interpret this story and the idols as the vestiges of a cult of fertility.

Meanwhile, about the same time that Gaudefroy-Demombynes' book on Muhammad appeared, Joseph Henninger, in a study of human sacrifice among the Arabs, briefly broached the topic of sacred prostitution in Arabia.[38] He states that the existence of sacred prostitution in Mecca has often been asserted and that it has been associated with a pre-Islamic rite of spring in which men and women circumambulated the Kaaba naked. He mentions several scholars who have made this assertion or association, but their evidence is nonexistent. The first is one W. F. Adeney, who mangled Robertson Smith, saying:

> The Byzantine writers regarded the worship of Aphrodite as the principal cult of Mecca. This idea is supported by recent research, the white stone being the original Meccan divinity, and the black stone her son, the very name *ka'ba* [which means "cube"] seeming to point to a supreme female deity [!]. Prostitution both by married and unmarried woman in imitation of the conduct of the goddess was a recognized custom in the ancient Arabian cult.[39]

A few writers from the early Byzantine period may have believed that the goddess al-ʿUzzā, who was worshipped in Mecca, was the planet Venus, which they identified with Aphrodite. However, attempts by modern scholars, including Robertson Smith, to identify al-'Uzzā with Venus, require "a tenuous series of equations with other deities in which each divinity is assumed to be endowed with all aspects of the others."[40] In short, the evidence is inconclusive if not completely unconvincing. The association of sacred prostitution with Aphrodite goes back to Herodotus. In a famous passage, he claimed that once in her lifetime every Babylonian woman had to resort to the sanctuary of Aphrodite and have intercourse with a foreign man.[41] Budin has demonstrated, however, that the sacred prostitution that Herodotus described was not real. It was a fiction.[42]

The second scholar mentioned by Henninger is Gaudefroy-Demombynes, whom we have discussed above. The third is Carl Rathjens. He emphasizes the lesser pilgrimage—the *'umra,* which also takes place in Mecca—as a vestige of a pre-Islamic spring festival which included sexual excess.[43] He provides no evidence, however, for any orgiastic celebrations or ritual sex. The *'umra* was indeed the pre-Islamic pilgrimage to Mecca. During the period of paganism it may well have occurred in the spring, but any such association of it with this season was apparently forgotten by the time of Muhammad. It was absorbed into the hajj proper, the "greater pilgrimage," shortly before his death. For Muslims the lesser pilgrimage basically consists of the ceremonies of circumambulating the Kaaba seven times and running seven times between the "hills" of al-Ṣafā and al-Marwa outside the shrine of the Kaaba. It differs from the hajj in not including the visit to 'Arafa outside Mecca.[44]

The fourth is Joseph Chelhod, who presents a more interesting hypothesis regarding ritual or sacred prostitution, that is, sexual intercourse as an act of desacralization after completing the ceremonies of the pilgrimage. Like Gaudefroy-Demombynes, he believes such practice occurred and marshals extremely tendentious evidence to try to prove it. In the hills east of Mecca on the way to 'Arafa is the place called Minā. In the pre-Islamic period this was where the concluding ceremonies of the hajj took place and where animals were sacrificed. Chelhod asserts that:

> It was at this very place of Minā where, after the sacrifices, supplicants entered into communion with the divinity by physical union with

> sacred prostitutes, called *mūmis*. A linguistic proof appears to militate in favor of this hypothesis. It is worthy of note that the root *m n y* [in Arabic], which is that of Minā, the place of immolation, gives rise to the word *many*, meaning sperm, which, according to [the lexicographer] al-Fīrūzābādī [d. 817/1415] was sometimes pronounced as *minā*. Thus the same word from the same root signifies at the same time the place of immolation of sacrificial victims and sperm, death and life, destruction and regeneration. Furthermore, this root, used in the first and fourth forms [of the verb] can mean, at the same time, to arrive at Minā and to spill sperm.[45]

Through such contortions, Chelhod links the ceremonies of the pre-Islamic pilgrimage with sacred prostitution. The word *mūmis* does, in fact, mean prostitute in Arabic. It does not, however, appear in the Qur'an and occurs only once, in two forms, in the hadith, which were the alleged traditions of Muhammad. In this tradition, the Prophet tells the tale of a man whose child was supposedly born of a prostitute. Here the plural forms of prostitute are given as *al-mayāmis* and *al-mūmisāt*.[46] Chelhod presents no evidence of the currency of *mūmis* in pagan Arabia—and I have not encountered it in any other work cited in the present study.

Mūmis is actually not an Arabic word, but Greek, from the feminine noun *mīmus*, meaning "mime." It apparently came into Arabic before the coming of Islam as the term for "female mime-player, strolling player > whore."[47] Such mimes were found in the Hellenized cities of the Levant but, as far as we know, not in Arabia. Nevertheless, Chelhod goes on to claim that at the pre-Islamic fairs, one could see, among other things, the nubile girls (*des jeunes filles nubile*) destined for sacred prostitution.[48] Through further linguistic gymnastics, Chelhod connects the root *w–m–s*, which is that of *mūmis*—assuming it to be an Arabic and not a Greek word for which such a root would be nonsense—by metathesis with *w–s–m*, which means "to mark." *W–s–m* in turn is related to the root *w–sh–m*, which means "to tattoo." This suggests that prostitutes were tattooed in order to indicate their sacred status and distinguish them from other women. Moreover, *w–s–m* is at the root of the word *mawsim*, which means season, or festival.

This, then, would account for seeing nubile girls at the fairs, and they were undoubtedly tattooed and destined for sacred prostitution.[49]

Chelhod summarizes his hypothesis by saying,

> The existence of marked prostitutes, and therefore sacred in view of the religious aspect that we have recognized in *w s m* and its synonym *w sh m* leads us to believe in ritual sex which must have completed the major manifestations of the public cult. It seems that this act must have terminated the hajj, as Gaudefroy-Demombynes has suggested. The *'umra,* festival of rejuvenation of nature, of youth, of abundance, of vegetation, of the birth of animals, of the sun, which regains its strength, and of love, which triumphs over death, marks the apotheosis of the mother goddess with all that this entails of unbridled joy and wild festivities and unlimited promiscuity.[50]

This is all very intriguing...but also extremely tenuous, to say the least. Before and after the appearance of Islam, some prostitutes may have worn tattoos for one reason or another, but there is no evidence to connect this body art with sacred sex. Moreover, in the research for this book, I have not come across a single reference to a public woman who was tattooed for her trade, either as an act of personal adornment or by compulsion. As we will see in later chapters, it was above all her dress that set her apart from other women and attracted customers. As a form of advertisement, a tattoo would have been ineffective or useless.

As for circumambulating the Kaaba naked, Henninger points out that Julius Wellhausen has indeed shown that this ritual was practiced in Mecca and elsewhere in Arabia before the rise of Islam.[51] However, Henninger goes on to state that there was no erotic sense to this ritual and it cannot be used as evidence of sacred prostitution. Robertson Smith says that the removal of garments before making the circuit was required by the need for ritual purity.[52]

Henninger does believe that there were professional temple prostitutes in the high culture of South Arabia, but he offers no proof.[53] A study that he mentions in this respect is worth describing, however, in some detail:

A. F. L. Beeston's "The so-called harlots of Ḥaḍramaut."[54] Beeston analyzes a curious passage called "The women who desired the death of Muhammad and their story" found in Muḥammad ibn Ḥabīb's *Kitāb al-Muḥabbar* (pp. 184–9). According to this story, when news of the death of the Prophet reached Ḥaḍramaut, a mountainous region running parallel to the southern coast of Arabia, six women who lived there began to celebrate, dying their hands with henna and playing the tambourine; and they were joined by some twenty harlots (*baghāyā*). When Abū Bakr, Muhammad's first successor (or caliph), was informed of this, he ordered that their hands be cut off. Because three of the harlots were described as members of the noble class and four as members of the royal tribe of Kinda, and they were vigorously defended by local tribes, Beeston states that they could not all have been common prostitutes. He proposes that at least some of them were priestesses of the old pagan religion of South Arabia;[55] and their singing and dancing were incitements to throw off the new religion. While Beeston acknowledges that the word harlot could simply be a term of opprobrium used by the Muslim enemies of these women (which is highly likely), he nevertheless suggests, citing cuneiform tablets, that, because religious prostitution was practiced in ancient Babylonian temples, this could also have been true of South Arabia. He admits though that there is no evidence for such a practice. Indeed, this would require a huge leap of faith in time (more than a thousand years) and space (more than two thousand kilometers), assuming there had actually been such religious prostitution in Babylonia. Moreover, one of the harlots was Jewish, Hirr (Kitty), who became proverbial for "adulterousness" (*zinā'*). She could not have been a priestess in a pagan temple (cf. Deuteronomy 23:17). Some of the original six women might have been priestesses while the others, from "respectable" lineages or not, were simply public women drumming up business during the celebration of the return to the old-time religion. We have, then, no solid evidence for sacred prostitution anywhere in pre-Islamic Arabia.[56] Moreover, it is important to keep in mind that the Western search for sexual excess among the Arabs is part of the long tradition of Christian polemic against Islam, for which pre-Islamic practices in Arabia were simply precursors.

"MARRIAGE" RELATIONSHIPS AT THE TIME OF MUHAMMAD

Before examining the status of public women in the light of the Qur'an, Muhammad's mission, and then early Islamic law, a few words are in order about the nature of "marriage" in Arabia. The modern Western study of this subject goes back above all to Robertson Smith's (1846–94) *Kinship and Marriage in Early Arabia*.[57] Despite its almost iconic status, it has been criticized for its evolutionary approach to the institution of "marriage" in Arabia.[58] In general, Smith traces the evolution of "marriage" from polyandry before the fourth century CE to limited polygamy at the time of Muhammad, with many different practices being concurrent. There is also a problem with the term "marriage" (which I have highlighted here) in his work. Robertson Smith was an Old Testament scholar, a professor of divinity, and a minister in the Free Church of Scotland. He was also very much a product of Victorian Britain and its view of marriage and morality. In Arabia "marriage" relationships, or—more accurately—accepted methods of male and female cohabitation for procreation and sexual pleasure, did not all fit the strict Victorian paradigm of a permanent legal bond between one man and one woman. One can sense his struggle to define for a Victorian audience various forms of "marriage" for which there were no English equivalents.

Nikāḥ, which was perhaps the most common form of "marriage" in Arabia, was at least recognizable to Victorians as such. This institution was intended to be a permanent union between a man and a woman, with witnesses, and it required the transfer of wealth (bride price) from the groom to the bride's kin. Procreation was the primary objective and inheritance was a major concern. Other forms of cohabitation, however, were not so familiar to Robertson Smith's audience. These included unregulated polyandry in which a woman received as many men as she wished; Robertson Smith viewed this as no different than prostitution.[59] The tribe of Hudhayl in the vicinity of Mecca and al-Ṭā'if supposedly asked the Prophet if they could continue this practice.[60] Al-Bukhārī (d. 256/870), whom later Muslims generally considered the most authoritative of the compilers of hadith, records on the testimony of 'Ā'isha, the Prophet's favorite wife, that, in addition to traditional *nikāḥ* (*nikāḥ al-nās al-yawm*) there were several other forms of "marriage" in pre-Islamic Arabia. The second was the custom of *nikāḥ al-istibḍā'* whereby a man, hoping for an exceptional child, might have his wife sleep with another man admired for certain qualities or abilities. The third was that of *nikāḥ al-rahṭ* whereby a group of up to ten men would have intercourse with one woman. If she gave birth, paternity was attributed to the man who was most desirous of naming the child. And the fourth, which was quite similar, was that whereby a woman had relations with a large number of men, refusing none (as practiced by the Hudhayl?). In this case, according to this hadith, "These prostitutes (*baghāyā*) raised banners at their doors which served as a sign. Anyone who wished could enter."[61] If such women gave birth, all their clients would be assembled and physiognomists would determine paternity. There existed, in fact, the profession of physiognomy (*qiyāfa*), whose practitioners could, when necessary, determine the father of a child if his identity were in doubt.[62] Apart from *nikāḥ*, these different arrangements sound incredible, especially with the inclusion of prostitution as a form of "marriage." Indeed, it would not be unreasonable to doubt the veracity of this hadith. It is possible that later Muslims put this description of these forms of "marriage" into 'Ā'isha's mouth in order to contrast, in an authoritative manner, the sexual license of the period of paganism with the modesty and restricted forms of cohabitation that would be required by Islam.[63]

Still, there is some evidence for various flexible arrangements for cohabitation. For example, a man might loan his wife to a guest for sexual hospitality or, if he were going on a long journey, find someone to take his place, or share conjugal rights with another man in return for a specific service.[64] In addition, a group of men might purchase a wife in common.[65] One or more men could also purchase one or more slave girls.[66] Finally, there was the practice of *mut'a*. This word is usually translated as "temporary marriage," but this is a misnomer. It literally means "enjoyment" or "pleasure." Specifically, it was an agreement between a man and a woman to live together for a certain period for sexual pleasure, in return for which the woman received compensation. There was no bride price paid to the woman's kin. No witnesses were required. There was no inheritance between the couple. And procreation was to be avoided. It was not "marriage" in any Western sense, or even in the traditional Arab sense. In the West, it might be somewhat like an arrangement between a man and his mistress. Wellhausen, one of the earliest scholars to comment on *mut'a*, considered it to be nothing more than a form of prostitution.[67] Given the definition of prostitution in the present study, that would indeed seem to be the case. In sixth or seventh-century Arabia, however, it appears to have been just another arrangement for cohabitation without negative connotations.

The Qur'an, in fact, seems to condone *mut'a* in the verse "And further, you are permitted to seek out wives with your wealth, in modest conduct but not in fornication; but give them their reward for what you have enjoyed of them (*istamta'tum*) in keeping with your promise" (4:24). Even Muhammad was supposed to have practiced it.[68] Furthermore, Ibn al-'Abbās (d. 68/686–8), the scholar we met above who was a contemporary of Muhammad and the father of Qur'anic exegesis, confirmed its permissibility.[69] One of the earliest reliable traditionists, the Meccan Ibn Jurayj (d. 150/767), another descendant of a Greek slave, corroborated Ibn al-'Abbās' opinion.[70] In fact, in addition to having a "regular" marriage to a pious woman, Ibn Jurayj entered *mut'a* arrangements with more than 60 women. This is attested by the great jurist al-Shāfi'ī (d. 204/820) himself.[71] In old age he injected himself with sesame oil to stimulate his sex drive.[72] The second caliph 'Umar (r. 13–23/634–44) forbade *mut'a* on his own authority.[73] The brilliant essayist al-Jāḥiẓ, writing in the third/ninth century, believed he had no right to do this. Moreover, he quotes 'Umar as saying, rather enigmatically, from the pulpit, "In the days of the Prophet there were two kinds of temporary marriage (*mut'atān*), the *mut'a* of women (*mut'at al-nisā'*) and *mut'a* of the pilgrimage (*mut'at al-ḥajj*). I forbid and shall punish both of them."[74] The first Umayyad caliph, Mu'āwiya (r. 41–60/661–80), entered a *mut'a* arrangement with a woman from al-Ṭā'if, and other contemporary cases are known.[75] 'Umar's action contributed to the later refusal of Sunni jurists to recognize the practice. The Shi'is, however, always regarded it as legitimate. Because there was no contract with the woman's kin, Robertson Smith concluded that they gave up no rights over her and she did not leave home.[76] But this is difficult to believe. *Mut'a* was especially well suited to a man who wished to travel for business, pilgrimage, or other reason and wanted female companionship. Henninger states that it was practiced not only in the towns but also among the Bedouin.[77] The fourth-century Roman historian Ammianus Marcellinus (d. after 391), who accompanied the Emperor Julian (d. 363) on a campaign in Mesopotamia in which the emperor was killed, mentions the practice of *mut'a* among the Scenitic Arabs (or Saracens). He says, "Their life is always on the move, and they have mercenary wives, hired under a temporary contract."[78] Al-Bukhārī reports a hadith in which Muhammad addressed men in the army and said, "You have been allowed to do the *mut'a*, so do it."[79]

A man could participate in as many of the aforesaid unions as he wished, or several different ones at the same time. There was no shame attached to a child born of any of these relationships. This was true, as we have seen, with Ziyād ibn Abīhi. And physiognomists were available to determine paternity if necessary.

This is not the place to try to explain why there were apparently so many bewildering—to a modern Westerner—arrangements for cohabitation in early Arabia. I can only speculate here that at certain times and places the ratio of males to females was out of balance and in favor of men. Female infanticide,[80] frequent death in childbirth (women were married quite young),[81] and the capture of women by raiders, garrisoning of troops, as well as environmental disasters, could have contributed to this. It goes without saying that trying to survive in the harsh conditions of desert Arabia had many risks. Furthermore, if a significant number of men practiced polygamy, this could have further reduced the number of women available to others. It could also happen that some men could not afford the price of a bride. Even slave girls could be expensive.[82] In some instances tribal endogamy or lineage might also have limited a man's access to women or the pool of his potential wives. Under these circumstances survival (reproduction) and the demands of sexuality required various and flexible arrangements for cohabitation. Traditional prostitution in our sense was simply one of many acceptable possibilities. This also seems to have been God's view.

PUBLIC WOMEN AND THE QUR'AN

In 622 CE, after failing to make much progress with his preaching in Mecca, Muhammad and a small group of followers took refuge in Yathrib (Medina) to the north. Sometime between then and 11/632, when he died, he received a revelation that mentioned prostitution in a single verse. This was, of course, one of the many revelations that later constituted the Qur'an. The verse in question, which was the only one to mention our subject in the entire noble text, states, "And constrain not your slave girls to prostitution [*wa lā tukrihū fatayātikum 'alā 'l-bighā'*], if they desire to live in chastity, that you may seek the chance goods of the present life" (24:33).[83] The text goes on to say that if slave girls were forced into prostitution, God would forgive them. Muslim ibn al-Ḥajjāj (d. 261/875), who compiled the most authoritative collection of traditions after al-Bukhārī, records a hadith describing the circumstances in which this verse was revealed. It seems that 'Abd Allāh ibn Ubayy ibn Salūl, a leading man of Medina and an antagonist of Muhammad, had two slave girls named Umayma and Musayka whom he forced into prostitution. They complained to Muhammad, and subsequently this verse was revealed.[84] The Arabic clearly indicates that those being addressed are males. In other words, men are forbidden to prostitute their slave girls—although no punishment is mentioned. Implicit in this is that pimping in general is also forbidden. Nothing is said about independent public women. Here the implication is that they should be left alone to go about their business as usual; they should not be exploited, and they should be allowed to keep their earnings. The revelation that contains this verse chiefly concerns the modesty of women and fornication. We should add here that the Qur'an also encouraged the manumission of slaves (e.g. 90:12–18). This could cause difficulties for female slaves, who had little means to support themselves. When slavery was abolished in Zanzibar in 1897, the British authorities noticed a steep increase in the number of prostitutes, especially among freed concubines, and a swollen brothel population.[85] In this instance the right of a free woman to sell her sexual favors was essential.

While the word "prostitute" (*baghīy*) does not appear in the Qur'an, the word *fāḥisha*, meaning "indecent act," is found in many places. Such an act is always forbidden.[86] In one verse (17:32) it is equated with fornication (*zinā'*). Elsewhere it is undefined, even when committed by a female, and the context is vague, although sometimes a sexual infraction is suggested (e.g. 4:15). In later works, the same word became a synonym for prostitute, but that is not the case in the Qur'an.[87] *Zinā'* and its derivatives appear much less frequently than *fāḥisha* in the noble text. It too is not clearly defined, but is translated as "fornication" in the sense of sexual intercourse between a man and a woman who are not married to each other, with the exception of intercourse between a man and his slave girls. Apart from this exception, *zinā'* includes the English concept of "adultery."[88] Indeed, all sexual relations outside these bounds appear to be subsumed within the term.[89] This is the way it has usually been interpreted in later Muslim legal discussions[90] and by Western scholars.[91]

But was prostitution really intended to be included within the definition of fornication, or was it in a different category of act? Fornication was considered a serious offense and was to be punished by flogging (24:2, later changed to stoning in light of certain hadith[92]). It was difficult, however, to prosecute. Four males of the highest moral and religious probity had to witness the couple in the very act of copulation. This requirement would have been difficult enough to fulfill in the case of "ordinary" unmarried lovers, but it was impossible in the case of a public woman and her client. Thus it would clearly exclude prostitution from the punishment of fornication, if not from the concept of fornication altogether.[93] The fact that God would forgive a slave girl (or perhaps any woman) forced into prostitution would also have helped make punishment for this trade moot. As we will see later in this book, no instances have come to light of women being flogged or stoned for selling sexual favors. Furthermore, we have a technical term for prostitution, *bighā'*, which sets it apart from *zinā'* in the Qur'an. Moreover, it is described in the Qur'an in the context of a certain kind of forbidden business transaction, namely, *the sale of the sexual favors of slave girls by their male owner.* In other words, this method of prostitution was forbidden, not prostitution itself. *Bighā'* was a legitimate profession for a woman, although it was despised along with certain other professions.[94] In this respect, it is important to point out that in the legal texts *mut'a* also fell under the heading of hire or lease (*ijāra*).[95]

The hadith say little about prostitution, but tend to confirm that it was to be tolerated. Al-Bukhārī records seven traditions in which the Prophet forbids money earned by prostitution, but in each case the implication is money earned by pimping.[96] He also records two hadith in which the Prophet briefly remarked that one day a prostitute drew water from a well with her shoe and gave it to a dog that was about to die of thirst. As a result, God pardoned her for her profession.[97] In one version the woman is described as from the Banū Isrā'īl (that is, as Jewish). One wonders if the thirsty dog might symbolize the woman's clients. Muslim relates essentially the same traditions about forbidding the earnings of a prostitute[98] and about the public woman who gave water to a thirsty dog.[99] Abū Dā'ūd al-Sijistānī includes similar accounts prohibiting earnings from prostitutes.[100] He also mentions a tradition according to which one Marthad ibn Abī 'l-Marthad al-Ghanawī, who used to take prisoners (of war) from Mecca (to Medina), made love with a public woman in Mecca named 'Ināq ("Embrace").[101] He later went to Muhammad and asked if he could marry her. The Prophet kept silent for a while, and then the verse declaring that only an adulterer could marry an adulteress (24:3) was revealed. As a result, Muhammad told him not to marry her.[102] In addition, Abū Dā'ūd records a hadith on the testimony of Ibn al-'Abbās in which the Prophet said, "There is no prostitution in Islam."[103] On the other hand, the traditionist al-Nasā'ī reports a hadith in which Muhammad condoned giving alms (*ṣadaqa*) to a prostitute (*zāniyya*).[104] Furthermore, there is also a hadith in which Muhammad says that God forgave the legendary Israelite Dhū 'l-Kifl (Job or Ezekiel, according to the *Encyclopaedia of Islam*) of his sins because when a woman who was in need offered herself to him for money, he paid her what she required but did not have sex with her. By implication, of course, the woman was also forgiven.[105]

PROSTITUTION IN QUR'ANIC EXEGESIS

For our purposes, works of Qur'anic exegesis, or *tafsīr*, add little to what is found in the compendia of hadith.[106] This is because these works themselves, although providing running commentary word by word or phrase by phrase on the Qur'an, rely heavily on the hadith for explications—and then not necessarily on those in the most authoritative collections. The earliest reliable *tafsīr*, and the most renowned, is that of al-Ṭabarī, his *Jāmiʿ al-bayān ʿan taʾwīl al-Qurʾān*. It was completed between 283/896 and 290/903. Commenting on 4:15, he equates *fāḥisha* with *zināʾ*; and on 17:32 he simply follows the Qur'anic text equating *fāḥisha* with it.[107] Concerning 4:24, he says that *mutʿa* is a form of marriage, yet if a man has enjoyed a woman he should give her the fee she required.[108] Regarding 24:33, he states that prostitution is *zināʾ*.[109] With respect to 60:12, he comments that a free woman should not fornicate. Here prostitution is not specifically mentioned.[110]

Almost as highly regarded as the *tafsīr* of al-Ṭabarī was that of al-Qurtubi (d. 671/1272), *al-Jāmiʿ li-aḥkām al-Qurʾān*, which relied even more heavily on hadith. For the verses of the Qur'an in question, al-Qurtubi's commentary differs from that of al-Ṭabarī in only a few respects. On 4:15 he equates *fāḥisha* with *zināʾ*. On 17:32 he too repeats the Qur'anic definition of *fāḥisha* being the same as *zināʾ*. On 4:24 he provides differing opinions on whether *mutʿa* is permitted. On 24:33 he states that prostitution is the same as *zināʾ*. And on 60:12 he does not clearly state that *fāḥisha* is the equivalent of *zināʾ*.[111]

A third commentary that was later widely used was Ibn Kathīr's (d. 774/1373) *Tafsīr al-Qurʾān al-ʿaẓīm*, which closely followed that of al-Ṭabarī. Explicating 4:15, he identifies *fāḥisha* with *zināʾ*; and regarding 17:32, he too simply follows the Qur'anic text equating *fāḥisha* with it. And on 60:12, he equates *fāḥisha* with it as well.[112] On 4:24, he says *mutʿa* was eventually forbidden.[113] And he comments on 24:33 claiming that prostitution is the equivalent of *zināʾ*.[114] These three leading examples of Qur'anic exegesis thus clearly do not provide any discussion of prostitution. It is ignored except for the commentary which is first found in al-Ṭabarī to the effect that it was the same as *zinā'*. This view, however, is based on two hadith of unknown veracity.

PROSTITUTION IN MĀLIKĪ AND ḤANAFĪ LAW

Resulting largely from different interpretations of the Qur'an and Ḥadīth, a number of distinct schools (s. *madhhab*) of Islamic law began to take shape some 150 years after the death of Muhammad. This diversity of doctrine in law came about because the original source of the law was often rather unclear and inadequate, which opened the door to a variety of uneven influences and opinions. Furthermore, diversity also resulted from geographical differences, the power of local customs and traditions, new problems and foreign ideas introduced by conquest, the failure of the ruling authorities to undertake or enforce any codification of the law, the lack of any hierarchy of courts, and finally from political differences. Controversy was inherent from the start.[115]

Here I will mention only the first two schools that emerged, namely the Mālikī and Ḥanafī, which came to dominate the Eastern Mediterranean littoral. The former was especially strong in Arabia and Egypt, and the latter in Syria and Anatolia. In the first compendium of law to appear in Islam, *al-Muwaṭṭa'* of Mālik ibn Anas (d. 179/796), prostitution is mentioned only once, under the rubric of business transactions. Here a hadith is cited according to which the Prophet reportedly said that the following were forbidden: "the cost (*thaman*) of a dog, the price of a prostitute (*mahr al-baghī*), and the payment (*ḥulwān*) to a fortune-teller."[116] Then Mālik, or perhaps his informant, states, "By the price of a prostitute he meant what a woman was given for fornication (*zinā'*)."[117] There is some ambiguity here. It is not clear if prostitution or pimping is being forbidden. Al-Bukhārī, in fact, records another version of this hadith, in which the phrase "the price of a prostitute" is replaced by "receiving the earnings of a slave girl put up for prostitution."[118] Mālik only adds that he, Mālik, disapproved of the price of a dog. Mālik, who was from Medina, was considered the founder of one of the first two schools of Islamic law, the Mālikī. It is worthy of note that in a much later commentary on this hadith, again under the topic of business transactions, Muḥammad ibn Ismāʿīl Ṣanʿānī (1688–1768) states that whatever a fornicatress (*zāniyya*) takes in exchange for fornication (*zināʾ*) is forbidden money (*māl ḥarām*). However, because the buyer purchased the "product" willingly and the seller cannot recover it, her earnings should be given as alms (*yajibu al-taṣadduq bihi*).[119] The implications of this are, of course, enough to raise one's eyebrows. In other words, such alms are legitimate and acceptable; indeed, a woman could sell her sexual favors for the sake of charity![120] At the very least, this is evidence of equivocation in the legal status of prostitution.

Mālik's contemporary, Abū Ḥanīfa (d. 150/767), who was from Kūfa south of Baghdad, was the eponymous founder of the other school, the Ḥanafī, which was the more liberal of the two. It was adopted by the central ʿAbbāsid government. In the most popular concise manual of Ḥanafī law, the *Mukhtaṣar* of al-Qudūrī (d. 972/1037), who became head of the Ḥanafī school in Iraq, prostitution is simply not mentioned.[121] We should add that, based on various traditions, both the Mālikī and Ḥanafī schools tried to avoid applying the punishments for *zināʾ* (flogging or stoning) to prostitution if it became a problem, such as when neighbors complained of its presence among them.[122] The Mālikīs preferred banishment, and sometimes the Ḥanafīs did as well.[123] This is further proof that, legally, prostitution was treated differently from fornication.

Finally, if one interprets the tightened rules in the Qur'an regarding marriage and sexuality—such as limiting the number of wives to four and forbidding fornication—as a means of introducing uniformity to marriage in contrast to the fluid arrangements of the time of paganism, then there was no reason to forbid *bighāʾ*. As a short-term sale of sexual favors, it did not threaten marriage. There was no bride price, inheritance, or transfer of property. The begetting of children was avoided. There was no problem of complicating tribal or family alliances. If a child were born it could be legally acknowledged. A long-term arrangement as in *mutʿa*, however, might be more problematic in some of these respects. And this may have contributed to the grounds on which Sunni jurists later refused to recognize it.

Therefore, based on the evidence, the practice of prostitution was not forbidden to the community of believers at the time of Muhammad. Indeed, the commercial regulation of prostitution in the Qur'an, which is corroborated by the hadith, is telling proof to the contrary. The Qur'an does not forbid a public woman from practicing her trade. It only forbids pimping. And in this sense, it could be said to have eliminated a means of the exploitation of women and to have improved their lot. Public women could continue to go about their business. As Noel Coulson has cogently and succinctly stated with respect to Qur'anic legislation, "It is a natural canon of construction, and one in full accord with the general tenor of the Qur'ān, that the status quo is tacitly ratified unless it is expressly emended."[124] This echoes the remarks of none other than the renowned Arab *littérateur* al-Jāḥiẓ (d. 255/869) of Basra who says, while speaking of the pleasures of singing girls, "All that is not forbidden in God's Book and the *sunna* [hadith] of the Prophet is lawful and permissible, and human approval or disapproval is not sufficient grounds to establish by analogy the propriety of some forbidden act and bring it within the lawful category."[125]

Judaism, Christianity, and Islam differed somewhat in their views on the legality of sexual relations with members of other religions. Jews were forbidden to have sex with Gentiles. For Christians, sex with non-coreligionists was frowned upon (but allowed) for men, while it was completely forbidden for women. A Muslim man was under no restriction concerning the religion of his sexual partner, while a Muslim woman could only sleep with a Muslim.[126] Presumably this would not have been an issue for pagans. It is impossible to know how these attitudes could have affected the sale of sexual favors in Arabia. As Kitty above demonstrates, there was certainly a difference between theory and practice. One factor that definitely affected the trade would have been the number of opportunities for independent women to earn a living, when necessary, outside the home or immediate family. In Byzantium in Late Antiquity, the alternative to prostitution was to work as an "actress" in the circus, which often meant the same thing. In Arabia the profession of actress did not exist, but that of "singing girl" would have been a close counterpart. More important, and in contrast with life in Byzantium, in Arabia both before and after Islam a woman—at least a pagan woman—could establish and manage her own business. The best evidence of this is that Muhammad's first wife Khadīja (d. 619) engaged in long-distance trade. Before he married her, she owned property and was actively shipping merchandise to Syria. This might suggest that before and after Khadīja, prostitution might have been a more willful profession for some women.

It is noteworthy that the status of prostitution in Islamic law was almost identical with that in Roman law. In both systems it was a legitimate occupation, and pandering was forbidden. Furthermore, as we have seen in the previous chapter, the testimony of a prostitute was not accepted in a Roman court. In Islamic law the general principle was that only the testimony of a sane, adult, free, male Muslim of good character, could be accepted in court, i.e. before a judge (qadi). In a few instances the testimony of two women could equal that of a man if they had the same qualifications.[127] In either case, public woman were effectively barred from bearing legal witness. Despite these similarities, however, it would be difficult to prove the influence of Roman law on Islamic law in the matter of prostitution.

THE PROBLEM OF MORALITY

It is important to state here that acts or behavior that are regarded as legal and those that are regarded as moral are not necessarily the same. Coulson says that in Islamic law, the sharia, there is no distinction between law and morality.[128] In other words, what is legal is moral and what is illegal is immoral. That perhaps puts too fine a point on it, because what is considered immoral is not always illegal. This is because the sources of Islamic law do not (as we have seen) address all forms of human behavior. Moreover, community values can differ widely over time and space, regardless of the law. Custom, population growth, urbanization, contact with different cultures, crises such as plague or famine, and other factors can affect one's sense of morality. Certainly the establishment of institutional religion has a powerful effect on its adherents in this respect. The creation of religious administrative structures and the elaboration and interpretation of religious law and its execution all come into play in shaping a believer's sense of morality. Thus the morality of prostitution in desert Arabia in the religious flux of the first century or two after Muhammad would seem to have been much less of an issue than later, especially after Muslim religious institutions became firmly established in such cities as Damascus, Baghdad, and Cairo, and the equivalent of morality police (the *muḥtasib*, who we will meet in the next chapter) were on the job.

The essence of morality for Muslims came to be summed up in the phrase *al-amr bi'l-ma'rūf wa'l-nahy 'an al-munkar*, "commanding right and forbidding wrong." This notion derived from several Qur'anic revelations (e.g. 3:104) enjoining the community of believers to do just that. Indeed, they should take action to prevent wrong behavior if they saw it. This charge applied to both the ruling elite and the common people. Exactly what is right or wrong (or good or bad) behavior is not, however, fully spelled out in the Qur'an or the hadith. Consequently, this phrase became the grist for dissertations by many later jurists and theologians who struggled to specify the proper behavior—above all, public behavior—for Muslims. Needless to say, opinions differed widely among law schools, theologians, and even between Sunnis and Shi'is.[129] Certainly, for the individual, what was good or bad behavior could be rather subjective. Much (perhaps most) of the discussion on the popular level boiled down to "wine, women, and song."[130] With respect to women, much attention was given to their behavior outside the home—how they dressed, comported themselves, or spoke. While the men who addressed these issues could go into great detail on such matters as whether a man should engage in conversation with a woman who was not a member of his family, little seems to be said about more serious infractions. The Mālikīs, for example, questioned nudity and the presence of women at public baths;[131] but fornication is rarely mentioned in these discussions,[132] probably because it was obviously deemed wrong behavior as stated in the Qur'an. Prostitution seems not to be specifically mentioned at all, although it could be a very public activity.

In an attempt to gauge the prevalent attitudes toward sex in medieval Muslim society, James Bellamy examined several works from the mass of didactic literature composed in the early centuries of Islam and two important later works that addressed sexual ethics. The didactic works were al-Bukhārī's *Ṣaḥīḥ*, which we have mentioned; al-Tirmidhī's (d. 279/892) *Jāmiʿ al-ṣaḥīḥ*, which ranked fourth in collections of hadith after those of al-Bukhārī, Muslim, and Abū Dāwūd; and Ibn Abī 'l-Dunyā's (d. 281/894) *Dhamm al-malāhī*, which is replete with edifying essays or anecdotes (*akhbār*) on various topics. The works on ethics were those of the mystic Abū Ṭālib al-Makkī (386/998), *Qūt al-qulūb*, and the great theologian al-Ghazālī (d. 505/1111), *Iḥyāʾ ʿulūm al-dīn*. Bellamy reached two conclusions. First, in the hadith, and *akhbār* in particular, sex is presented in "a rather naïve and simplistic, even innocent, view, devoid of complications, free of doubts, and quite unaware of some of the darker aspects of human sexuality."[133] Second, in all this literature there is "a strong sense of pudency, equaling anything we can find among the Victorians."[134] In this respect he detected, over the centuries, both an increasing sense of modesty with regard to sex and an increasing severity with which sexual offenses were viewed. Prostitution as such was not discussed in these works, only *zināʾ* and certain sexual acts such as sodomy. Nevertheless, given these trends, it is easy to see how, over time, prostitution could increasingly be seen as immoral if it gradually lost its distinction from *zināʾ*. Thus, in the minds of many, it could have come to be regarded as illegal, although this was not the case (as we have seen) in the sources of Islamic law and its early development. In fact, one wonders if the shift in morality that Bellamy detected within Muslim society might have been influenced by Christianity. The early conquests of the Muslims brought vast Christian regions under their control, and it took centuries for the majority of the Christian inhabitants of these regions to convert to Islam. It would seem unlikely that Christian converts would not have brought their attitudes toward sexuality, including the view that prostitution was immoral, with them.[135] In any case, in subsequent chapters we will see examples of attacks on prostitution based primarily on its immorality, not its illegality. Again, the immoral and the illegal should not always be equated.

PUBLIC WOMEN IN ARABIA AFTER MUHAMMAD'S MISSION

Fred Donner has described how the believers' movement that was launched by Muhammad did not begin to crystallize into Islam until several generations after his death around the beginning of the second/eighth century.[136] Even then, it probably took several centuries for most of the inhabitants of Arabia to become at least nominally Muslims. Some never did. Moreover, the Bedouin were notorious for their laxness toward the faith up to modern times. A significant number of Jews remained in Yemen. Scattered groups of Christians, and perhaps even a few pagans, may have survived for a long time. Needless to say, there was no reason that these non-Muslims, or non-believers, could not have continued to practice prostitution in their traditional ways. The Qur'anic proscription of prostituting slave girls would not have applied to them. Unfortunately, we have virtually no information on this matter. We can only assume, for example, that the Christians of Arabia would have more or less accepted public women in the same manner as those along the Mediterranean littoral.

Ignaz Goldziher (and especially Joseph Schacht) held that some 150 years passed between the time that the Qur'an was committed to writing and the appearance of the earliest hadith that are recognized as authentic. The research of Harald Motzki has reduced this gap by about 75 years.[137] Still, the earliest schools of Islamic law, the Mālikī and Ḥanafī, which were based on the study and interpretation of the Qur'an and the Ḥadīth, did not arise until the late second/eighth century. It was the elaboration of law—the explication of fundamental beliefs and rituals—and its application that turned a believers' movement into a distinct religion. It was adherence to law and ritual that made one a Muslim. Thus, during the first seven or eight decades after the death of the Prophet, "Islam" must have been largely inchoate. There was no centralized religious authority to instruct followers on proper behavior nor was there any centralized administration to enforce religious uniformity. This was true both in Arabia and in the territories that the Arabs conquered within the first two centuries of Muhammad's death. For example, as Goldziher pointed out, during the first years of its existence the community of believers in Basra did not know how to pray.[138]

Consequently, during this time it is certain that the effectiveness of banning Muslims (or believers) from prostituting slave girls in Arabia would have been uneven, while independent public women would have gone about their business as usual. In fact, as we will see in subsequent chapters, this ban frequently fell into abeyance in various regions of the Eastern Mediterranean littoral that later came under Muslim rule. Among contemporary "outside" views of events in Arabia, there is a curious Coptic homily of the 640s that describes the Saracens (Arabs) as oppressors who, among other things, "give themselves up to prostitution, massacre, and lead into captivity the sons of men."[139] This may be simply an expression of calumny, or even a confusing reference to polygamy. On the other hand, al-Thaʿālibī (d. 429/1038), a renowned scholar and authority on the Arabic literature of his time, made a short list of nine members of the Quraysh, which was the tribe of the Prophet Muhammad, who were notorious "fornicators" (*zunāt*). Among them were sons of the first two caliphs, the "Rightly Guided," Abū Bakr (d. 11/634) and ʿUmar (d. 13/634), and a brother of Muʿāwiya.[140] The renowned poet ʿUmar ibn Abī Rabīʿa (d. 93/712 or 103/721), who was from the Meccan aristocracy, took advantage of the pilgrimage for sexual adventures.[141]

Because the material that I have collected on prostitution in Arabia after the rise of Islam is extremely sketchy, it does not allow us to follow the vicissitudes of this trade with respect to the political, economic, and social changes there over the following centuries. Prostitution was surely disrupted by the Ridda ("Apostasy") Wars that began after Muhammad's death and continued for several years, above all in Western and Southern Arabia. The Qarmaṭian invasion of Arabia that took place later must have been nothing short of catastrophic for public women. The first political manifestation of the Qarmaṭian movement was connected with Ḥamdān Qarmaṭ (d. after 286/899) from Kufa. He was a leader of the schismatic branch of the Shiʿis known as the Ismāʿīlīs. Around the time of Ḥamdān's death, his followers took control of Bahrain. From there they began to attack caravans of pilgrims. Developing exceptional striking power, they soon threatened Baghdad, and in 317/930 marched through Arabia to perpetrate mass slaughter on the pilgrims and people of Mecca itself. They even carried off the Black Stone of the Kaaba. Over the following centuries responsibility for the security of Mecca, Medina, and pilgrimage routes in Western Arabia was assumed by the different dynasties ruling from Cairo. They could not, however, always guarantee the safety of pilgrims from marauding Bedouin.[142]

In contrast to such crises, new opportunities for public women also appeared in Arabia in the centuries following the rise of Islam. For example, the renowned ʿAbbāsid caliph Hārūn al-Rashīd (r. 170–93/786–809) made nine pilgrimages to Mecca, and each time he expended vast sums in the city. Later caliphs and other Muslim rulers were also extravagant in their largess. This had a deleterious effect on the "moral fiber" of the population. In addition, the rise of mysticism (Sufism) as the popular version of Islam made the tombs of its outstanding practitioners, who were called saints, objects of pilgrimage. Like other holy sites, their tombs, many of which were around Mecca, would have attracted prospective clients for prostitutes. We will see a few examples of this in other regions in later chapters. The coming of Islam also resulted in some new holidays or festivals, which would have been good for business.[143] During the month of Ramadan, believers are, among other things, required to refrain from sexual relations during the day. We can surmise that under such circumstances some men might have had a heightened libido after the sun went down and that prostitutes were available to serve them. The feast of breaking the fast of Ramadan, ʿĪd al-Fiṭr, was especially carnivalesque. Furthermore, by the sixth/twelfth century, Mawlid al-Nabī, the birthday of the Prophet, had become an important popular festival in much of the Muslim world, especially in his birthplace of Mecca. This celebration often also took on a carnival atmosphere.[144]

The Qur'anic requirement that believers make a pilgrimage to Mecca at least once in their lifetime, of course, increased the traffic to the city along various routes across Arabia. This was no doubt a boon to women (or their owners) who sold their sexual services at the inns and taverns along the staging points of these routes, not to mention in Mecca itself.[145] The renowned *littérateur* Abū 'l-Faraj al-Iṣbahānī (d. 356/967) sheds some light on this. In his *Kitāb al-Aghānī* ("Book of Songs"), which is a kind of panorama of early Arab civilization, especially in the Baghdad of the early 'Abbāsid period, he includes a detailed entry on Dhū 'l-Rumma (d. 117/735–6), a famous poet whose tribe was from Central Arabia and who spent time in Basra. Dhū 'l-Rumma had a love affair with a certain Kharqā', about whom he rhapsodized. She was a woman from the Banū 'Āmir ibn Rabī'a and took up residence at a place called Falja, a station on the pilgrimage road from Basra to Mecca. She engaged pilgrims who passed by, saying, "I am one of the [religious] rituals on the pilgrimage" (*anā mansak min manāsik al-ḥajj*). Or, as Dhū 'l-Rumma said in verse, "The completion of the pilgrimage is when mounts halt before Kharqā' the unveiled."[146]

The centrality of the pilgrimage to Mecca for Muslims meant that travel by sea as well as by land increased to the holy city. The ports on the Red Sea, such as Jidda (Jeddah), and on the Arabian Sea, such as Aden, had to expand in order to accommodate this traffic. By the fourth/tenth century, the geographer al-Muqaddasī (d. ca. 381/990) was reporting that Aden—and indeed every town located next to a sea or river in the realm of Islam—seethed with fornication (*zinā'*) and pederasty.[147] Ibn al-Mujāwir also comments on this in his remarkable *Ta'rīkh al-Mustabṣir,* which was probably written between 624 and 627 (1226 and 1230). It is the most important source on life in medieval Arabia.[148] The author was a merchant who traversed the peninsula on various routes and described what he saw and heard. He describes Aden, for example, as a city teeming with people from many lands; he adds that "there is no one in the known world, on land or sea, more amazing and more shameless than Somali women," who were found there.[149] Off the Horn of Africa and some distance from the southern coast of Arabia is the island of Socotra. He relates that the way of life of the people who lived in its coastal areas was bound to piracy. Pirates would remain with them six months at a time and sell them their loot. The people of Socotra were a "hateful, debauched lot, procurers, and their old women more active in this than their men."[150]

In addition, the growing population of Mecca and Medina, combined with more and more pilgrims, eventually forced these cities to import grain from Egypt via the Red Sea ports. This, of course, added to seaborne traffic and commercial activity in the ports. At the same time, maritime trade from the ports of Arabia to India, the Far East, and down the east coast of Africa would have increased with the growing population, not to mention the demand from major urban centers north of Arabia, such as Damascus, Baghdad, and later Cairo, for goods from those regions. Altogether, these populous and lively ports, where many men were concentrated, would have ensured that prostitution would thrive.

In short, no matter what the stipulations of the Qur'an and the Ḥadīth, such as the one banning the prostitution of slave girls, the sale of sexual favors continued unabated. There was an amusing tale in early Arabic literature, which was circulated in several different versions, that may testify to the continuing presence of prostitution in the holy cities of Arabia in the early centuries of Islam. It goes back at least as far as al-Madā'inī (d. ca. 228/843), who specialized in the early history of the Arabs. According to this tale, there was a panderer in Mecca (Medina in some versions) who used to couple men and women in his house. He was a sharif (descendant of Muhammad) of the Quraysh. The people of Mecca complained to the governor who then banished him to 'Arafa, right outside Mecca (or Qubā' outside Medina). However, he slipped back into Mecca to solicit men and women, telling them it was only a two-dirham (silver coins) donkey ride to his new establishment. He attracted so much business from Mecca that once again the people complained to the governor, and once more he was brought before the governor, who denounced him. However, the panderer claimed that the Meccans had no evidence against him. The Meccans retorted that one only had to give rein to the donkeys that were hired and they would go straight to the panderer's house. This was done, and—sure enough—the donkeys stopped in front of his house. Just as the governor was about to have him whipped, the panderer remarked to the governor that he would become a laughing stock in Iraq because they would say that the Meccans accepted the testimony of donkeys in their law courts. The governor laughed and let him go.[151]

More solid evidence of the practice of prostitution in Mecca in the Islamic period comes again from Ibn al-Mujāwir. He reports that the people of Mecca say "we are all involved with pilgrims in every kind of activity, both legal and illegal" and, in Mecca,

> the women imposed a contribution on their slave girls in order to get money. So the slave girl [simply] hopes for alleviation [from her financial burden] or she gives freely of her vagina to the man and promiscuity runs amok. This is still found in Aden among outsiders and locals and they do not regard this practice as a shameful act. On the contrary, women [even] boast of doing this.[152]

The Ottoman traveler Evliya Chelebi, who made the pilgrimage to Mecca in 1672, reports that the Meccans were said to practice *mut'a* "in olden times." He did not notice it during his visit, but he was familiar with the practice and gives an interesting account of it, saying:

> This is an arrangement whereby a man on a campaign or journey can contract to have sexual relations with a woman for up to one month for one *gurush* [a piaster, silver coin]. At the end of the month he contracts with the same woman for one *gurush* or five *gurush,* or else with a different woman, and they can do what they will. This is called a *mut'a* marriage.[153]

Ibn al-Mujāwir goes on to record that pilgrims are fleeced en route from Yemen to Mecca and that "all shameful acts are done."[154] Staging points served merchants, of course, as well as pilgrims. The same writer reports that at the staging point of al-Ḥalīla, between the ports of Zabīd and Aden, there were pretty girls and beautiful women, "some evil."[155] He also remarks that the Persians called the women who were brought up in caravanserais—which would have been found at many staging points as well as in cities and towns—*kām-sarwānī,* "the gratification of the cameleer."[156] Furthermore, fairs continued to be held periodically in Arabia in the Islamic period. Ebu Bekir ibn Behram el-Dimeşkî (d. 1691), a geographer of the Ottoman period, mentions several fairs in addition to those going back to the period of paganism. One was at Ṭawīla, north of Ṣan'ā'. Another was at

Wādī 'l-Dawāsīr, east of Ṣa'da (northeast of Ṣan'ā'). Once a year, the people of Yemen, Najd (a region of Northwestern Arabia), and Oman gathered there to hold a great fair. People came from India, Yemen, and the Ḥijāz to buy and sell everything from common goods to precious stones. A third was at Ghatūd, in the Ḥijāz on the Gulf of Suez, through which pilgrims no doubt passed.[157] He also mentions major markets at Sabā near Ṣan'ā', Jidda, and Aydām near Mecca.[158] Public women surely continued to do business at these fairs and markets up to modern times.

During his extensive travels in Arabia in the late nineteenth century, Charles M. Doughty (d. 1926) witnessed "an excess of ribald living" in Medina,[159] despite the puritanical views of the Waḥḥābī religious authorities, and noted that in all the Turkish-Arabic towns (towns where Turkish troops and administrators were posted) there were those who fell into loose living. As he says, "In the lands of Christians such would be haunters of the licensed stews [brothels] and taverns." Both drunkenness and harlotry (Doughty liked to use Biblical English) were present.[160]

Some 50 years later, H. R. P. Dickson, a longtime resident of Arabia and an authority on the Bedouin, stated that among the town dwellers in Najd, gaily dressed prostitutes were often invited to sing and dance and entertain guests at circumcision parties. No one was shocked by their presence.[161] During holidays public women occasionally accompanied groups of "respectable" women and children on picnics.[162] In town their presence was believed to ensure the safety of respectable women when they left the house. They were also regarded as an outlet for the young men.[163] Prostitutes were generous to each other and often to young unmarried men out of work. They usually relied on male and female servants to bring customers, shop, and expel unruly visitors. A procurer was called *qawwād* and, curiously, this word was frequently used as a term of endearment for newborn boys.[164]

CONCLUSION

We have sufficient (albeit very fragmentary) material to demonstrate that prostitution was a common practice in Arabia before and after Islam.

This material is enough to show, in fact, that the working conditions and legal status of public women in Arabia were similar in many ways to those of their counterparts who lived in the Eastern Mediterranean coastlands in Late Antiquity. In both regions, prostitutes could be slaves who were managed by their owners or free women. In both regions they worked at ports, market centers, taverns and inns, festivals, and pilgrimage sites; basically, wherever large numbers of men congregated. And men of the highest positions of power and authority had liaisons with them. In both regions prostitutes could be itinerant. As far as we know, women of all religious backgrounds—Jewish, Christian, pagan, and later Muslim—participated in the sex trade. In Arabia, Greek and Somali women are specifically mentioned in addition to natives. There were no circuses in Arabia, but there were many periodic fairs which had a similar carnival atmosphere. And in Arabia the role of actress was taken by that of singing girl.

There was no sacred prostitution in either region, and the status of prostitutes in Roman and Islamic law was almost the same. In both cases prostitution was a legitimate but morally questionable profession, and pimping was forbidden. Neither the Qur'an nor the Ḥadīth clearly forbade prostitution, instead introducing some commercial regulation of it. In general, both Christianity and Islam tended to be ambivalent toward public women. Many Christians and Muslims regarded Jerusalem and Mecca, respectively, as immoral cities, as places of sexual temptation and adventure.

In Arabia, unlike the Eastern Mediterranean region, some towns had quarters reserved for prostitutes, where special banners were hung to indicate their place of business. Local authorities probably taxed them, but we have no record of it. Free women had more career opportunities in Arabia than in the eastern Christian world, which could have made prostitution a more willful line of work.

The coming of Islam provided some additional opportunities for public women. It made the pilgrimage to Mecca a requirement of the faith and thus brought more people (especially men), commerce, and wealth to that holy city and other places in Arabia. The new Muslim holidays were also good for the trade.

It is striking that there is nothing in early Arabic Muslim literature that is remotely comparable to the edifying Christian stories of holy harlots—public women who gave up their profession for a saintly life—or even tales of women who had committed "fornication," seen the error of their ways and then had become virtuous examples to others.[165] Indeed, given the required Qur'anic or divine punishment for fornication, the latter would have been impossible.[166] This might be further evidence that prostitution, again in contrast to fornication, was accepted and tolerated within Islam. It is related in the Qur'an that "some of Mary's people" accused her of being a harlot, but the infant Jesus spoke up and defended her (19:20–30). Even this stands in isolation.

In the next chapter, on Egypt, we have, happily, much richer sources on public women. We will also be able to examine their profession in a much more urbanized setting, above all following the rise of the great city of Cairo. In Egypt prostitution becomes big business; indeed, a state enterprise.

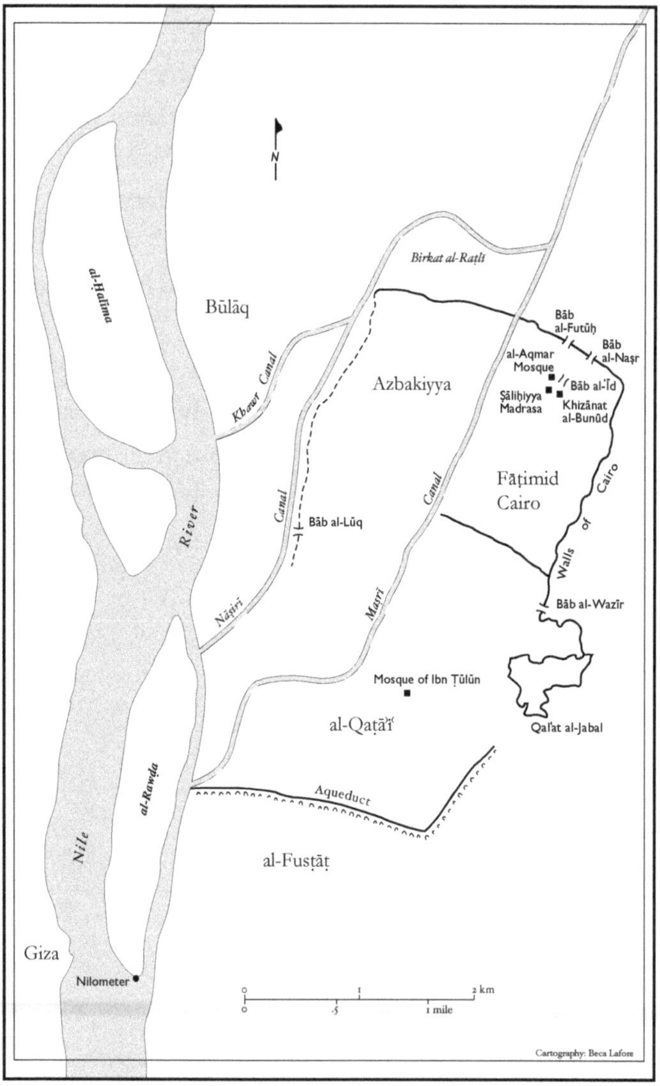

MAP 2

Cairo in the Mamlūk period

THREE

Public Women in Medieval Egypt

POLITICAL AND SOCIAL CONTEXT

In 21/642, after striking across Sinai from Palestine, an Arab army under the command of ʿAmr ibn al-ʿĀṣ (d. 42 or 43/662 or 664) captured Alexandria from Byzantium. The Byzantines managed to recapture it in 25/645, but a few months later in 25/646 the city fell permanently to the Arabs. At the time of its conquest, Alexandria was the capital of the Byzantine province of Egypt. It was not only the administrative and military center of the country but also the most important intellectual and cultural center in the East. Moreover, it was the leading commercial emporium of the Eastern Mediterranean and the main outlet for Egyptian grain shipments to Rome and Constantinople. Its loss sealed the fate of Egypt.[1]

When the Arabs conquered Alexandria, its population may have been as high as half a million. Greeks constituted most of the population. The rest were Egyptians, Syrians, and Jews. The Jewish community in Alexandria was, in fact, one of the largest in the Mediterranean world. The dominant language of the city was Greek, followed by Coptic. After the conquest, much of the Greek population, especially the Melkites, who were loyal to the Orthodox Patriarch in Constantinople, departed for that city. The Patriarch of the Egyptian (or Coptic) Church then consolidated his position with respect to the other Christians. Alexandria remained the seat of the

Coptic Patriarch until the second half of the fifth/eleventh century, when it was transferred to Cairo.

In 22/642 the Arabs built a new capital and military center, al-Fusṭāṭ, near the apex of the Nile Delta. During the first centuries of Arab political control, Egypt was ruled by a governor who sent revenue to the Umayyad caliphs in Damascus and later to the ʿAbbāsid caliphs in Baghdad. The native population seems to have remained peaceful except for a few revolts resulting from heavy taxation. Apart from these uprisings, the only disturbance of note occurred in 202/818 when Arab exiles from Cordoba in al-Andalus seized Alexandria and controlled it as a kind of city-state until they were expelled in 212/827.[2]

ʿAmr ibn al-ʿĀṣ built the first mosques in both al-Fusṭāṭ and Alexandria. Initially there was almost no conversion—and no attempt at mass conversion—of Christians and Jews. Instead they were treated as protected peoples, or *dhimmīs*, who were subjected to certain taxes and other obligations; and life generally continued as before. They continued to speak Greek or Coptic, and it took at least a century for Arabic to begin to spread among them. Moreover, as *dhimmīs* they were allowed to manage their own religious affairs. Meanwhile, the Mālikī school of law eventually came to predominate among the Muslims of Egypt. It was later followed by that of al-Shāfiʿī (d. 204/820), who had been a student of Mālik. He came to differ from the Mālikīs (and Ḥanafīs) chiefly because of his strong emphasis on using solidly established hadith as a major source of law. But over the centuries this difference gradually faded, since the greater part of the doctrine of the Mālikīs (and Ḥanafīs) had already been expressed in the form of hadith.[3]

In 254/868 the Turkish commander Aḥmad ibn Ṭūlūn (d. 270/884) entered al-Fusṭāṭ as a lieutenant of the new governor. Talented and ambitious, he managed to establish the first local and autonomous dynasty of Muslim Egypt, that of the Ṭūlūnids (254–92/868–905). He created a large army and invaded and annexed Syria. He also built a navy that operated as far as Palestine. Apparently because of the large size of the army, he built a new capital, al-Qaṭāʾiʿ, northeast of al-Fusṭāṭ. A large number of workers were, no doubt, needed for construction. Afterward, each military unit was assigned a section of the city as its residence. Al-Qaṭāʾiʿ soon became a major marketplace and attracted merchants of all kinds, drawing business away from al-Fusṭāṭ. Ibn Ṭūlūn's successor, his son Khumārawayh (270–82/884–96), had a reputation for luxury and dissipation. He was assassinated by his court eunuchs, "who had taken advantage of his absence to satisfy the insatiable sexual appetites of his harem women."[4]

Apart from Alexandria and al-Fusṭāṭ, the only other towns were the modest ports of Damietta on the eastern branch of the Nile where it enters the Mediterranean, and Tinnīs to the east of it. Alexandria continued to flourish as the major emporium. The Red Sea ports of Quṣayr and, south of it, 'Aydhāb were active in the grain trade with the Ḥijāz and growing pilgrimage traffic from Egypt, North Africa, and al-Andalus. In addition to pilgrims, many refugees, merchants, and students from the Far West also passed through Egypt, usually via Alexandria, to Mecca. Many settled permanently in Alexandria or the capital city.[5]

After an interregnum of three decades, Ṭūlūnid rule was followed by that of another Turkish military family, that of the Ikhshīdids (323–58/935–69). It was ultimately undermined in large part by low floods of the Nile. Such catastrophes, which could result in famine, were the most serious threat to the economy, not to mention social and political stability. Some of the most severe low floods occurred in 352–9/963–9.[6]

Meanwhile, a movement of the Ismā'īlī branch of Shī'ism had taken hold in North Africa with the support of the Kutāma Berbers. Its leader was 'Ubayd Allāh al-Mahdī (d. 322/934) who, in a challenge to the Sunni 'Abbāsids, was recognized as caliph by his followers in 297/910. Claiming descent from the Prophet's daughter Fāṭima and his son-in-law 'Ali, al-Mahdī established a dynasty known as that of the Fāṭimids. He and his first three successors gradually took political control of most of North Africa and then, after several failed attempts, the Fāṭimid army conquered Egypt. In 358/969 its commander Jawhar entered al-Fusṭāṭ, removed the last Ikhshīdid, and founded a new capital, Cairo, on the northern edge of al-Qaṭā'i' and a number of kilometers east of the Nile. A few years later, the fourth caliph al-Mu'izz (r. 341–65/953–75) entered Egypt in triumph and established his court and a large army of Berbers in Cairo. For the next two centuries (297–567/909–1171) Egypt would be, politically, a Shi'i country.[7]

From Egypt the Fāṭimids expanded their empire to include Syria. They even threatened Baghdad and dominated Western Arabia. On the whole the economy of Egypt thrived under their rule. There was great prosperity and cultural vitality.[8] Cairo grew to become a substantial city and, combined with the larger al-Fusṭāṭ and the incorporation of al-Qaṭā'i' between them, formed a great metropolis as the political, administrative, and commercial center of the country and capital of an empire. It was the hub of the Mediterranean Sea–Indian Ocean trade continuum between Alexandria and Qūṣ, which was on the Nile in Upper Egypt and the jumping-off point for the Red Sea ports. Alexandria attracted large numbers of merchants from around the Mediterranean, especially from North Africa, Italian city-states, and Syria. There were, in fact, resident merchants from all along the route to India.[9] Refugees, pilgrims, and students also continued to enter Egypt, which remained the transit point for Muslims from North Africa and al-Andalus who were on their way to Mecca and Medina. But Egypt had its own places of pilgrimage. These included, for Muslims, the tombs of several companions of Muhammad and, for Christians, the burial place of St. Mark, all of which were in Alexandria. Muslims also flocked to the tomb of the female saint al-Sayyida Nafīsa (d. 208/824) south of Cairo.[10]

The Fāṭimids devoted considerable energy to trying to convert the Sunni population of Egypt to their Ismā'īlī version of Shī'ism, but failed. Needless to say, their efforts had no effect on non-Muslims. Al-Mu'izz supported a new interpretation of Ismā'īlī doctrine and law, and he and subsequent caliphs engaged in elaborate processions to impress the population. The Fāṭimids introduced new celebrations, such as the commemoration of Ghadīr Khumm, a place between Mecca and Medina where the Prophet supposedly made a statement that was interpreted by Shi'is as supporting 'Alī's right to the caliphate. They also stressed the emotional mourning of 'Ashūrā' (the tenth of al-Muḥarram), which was the anniversary of the day in 60/680 in which 'Alī's son al-Ḥusayn was killed fighting the Umayyad caliph. In addition, the Fāṭimid caliphs were apparently the first to go in procession to the Nilometer on the island of al-Rawḍa opposite al-Fuṣṭāṭ to mark the annual flood of the Nile in the fall, which was always a cause for rejoicing by all Egyptians.[11] They celebrated the Islamic New Year with great fanfare, and especially the holidays of Eid al-Adha (ʻĪd al-Aḍḥā, the sacrifice during the annual pilgrimage to Mecca) and Eid al-Fitr (ʻĪd al-Fiṭr, breaking the fast of Ramadan), which were characterized by great distributions of food, ceremonial clothing, and money. The Coptic New Year, or Nawrūz, was also celebrated as a major holiday and all Egyptians participated in it.[12] This was true too of Epiphany, which was called ʻĪd al-Ghiṭās (Festival of Immersion). On this day the Christians bathed in the Nile. During the night the river was illuminated with candles and fires, and the caliph himself gave the signal for them to be lit. There was much eating, drinking, music, and dancing.[13]

At the beginning of the Fāṭimid period the population was still mostly Christian. This was especially true in the countryside, where Coptic continued to be spoken. Islam and Arabic spread first in the cities. By the end of the Fāṭimid period, the sixth/twelfth century, the balance throughout the country tipped in favor of Sunni Muslims and Arabic. The large Jewish communities of Alexandria and al-Fusṭāṭ maintained their integrity, but also became Arabic-speaking. Christians and Jews as well as Muslims participated in commerce of all kinds and held important administrative positions.[14]

Apart from a low flooding of the Nile, Egypt's economy and political stability under this dynasty were affected mainly by oppressive actions of the supposedly unbalanced caliph al-Ḥākim (r. 386–411/996–1021), who ordered troops to plunder and burn al-Fusṭāṭ, crises over succession to the caliphate, splits within the Ismāʻīlī movement, factional fighting within the army, and finally Crusader invasions. In the course of these invasions, which occurred between 559/1163 and 565/1169, the Franks briefly entered and "toured" Alexandria and besieged Cairo. The Fāṭimid vizier Shāwar, unable to defend al-Fusṭāṭ, set it ablaze. Meanwhile, the child caliph al-ʻĀḍid (r. 555–67/1160–71) was helpless in the midst of these events. In 564/1169, Ṣalāḥ al-Dīn Ibn Ayyūb became vizier. When al-ʻĀḍid died, he proclaimed the end of the Fāṭimid caliphate and the restoration of Sunnism as the official version of state Islam, and seized complete control of Egypt.

Ṣalāḥ al-Dīn (d. 589/1193), who was called Saladin in Europe and became renowned for his exploits against the Crusaders, proceeded to establish his own dynasty, the Ayyūbid, based on Egypt. He created an empire that included most of Syria, Southeastern Anatolia, Northern Iraq, the Ḥijāz, and Yemen. He parceled out these regions to members of his family, who ruled them as their own principalities. The Egyptian branch of the dynasty remained in power until 650/1252.

Like the Fāṭimids, the Ayyūbids controlled commerce between the Mediterranean and Indian Ocean, to the great benefit of Egypt. The travel of merchants, pilgrims, students, and others to the country and beyond continued. Saladin undertook a large-scale building program in Cairo, especially the construction of fortifications. He also expanded the port facilities of Alexandria and invited the Doge of Venice to open a warehouse. After the Doge did so, merchants from other Italian cities, France, Catalonia, and elsewhere settled in Alexandria in fairly large numbers. Furthermore, Saladin stationed a fleet there, which raided the Crusader states on the Syrian coast. Later, between 595–8/1199–1202, the economy was severely undermined, however, when low floods once more brought famine and devastation to the countryside. This was exacerbated by a major earthquake in 597/1200. Apart from natural disasters, the threat to Egyptian prosperity came, again, mainly from the Crusades. In 578/1182–3 the notorious Reginald of Châtillon, who had arrived in Palestine with the Second Crusade, launched raiders into the Red Sea from Palestine. They seized ships, cut the pilgrimage route from Egypt, and briefly caused panic in Mecca and Medina. It was with some difficulty that Saladin had them tracked down and annihilated.[15]

A much greater danger came from full-scale Crusader invasions. In 615/1218 the army of the Fifth Crusade attacked the port of Damietta, and captured it the following year. The Crusaders were not compelled to surrender until 618/1221. In the course of this campaign, the city suffered enormous damage. Another consequence of it was that the European merchants in Alexandria were arrested. Then, in 647/1249, Louis IX attacked Damietta in the Seventh Crusade. He too managed to capture it, but the next year he was defeated and taken prisoner.[16]

Because of the need for defense against the Crusaders, Saladin mobilized a large army composed mostly of Kurds and Turks, many of whom were stationed in Egypt, above all in Cairo. After al-Ṣāliḥ became sultan (r. 637–47/1240–9), he began to import many young Turkish slaves through

Alexandria. These slaves, or *mamlūks*, were quartered on the island of al-Rawḍa. There they were given strict military training and transformed into elite troops. These men, who became known as the Baḥriyya (Nile) Mamlūks, quickly became the power behind the throne. In 648/1250–1, immediately after al-Ṣāliḥ died, they demolished Damietta as a precaution against a future Crusader invasion. Then, in 650/1252, the Mamlūks seized power and put an end to the Ayyūbid dynasty.[17]

The real founder of the Mamlūk regime was Baybars (r. 658–76/1260–77), who seized the sultanate after helping to lead the Egyptian army to victory over the Mongols at the Battle of ʿAyn Jālūt (Goliath's Spring) in Palestine. The Mongols had sacked Baghdad and killed the ʿAbbāsid caliph in 656/1258. The Mamlūks then blunted their drive to the West. In the aftermath, Egypt—and Cairo in particular—became the bulwark of Muslim orthodoxy and the center of Arab culture, with a population perhaps as high as 200,000. Indeed, an ʿAbbāsid pretender made his way to Cairo, where Baybars established a shadow-caliphate in 659/1261.

Given the nature of their origin, the Mamlūks did not establish a seamless dynastic succession in the traditional sense. Instead, the most powerful among them assumed or seized the throne with the backing of a coalition of forces. The greatest of the strongmen who reached the sultanate passed it on to their descendants. Such continuity was frequently interrupted, however, by rival military men who had their own supporters. Coups, assassinations, and revolts resulted in short reigns and frequent political turmoil as the strongmen of the corps jockeyed for power. Because of the inherent instability of the regime, Sultan Qalāwūn (r. 678–89/1279–90) began to import Circassian slaves from the Northern Caucasus as a counterweight to the Turkish *mamlūks*. He used them to create a new regiment, which he quartered in the Cairo citadel. Thus they were called the Burjiyya (Tower) Mamlūks. Eventually, however, a Circassian commander, Barqūq (r. 784–91/1382–9, 792–801/1390–9), seized power and inaugurated a second line of Mamlūk rulers, most of whom ruled rather briefly and usually in name only.[18]

Baybars and subsequent sultans assimilated most of the Ayyūbid domains outside Egypt to their rule. The Mamlūk Empire eventually stretched to the Euphrates in the East and to Dongola in Nubia (Sudan) in the South, with the Ḥijāz, again, as an Egyptian protectorate. The Mamlūks put relentless pressure on the Franks in Palestine and eventually snuffed out the last of the Crusader states, Acre, in 690/1291. Afterward, they faced no major external challenge until the appearance of Tīmūr (Tamerlane), who invaded Syria with great ferocity in 803/1400. Egypt was saved from his onslaught when he turned against the nascent Ottoman state in Anatolia. There at Ankara in 804/1402 he crushed the Ottoman army and then pillaged Anatolia before returning to Samarqand. Within 50 years, however, the Ottoman phoenix rose from the ashes to become a leading European and Middle Eastern power. In 922/1516 Selim I, the sultan of a now robust Ottoman Empire, shattered the Mamlūk army near Aleppo in Syria and in the following year proceeded to conquer Egypt. He hanged the last Mamlūk ruler, Ṭūmānbāy II, and made Egypt a governorate of the Ottoman state.[19]

The Mamlūks, like their predecessors, continued to benefit from (and encourage) trade and other transit traffic between the Mediterranean and the Indian Ocean. The looming commercial threat from the Portuguese in the Indian Ocean and Red Sea did not begin to materialize until the end of the Mamlūk period. On the Mediterranean, Alexandria boomed. It had no rival, especially after Baybars blocked the mouth of the Nile next to Damietta to seagoing ships, again as a precaution against the Crusaders. Cairo, the hub, flourished and essentially merged with al-Fusṭāṭ. Quṣayr and ʿAydhāb continued as the prominent ports on the Red Sea. Some of the leading sultans, such as al-Nāṣir Muḥammad ibn Qalāwūn (r. 693–4/1293–4, 698–708/1299–1309, 709–41/1310–41), undertook major construction programs and improved the country's infrastructure by building new canals and other facilities. Indeed, he had to rebuild much of Alexandria after a massive earthquake struck it in 702/1301, and Cairo after a great conflagration swept it in 721/1321. Yet on the whole trade, agriculture, and the population grew.[20]

This trend suffered serious reversals after the middle of the eighth/fourteenth century. In 748/1347, the Black Death arrived in Alexandria on Italian ships from the Crimea. It spread with devastating effect throughout Egypt. The cities endured great losses, and much of the countryside was depopulated. Between then and 864/1459, pneumonic plague visited the country with almost cyclical recurrence. In 767/1365 Alexandria experienced another disaster and one from which it never fully recovered. In that year the king of Cyprus, supported by Venice and Genoa, stormed and sacked the city. In the early ninth/fifteenth century pirates raided the city. The economy of Egypt was further disrupted by periodic street riots and revolts of the troops, who demanded more and more pay. The sultans, who could not survive without their support, were compelled to devise new taxes and other fiscal policies in order to extract as much revenue as possible from the populace. Barsbay (r. 825–41/1422–38), for example, established a monopoly for the sultanate on the spice trade through the Red Sea, undermining local merchants. He even destroyed ʿAydhāb in retaliation for the pillage of a caravan on its way to Mecca.[21]

Despite these stresses, Egypt enjoyed a fairly exuberant popular life under the Mamlūks. The Sunni holidays of the Ayyūbid period continued. Even the birthday of the Prophet, which had originated in the Fāṭimid period, became an increasingly important celebration.[22] And a new Egyptian holiday was introduced in 664/1266 when Baybars sent a richly adorned litter on camelback overland to Mecca. This was meant to symbolize the reopening of the land route between Egypt and the holy cities that had been closed since the Crusades. The departure of the litter evolved into an annual celebration, with much revelry, of the procession of the palanquin through Cairo at the approach of the pilgrimage season and then the actual departure for Mecca. Its return was also cause for celebration. Other festive occasions, especially in Cairo, were processions marking the accession of a new sultan—which could be frequent—and triumphal ceremonies following successful military campaigns.[23] New pilgrimage sites also came into being in Egypt during Mamlūk rule. The most important was the tomb of the Sufi saint Aḥmad al-Badawī (d. 675/1276) in Ṭanṭā in the Nile Delta. Sometimes the celebration of his birthday reportedly drew more people than that of the Prophet or the pilgrimage to Mecca.[24]

By the end of the Mamlūk period, the great majority of the Christians had converted to Islam, although they remained a significant component of the population. Coptic ceased to be a spoken language. The Jews seem to have been relatively immune to conversion and maintained themselves mainly in Alexandria and Cairo/al-Fusṭāṭ. Again, both Christians and Jews were active in trade and held posts in the government, above all in fiscal administration. The commercial centers continued to attract merchants from around the Mediterranean, sub-Saharan Africa, and as far east as India. Many of them settled permanently and contributed to the ethnic diversity.

OPPORTUNITIES FOR PUBLIC WOMEN

The early centuries of Muslim rule

The business opportunities or places of trade for public women in Egypt after it came under Muslim control generally paralleled those under previous Christian rule. These opportunities were also similar in some respects to those in Arabia. Again the principle applied that prostitutes worked wherever large numbers of men gathered. These women sold their services primarily in the major commercial centers, especially the ports. In the cities they worked at taverns, inns, public baths, brothels, and even in their homes. They also conducted business along the main roads at taverns, inns, staging posts, and caravanserais. Prostitutes did a brisk trade during popular holidays and at pilgrimage sites. Egypt generally lacked fairs like those in Arabia, but the needs of standing armies, especially the regiments of the Mamlūks, easily compensated for this. Moreover, by the time of the Fāṭimids, public women, either as independent contractors or under the management of their owners or brothels, were monitored or supervised by the government. Like the Romans and Byzantines, the Fāṭimids in fact may have taxed prostitution and made it a state enterprise. Subsequent dynasties unquestionably did so.[25]

It is important to keep in mind that, for at least the first 400 years of Muslim rule (from the first/seventh to the fifth/eleventh century) the majority of Egypt's population remained Christian. It is reasonable to assume that among this segment of the population the practice of—and attitude toward—prostitution would have remained as it had been under Byzantine rule. In other words, public women would have continued to pursue their profession as usual.[26] The Coptic Church, like its sister churches in the East, threatened with excommunication those who forced their slave girls into prostitution, either directly or by refusing to maintain them.[27] But this did not stop the trade. As late as the early thirteenth century, the canons of the Coptic Church stated that a man who was the son of a prostitute slave girl who had not been married could not be ordained to any of the holy orders.[28] This suggests, of course, that Christians continued to prostitute slave girls. Moreover, as we have seen, the new Muslim rulers of Egypt preferred to tax non-believers rather than convert them, and they allowed these "protected people" to manage their own religious affairs. The Muslims, therefore, would have been under absolutely no legal or moral obligation to forbid non-Muslim women from selling sexual services. Indeed, because their main concern was to extract revenue from non-Muslims, the new rulers would, on the whole, have been ambivalent about how they made their money.[29]

Contemporary sources for the social and economic history of Egypt are rather sparse until the fourth/tenth century and the establishment of the Fāṭimid dynasty. We have virtually no references to prostitution during this time. This may in part be a reflection of the fact that this trade was largely in the hands of the Christian majority, meaning that Muslim writers were indifferent to it. In any case, our sources become somewhat richer with the advent of the Fāṭimids. The earliest reference to prostitution under Muslim rule that I have come across might be found in the geographical work of al-Muqaddasī (d. ca. 381/990). Born in Jerusalem, he visited Egypt shortly after the Fāṭimids came to power. He remarks that the majority of the people were Copts, and their customs predominated. He goes on to say that Alexandria, Damietta, and Tinnīs were flourishing ports attracting shipping from throughout the Mediterranean. Damietta also had a festival (*mawsim*) every year which drew *murābiṭūn* (warrior-"monks" who lived in fortified convents on the frontiers of Islam) from all around.[30] Al-Fusṭāṭ was a metropolis in every sense. Countless ships reached it from the Nile. Altogether the people were prosperous. Their greatest fear, a constant one, was a low flood of the river and the ensuing dearth of food. As a result of the population's prosperity, their *mashāyikh* (elders, religious leaders) did not refrain from drinking wine nor did their women refrain from immorality (*fujūr*). In fact, says, al-Muqaddasī, "each woman had two husbands."[31] This might be his way of saying that prostitution was widespread. Presumably he was speaking of the entire population, both Muslim and non-Muslim. As we saw in the previous chapter, he also asserted that fornication and pederasty were common in virtually all towns located next to seas or rivers. In addition to Aden, he gave as examples Sīrāf on the Persian Gulf and Bukhara on the Zarafshān River in Central Asia.[32] He no doubt would have included such Egyptian ports as Alexandria and al-Fusṭāṭ.

The Fāṭimid period

No sooner did the Fāṭimid caliph al-Mu'izz take up residence in Cairo in 362/973 than he proclaimed a new age. He spoke against the alcoholic, sexual, and musical diversions of his subjects and, in light of the mission God had conferred on his line, was determined to "command right and forbid wrong."[33] Presumably this led to a crackdown on public women, although it is unlikely that non-Muslims would have been affected very much. Whatever success there may have been in curbing prostitution, it was temporary; we will see later that subsequent caliphs had to renew the effort to suppress this trade.

It is important to point out that, with regard to the nature of marriage, Ismā'īlī law differed from that of the other Shi'is concerning *mut'a*. Al-Mu'izz worked closely with al-Qāḍī al-Nu'mān (d. 363/974), the leading Fāṭimid jurist, to codify a complete corpus of Ismā'īlī law. In al-Nu'mān's great digest *Da'ā'im al-Islām*, *mut'a* was forbidden, supposedly on the authority of the Prophet. Thus, the Ismā'īlī Fāṭimids did not encourage a resurgence of temporary marriage.[34] In addition, around the same time, a new school of law had begun to emerge among the Sunnis of Egypt based on the legal thought of al-Shāfi'ī. He had attempted to resolve the conflicts between the Mālikī and Ḥanafī schools and reach a compromise by emphasizing, in particular, the Ḥadīth as a source of divine will complementary to the Qur'an. The result, however, was the creation of another school. His legal thought was epitomized in his *Risāla* (Treatise). Here he cites, without comment, the passage in the Qur'an condoning *mut'a*. Later, however, he claims, like al-Nuʿmān, that the Prophet had prohibited this practice.[35] In any case, neither al-Nuʿmān nor al-Shāfiʿī mentions prostitution.

Meanwhile, it seems that with the advent of the Fāṭimids the old state-appointed position of *muḥtasib*, the supervisor of the marketplace and public behavior, became more prominent in Egypt.[36] Among his duties was the charge to "command right and forbid wrong." By the Mamlūk period, there was a *muḥtasib* for Cairo and Lower Egypt, with the exception of Alexandria which had its own, and one for al-Fusṭāṭ and Upper Egypt.[37] The *muḥtasib* came to be found throughout most of the Muslim realm. It is curious that the rise in the importance of this position, and works describing its responsibilities, coincided with the fifth/eleventh century. This was long after the appearance of this office, but a time of intense competition between Sunnis and Shiʿis. One wonders if it was a factor (at least for a time) in the competition between them for claiming the "moral high ground"?[38]

References to specific incidents of prostitution in the Fāṭimid period are rare. In 381/991 al-ʿAzīz (r. 365–86/975–96), who succeeded al-Muʿizz and firmly established the dynasty in Egypt, forbade people from going to Banī Wāʾil outside al-Fusṭāṭ during the Coptic Feast of the Cross (ʿĪd al-Ṣalīb) because "it was a place of immorality and iniquity that defied description."[39] It is noteworthy that al-ʿAzīz's Christian vizier ʿĪsā ibn Nasṭūras, who held office from 383/993 to 386/996, "commanded and forbade" (*amara wa nahā*), which suggests that he was expected to follow the caliph's orders to command right and forbid wrong.[40]

Al-ʿAzīz's successor, the notorious al-Ḥākim (r. 386–411/996–1021), whose mother was a Christian, took the injunction to command right and forbid wrong to an extreme (if that, indeed, helps explain his erratic behavior; one wonders if he was bipolar). He took numerous extraordinary measures against the behavior of Egyptian society, some of which he then mitigated or abolished and then reintroduced. Many of these measures were directed at women and probably public women in particular, although this is usually implied rather than explicitly stated. Between the years 395/1004 and 404/1014, he issued a series of decrees that suppressed houses of ill fame (*ḥawānīt*?), closed taverns, prohibited the sale of alcoholic beverages and the sale of singing girls, banned musical instruments and performances by

FIGURE 3.1
Dancing girl on Fāṭimid bowl, fifth/eleventh century.

singers and musicians, and forbade people to appear in the baths without wearing a loincloth. Women were even forbidden to adorn themselves and to go to the baths altogether. Al-Ḥākim went so far as to prohibit shoemakers from making shoes for them, so women were forced to remain indoors (as we will see later, prostitutes adorned themselves with special clothing, including shoes). He even banned women from: going into the street and looking out from archways (*ṭīqān*); from sitting next to streets and looking out (all of which may be references to streetwalking);[41] from riding in boats with men on the Nile (again, as we will see, a boat was a favorite place for a prostitute to entertain a client);[42] and from "going with men to places of sin (*ḥaraj*)." Al-Ḥākim also forbade parties on the banks of the river, including the Coptic Procession of Epiphany.[43] In addition, he banned the tents that women erected in the cemeteries during days of visitation (to places of pilgrimage; again, this was a business practice of prostitutes).[44] In 401/1010–11, he killed a great many scribes (*kuttāb*, secretaries), tribal chiefs (*ru'asā'*), servants (*khuddām*, attendants), common people (*'āmma*), and women (presumably those who violated his bans). Obviously, these measures would have seriously undermined the business of prostitutes, who may in fact have been one of their primary targets.[45] If this were so, then prostitution must have been quite common.

These and other decrees issued by al-Ḥākim were extremely unpopular—they certainly would have infringed on certain economic interests—and no doubt contributed to his eventual assassination. Consequently, they did not long outlive him. Furthermore, because he had to reimpose some of his own policies against women, their effectiveness was only temporary. In any event, the eradication of prostitution was impossible. The Fāṭimid historian al-Musabbiḥī (d. 420/1030), who was closely attached to the personality of al-Ḥākim and worked in his government, records two instances of prostitution that followed closely after the caliph's death. In his history of Egypt, *Akhbār Miṣr*, he states that in the year 414/1023 an officer of the police (*mutawallī 'l-shurṭa*) arrested a man and his wife and had them beaten and paraded (through al-Fusṭāṭ) while a crier shouted, "This is the punishment of one who pimps his wife to Jews and Christians."[46] Presumably the couple were Muslims. The punishment seems to have been chiefly for pimping one's wife to non-Muslims, rather than for pimping or prostitution in general. In the following year, 415/1025, al-Musabbiḥī records that another officer of the police had a bisexual man (*mukhannath*) beaten and paraded because he was accused of pimping five women in his house.[47] He appears to have operated a brothel. No punishment of the women is mentioned. Unfortunately, only a fragment covering these two years of al-Musabbiḥī's history has survived. Otherwise, we would undoubtedly have other examples of public women during and after the reign of al-Ḥākim. The fact that these instances of punishment for prostitution are mentioned at all naturally raises the question of whether they were unusual. Again we can't know for certain. What they have in common is punishment for pimping. The writer's message may be that prostitution itself was commonly accepted and not worth reporting, but there was edification in recording the punishment of pimping, which was illegal.

Ibn al-Ma'mūn al-Baṭā'ḥī (d. 588/1192), the son of the Fāṭimid vizier al-Ma'mūn al-Baṭā'ḥī (served 515–19/1121–5), wrote a history of Egypt that is important for describing Fāṭimid ceremonial. Unfortunately, only fragments of it have survived. But in one of them he says:

> It had been the custom since the vizierate of al-Afḍal [487–515/1094–1121] to close each year at the end of [the month of] Jumādā al-Ākhir the halls of the wine sellers in Cairo and al-Fusṭāṭ and to seal them and to warn people against the sale of wine. When al-Ma'mūn became vizier after al-Afḍal, he decided that this custom should apply throughout the realm. He sent a letter to the governors of all the provinces [to this effect] and had it proclaimed that anyone who tried to sell or buy alcoholic drinks publicly or secretly would expose himself to ruin, but this did not apply to *dhimmīs*.[48]

This custom would certainly have affected the business of prostitutes, although they are not mentioned. The taverns were probably closed (symbolically?) each year at the end of Jumādā al-Ākhir because the following three months—Rajab, Shaban, and Ramadan—had a special sanctity among Muslims.[49] We don't know how long this policy lasted.

Apart from passages such as the one above, from which certain inferences can be made, all other sources tend to be silent about matters directly related to public women in the Fāṭimid period. This is true of the richest source on the economic and social life of Egypt between the fourth/tenth and seventh/thirteenth centuries, the famous Geniza documents that have survived in the thousands from the storeroom of the Synagogue of the Palestinians in al-Fusṭāṭ. These documents consist mainly of letters concerning business and family matters of Egyptian Jews. Given their nature, prostitution would clearly not have been a topic of discussion. Nevertheless, some letters hint at its presence. At least one has surfaced that mentions an encounter with a public woman in a caravanserai (*funduq*) in Alexandria.[50] Caravanserais, which served as both warehouses and inns, were especially numerous at such ports as Alexandria and al-Fusṭāṭ, where they catered to the needs of a great many merchants from home and abroad. As we have seen, these establishments were one of the main workplaces or residences of prostitutes. One Muslim author actually defined the term "prostitute" as "a woman living in a *funduq*." Some Jewish writings of the early Byzantine period referred to Helena, the mother of Emperor Constantine, as a *funduqiyya*, with the same meaning.[51] In the event, a few other Geniza documents seem to refer only obliquely to prostitution in the ports of Alexandria and Acre in Palestine in general.[52] At that time both Alexandria and al-Fusṭāṭ had a reputation for "loose morals."[53]

In his classic work, *The Renaissance of Islam*, Adam Mez (d. 1917) stated that the Fāṭimids followed the example of the Būyid ruler ʿAḍud al-Dawla (r. 338–72/949–83) in taxing prostitutes and dancing girls and farming out the collection of the tax.[54] Originating from the hills of Daylam near the southern shore of the Caspian Sea, the Būyids, a rival Shiʿi dynasty, seized Baghdad in 339/945, made the ʿAbbāsid caliph a puppet, and established sway over Southern and Western Persia and Iraq. They reached the height of their power under ʿAḍud al-Dawla. His contemporary, the geographer al-Muqaddasī, reports that during his rule houses of prostitution (*dūr al-zināʾ*) in Shīrāz were open by contract.[55] A near contemporary, the scholar al-Biruni (d. after 442/1050), says that in order to help pay for his large army ʿAḍud al-Dawla taxed prostitution on a large scale. Furthermore, he organized prostitution (that is, took it under state control or sponsorship) in order to keep his troops from molesting women on the street or in their homes.[56]

The Fāṭimids probably were familiar with Aḍud al-Dawla's policies in this matter and perhaps had adopted the same practices, at least intermittently. In fact, even before the Fāṭimids, Egyptian governments may have taxed the income of public women. In the aftermath of dynastic changes in the Muslim world, most taxes tended to remain in place and many that were abrogated in order to gain popular or religious support were later reinstated. Thus, if the Fāṭimids taxed prostitution, they may have simply been following local precedent. Whatever the case, despite Mez's assertion, I have not come across any statement in the sources verifying that the Fāṭimids taxed this trade, no matter how likely. Mez cites the Mamlūk historian al-Maqrīzī (d. 845/1442) to support his claim. In the reference in question, al-Maqrīzī describes certain taxes that were abolished by Sultan al-Nāṣir in 715/1315. They included a tax on brothels (*buyūt al-fawāḥish*), which was collected by a tax farmer (*ḍāmin*) who had a number of assistants. The right to collect this tax, for a percentage, was held by various members of the Mamlūk military establishment.[57] Al-Maqrīzī does not tell us the history of this tax. We only learn that it had previously been in existence. As we will see, the

Ayyūbids, who preceded the Mamlūks, definitely taxed prostitution (perhaps following Fāṭimid practice), as did some Mamlūk sultans prior to al-Nāṣir. For now, Mez's assertion awaits confirmation.[58]

Nevertheless, if we cannot state for certain that the Fāṭimids taxed prostitution, we have indirect or "circumstantial" evidence that they profited from it through rents or fees. The Persian traveler Nāṣir-i Khusraw, who was in Cairo and al-Fusṭāṭ in 439/1047–8, says:

> I estimate that there were no less than twenty thousand shops in Cairo, all of which belong to the sultan [*sic*]. Many shops are rented for as much as ten dinars (gold coins) a month, and none for less than two. There is no end of caravanserais, bathhouses, and other public buildings—all property of the sultan, for no one owns any property except houses and what he himself builds. I heard that in Cairo and Old Cairo (al-Fusṭāṭ) there are eight thousand buildings belonging to the sultan that are leased out, with the rent collected monthly. These are leased and rented to people on tenancy-at-will, and no sort of coercion is employed.[59]

Because public women commonly conducted business in caravanserais, at public baths, and in certain "public" buildings—and would have paid for the privilege—they must have contributed to the coffers of the Fāṭimid caliphs. Indeed, it is reasonable to assume that some of the many shops and other buildings that the caliphs leased out were used as brothels. Nāṣir also reports that in al-Fusṭāṭ there were many houses where rooms could be rented.[60] The same would have been true of Cairo. Such rooms, of course, could serve the purposes of independent prostitutes.

The Ayyūbid period

We are much better informed about the taxation of prostitution in Egypt under the succeeding Ayyūbid dynasty. The Ayyūbids taxed this trade, with few interruptions, throughout their rule from 564/1169 to 648/1250. This suggests, of course, that prostitution was a significant business and that it generated a sizeable income which was important to the state. Al-Maqrīzī informs us that in 564/1168, when Saladin became the Fāṭimid vizier, he renounced drink and amusement (*lahw*), certainly as a symbolic act of following the dictum of "commanding right and forbidding wrong."[61] He maintained this posture after he overthrew the Fāṭimid dynasty a few months later, and issued a decree abolishing numerous non-canonical taxes (*mukūs*). It is possible that there was such a tax on public women.[62] He closed all taverns and presumably brothels. As we have seen, of course, taverns served as places of business for prostitutes. Their closure proved, however, to be short-lived. In 567/1171, while Saladin was in Syria, his father Najm al-Dīn Ayyūb, who was helping to administer Egypt, allowed them to be reopened in Alexandria upon the payment of a sum to his government department (*dīwān*, treasury). Wrongful practices (*manākir*) then reappeared.[63] There is no indication that Saladin opposed this change in policy. In fact, at that time Saladin's nephew Taqī 'l-Dīn 'Umar owned several places were beer (*mizr*) was sold.[64] The reopening of taverns in Alexandria may have been related to the growing presence of Italian merchants in that port city. By 568/1173 Saladin had signed a treaty with Pisa allowing its citizens to establish commercial buildings, housing, and bathhouses there. Similar privileges were later extended to other Italian republics.[65]

Saladin's acceptance of taverns and other places of "immorality," and their taxation, waxed and waned during his reign. In 574/1178, again when he was in Syria, his renowned secretary al-Qāḍī 'l-Fāḍil sent him a letter from Egypt informing him that his brother al-'Ādil, who had been left in charge, was attempting to close the brothels. He says that al-'Ādil had summoned one of his police officials (a *wālī*), showed him a decree from Saladin informing him of his strong objection to reprehensible acts (*munkarāt*), and had then given the governor a dressing-down for not complying with Saladin's wishes. The governor then made excuses for not closing the "houses of reprehensible acts." In response al-'Ādil accused him of being a partner in their operation and threatened him with punishment. Afterward, the governor assured him that he would arrange for al-'Ādil's officials (*al-aṣḥāb al-'ādiliyya*) to close places of prostitution (*al-khanā'*) and prohibit the immoral behavior of women (*fawāsid al-nisā'*). Al-Qāḍī 'l-Fāḍil's letter then denounces, in religious terms, any profiting from this behavior.[66] The impetus for Saladin's change of heart in this matter is not given. In 577/1181, in reaction to a multitude of beer houses (*buyūt al-mizr*) that had been opened in Alexandria, no doubt in response to the stationing of the fleet there, not to mention the growing number of European traders, 120 were demolished.[67] In 580/1184, once more while Saladin was in Syria, the farming out of revenue from beer, wine, and places of entertainment (*al-malāhī*) was prohibited and the income that the sultan had received from this throughout Egypt was forgone.[68]

The crackdown on the "usual establishments" soon proved once more to be ineffective or, more likely, it simply lapsed. Al-Maqrīzī relates that there was a particular display of immorality during a conjunction of several festivals in 590/1194 combined with severe economic stress during the reign of Saladin's successor, his son al-'Azīz (r. 589–95/1193–8). In Ramadan the dike of the Abū 'l-Munajā Canal was cut to mark the annual flooding of the Nile. This occurred seven days after the Festival of the Cross. During the month of these events the people openly indulged in all kinds of "reprehensible acts" (*munkarāt*) without fear of any consequence. In the same month there was an outbreak of disease that killed large numbers of cattle, camels, and asses. Then there was an increase in the export of cereals to North Africa, which drove up prices in Alexandria. Meanwhile, the Nile rose somewhat but then fell again, and a shortage of wheat followed, making bread dear. All of this in turn contributed to an increase in reprehensible behavior. The demand for wine drove up the price of grapes and a mill was opened to grind hashish. Beer shops were crowded and a tax was imposed on them, some paying as much as 16 dinars a day. At the same time the making of home-brewed beer was banned in order to control more effectively—and increase the revenue from—the taxation of taverns. Altogether the entire population gave itself up to shamelessness. Some wise men saw this behavior as a portent of a major natural calamity.[69] Needless to say, public women would have seen this quite differently, as it would have provided the context for excellent working conditions.

However, the wise men were right in their prediction. Two years later, in 592/1196, a plague arrived in Egypt and struck Alexandria especially hard. At the same time, there had been a lack of rain, and famine stalked the land. As a consequence of these combined calamities, there was a shortfall in the revenue for al-ʿAzīz's household. In order to help compensate for this, breweries and wineries were farmed out at 12,000 dinars each, the income going to the sultan. Such was the need for money, in fact, that no thought was given to its source.[70] Even during Ramadan, which was near the end of the Muslim year, beer and wine were sold openly in well-stocked shops and there was no inhibition from "revealing what should be veiled,"[71] which is doubtless an allusion to (or euphemism for) prostitution. This also happened to be the month in which the dike was opened to mark the annual flood of the river, the celebration of which simply contributed to further hedonism. Al-Maqrīzī tells us that many men and women met at the dike and on the bank of the Nile at al-Fusṭāṭ at that time and the river became polluted with shameful sins. In the following month Nawrūz occurred, and again the people indulged in an excess of immorality without reproach.[72] During the next two years there was little improvement in the economy and the sultan's monopoly on the sale of alcohol and the taxation of other vices remained in force. Indeed, conditions were so dire that some Muslim jurists even reinterpreted Islamic law so that "[w]hat had been forbidden became permissible by opening the doors of legal justifications."[73] In 594/1198 the same holidays again occurred close together. And once more, during all of them, the people indulged publicly in unrestrained improprieties. It is curious that in the month before Ramadan, al-ʿAzīz prohibited certain military commanders (*amīrs*) from erecting buildings on the edge of the Nile.[74] Perhaps they had hoped to use these buildings as places of "entertainment," which would have undermined the sultan's income. In any case, the tax on vice, including prostitution, seems to have remained in place throughout the remainder of Ayyūbid rule in Egypt. The vizier al-Ṣāḥib Ibn Shukr, who was notorious for his extortionate, confiscatory, and austere fiscal policies while serving al-ʿĀdil, al-ʿAzīz' successor, between 596/1200 and 609/1212–13, and then his successor al-Kāmil, between 615/1219 and 622/1225, "associated with base people and the worst jurists." He would have had no scruples about taxing prostitution.[75]

The religious authorities, the Muslim jurists, were never happy with this state of affairs, and there was continuous tension between them and the rulers over the permissibility of vice taxes. The sultans' chronic need for money, however, always trumped Islamic law and the sense of religious propriety. The firebrand Shāfiʿī jurist Najm al-Dīn al-Khabūshānī, who was the first to announce the Friday prayer (*khuṭba*) in Egypt in the name of the ʿAbbāsid caliph and thus signal the end of the Fāṭimid caliphate in 565/1169, castigated Saladin's nephew Taqī ʾl-Dīn ʿUmar for owning taverns.[76] Equally pugnacious, near the end of the Ayyūbid dynasty, was the Shāfiʿī ʿIzz al-Dīn Ibn ʿAbd al-Salām al-Sulamī. The Ayyūbid sultan al-Ṣāliḥ Najm al-Dīn (r. 637–47/1240–9) appointed him judge (qadi) of al-Fusṭāṭ and preacher in the Mosque of ʿAmr. Incensed at learning that there was a tavern (in al-Fusṭāṭ?) where, undisturbed by the government, wine was sold and reprehensible things occurred, he marched straight to the sultan and denounced him for permitting it to operate. The sultan excused himself by saying that this was not his doing but had been the practice since the time of his father. Nevertheless, he was compelled to close it—but not for long.[77] There may be some irony here in the fact that the Ayyūbids, touting their loyalty to Sunni orthodoxy after Saladin overthrew the Fāṭimids, built dozens of law schools (*madrasas*) in Egypt, especially in Cairo and al-Fusṭāṭ, to support and gain patronage over Sunni theologians.

During the reign of al-Ṣāliḥ, the poet, historian, and geographer Ibn Saʿīd al-Maghribī (d. 685/1286) wrote a short description of popular life in Cairo/al-Fusṭāṭ that reveals great casualness toward—if not avidity for—certain behavior that the religious class frowned upon, that is, toward vice in general. It would seem that there was both popular and governmental resistance to prohibiting certain pleasures. Ibn Saʿīd departed al-Andalus for Egypt in 639/1241 on the way to making the pilgrimage to Mecca. He remained for a time in Cairo and al-Fusṭāṭ, and there wrote the final supplement to *Kitāb al-Mughrib fī ḥulā ʾl-Maghrib* in 641/1243. One Abū Muḥammad ʿAbd Allāh ibn Ibrāhīm al-Ḥijārī had begun this book in 530/1135 in al-Andalus and it was continued by others. In his supplement, Ibn Saʿīd bore witness to behavior the like of which he had never seen, so he claimed, in his native land.

The naked poor there [in al-Fusṭāṭ] is content, thanks to an abundance of cheap bread, the presence of musical performances and festivities both outdoors and indoors (*fī ẓawāhirihā wa dawākhiliha*, or outside and inside al-Fusṭāṭ?) and little to prevent him from fulfilling his desires. He acts however the spirit moves him, whether it is dancing in the markets, stripping himself naked, becoming high from hashish, associating with youths [that is, having homosexual relationships], or other such things. All of this is in contrast with [the behavior] in the other cities of the Maghrib [North Africa][...]

The masses drink white beer (*mizr*) which is made from wheat. The demand is so great that the price of wheat is high among them. Then (when the price gets high) the governor has the crier proclaim its prohibition and the breaking of beer vessels. But there is no censure of openly displaying wine vessels, or of stringed musical instruments, or of adorned whores (*al-ʿawāhir*), or of other such things censured in the other cities of the Maghrib.

I entered the canal (*khalīj*) which is between Cairo and al-Fusṭāṭ. It is especially crowded on the Cairo side. I saw remarkable things there. Sometimes murder occurred as the result of drunkenness. Drinking was forbidden but only from time to time. The canal is narrow and on both sides are many pavilions full of people devoted to pleasure, revelry, and wantonness. It is such that respectable people and leading officials refrain from crossing it by boat. At night the lamps on both sides create an enchanting spectacle. Frequently, people come in disguise (*ahl al-sitr*) to enjoy the scene. I will mention here (in verse) what was said to me by an official who invited me to cross it during the day:

Don't go by boat on the canal of al-Fusṭāṭ until after darkness has descended
You know the type of people who congregate there, all the people of the low class
The two banks face off for war, the weapons used between them are words
Sir, don't go there before most people have gone to sleep
And before the night has cast its curtain over desire, thanks to the night the canal is veiled
And the lamps cast over it endless golden reflections

> Here it is spread before you and the buildings flanking it are at the service of those who rebel [against propriety]
> God, how many branches have we gathered there, of which the fruits were sins[78]

As we have already seen (and will see again in subsequent chapters), descriptions of public women actually consorting with customers, or engaging potential customers, are extremely rare in the sources. A contemporary of Ibn Saʿīd has left us two rather unique anecdotal accounts of prostitutes and their clients in Cairo, however, which might be indicative of some of their common business practices. ʿAbd al-Raḥīm al-Jawbarī (fl. first half of the seventh/thirteenth century) visited Egypt, initially from Syria, several times between around 613/1216 and 624/1227. Between 629/1232 and 646/1248–9, he composed *al-Mukhtār fī kashf al-asrār* for the Artuqid ruler of Āmid and Ḥiṣn Kayfā in Eastern Anatolia. In this work he described the tricks, ruses, and modi operandi of the medieval Islamic underworld—in the political rather than the religious sense, since not all of its members were Muslims.[79]

In the last chapter of this book, entitled "On Revealing the Secrets of Women with Respect to How They Trick, Deceive, and Cheat," al-Jawbarī records two stories which seem to shed light on the tactics of prostitutes, the first told from personal experience. At the very least they are evidence of a deep-seated misogyny which helped to rationalize prostitution. He says:

> It should be known that women are more deceitful, cunning, treacherous, and masterful [in such behavior] and less shameful than men. Their hearts know no fear. This is because they lack intelligence and [grounding in] religion, have little sense of honor and loyalty. If a man wants to do something or encounters something unpleasant, he may forego following through with it out of fear of God, or fear of punishment (the sword), or out of shame or sense of honor. The eminent sage Aristotle said, "Injustice is in the nature of the human psyche. It is prevented by one of two means, either religion, out of fear of antagonizing [the God], or the authorities (*siyāsa*) and out of fear of punishment." As for women, they have no fear in these

respects. They have no sense of honor or shame. Because they lack these praiseworthy qualities, they are able to do base things and become masters of them. Given the chance, they indulge in every vice. They are more inclined to do this than men. She who has no sense of honor in order to ground herself [against such behavior] is not safe from any misfortune that might occur to her or from any despicable action that might originate from it. I mention [below] some things that I have experienced.

FIRST ANECDOTE

As for revealing their secrets with regard to what I have experienced, I was once at a party where a group of us were having a good time and carousing. I had a companion from Aleppo. He had a woman (*wāḥida*) with him. She had parted company with him while we were heading for Yemen. So, that day we gave ourselves up to pleasure and saying farewell to our good companions and friends. When we got together, whoever had a male or female companion brought that person along. I then said to my companion, whose name was ʿĪsā, "Fetch such and such woman [the one who had left] so we can say farewell to her. And we ask that she come right away." But he said, "She won't come." So I said to my slave boy (*ghulām*), "Take this seal ring and go to her and say, 'My master is at your service and says to you, "We are going to Yemen tomorrow. We have gotten together today to say farewell and I long for the presence of our sister so we can say farewell to her and we ask that she come right away. It is absolutely essential that you come."'" The slave took the seal ring and left. An hour passed. He [returned and] said, "She is coming. It will only be a moment." She entered while we were in a room. Inside was the gathering. Next to the group was a stone bench. She came in and sat on it and revealed part of a leg. Indeed, she [completely] bared one of her legs. Then she saw her husband sitting with us in the group. When she saw him she showed no care and did not conceal her face. She did not cover herself on his account. Instead, she took off one of her shoes and attacked him [with it] while the other remained on her foot. She

> did not put it back on and conceal her foot. Instead she grabbed his skullcap and started to strike him with her shoe until he took leave of his senses. Then she grabbed him by the beard and took him aside from the gathering while saying, "You pimp! You have sneaked off to one place after another. This is the thirteenth drinking place that you have visited today. Look how many you have set foot in!" Then she took him into the alley and said to someone, "Take this dirham [a silver coin]. Bring me the slave of the judge." Then we went over to her. I asked her [about all of this] and we took her by the hands. She said, "You are the ones who have corrupted my husband. That prostitute (*qaḥba*) who is with you is his." Then we swore an oath to her [that we had nothing to do with this?] and asked her about this. She said, "I won't leave him alone until he swears on pain of divorce that he will never set foot in this alley again." He swore to her then and said to her, "Go home!" Then she said, "By God, I'm not going back home with you today or tonight. I'm going to my sister's in Miṣr (al-Fusṭāṭ). Take your keys and leave! By God, don't follow me or send anyone for me. Don't return and expect me to be part of your messed up life. I want 100 Egyptian dinars from you." I told her to settle down and go to the home of her sister until her anger abated and the women [there] calmed her down, and she could come back the next day. Then he said, "Take these 10 dirhams and buy something for yourself. Go!" And she took them and said, "Go! Go out before me. I'm not leaving. Perhaps you'll take the prostitute and go." She continued to badger him until he left. Then she came over to us, disrobed,[80] and sat down. She said to my slave boy, "Take this silver piece and buy something for us to nibble." He did so. She stayed with us that day and night. So beware of this deception and this [type of] prostitute, the lack of shame and mastery and boldness in doing things that would be shocking to you. Learn from this.[81]

With few changes, al-Jawbarī's story could pass as a scene from a modern American television soap opera or a scandal in a British tabloid. It does have a number of ambiguities, not the least of which is whether the wife herself was a prostitute. Certainly her behavior was quite brazen. What is clear is that a group of male friends had a farewell party in a room off an alley in Cairo or al-Fusṭāṭ and brought prostitutes (male and female?) with them to help celebrate. The "husband," in fact, may have procured them. It appears that the women were free and independent workers, not slaves, or the author would surely have mentioned that status. There is no hint of any inhibition about such carousing, much less any fear of the "authorities."

In the second anecdote, the author describes a story told to him by a friend from Damascus who set up a shop selling candied almonds and nuts in Cairo. He was looking for female companionship. One day he asked an old woman who frequented his shop if she could find him a young girl "who was not from among these prostitutes," apparently meaning those who were milling around his shop. She did so and procured a girl aged 15, "who did not know her right from her left." The procuress then set up a love nest for them in her home during the time when her husband was at work. One day, her husband came home early and discovered the two. His wife then concocted an elaborate tale, not without humor, to explain their presence.[82] Here the procuress acts independently from her home. She does not operate from a brothel or take clients to women at caravanserais, taverns, or other places of work. The reference to the girl as not knowing her right from her left might mean she was a virgin, rather than simply uneducated.

Prostitution and the Crusades

Other accounts of the social context of prostitution in Ayyūbid Egypt come from distinctly Christian sources concerning the Crusades. Toward the end of his life, Pope Innocent III (r. 1198–1216) and his successor Honorius III (r.1216–27) organized what became the Fifth Crusade. Initially led by Andrew III of Hungary and Duke Leopold V of Austria, the invading armies departed Europe for Acre in 1217. There John of Brienne, who was the king of Jerusalem, and others joined them. After some local expeditions and the return of Andrew to Hungary, the Crusaders decided to attack Egypt, the main source of Muslim power. In May 1218 they sailed to Damietta and besieged it. In November 1219 they finally took control of the city, where they remained inactive until July 1221. They then set out for Cairo and managed to reach the town of Manṣūra, about one-third the distance to their goal, before they were defeated by Sultan al-Kāmil. Shortly thereafter, in September, they evacuated Damietta.[83]

One of the leading preachers of the Fifth Crusade was James of Vitry (Jacques de Vitry). He had been an effective preacher of the crusade against the Albigensians in France. As a result he was made bishop of Acre and sent there in 1216 to rouse the faithful in the Latin settlements of Syria to the new crusading enterprise. Shocked by the immorality that he found there, he nevertheless recruited for the cause women as well as men of dubious character. He called on women to put themselves at the service of the army "according to their ability" and promised not to impose any penance for their sins.[84] It seems that he was recruiting camp followers in the widest sense. Prostitutes from Syria, if not also Europe, did, in fact, accompany the crusading army and were with it at the siege of Damietta. James reports that the papal legate Pelagius broke up the brothels in the army camp in order to help ensure that God would grant them the conquest of the city.[85]

No sooner did God do so than the troops and their followers relaxed to enjoy the spoils and reverted to their old habits. Oliver of Paderborn, who also preached this crusade and composed a remarkable account of it, was an active participant in the siege and a keen observer of its aftermath. As he stated, "No one can describe the corruption of our army after Damietta was given to us by God, and the fortress of Tanis was added. Lazy and effeminate, the people were contaminated with chamberings [[*sic*], lewd behavior] and drunkenness, fornications and adulteries, thefts and wicked gains."[86]

A similar phenomenon was recounted 30 years later in Joinville's *Life of St. Louis*. In 1248 Louis IX of France set out on crusade, the Seventh. He went first to Cyprus. Then, after assembling his troops, stocking supplies, and arranging for the local Italian merchant colonies to provide him with ships, he too decided to attack Damietta. In June 1249 he and his army landed on the beach near that city. After the initial clash, the Muslim commander decided to evacuate it. All the Muslim inhabitants fled and burned the markets. Some native Christians, however, remained behind. Louis then quickly and easily occupied Damietta and turned it into a Frankish city, giving markets to the Genoese, Pisans, and Venetians. Flushed with this success, Louis decided to march to Cairo in November after the flooding of the Nile had subsided. In the course of this invasion, Sultan al-Ṣāliḥ died, but progress was slow because of the many canals and harassment from the Egyptians. Then history repeated itself. At Manṣūra an obscure *mamlūk* commander named Rukn al-Dīn Baybars checked his advance, and Louis' counterattack ground to a halt. He was forced to retreat and in April 1250 he surrendered before he got back to Damietta.[87]

During the five months that Louis spent in that port city before marching south, his troops indulged in the usual garrison vices. In fact, these vices continued even while the army was on campaign. Joinville, who accompanied Louis on this crusade and wrote a vivid account of it, criticizes the army's behavior, saying:

> The barons, who should have kept their money so as to spend it to the best advantage at a proper time and place, took to giving great banquets at which an excessive amount of food was consumed. As for the main mass of the troops, they took to consorting with prostitutes, and because of this it happened that, after their return from captivity, the king discharged a great number of his people. When I asked him why he had done this, he told me that he had found out for certain that those he had discharged from his army had gathered for their debauches at a place no more that a short stone's throw from his own pavilion, and that at a time when the army as a whole was suffering the greatest distress and misery it had ever known.[88]

The reports of James and Joinville are especially remarkable for showing that public women set up shop in camp while the army was on the march. Indeed, in the Crusade of Louis IX they went to work right next to the tent of the king and future saint himself. In light of what happened to the armies of both crusades, they must have suffered much the same distress and misery as the men. Many must have been captured by Muslim soldiers. What happened to them? We don't know. We can only speculate that they were probably sold as slaves rather than ransomed and that some may have even been put out to prostitution by their owners—the same fate could be imagined, of course, for the captured women who were not prostitutes. In any case, the Crusades definitely brought European public women to Egypt. We will have more to say about harlots and Crusaders in the next chapter, on Syria.

The Mamlūk period

Rukn al-Dīn Baybars, who defeated Louis at Manṣūra, was an ambitious man. In the midst of the negotiations over the surrender of Damietta, al-Ṣāliḥ's son Tūrān Shāh, who had succeeded him, arrived from Syria. Within a few weeks, before the city was handed over, Baybars and a group of conspirators assassinated him. This was the beginning of Baybars' ruthless climb to the sultanate. The Baḥrī *mamlūk* commanders then placed al-Ṣāliḥ's widow Shajar al-Durr on the throne and married her to one of their own, 'Izz al-Dīn Aybak, who was then declared sultan in 648/1250. He immediately imposed wide-ranging taxes called "sultanal" taxes, and he "farmed out (*ḍimn*) those on *munkarāt*, namely, on wine, beer, hashish, and brothels (*buyūt al-zawānī*)."[89] Uneasy with their selection as sultan, the commanders soon replaced Aybak with a distant member of the Ayyūbid family. Aybak became commander-in-chief (*atābak*), but coveted the sultanate. To that end, he began to eliminate his rivals, among whom was Baybars. Fearing foul play, Baybars fled to Syria. Aybak proclaimed himself sultan, but Shajara Durr promptly murdered him. The commanders then selected Aybak's young son as his successor and plotted against Shajara Durr. She was killed by another of Aybak's wives in 655/1257. Shortly thereafter, in 657/1259, Aybak's leading *mamlūk* commander Sayf al-Dīn Quṭuz deposed the sultan and seized the throne.[90]

Baybars followed these events closely, hoping for an opportunity to intervene. He twice attempted to march into Egypt against Quṭuz, only to be thrown back both times. The Mongol invasion of Syria, however, led to a reconciliation of the two men. As the troops of Hülegü entered Damascus in 658/March 1260, Baybars returned to Egypt. A few months later, Quṭuz and Baybars set out for Syria with a large force. In September, at ʻAyn Jālūt near Nābulus (modern-day Nablus in the West Bank) in Palestine, they shattered the Mongol army. It was the first time that the Mongols had tasted defeat. After overcoming the Mongols, Quṭuz became ruler of both Egypt and Syria; but the old rivalry between him and Baybars soon reemerged. They both realized that the sultanate would go to whomever eliminated the other. Baybars struck first, killing Quṭuz on their way back to Egypt in October. Soon afterward, he was confirmed as sultan.[91]

Baybars' violent rise to power was to be emblematic of subsequent successions of sultans of the Mamlūk dynasty, which he firmly set in place during almost two decades of rule. Apparently having no sense of irony with respect to his own actions, Baybars immediately issued various decrees "commanding right and forbidding wrong."[92] Like the Fāṭimid caliph al-Muʻizz and the Ayyūbid sultan Saladin, he announced a new era (and no doubt sought to help legitimize his rule) by taking measures against vice. This meant, of course, trying to put public women, who were among the usual targets, out of business—four times!

Baybars' secretary and biographer Ibn ʻAbd al-Ẓāhir (d. 692/1292) states that late in 661/1263 the sultan sat in the Court of Justice in Alexandria and administered justice, and after that "issued orders for the port to be purified of the Frankish women sinners (*taṭhīr al-khawāṭi' al-faranjiyyāt*)."[93] The presence of European prostitutes in Alexandria must go back at least to the time of Saladin, who encouraged merchants from various Italian city-states to settle there. These women would have arrived with the merchants to that port, or followed them.

Olivia Constable has drawn attention to an interesting document related to this phenomenon, namely the Statutes of Marseille, dated 1228. It states that no prostitutes were allowed to take up residence in the inns (*fondacos*) of the merchants from Marseille in Syria, Egypt, and North Africa. Furthermore, "consuls who go to the said places must swear [...] that they will not send prostitutes, nor allow them to be sent, to any *fondaco* in these lands, nor allow the said prostitutes to take up residence there."[94] Thus, Europeans had obviously been importing public women to staff their inns. Perhaps they pimped some of them to Egyptians. It is possible that some of the Frankish women in Alexandria were itinerant, selling their services from port to port around the Eastern Mediterranean. They would surely have been in demand in all the ports, especially those controlled by the Crusaders where European women were few. Some itinerant public women may have found their way to Damietta. It seems unlikely that any of the European prostitutes in Alexandria were slaves. For the most part, they probably carried on their trade in taverns, inns, and caravanserais rather than brothels, but we can't be certain.

We do not know the fate of these women following Baybars' decree. Were they arrested? Were they forced to leave the country or take up other professions? Were native Egyptian prostitutes left undisturbed, and if so, why were European women singled out? Did Egyptian prostitutes or their managers object to the competition? Did the decree apply only to Alexandria? Our sources are, unfortunately, silent on these matters. It is curious that in 662/1263 Baybars "ordered it to be proclaimed in the cities of Cairo and al-Fusṭāṭ that no woman should wear a turban or dress in men's clothing, and that if anyone three days after this proclamation did so, the clothes she was wearing would be taken away from her."[95] One wonders if this decree was related to the ban on European prostitutes, who perhaps wore different clothing from native women. The famous traveler Ibn Battuta, who was in the town of Lādhiq (near modern-day Denizli in Turkey) in Southwest Anatolia in 733/1331, reports that Greek women there wore capacious turbans.[96] Were public women going about their business in disguise and escaping taxation?

Whatever became of the European women, the issue of prostitution did not rest. Three years later, in 664/1266, Baybars once more cracked down on vice, which clearly indicates that his earlier decree was ineffective or ignored—or perhaps he was focusing on native Egyptians this time. He closed places of debauchery (*khānāt*, cabarets) and forbade "women sinners." This policy was to apply throughout Egypt and Syria, which would thus be purified. When the order reached Alexandria, its governor "eliminated all trace of forbidden things."[97] In 662/1264 Egypt had been threatened with famine. The difficulty in eliminating vice may be related to this. The struggle to survive may have forced public women to continue their trade and forced other women into prostitution for the first time. In any event, again there was backsliding. Consequently, in 667/1269 Baybars had to try again, this time much more forcefully. In that year

> [t]he Sultan issued a decree banning wine, abolishing iniquity (*fasād*), and putting women sinners out of work in Cairo, al-Fusṭāṭ, and the rest of Egypt, purifying all of it of wrongdoing. The *khānāt*, where people of iniquity were in the habit of gathering, were ransacked. Some of the iniquitous were banished. The women of iniquity (*mufsidāt*) were dispossessed of their property and imprisoned until they married.[98]

Al-Maqrīzī, perhaps the greatest of the Mamlūk historians, tells us that as a result of these measures putting prostitutes out of work, "there was a drop in the revenue of the *muqṭaʿīn* who were then compensated with lawful sources of revenue."[99] A *muqṭaʿ* was one, usually a high-ranking military officer, who held an *iqṭāʿ* (land over which the state delegated fiscal rights to the officer in return for military service). An *iqṭāʿ* system for rewarding civil officials had existed in Egypt since at least Fāṭimid times, but Saladin was the first to use it to support the army, and in this form it passed to the Mamlūks.[100] With the income he received from an *iqṭāʿ*, its holder had to provide troops in time of war, perform some personal service to the sultan, and fulfill other duties, such as making sure his land prospered. In this case he also paid cash to the government.[101] Al-Maqrīzī's remarkable statement here that revenue generated by prostitution was granted as an *iqṭāʿ* to military officers, like that generated from land, is telling evidence of how institutionalized the taxation of public women had become and how important their trade was to the fiscal and military strength of the state. Because the word *muqṭaʿīn* is plural in the aforesaid statement, there were obviously a number of holders of such *iqṭāʿ*s. Perhaps these grants were made city by city. *Iqṭāʿ*s for revenue from prostitution probably originated with the Ayyūbids, who squeezed all possible sources of income to pay for their campaigns against the Crusaders.

Al-Maqrīzī's account of granting *iqṭāʿ*s for revenue from prostitution in order to support the army is corroborated by a surprising source, a contemporary Dominican friar, William of Tripoli. He was born in Tripoli around

1220, served in the Dominican convent in Acre, and died after 1273. In his *Tractatus de Statu Saracenorum*, composed in 1273, he provides a rather admirable estimate of the rule of Baybars, saying:

> He detests and hates wine and prostitutes, saying that these make strong men silly, and effeminate them. For five years, therefore, in virtue of his proclamation, no brothel with prostitutes has been found in the land which is subject to him, and no one dares to drink wine, except secretly. When he was told that his predecessors were accustomed to employ five thousand mercenaries out of the rate, or farm, on wine and prostitutes, he replied, "I prefer to have a few chaste and sober soldiers, rather than many who are baser than women, and who war for Venus, rather than for Mars, the god of wars and battles."[102]

One wonders how William came by his information. Because he was born in Tripoli and spent much of his life in Acre, he probably knew Arabic. Moreover, he would have been well aware of Baybars, who campaigned frequently in Syria, whittling away at Crusader territory. In 661/1263 he threatened Acre. William was in touch with the Pope and carried out some diplomatic duties. In 670/1272, while in Syria, Baybars negotiated a ten-year treaty with Acre. Thus William may have met Baybars' envoys, if not the sultan himself. When William speaks of the employment of "mercenaries" from the revenue generated from prostitution, he probably means *mamlūk* troops of the Ayyūbids.[103] At that time an army of 5,000 men was very large. For that number to have been supported strictly by taxes on wine and public women would be truly astonishing. Perhaps we should just interpret William to mean that revenue from wine and prostitution contributed significantly to the military budget.

In Dhu'l-Hijja, 669/July 1271, back in Cairo after campaigning in Syria, Baybars once again attempted to stamp out vice. Wine was poured out and its farming was abolished. A decree to this effect was read from the pulpits (*minbars*) of the mosques. A few weeks later, in August, the year 670 opened with more wine being poured out combined with a great effort against wrongful acts (*munkarāt*). This, of course, would have included measures against prostitution. The launching of this attack on vice was a "memorable day."[104] The sultan's great difficulty in permanently ending the business of public women shows how deeply ingrained it was in society. His difficulty probably also reveals that there was considerable money at stake and that those who profited from holding the *iqṭā*'s assigned to it—important military officers in Baybars' own ranks—resisted giving up a lucrative income.

Furthermore, we have no evidence that there was any popular support for Baybars' actions. Surely speaking for the masses (or at least the lower classes), who were the great majority and who were not keen to give up their pleasures, the writer Ibn Dāniyāl satirized Baybars' campaign against vice in a famous poem. Ibn Dāniyāl was born in Mosul around 646/1248. From roughly 666/1267 on, he lived in Cairo, and died in 710/1310. In the poem he laments the sultan's attack on drinking, hashish, and public women in 667/1269. With respect to the last, he says:

> 22. "Away! Now this country is a land of virtue and chastity,
> where a rake's fortune is loss."
>
> 23. Where are his eyes that would gaze at whores,
> when brothel's roof has been splintered by axes.
>
> 24. "Dick" (*Qaḍīb*), Zaynab, and "Noisy" (*Kahār/Gahār*)
> are all crying,
> so are "Pleasant Walk" (*Nuzha*) and "Little Bride" (*'Arūs*).
>
> 25. One is now saying farewell to her lover:
> "From now on, there will be no more hug, no
> more f—— (*nayk*), and no more kiss!
>
> 26. "All has become a thing of the past; and after that,
> I am stumped by this taste!
>
> 27. "Where is 'Madam' (*Zāmurd*)? Please summon for
> me, O Mamma!
> or else Ḥamdūn, O peacock!!

28. Their pimp lord cries: "Shit! What fault is it of ours?!
Our lady's star is screwed by catastrophe (*al-nuḥūs*)!

29. "God shot down our lady's star, and at the seventh
try the arse (*ist*) of the geomancy game is screwed (*inkīs*)."

30. Where can we go now? We are at such a loss,
Damn Time!
when there are no call-girls, no wine!...[105]

Apart from, or perhaps despite, its "earthiness," Ibn Dāniyāl's poem actually describes the prostitutes rather sympathetically, if not affectionately, using pet names of endearment to personalize real people. Indeed, he seems to take us right into a brothel which, he tells us, was run by a woman while a pimp brought in customers. The expression "pimp lord" might even suggest that the brothel had a chief pimp who oversaw others. Elsewhere in the poem, in the section not cited above, the author states that Baybars' orders were carried out by a certain officer, who was probably the governor of Cairo or the chief of police (*wālī 'l-shurṭa*). In his analysis of the complete poem, Li Guo states that Ibn Dāniyāl was not only nostalgic for the "good old days" but also was actually sad about their passing. Furthermore,

> [i]n Ibn Dāniyāl's eyes, the violent Mamluk campaign against vice in Cairo created a circus-like atmosphere; it was scary, but at the same time absurd and comic. The public outcry as an immediate reaction must eventually be transferred to laughter, otherwise the poet's role as a jester [...] whose duty is to entertain the public through societal lampooning, is not fulfilled.[106]

The crux of the lampoon is that whereas the Qur'anic version of paradise is a place of wine, honey, and dark-eyed houris, Baybars' action resulted in a "paradise lost."[107] But not for long.

Ibn Dāniyāl also wrote several shadow plays set in Baybars' era (although completed later) which include vivid characters from the lower levels of urban society and reflect the mores of late seventh/thirteenth-century

Egypt. In the farce *Ṭayf al-Khayāl* (The Shadow Spirit), there is a matchmaker who dies in a brothel. Her last words were "to counsel someone present to take her place in bringing together men and women in the pursuit of love and physical union."[108] A doctor recites an elegy on her in which "he enumerates her various achievements in procuring women for men and many aspects of her dissolute life."[109] In other words, she brought men and women together and derived vicarious pleasure from the experience. In the comedy of manners *'Ajīb wa Gharīb* (The Amazing Preacher and the Stranger), Ibn Dāniyāl presents a parade of characters—rogues and disreputable types—from the marketplace who are cleverly indicated by their names and the language of their professions. One is a phlebotomist/prostitute who describes how she treats the minds of men and compares cupping with lovemaking.[110] Like his poem, Ibn Dāniyāl's plays show public women in a sympathetic light and we see them as a common and acceptable feature of daily life.

It seems that no sooner did Baybars pass away in 676/1277 than the usual vices returned to Egypt (if in fact they had ever completely disappeared), thus mollifying Ibn Dāniyāl. Some two decades later Sultan Lājīn (r. 696–8/1296–9) reintroduced their prohibition. Ibn Dāniyāl was still on hand to compose an ode which was a parody on such action. In it he once more praised prostitutes.[111] Between Baybars and Lājīn, six sultans sat on the throne. They were surely more concerned with trying to retain power than prosecuting vice. This instability perhaps helps to account for the reappearance of the usual pleasures.

After Lājīn, prostitution returned to its usual role in the fabric of society. Once again it became fully institutionalized and taxed as a major source of government revenue. This state of affairs continued until early in the third reign of Sultan al-Nāṣir. In 715/1315, he carried out a cadastral survey which resulted in a new distribution of land and modified the *iqṭā'* system. These measures greatly increased the sultan's revenue and allowed him to reform the tax system (and in fact abolish certain taxes). Henceforth *iqṭā'*s that were not based on taxes from land and agriculture were abolished.[112] Al-Maqrīzī lists the taxes that were abolished. Among them, he says, were:

> [arbitrary?] taxes of the police (*wilāyāt*), the military officers (*muqaddamīn*), the prefects/viceregents (*nuwwāb*), and the constabulary (*shurṭiyya*) and this was because they were connected with the governors (*wulāt*) and military officers who collected them from those who know (*'urafā'*) the markets and whore houses (*buyūt al-fawāḥish*). And for this purpose there was a tax-farmer who had a number of agents. A corps of *iqṭā'* holders (*jund mustaqṭa'a/jund mustaqṭa'ūn*?) and Mamlūk commanders (*umarā'*) were responsible for them (*'alayha*).[113]

He adds that, with respect to these taxes, there was corruption beyond description. He goes on to recount sundry other taxes that were abolished, and then returns to those on vice. They included:

> a tax on female singers (*huqūq al-qaynāt*) which consisted of what was collected from whores and which the head of the sultanal pantry (*mihtār al-ṭashtkhāna*) collected from prostitutes (*baghāyā*); he collected it for wrongful acts (*munkarāt*) and from the whores (*fawāḥish*) from the riff raff of al-Fusṭāṭ (Miṣr) and the tax-farm receipts (*ḍumān*) in al-Fusṭāṭ. [...] And a specific tax was collected on every male and female slave when they resided in caravanserais (*khānāt*) to practice prostitution. It was collected from every male and female. And this was a despicable thing (*wa kānat jiha qabīḥa shanī'a*).[114]

Clearly the taxes farmed out on prostitution were important. There are some ambiguities in al-Maqrīzī's account, but several things seem clear: 1) the military monopolized most of the taxation of public women, but some went directly into the sultan's coffers; 2) female singers worked as prostitutes; 3) al-Fusṭāṭ was then the center of prostitution; and 4) male and female slaves were prostituted in caravanserais throughout the country. Muḥammad Muṣṭafā Ziyāda, who edited the volume of al-Maqrīzī's *al-Sulūk* containing these passages, says that the sentence stating that taxes collected for wrongful acts and from the whores from the riffraff of al-Fusṭāṭ and the tax-farm receipts in al-Fusṭāṭ refers to a district (*khiṭṭa*) of al-Fusṭāṭ where descendants of the tribe of Tujayb lived, and perhaps this district contained the abodes of the people of wrongful acts.[115]

Al-Nāṣir may have abolished the taxation of prostitution, but there is no record that he banned public women from their trade. Indeed, his actions were not compelled by any feeling of moral rectitude; instead, he was trying to reform the tax system in order to raise more money, which would have compensated for the loss of revenue from prostitution. Still, he may have exploited the abolition of this tax publicly or formally, thus demonstrating that his government was not a partner in profiting from the sex trade. Early in his third reign, al-Nāṣir's relations with the ruler of Mongol Iran, Abū Sa'īd (r. 716–36/1316–35), were tense as they competed for influence in Anatolia. In 1318–19, Anatolia and nearby regions were afflicted with famines, and 1320 brought terrible hailstorms. Alarmed, Abū Sa'īd consulted the theologians for the reason for these disasters. They ascribed them to laxity in eliminating wine drinking and prostitution, especially because taverns and brothels were often located close to mosques and law schools; thereupon he closed all disorderly houses and had a great quantity of wine destroyed. Only one wine shop in each district was left open, for the benefit of travelers. These measures supposedly produced a good effect in Egypt and helped facilitate a peace treaty between al-Nāṣir and Abū Sa'īd in 1323.[116] Perhaps prostitution had been an element in a propaganda war between the two rulers.

We have solid evidence, however, that (as we would, of course, expect) the business of public women continued to flourish in Egypt after its taxes were abolished during the rule of al-Nāṣir. Indeed, it might even have dramatically increased. This evidence is provided in al-Maqrīzī's *al-Sulūk*, where he describes the building called Khizānat al-Bunūd (Storehouse of the Banners/Arsenal of the Troops) near the Bāb al-'Īd (Festival Gate), which was at the northeast corner of the eastern section of the Fāṭimid palace in Cairo. It was, in fact, originally built by the Fāṭimids as a place where weapons were made. It burned down in 461/1068–9 and a prison, which took the same name, was erected on the site. When al-Nāṣir returned to Egypt from Kerak in Transjordan in 709/1310 to take the throne for the third time,

> he had a zeal for building and so he took prisoners and brought them to Egypt from Armenia and elsewhere and housed many of them in the Qal'at al-Jabal [the "Citadel of the Mountain," which overlooked Cairo] and many others in Khizānat al-Bunūd. He filled it with Armenians and it ceased to be a prison and the Sultan [re]built it as homes for them. They had children there and made wine which reached the amount of 32,000 jars annually. They sold it openly. They even sold pork at the meat counter and it was sold without shame. They set up places where people could congregate for forbidden things. They were occupied with depravity, spending days drinking wine and associating with prostitutes (*fawājir*) and doing other misdeeds. Many people were terribly corrupted including their *awlād* and many *mamlūks* of the *amīrs*. Indeed, if a woman left her family or husband, or a slave girl left her master, or a boy left his father and went to the Armenians at Khizānat al-Bunūd, they could not be taken back no matter who they were.[117]

Al-Maqrīzī also mentions the Khizānat al-Bunūd in his *al-Khiṭaṭ*, but only in a few sentences. Curiously, there he characterizes its inhabitants in a rather different fashion. He says: "During the reign of al-Malik al-Nāṣir Muḥammad ibn Qalāwūn, the prison was transformed into a residence for the *amīrs* of the Franks, along with their families and children after his [the sultan's] return from Kerak."[118] Now, in Arabic the words "Armenians" (*arman*) and "Franks" (*faranj*) are very different from each other, so a copyist's error is unlikely. In *al-Khiṭaṭ*, perhaps the author is euphemistically referring to Armenians as Franks because the Armenian Kingdom of Cilicia was frequently allied with the Frankish (that is, Crusader) states in Syria, and both the Armenians and Franks were Christians. In any case, he certainly means Armenians. The transfer of Frankish *amīrs* per se with their wives and children to Egypt makes no sense. The last Crusader stronghold, Acre, along with all Frankish towns in Syria, had surrendered in 1291, before al-Nāṣir came to power. He was actually preoccupied with the Mongols. In this respect he attacked and invaded the Armenian Kingdom of Cilicia on several occasions—as early as 701/1302—because of its alliance with them, and he no doubt took many captives.[119] Moreover, the Armenians were well known for their building skills and craftsmanship. In Cairo in the late fifth/eleventh century of the Fāṭimid period, and afterward, Armenian architects were engaged in the construction of numerous monumental buildings.[120] Indeed, there was a notable Armenian presence in Cairo and Armenians were an important factor in both the army and the government.

The Khizānat al-Bunūd continued to function as an Armenian Christian "den of iniquity" until 744/1343. In that year the newly enthroned and very young Sultan al-Ṣāliḥ Ismāʿīl (r. 743–6/1342–5) bestowed a robe of honor on the Amīr al-Ḥājj (leader of the annual caravan of pilgrims from Cairo to Mecca) Āl Malik and made him deputy sultan (*nā'ib al-sulṭana*). Āl Malik immediately demanded that the sultan do nothing without his approval, ban the sale of wine, and strictly adhere to the canonical law of Islam. He later convened a meeting to listen to judicial proceedings, and one of the first things to emerge from it was that he ordered the chief of police (*wālī*) of Cairo to go to the Khizānat al-Bunūd and investigate the wine-drinking and prostitution that occurred there.[121] Furthermore, he was to remove the Christian prisoners from the site, destroy the wine, and level the building to the ground. Āl Malik had earlier tried to get al-Nāṣir to close it, but he was rebuffed. Now he went at it with a vengeance. The *wālī* of Cairo, the chamberlain (*ḥājib*), and associates of Āl Malik descended on it and attacked it. They expelled the inhabitants, destroyed the wine jars, and razed the building. It was a glorious day. Their action "was equivalent to the capture of the cities of Tripoli and Acre [from the Crusaders] because of the many things that were done in it that were odious to God."[122]

Āl Malik then summoned the *wālī* of the Qalʿat al-Jabal, where the other Armenian "prisoners" were housed. Like those in the Khizānat al-Bunūd, they had originally been special prisoners (*min khawāṣṣ al-asrā*) on whom al-Nāṣir relied for their construction skills. However, they too began to operate a similar "den of iniquity" and were corrupting the troops (*mamlūks*) in the very heart of the major garrison of the city. Indeed, the Qalʿat was where the sultan himself was frequently in residence! So, the Armenians who were there, along with those in the Khizānat al-Bunūd, were then relocated to a place near al-Kūm, which was south of Cairo between the

Mosque of Ibn Ṭūlūn and al-Fusṭāṭ. They still lived there in al-Maqrīzī's time, the mid-ninth/fifteenth century.[123]

Seemingly driven by a puritanical view of Islam, perhaps related in part to his former post as head of the pilgrimage caravan to Mecca, Āl Malik did not stop there. He then issued an order to crack down on "people of corruption" (*ahl al-fasād*) in general. Al-Maqrīzī states in his *al-Sulūk* that he banned people from pitching tents on the bank of the Nile at "the island," because this was "a place of great corruption where men and women mingled and were ruined by wrongful acts."[124] The island in question might be that of al-Rawḍa, opposite al-Fusṭāṭ.[125] On the other hand, the same author says in his *al-Khiṭaṭ* that there was an island popularly called al-Ḥalīma between Būlāq, which was the port of Cairo, and the "middle island"—al-Ḥalīma being actually downstream from the middle island and al-Rawḍa being upstream from it. He goes on to report that this island was destroyed in 747/1346–7, apparently as a result of the Nile flooding or a change in its current. Before that occurred, many huts, some quite luxurious, had been erected there, and around them were cultivated *al-maqā'ī* (a narcotic?) and other things that were disapproved of. People of depravity and shamelessness lived there, and "they revealed all kinds of things that were forbidden" (an allusion to prostitution). This island was such a popular place that there was hardly anyone in Cairo who had not visited it. The price for a single "pipe" there and on the island known as al-Ṭamiyya between al-Fusṭāṭ and Giza, which was on the west bank, was 20 dirhams with *nuqra* flans.[126]

> People squandered there what could not be described. When their wickedness became public, Amīr Arghūn al-'Alā'ī [the step-father of Sultan al-Ṣāliḥ] and [Sultan] al-Malik al-Kāmil Sha'bān [the brother and successor of al-Ṣāliḥ in 746/1345] destroyed the huts on the island. The *wālīs* of Cairo and al-Fusṭāt raided the place, poured out the wine, and burned the huts, destroying much property.[127]

Clearly the banks of the Nile and the islands offshore were the haunts of public women in the Mamlūk era.[128]

While he was in charge, Āl Malik also banned musical instruments and female mourners from Cairo and al-Fusṭāṭ.[129] He was especially outraged over drinking and compelled the *walīs* of Cairo and al-Fusṭāt to take extreme measures against it, even arresting people for selling grapes.[130] Furthermore, he tried to forbid the Franks from importing wine to Alexandria, no doubt for their merchant communities.[131] But in 744/1343–4 alone the duty on the wine was 40,000 dinars. As a result, when the import of wine was banned it had a negative effect on the economy of Alexandria. Finally, al-Ṣāliḥ Ismāʿīl, who enjoyed his wine and many concubines as much as the next sultan, managed to stop him from carrying out this ban.[132] Al-Ṣāliḥ wanted to get rid of him, but he died before he could take action. In 747/1346, during the short reign of al-Kāmil Shaʿbān (r. 746–7/1345–6), Āl Malik was killed in Alexandria. The circumstances are not described.[133]

In the fall of 748/1347, the Black Death arrived in Alexandria on Italian ships from the Crimea and spread throughout Egypt. It had been preceded by famine resulting from a low Nile and then heavy flooding from an exceptionally high Nile. The combined effects were catastrophic. As a result of natural disasters such as plagues and earthquakes, it was common for Muslim rulers to summon the leading religious authorities, as Abū Saʿīd did above, and ask why Providence had brought such suffering. Inevitably, it would be explained as God's punishment for sin, above all moral laxity with respect to alcohol and sex, and the closure of taverns and brothels would then follow. I have not come across a reference to such a reaction to the plague of 748/1347, although the sultan seems to have spent a lot of time praying.[134] The populace may have come to view the plague fatalistically and adopted an attitude of "eat, drink, and be merry" or "wine, women, and song." But again the sources seem to be silent on this. In any case, in light of such terrible circumstances, we can easily surmise that many women, professionals and others, would have had to sell their favors in order to survive.

Less than 20 years after the plague struck Alexandria, it received another blow from which it never fully recovered. In 767/1365, the king of Cyprus, Peter I de Lusignan, supported by Venice and Genoa, sailed with an armada from Rhodes and stormed and sacked the poorly defended city. Peter had hoped to make this the first step in a Crusade that would eventually recover Jerusalem. He could not hold the city, however, and as he withdrew he destroyed whatever he could not carry away.[135] Alexandria was left in ruins. The walls were never restored, and much of the city became derelict. Alexandria continued to be an important economic hub, but it was never again the beacon of opportunity for public women that it was in the Middle Ages.

Still, they continued to practice their trade in Alexandria and elsewhere. Sometime after al-Nāṣir abolished the tax on prostitution, it was reintroduced, only to be abolished again in 778/1376 by Sultan al-Ashraf Shaʿbān (r. 764–78/1363–77). Al-Maqrīzī seems to give us two accounts of this. In his *al-Khiṭaṭ* he says that in that year the sultan annulled the tax farming of singing girls (*al-aghānī* [*sic*], literally "songs") because it had become a great affliction:

> It consisted of taking money from women prostitutes (*al-nisāʾ al-baghāyā*). If the most upstanding woman in Egypt (*Miṣr*) wanted to be a prostitute, all she had to do was register her name with the tax farmer (*al-ḍāmina*) and do what was required of her; and not even the most powerful people in Egypt could prevent her from working as a harlot (*al-fāḥisha*). It was up to the women.[136]

This passage may, however, be out of context in *al-Khiṭaṭ*. Ibn Iyās reports that what al-Maqrīzī describes actually occurred during the reign of al-Nāṣir, but he gives no date. Perhaps al-Maqrīzī is restating the abolition of the tax on female singers that followed al-Nāṣir's cadastral survey. Ibn Iyās adds that the ease of registering to work as a prostitute led the women and daughters of the illustrious families of Egypt (*aʿyān Miṣr*) into corruption. Consequently, al-Nāṣir abolished this practice, although the amount of revenue generated by it was enormous.[137] This suggests, of course, that this practice was widespread.

Al-Maqrīzī sheds more light on this subject in his *al-Sulūk*. Here he says that at the beginning of the month of Jumada al-Awwal (778/mid-September 1376) a decree was issued to abolish the tax farming of singing girls (*al-maghānī*) and (wedding) celebrations (*al-afrāḥ*) in all provinces of Egypt from Aswan to al-ʿArīsh. It had been restored by "ministers of iniquity" (*wuzarāʾ al-sūʾ*) because of the great amount of income to be derived from it.[138] As for the tax on singing girls,

> A fee (*qaṭīʿa*) was imposed on every singing girl, which she paid to the tax farmer (*ḍāmina*). If she spent the night in a house that was not hers, she paid a fee to the *ḍāmina*. The *ḍāmina* sent out a patrol every night to the homes of the singers to see who was not at home. There were specific taxes (*ḍarāʾib*) on prostitutes. As for upper and lower Egypt, streets were set aside for singers and prostitutes and each paid a tax. These places were notorious for fornication, drinking wine, and things too horrible to mention. Indeed, even if a stranger should pass through one of these places without intending to commit fornication, he would have to take up with one of these prostitutes even if he detested it, or he would have to ransom himself with the money he would pay her. In fact, her charge would be the price of the tax.[139]

Al-Maqrīzī's two accounts are of great interest in several respects. In the first, he confirms that professional singing girls were still considered to be identical with prostitutes. Moreover, it was easy for a woman to sell her sexual favors if she wished. All she had to do was register with the tax farmer who held the concession on prostitution. A woman of any class could do this of her own free will, and no one could stop her. This suggests, of course, a rather casual attitude toward the business of prostitution and that it was commonly accepted.[140] Al-Maqrīzī also tells us that the tax farmer was a woman, *ḍāmina* being the feminine form. This is confirmed by his use elsewhere of the masculine form, *ḍāmin*.[141] In the second, he reiterates that the tax farmer was a woman and that she closely monitored the singing girls' activities, since these girls worked outside their homes. Furthermore, he states that public women were found throughout Egypt, and not just in the large cities. In each place a street was set aside for them. Their charge for a visit was the amount of the tax they paid. Thus the tax, which was probably paid daily, was not onerous and easily recouped. It is noteworthy that this tax rate was the same as that for the prostitutes in Palmyra in the second century.

Al-Ashraf apparently abolished the tax on prostitution for pious reasons. No sooner did he do so than the master of the sultan's household (*ustādār*), Nāṣir al-Dīn Muḥammad ibn Āqbughā Āṣ, forced the chief judge to refuse to enforce the order to rescind it. The sultan called the judge to account, saying the tax farming of singing girls resulted in sin (because the government profited by it, and this was tantamount to pimping).[142] The *amīr* must have had a financial stake in the matter. Prior to the nullification of the tax, there had been a low Nile (776/1374) followed by famine. And around the time of the nullification, there was a terrible outbreak of pneumonic plague. These events perhaps contributed to the ease with which women could turn to prostitution. Al-Ashraf's action would therefore have been good for their business.

Al-Maqrīzī provides a number of glimpses into prostitution in his own time. For example, he reports that in 822/1420, during the reign of al-Mu'ayyad Shaykh (r. 815–24/1412–21), Ṣadr al-Dīn Ibn al-ʿAjamī, the *muḥtasib* of Cairo, personally set out with the *wālī* of Cairo to crack down on places of corruption. He poured out thousands of jars of wine and broke them. He forbade the public use of hashish and banned prostitutes from soliciting customers in the markets and in "seedy places" (*mawāḍiʿ al-rayb*, "places of suspicion").[143] Three years later he also forbade women from sitting in the shops of vendors in order to watch the festivities of the departure of the annual pilgrimage caravan to Mecca. On this occasion women would customarily go to a shop the morning before the event, spend the night there, and watch the caravan and merrymaking the next day. In the course of this, "they mixed with men for two days and a night and thus unacceptable behavior occurred."[144] There was, indeed, much carousing with sexual overtones during this holiday.[145] And, in general, the carnivalesque atmosphere offered public women excellent business opportunities, although respectable women certainly enjoyed it as well. Banning women from sitting in shops to watch the caravan was considered to be one of Ibn al-ʿAjamī's most admirable measures. It almost immediately lapsed, however, because women ignored it.

The same author informs us that in 827/1424, during the reign of Barsbay (r. 825–41/1422–38), prostitutes were tracked down and compelled to marry. Their dowry was set at no more than 400 *fulūs* (copper coins), half of which had to be paid immediately and half of which could be paid later. This was proclaimed throughout Egypt, but nothing came of it.[146] The amount of the dowry was extremely low, and no explanation is given for why this policy failed. We can only guess that the women—or their managers—were making too much money and that potential husbands sought more respectable matches. Perhaps the Qur'anic verse that only an adulterer could marry an adulteress (24:3) was also a factor. Still, marrying off public women in an attempt to put an end to their trade comes across as a fairly enlightened policy compared to trying to do so by means of punishment. It even suggests a certain sympathy for the women.

Al-Maqrīzī also tells us something about where prostitutes worked in Cairo. One place where their services were available was the Rabʿ al-Zaytī. A *rabʿ* was a large apartment house or complex of residences. As we will see, such apartment houses were well suited as brothels. This one was located near the Chamberlain's Bridge on the Nāṣirī Canal, which ran somewhat parallel to the Nile on the west side of Cairo and not far from the river. Our author states that it contained many residences where "people of depravity" went to carouse. However, the Nile had flooded it.[147] His contemporary Ibn Ḥajar al-ʿAsqalānī (d. 852/1449) remarks in a biography of one of the judges of Cairo that there was a place in his time called Birkat al-Raṭlī (Pool of al-Raṭlī), which was frequented only by people of corruption.[148] Al-Maqrīzī adds that the pool was connected to the Nāṣirī Canal and that this place was a resort of pleasure beyond description and very crowded. People would go out in boats and participate in all kinds of forbidden things. There was drinking, and debauched women would display themselves and mix with men without censure.[149]

Furthermore, al-Maqrīzī provides a unique, but far too brief, description of the comportment of public women in the marketplace. He does so in the course of his account of the candle-makers' market in Cairo. He says that this market extended from the al-Aqmar Mosque, which was built by the Fāṭimid vizier Ma'mūn ibn al-Baṭā'ḥī in 519/1125, to the market of the chicken sellers. In the time of the Fāṭimid dynasty, it was known as the market of the grain merchants. The mosque was built above shops and storerooms and was located on the street that led to Bāb al-Futūḥ, one of the main northern gates of Cairo. Al-Maqrīzī says he knew the candle-makers' market when it was full of shops on both sides of the street. They sold candles used in processions, in lanterns, and for walking about at night. The shops remained open until midnight. Here, in this market, prostitutes congregated. Our author says:

> Prostitutes would sit there at night. They were called the "wanton women" of the candle makers.[150] They had a mark (*sīmā'*) by which they were recognized and a dress by which they were distinguished. This dress was a large enveloping outer wrap (*mulā'a*), a long head-veil that draped down the back (*ṭarḥa*), and pantaloons (*sirwāl*) over the legs made of red leather. They were single-minded of purpose in debauchery. They would consort with men who would throw them on their backs[151] when they were in the mood to enjoy themselves. Some of the women carried the *ḥadīd*. In the past candles were sold for great sums every night in this market. Today, however, it is deserted and there are not more than five shops, whereas I have seen it with as many as twenty. This must be attributed to the decline in the opulence of the people and their abandonment of the use of candles.[152]

As for the appearance of public women, it was clearly quite distinct. These women stood out from the crowd. Unfortunately, al-Maqrīzī does not specify the nature of the "mark" by which they were recognized. *Sīmā'* can also mean "sign, characteristic, or mien." It was not a tattoo (*washm*). Presumably these women either wore something special, such as an emblem, to indicate their business[153]—which was a common feature of various trades—or, if "mien" is intended, they behaved in a certain manner, unlike "respectable" women, to attract customers.[154] The *mulā'a* was an outer garment that covered the entire body. It was described in the *Description de l'Égypte*, compiled by French savants who accompanied Napoleon when he invaded Egypt in 1798, as a piece of cotton cloth decorated in blue and white, measuring eight feet by four feet, and which one wore as a kind of mantle.[155] Writing about the dress of upper-class Egyptian women shortly thereafter, Edward

Lane described the *mulāʾa* as a kind of plaid "composed of two pieces of cotton, woven in small chequers of blue and white, or cross stripes, with a mixture of red at each end."[156] Perhaps the prostitutes of al-Maqrīzī's time wore a *mulāʾa* of special colors.

The *ṭarḥa* was a veil that rested on the head and flowed down the back. It was very long. The Egyptian historian Ibn Taghrībirdī, who died in 874/1470, some 30 years after al-Maqrīzī, records that the women of Egypt adopted it during the reign of al-Nāṣir and that it was very expensive.[157] It was made of linen or cotton. According to Lane,

> [a] long piece of white muslin embroidered at each end with coloured silks and gold, or of coloured crape ornamented with gold thread, etc., and spangles, rests upon the head, and hangs down behind, nearly or quite to the ground; this is called '*ṭarḥa*'—it is the head veil.[158]

Again, it is possible that the *ṭarḥa* of public women was of a unique color or design.

Pantaloons of red leather would have been quite striking (if that in fact is what is meant here). Pantaloons were a common article of women's clothing, especially as an undergarment, but they were usually made of cloth.[159] They would certainly have been worn under a *mulāʾa*. In the Būlāq edition of *al-Khiṭaṭ*, the term in question is *sarāwīl*, plural of *sirwāl*. In the manuscript of this work, however, this word is corrupt. One could conjecture that it might actually be *ṣanādil*, plural of *ṣandal*, meaning "sandals," especially because the word for feet and legs in Arabic is the same. Thus one could understand the relevant passage to mean that prostitutes wore sandals of red leather on their feet.[160] Either way, the pantaloons or sandals would have been distinctive, although the former would have been more so. Altogether, the costume of public women would have made them easy to spot, whereas that of other women would have been utterly unremarkable.[161]

Also problematic is what the public women carried. Dozy believes *al-ḥadīd* (iron), which is in the Būlāq edition of *al-Khiṭaṭ*, is a mistake for *al-jadīd*, which he translates as "sack" (specifically, a sack containing objects for divination).[162] Raymond and Wiet, however, find Dozy's reading highly implausible and believe *al-ḥadīd*, which they translate as "dagger," to be more satisfactory.[163] As we have seen in the second chapter, there is a hadith in which the Prophet supposedly denounced paying money to a soothsayer and a prostitute in the same breath. Prostitutes could certainly have practiced white magic or fortune telling in order to supplement their income.[164] Dozy claims that *al-jadīd*, which literally means "new," also connotes "happy," which leads him to *fortunatus* and on to divination. Needless to say, this pushes the bounds of credulity. Dozy also identifies the "wanton women" in the candle-makers' market with Gypsies and cites Lane's description of them in Cairo as fortune tellers who use a bag of objects from which they make prognostications.[165] Here Dozy makes a leap of faith based on an unsubstantiated assumption about our wanton women. In short, André Raymond and Gaston Wiet are right in declaring Dozy's explication to be implausible. Their acceptance of the word as it is in the text and their translation of it as "dagger" are much more reasonable, since some of the women may have wanted to protect themselves. Still, we have to admit that the word may be corrupt and that we don't know what it is.

Public women and candle makers clearly had a symbiotic relationship with each other. The women benefited from the candle makers in several ways. The nature of the latter's products, various candles and lanterns, required them to keep their shops open until midnight, and the combined glow of their shops would have been a beacon for some distance. One can imagine that this market was a rather delightful place. Few "respectable" women would have been out late at night, so the market would have attracted mostly men, some of whom were potential customers for the prostitutes. Moreover, those men seeking female companionship rather than candles would have known exactly where to go, and the darkness and low flickering lights would have provided a veil of discretion. The candle makers benefited from the public women by selling them lights to carry on their business, and the women's clients probably purchased lights as well. We have mentioned above the carnivalesque atmosphere of certain holidays and festivals, such as Epiphany and the end of Ramadan, when the banks of the Nile were gloriously illuminated at night. At such times the entire market place would have been lighted on a grand scale and would have drawn huge crowds of customers and spectators, to the great benefit of both prostitutes and merchants.

The relationship between public women and candle makers highlights the integration of these women into the business community as a whole. This is a subject that (as far as I know) has received no attention in studies of the economic history of the Eastern Mediterranean world in our period. More will be said of this in the Excursus. For now, suffice it to say that prostitutes wore special and expensive clothing, including shoes and perhaps leather pantaloons. They also wore expensive ornaments (gold, silver, jewels, and the like), cosmetics, and perfume. They were thus excellent customers of the sellers of those goods. And, of course, wine merchants, tavern and bath operators, landlords, pharmacists who sold drugs for birth control or abortifacients, and even boatmen on the Nile benefited from their presence.[166] It was this economic integration combined with the continuous demands of male sexuality that made the eradication of prostitution—as urged by certain religious authorities, who were a very small but vocal minority—impossible and government capitulation (to be charitable) to taxation inevitable. The religious authorities recognized that they challenged powerful economic interests in their periodic attempts to compel the rulers to ban prostitution. Some of these authorities, in fact, tried to suppress prostitution by placing restrictions on those who had non-sexual business relationships with public women. For example, the Mālikī jurist Ibn al-Ḥājj (who was born in Cairo in 737/1336 and may have known al-Maqrīzī) demanded that the tailors of his time refrain from sewing any dress for a prostitute, or a dress that would facilitate fornication by making a woman attractive to someone other than her husband. Moreover, tailors should not sew for women who adorned themselves, for that could lead a woman to forbidden behavior even if she were not known as a harlot.[167] The dress for proper women should be undistinguished, long and draping, not tight-fitting or short.[168] As we saw in the first chapter, St. John Chrysostom would certainly have agreed with these measures. Also as mentioned earlier, the series of decrees issued by the Fāṭimid caliph al-Ḥākim at the beginning of the fifth/eleventh century against wine, women, and song included a ban on shoemakers from making shoes for women and on female adornment. These bans might be seen in the same light.

Finally, al-Maqrīzī's above account raises the interesting question of exactly where the public women entertained their clients. He seems to say they did so right in the candle-makers' market, virtually in public! Did they rent rooms somewhere in that market? More intriguing is the fact that this market was next to the al-Aqmar Mosque, one of the most important in Cairo, and that this mosque was built above shops (including, presumably, those of candle makers). Can we go so far as to propose that prostitutes conducted business almost on the premises of the mosque? Even if they did not, their close proximity to it could be taken as further evidence of the tolerance for—and ubiquity of—their trade. We should mention that the candle-makers' market was a very short walk from the Khizānat al-Bunūd, which the Armenians had turned into a brothel but which had been razed in 744/1343. In al-Maqrīzī's time the candle-makers' market was also a short distance from a large concentration of caravanserais (khans, *wakālas, funduqs*), and probably taverns, which could have provided lodging or rooms for public women as well as merchants, both native and foreign.[169] Indeed, the northeastern corner of Cairo, where all of these places were located, must also have been a district where the sale of sexual favors was readily available.[170]

For the remainder of the Mamlūk period, prostitutes seem to have worked more or less as usual. In 841/1438, shortly before al-Maqrīzī died, Egypt was again ravaged by plague. Sultan Barsbay (r. 825–41/1422–38) assembled the leading religious authorities—judges, jurists, and scholars—and asked them if God was punishing men for their sins. One of them claimed, as had been done in the past (if not in Egypt, then elsewhere), that in fact the plague was caused by fornication and prostitution. Consequently, the sultan prohibited all women from going out into the streets, and a decree to this effect was announced in Cairo, al-Fusṭāṭ and their suburbs. It was enforced by a ruthless *muḥtasib*. There were widespread complaints, especially because the plague did not abate. The contemporary historian Ibn Taghrībirdī claimed this decree resulted from the ineptitude of the sultan, who himself was a victim of the plague, and the bad judgment of his officials. Banning all women, young and old, from going into the streets was, he thought, absurd. And he states, "Surely the virtuous woman is recognized even if she is in a tavern, and a harlot is recognized even if she is in the Sacred House [the Kaaba in Mecca]."[171] This, of course, is further testimony that public women dressed or adorned themselves differently from respectable women.

We have a curious contemporary report on the sexual mores in Egypt from the German nobleman and traveler Johann Schiltberger (d. ca. 1440). He was captured by the Ottoman sultan Bayezid I at the Battle of Nicopolis on the Lower Danube in 1396. He remained in Ottoman captivity until 1402 when Tīmūr (Tamerlane) defeated Bayezid at Ankara. Schiltberger then served Tīmūr and other masters for some two decades before escaping. During this time he traveled through much of Southwest Asia. At one point Bayezid apparently sent him to Egypt with some Ottoman troops to assist Sultan Faraj (r. 801–8/1399–1405, 808–15/1405–12). Later, after his escape, he returned once more to Egypt and claims to have been present at the wedding of the daughter of Barsbay. On this occasion he remarks:

> It is the custom in the country of the king-sultan, that during the week of their feast [Ramadan?], married women are at liberty to be wanton with men if it be their desire, without their husbands or anybody else having anything to say, because it is their custom.[172]

While this sounds suspiciously similar to Herodotus' description of the so-called sacred prostitution of Babylonian women, Schiltberger may well have witnessed the free mingling of the sexes along the Nile during a festival, which he interpreted in his own fashion.

The "free mingling of the sexes" may sound to us today as harmless or unremarkable, but at that time it could be risky. In particular, the life of a public woman had very real dangers, especially if she had acquired considerable wealth. These dangers are epitomized by a horrible crime that was committed in Cairo in 876/1471. It was described by a contemporary historian, al-Ṣayrafī (d. 900/1495), who was a student of Ibn Ḥajar al-ʿAsqalānī whom we met earlier. As he states,

> [o]n Tuesday the twenty-ninth (of Jumādā II 876/December 11, 1471), a strange event occurred in the quarter of Bahāʾ al-Dīn

> Qarāqūsh. Near the house of our shaykh, Ibn Ḥajar (al-ʻAsqalānī), stood a den of long-standing iniquity where resided a man from Ḥalab [Aleppo], a peculiar celibate. The den belonged to a person of Bedouin descent. The Ḥalabī enriched a woman among the daughters of sin and her mother. He paid the two a measure of silk and gold given him by an elderly panderer *(ʻajūz quwwāda)*. The two wore outfits of silk embroidery, with gold bracelets and ruby or turquoise rings, gold hairnets and perfume (*misk*). He plied them abundantly with wine and indulged them in illicit behavior. He strangled them, seized what they had (gained) and fled, leaving them dead in the den. They remained there (undiscovered) for eight days and their stench dispersed. Local residents hastened there and found them—in a nude state—strangled among the wine vessels. The prefect (*wālī*) rode forth with his deputy and buried them. He interrogated those familiar with the victims. They also arrested the owner of the property and fined him a trifle. It was rumored among the masses some days later that they had arrested a group selling the victims' personal effects, but this was unverified.[173]

I have come across no such crime—indeed, no crime at all against prostitute—in any earlier source. This silence certainly does not mean that it did not occur; the historians simply did not believe that crime in general was worth recording, especially if it occurred between members of the underworld. The deed had to be unusual or horrendous in order to attract their attention. In his analysis of this passage, Carl Petry points out that al-Ṣayrafī was more shocked by punishment for lewdness than for theft. Petry also indicates that al-Ṣayrafī reported the indifference of the prefect toward this case, for he did not exert himself in pursuing the murderer.[174] It was as if the victims were non-persons.

Apart from the details of the crime, al-Ṣayrafī clearly describes the rich attire of the two prostitutes, which made them a target and resulted in their deaths. He also says that the elderly panderer was a woman, *ʻajūz quwwāda* being feminine. Furthermore, it appears that the two women were independent operators. They were neither slaves nor did they work in a brothel, although "den of long-standing iniquity" might suggest otherwise. It was the residence of the murderer, a celibate (?), and was owned by a man of Bedouin descent. It was located in the part of Cairo called "the quarter of Bahā' al-Dīn Qarāqūsh," who had been Saladin's master builder. Qarāqūsh (d. 597/1201) built the citadel of Cairo and extended the city walls to include both Cairo and al-Fusṭāṭ. Among his other structures was a grand khan or caravanserai called Khān al-Sabīl (Khan of the Fountain), which had a well of potable water and a basin. The building contained warehouses, shops, lodgings, and stables. It was located outside the city walls, that is, outside the northern gate called Bāb al-Futūḥ. No fee was charged to poor wayfarers who stayed there.[175] Because of the size and importance of the khan, the area around it was named after its founder. As a hub for merchants, locals and foreigners, the quarter of Bahā' al-Dīn Qarāqūsh would have offered excellent opportunities for public women, some of whom may have entertained clients in the khan itself.

FIGURE 3.2
Wakāla *of Sultan Qāyit Bāy, built in Cairo in 885/1480–1.*

For the remainder of the Mamlūk period, specific references to only two brothels, both in Cairo, have come to light so far. The first is mentioned by two historians, al-Sakhāwī (d. 902/1497) and ʿAbd al-Bāsiṭ ibn Khalīl (d. 920/1514). Al-Sakhāwī, who was from a Cairo family and known primarily as a biographer, says it was a beautiful *wakāla* (inn, khan) called Rabʿ al-Bārizī.[176] It was located between the booksellers' market and the Khān al-Khalīlī, which was in northeastern Cairo a short walk south of the site of Khizānat al-Bunūd. In other words, it was in a thriving commercial area. Al-Sakhāwī adds that some daughters of sin (*banāt al-khaṭā'*) had rented this building and entertained customers there.[177] ʿAbd al-Bāsiṭ, who was a government official, says that in 896/1491 the *atābak* (marshal, the second-ranking military officer, after the sultan, of the Mamlūk state) Azbak closed the Rabʿ al-Bārizī. He also says that it was located behind the Ṣāliḥiyya Law School (*madrasa*), which was between the booksellers' market and the gold-sellers' market.[178] Al-Sakhāwī states that about 20 women, some of whom were slaves (*imā'*), were expelled when this establishment was closed.[179] It was closed because the door of the brothel opened toward the lecture room (*qāʿa*) of the Ḥanafī judge in the Ṣāliḥiyya, who complained![180] Presumably the women moved on.

The second brothel is mentioned by Ibn Iyās. He says that it was at the center of a dispute that broke out in 914/1509 between the grand chamberlain (*ḥājib al-ḥujjāb*) Anaṣbāy and Nawrūz, one of the most senior army commanders. The affair concerned a house that apparently belonged to Nawrūz. It was next to the Mūskī Bridge, which was over the canal that bordered the western edge of Cairo and very close to the home of Nawrūz. This house was occupied by prostitutes, and Anaṣbāy wanted to close it. The property in question had belonged to another high-ranking army officer, the aforesaid *atābak* Azbak. Anaṣbāy sent his secretary (*dawādār*) with some troops to disperse the women. When they arrived on the scene, the grooms and black slaves of Nawrūz attacked them and drove them off. When informed of this, Anaṣbāy went there in person. He beat the women whom he found in the house and paraded them through Cairo on donkeys. Nawrūz then complained to Sultan Qānṣūh al-Ghawrī (r. 906–22/1501–16) about Anaṣbāy, but the sultan sided with the grand chamberlain. He had Nawrūz caned, and even wanted to put him to death.[181]

Bernadette Martel-Thoumian, who has tabulated incidents of different kinds of vice in Egypt and Syria from the beginning of the reign of Sultan Qāytbāy (r. 872–901/1468–96) to the end of the Mamlūk dynasty in 923/1517, raises the important question of the ownership of the brothels. Who were the landlords? A few public women earned enough money to purchase and operate their own establishment, and we will mention one shortly. Most brothel operators, however, had to pay rent. A residential building with many rooms located in a high-traffic commercial area was very expensive; the landlords had to be from the class of wealth and power, which, of course, included prominent families and government and military officials. The Bārizī, for example, were an important family of notables in the ninth/fifteenth century.[182] Nawrūz was clearly an important military officer. Renting out facilities for large-scale prostitution was a good investment, and was probably commonplace. Moreover, the class that did so was also the only one that had the power to close brothels. They did close them from time to time when there was a complaint from the neighborhood or a religious official, but the houses were promptly reopened or the women simply moved elsewhere. One of the most popular places where the elite built residences was along the Nile.[183]

Furthermore, it seems to me that there is a high probability that not only the rich and powerful but also Muslim (and perhaps Christian) institutions benefited from prostitution—at least indirectly—to some degree. As Petry and other historians of the late Mamlūk period have noted, over the years the elite increasingly tried to shelter their revenue-generating property from direct taxation by the central government. They did this by placing such property in endowments (s. *waqf*, pl. *awqāf*) that were supposed to be for charitable purposes.[184] Both Muslims and Christians could do this. Typically, for Muslims, the income generated from these endowments was used to support mosques, *madrasas*, and Sufi hospices as well as hospitals and even to build bridges and public fountains. The ruling establishment learned to abuse this institution. They managed to create endowments that provided income for themselves and members of their family, sometimes in conjunction with providing income for the public good. No matter if the beneficiary was oneself or a mosque, the objective of the endowment was to produce as much revenue as possible. Among the most popular urban investments in *waqfs* were apartment houses (*rabʿ*) and commercial buildings (khans, *wakālas*, and *funduqs*) that yielded reliable rents.[185]

With extremely few exceptions, the earliest *waqf* documents that have come down to us in Egypt are from the Mamlūk period. This is not the place to attempt to examine all of them. We can say, however, that they usually contain the same kind of information and often follow the same format. They begin with honorifics concerning the founder, followed by the purpose of the endowment, a delineation of its properties (but often without exact measurements or well-defined locations), an explanation of the function of the endowed institution, a description of its staff, services, salaries, and expenses, oversight and relationship to the founder's family, and finally the signatures of those who witnessed the document. The urban properties that were commonly included in *waqfs* were, as mentioned, apartment houses and commercial buildings, plus a large number of "shops." It seems that there was no restriction in the endowment documents on who could rent these properties or on the nature of the business conducted therein. This certainly made convenient (and could help conceal) investment in any particular trade. In the endowment document of Sultan Barsbay, for example, there are only the vaguest conditions imposed on the administration of his properties and these are directed toward maximizing income.[186] Muslim endowments were often administered by judges, but that was no guarantee that the renters of endowed properties conformed to the judges' view of morality. Some judges could have been faced with a conflict of conscience while others may have looked away, especially when a lot of money was at stake.[187] It is likely, therefore, that public women sometimes rented apartment houses, other lodgings, or shops that were *waqf* properties.[188] Both the Rabʿ al-Bārizī and the house of Nawrūz could have been such properties.[189]

A glance at the endowment document of Sultan Barsbay, which was originally drawn up in 827/1424 and afterward frequently supplemented, is instructive in this respect. His *waqf* provided revenue for members of his family and Muslim religious institutions. It included a number of properties that would have been excellent locations from which prostitutes could have worked. For members of his family, he endowed a building of unspecified type inside Bāb al-Naṣr, one of the main entrances to the commercial heart of Cairo. It was on a main artery and contained ten shops.[190] Outside the walls of Cairo, again near the northeastern commercial center, he endowed a building consisting of shops and storerooms (s. *makhzan*) on the ground floor and lodgings above them.[191] Among the properties that he set aside to support his mosque (al-Jāmiʿ al-Ashrafī) was a triangular-shaped apartment house at the intersection of several streets in the northeastern commercial section of Cairo. One side faced the main entrance to the shearers' market and another faced the shop of a brewer.[192] Another property that supported the same mosque was a former mansion outside the Bāb al-Wazīr. It faced a *funduq* above which were apartments.[193] The sultan endowed a neighborhood mosque (*masjid*) with a building in the same area south of Bāb al-Naṣr. It consisted of 17 shops and a *wakāla* containing 18 storerooms. It was near a public bath.[194]

Furthermore, a relevant inscription survives on the wall of Barsbay's *madrasa* in Cairo. Around the college were the tombs of several members of his family, including his brother Yashbak. The inscription states that revenue for the maintenance of Yashbak's tomb was to come from a *waqf* consisting of one-fourth of two merchandise markets (s. *qaysāriyya*, covered market) and one-fourth of the shops at Bāb al-Lūq,[195] which was a gate at one of the main approaches to Cairo west of its old walls. While describing the events of 1502, Ibn Iyās remarks in passing that people of the basest class lived in the quarter of Bāb al-Lūq.[196] As we will see shortly, subsequent visitors to Cairo confirm this. In particular, the Ottoman traveler Evliya Chelebi, writing in the late seventeenth century, reports the presence there of numerous brothels.

As for brothel operators, Ibn Iyās mentions three. In the year 915/1509, he says:

> the *wālī* arrested a woman of wicked life named Anas [or perhaps Uns, "Sociable"] who ran a house of prostitution. She had been established in Azbakiyya, but then had moved to Qalyūb when Qurqmās became

> marshal (*atābak*); and it was there that the sultan ordered her to be arrested. The sovereign condemned her to be drowned, but by paying 500 dinars her punishment was commuted to banishment.[197]

Azbakiyya was a suburb of Cairo just beyond its old northwestern wall and just north of Bāb al-Lūq. This quarter was founded by the *atābak* Azbak, whom we met above, in 880/1476, and was almost adjacent to the Nāṣirī Canal.[198] Qurqmās was marshal from 910/1505 until his death in 916/1510.[199] Qalyūb was a town about a day's march on the main road north of Cairo. It was next to the Nile, near the tip of the Delta. There the traffic coming from the Mediterranean on both branches of the Nile merged and the traffic going to the Mediterranean from Cairo divided. This was probably a good place for Anas and other public women to go into business. The reason for the sultan's action against the woman was clearly to extort money from her; the 500 gold dinars that he extracted indicate that she had accumulated considerable wealth. Undaunted, she was soon back in business in Cairo.

In 925/1519, after the Ottomans had conquered Egypt, the same author records that the Nile did not significantly flood. This natural disaster was then interpreted as punishment for the people's sins. Consequently, the Ottoman governor, Amīr al-Umarā' (commander-in-chief) Khayrbak, prohibited the usual vices including prostitution. The *wālī* then arrested Anas in the Azbakiyya quarter. She was again managing prostitutes whom she had gathered around her, and paid a monthly fee for a license to do so. "This," says Ibn Iyās, "was common knowledge." Nevertheless, the governor

> ordered her to be thrown into the water with another woman named Badriyya, the wife of a certain Baghīdī [or Baghdādī?]. Like Anas, she had turned her house into a center of prostitution. The *wālī* therefore arrested the aforesaid Anas and took her to Qaṣr Ibn 'Aynī at Manshiyya and drowned her on the spot in the afternoon. A considerable crowd assembled to enjoy the spectacle of the drowning. This woman was thrown into the water with all the desired publicity. God save the Muslims from her presence and purify the land.[200]

Presumably Badriyya met the same fate.

Had the authorities waited a few more days, this execution would have been unnecessary (unless one believed God had accepted it as atonement); within a week or so, the Nile rose and the people returned to their old habits. In fact, the governor stated that there should be no opposition to the sons of Anas if they decided to gather together prostitutes as their mother had done, although she had been drowned for doing so![201] This might be evidence that the governor or other powerful figures had a financial interest in the sex trade. One of Anas' sons did, indeed, follow in her footsteps and become a keeper of a house of joy. In 928/1522, however, he was impaled in the Azbakiyya quarter, not for operating a brothel but on suspicion of participating in the murder of a janissary (a member of the elite Ottoman infantry). The chief of police of that quarter was also impaled because the assassination had occurred in his district. The circumstances of the murder are not explained.[202]

Apart from brothels, public women continued to sell their favors at the usual places. According to al-Ṣayrafī, in 875/1470 the banks of the Nile and the island of al-Rawḍa, al-Jisr ("the Bridge," probably over one of the canals west of Cairo) and al-Jazīra ("the Island," one of those downstream of al-Rawḍa) were among the main places of corruption. He says there were others, but he does not give their location. These were haunts of fornicators, sodomites, wine drinkers, and hashish eaters. In addition, carnal relations with women took place on boats beyond the promenades. In 879/1475, ʿAbd al-Bāsiṭ confirms that the banks of the Nile were places of depravity; at Būlāq people amused themselves continuously. The immorality was immense. In 890/1485 the situation was apparently no better and perhaps worse, for he says he saw an increase in corruption not only in Cairo but also in its environs.[203]

As for Ibn Iyās, he records that in 917/1511, when the Nile once again failed to rise to its proper height at the proper time, Sultan al-Ghawrī ordered the grand chamberlain and *wālī* of Cairo to go to the island of al-Rawḍa and arrest those who had set up tents there for the purposes of vice. These officials arrived on the scene but did not bother anyone who patronized the tents and they guaranteed their safety. They did, however, forbid people from indulging publicly in reprehensible acts and had some of the tents torn down. "This," says Ibn Iyās, "was a deplorable day; and all this zeal was expended because the Nile failed to reach its maximum of five cubits."[204] Over the next two nights the river finally rose to the necessary level. Meanwhile, the population (of the island?) was upset by the reports that al-Rawḍa had become a place of perdition and dissolution, causing the sultan to take action.

No sooner did the Nile properly flood than the usual festivities occurred at the Nilometer and along the river after the dike was cut on the canal to mark the occasion. As always, public women joined the revelers. Ibn Iyās states that in 918/1512 there was much gaiety throughout the night after the dike was opened. The *wālī* of Cairo and his agents asked the people to remain calm, not to molest their neighbors, and asked the Mamlūk troops to avoid seizing women.[205] Any pleasant promenade or park-like area could be a place for a rendezvous. Ibn Iyās tells us that in 909/1504 the *wālī* surprised five people in a garden, including a woman, who were eating salted fish in broad daylight, or perhaps were found drunk. The woman fled, but the men were arrested, beaten with rods, paraded through the city, and imprisoned for some time.[206] The author does not explain if the woman was a prostitute or why the men were punished (in fact, punished severely), although the *wālī* was certainly angry about something.[207]

Ibn Iyās also reports that in 909/1504 there was an especially grand celebration of the procession of the caravan departing Cairo for Mecca. The sultan set up his tent at Rumayla Square below the citadel for the event. "Even the young girls, despite their natural modesty, were stirred to go see the parade, the like of which had not been seen in a long time." Huge crowds arrived from various places. The people danced and sang. Everyone had a happy heart.[208] A decade later, however, the celebration was not so gay. Ibn Iyās says the procession of the caravan of 920/1514 drew a large crowd, but it included a multitude of "loiterers."[209]

Ibn Iyās detested the Ottomans, believing their rule was a disaster; he denounced their troops, in particular, for behaving abominably, and records a number of their assaults on respectable women.[210] He also reports, almost gleefully, how these troops consorted with public women. For example, he states that in 923/1517 four women were found guilty of procuring "foreign" women for some "Turkmen" (Ottoman soldiers) whom the four women had invited to their abode during Ramadan. The procurers were denounced, their faces were blackened, and they were paraded across Cairo riding on donkeys.[211] The same writer records that in the following year the troops brought women to the citadel and then joined them in the Mamlūk barracks, which were amply supplied with beer and became cabarets for parties of debauchery.[212] Furthermore, by the end of that year, the Ottomans had transformed the delightful island called al-Wusṭa, which was just downstream of al-Rawḍa, into a place of perdition and debauchery. Needless to say, the garrisoning of a large number of Ottoman troops in Egypt, mainly in Cairo and Alexandria, would have provided new business opportunities for prostitutes. They no doubt served the Ottoman soldiers just as they had served those of the Mamlūks.

In stark contrast with the actual conduct of the Ottoman troops was the official position on reprehensible behavior taken by the new Ottoman rulers. As we have seen, new rulers often proclaimed their determination to "command right and forbid wrong" in order to help establish their legitimacy. The Ottomans did the same. After his conquest of Egypt, Sultan Selim sent a new judge of the army (*qāḍī 'l-'askar*) to Cairo from Istanbul in 928/1522 in order to enforce a new morality. The judge immediately declared that in Egypt he wanted to establish the marriage customs of the women of Istanbul, and specified the new rules. In addition, he and the governor Khayrbak declared that

> women must refrain from going to the markets, from riding on donkeys followed by the donkey master. Only old women were authorized to go to market. Women who flouted this prohibition were given the rod. Then they were attached by the hair to the tail of a draft horse and dragged across Cairo. The women were quite upset with this measure.
>
> A few days later the *qāḍī 'l-'askar*, while going up to the citadel, saw some women talking with some cavalry soldiers (*sipahis*) in the middle of a market. This scene offended him. When he reached the

> citadel he said to the Commander-in-Chief [Khayrbak], "The women of Cairo debauch the soldiers of the emperor [that is, the sultan] and they will not be capable of fighting." He then described what he saw. The Commander-in-Chief was infuriated with these women and had the prefect (*wālī*) proclaim throughout the city that no woman was allowed to set foot outside the house and he forbade women from riding on a donkey followed by a donkey master; and any muleteer who rented an animal to a woman would be hung the same day without pardon. Afterwards a woman was found on a rented animal at the edge of the desert. She was made to dismount and the donkey master took flight. The woman was beaten, her veil was torn, and she only extracted herself with great difficulty after having paid about two *ashrafīs* (which were gold coins). While this measure was in force, the donkey masters sold their donkeys and bought draft horses on which they put half pack-saddles and the women sat on a saddle blanket while the muleteer led the animal with a bridal. Such were the new practices. Donkeys for rent disappeared from Cairo. The princesses and great ladies rode on draft horses, as in Istanbul, but some still used mules.[213]

Within the year, the judge left by sea for Mecca, to the great relief of the women of Egypt. As Ibn Iyās happily remarks, the women sang the following refrain: "Let's go! Let's prostitute ourselves and defile ourselves! The *qāḍī 'l-ʿaskar* has departed."[214]

Public women in the Arabian Nights

Before providing a postscript on prostitution in Egypt under Ottoman rule and then concluding this chapter, it is illuminating to briefly examine the portrayal of public women in the most famous work of Arabic literature, the *Arabian Nights* or the *One Thousand and One Nights*. The tales that constitute the *Nights* have a rather long and complex history, which is outside our subject. What is important for us, however, is that the tales in our possession seem to have two major strata: a Baghdad stratum of stories about Caliph

Hārūn al-Rashīd and the time of the 'Abbāsid dynasty, and a Cairo stratum from the Mamlūk period. The Baghdad stratum seems to represent the first phase of compilation between the fourth/tenth and sixth/twelfth centuries, while the Cairo stratum represents the second phase between the eighth/fourteenth and tenth/sixteenth centuries. Earlier stories were often later reworked. By the time the tales reached their more or less final form under the Mamlūks, their elements were all recognizable to an Egyptian audience.[215]

Although it can be hazardous to read too much social history into the *Nights*, some of the tales are useful for providing the usually brief and dry references to daily life found in historical works with a touch of verisimilitude.[216] Two stories from the *Nights*, as told by Shahrazad (who herself can be seen as a courtesan or prostitute), portray public women and how they went about their business in some detail. The first is the story of "Hārūn al-Rashīd and Abū 'l-Ḥasan the Merchant of Oman." The second is "The Third Constable's Story."

In the story of Hārūn al-Rashīd, the caliph is unable to sleep, so he and some companions set out from Baghdad on a boat down the Tigris, seeking amusement. They reach an apartment house from which they hear a girl singing to the accompaniment of a lute. The owner of the establishment, Abū 'l-Ḥasan, greets them and asks them to enter. Inside they find a salon whose ceiling is covered with gold and whose walls are decorated with lapis lazuli,[217] and within is a hall with a couch on which 100 girls are sitting. Their master calls them down from their seats, and offers his guests a feast of various delicacies served by several of the girls. After the meal, a black slave girl fetches the singing girl who was playing the lute. At this point, the caliph asks the master how he came by his present occupation.

Abū 'l-Ḥasan says he was originally a seafaring merchant from Oman, the region near the entrance of the Persian Gulf. He went to Baghdad to trade and rented a place in the Karkh district,[218] where the merchants resided. One day he saw a stately mansion with a large window overlooking the river, and in front of the house sat a handsomely dressed elderly man who was in the company of four slave girls and five pages. The man was in fact a keeper of girls, and Abū 'l-Ḥasan requested permission to enter his establishment. At this point the keeper informed him that he had many girls. The nightly fee for some was ten dinars, for some 40, and for others more. Abū 'l-Ḥasan chose a girl whose price was ten dinars, and paid for a month. A page took him to a bath in the house and then to the girl's chamber, which was decorated with gold. The girl was beautiful and was attended by two maids who served them wonderful dishes. After spending a month with her, Abū 'l-Ḥasan decided to spend a month with a girl whose price was 20 dinars a night, and then with a girl whose price was 40 dinars. One evening, he went to the roof of the building to watch the spectacle of a festive occasion along the river. There he saw a dazzling beauty whose price was 500 dinars a night. At that moment Abū 'l-Ḥasan decided to spend all his money on her. She turned out to be none other than the daughter of the keeper of the girls, and they fell in love. When Abū 'l-Ḥasan ran out of money, she confessed to him that she controlled her father's funds and secretly gave Abū 'l-Ḥasan enough money to remain with her. A year later, however, after nursing a grievance, one of her maids exposed her scheme. Her father then evicted Abū 'l-Ḥasan after giving him pocket change and an old suit of clothes. He took a ship to Basra, where he met one of his father's friends who helped him to go back into business. He recouped the money he had spent in the brothel and returned to where he had lived in Baghdad. One day he decided to return to the brothel to see if he could find the owner's daughter. He discovered that the owner had sold all his girls and gone out of business because of his daughter's grief over the loss of her lover. Abū 'l-Ḥasan then revealed his restored wealth, married the owner's daughter, and took over his business.[219]

Setting aside the fact that this tale is largely a male fantasy, it does portray brothel operations and life in a fairly realistic fashion in certain respects. Moreover, the elements of the tale do not conflict with the information on prostitution concerning Egypt that we have reviewed to this point: a brothel could be a large and opulent building (in this case one fit for a caliph); it could be located in a popular place, such as a site next to a river; it could be run by a man who, as the keeper, collected the fees for the girls (in this case, he even sold the services of his daughter); the women who worked there might be slaves, or they could be singers and musicians; they charged different rates; the clientele were chiefly merchants; the potential income from the operation of a brothel could be enormous, and ownership was a good investment; a customer could easily spend all his money there; and like the owner's daughter, a prostitute could give up her trade and contract a respectable marriage. Finally, there was no shame, not even for a caliph, in visiting a brothel.

"The Third Constable's Story" is apparently set in Cairo. It is one of 16 tales told by a chief of police (*muqaddam*). In this story a nameless constable is out on business one day in the city with some friends. As they walk along they fall in with a group of attractive women. The most beautiful of them and the constable glance at each other. This woman then lags behind her companions and waits to speak with the constable. He tells her (falsely) that he is from out of town; she declares that she is smitten by him and suggests that they take a room. He agrees, and she leads him to an apartment house (*rabʿ*), which is clearly used as a brothel. There she takes a room key from the woman who keeps the house and pays her a fee. In the room the two dally a while. The woman then goes to a bathroom to wash before making love. After bathing she gives her name as Rayḥāna[220] and says she lives elsewhere in the city. Next, the constable also decides to wash. After he has finished, he calls for Rayḥāna to bring him his clothes, but there is no answer. He then discovers that she has disappeared with his clothes and his money. Naked and penniless, he begs the mistress of the house to give him something to cover himself. She laughs and calls all the women in the house—naming Fāṭima, Khadīja, Ḥarīfa, and Sanīna—to come and see him. They all mock him, and one of them ridicules him for believing Rayḥāna when she said she was infatuated with him. At last, however, another woman takes pity on him and gives him a rag to wear. Fearing the husbands of these women will appear, the constable slips out a side door of the building and races home. When he knocks on the door of his house, his wife answers and screams "A maniac! A satan!" Nevertheless, while saying nothing about the true circumstances of his condition, he manages to convince her and his family that thieves have stripped him bare.[221]

This story in which no less than a chief of police is captivated and rolled by a prostitute must have delighted those who heard it.[222] With regard to the practice of prostitution, we learn from it that groups of public women, who were clearly unveiled, solicited customers in the street. Having secured a client with her beauty and sugared words, such a woman would then take him to an apartment house that served as a brothel. There she paid a fee—in this case to a madam—for the use of a room, perhaps paying by the customer. She did not live in the house, simply using it for her trade. Because the constable and his friends are out on business in the tale, the setting must have been a commercial district. In this story, the prostitutes are not slaves but free and independent women, and some are married. Two of the named women in the house, Fāṭima and Khadīja, are clearly Muslims, while the names Ḥarīfa and Sanīna are not religiously specific. Finally, of course, the story tells us that those who were responsible for policing vice were easily ensnared in it. In addition, we should not discount the possibility that the audience may have understood that the constable wore clothing that was distinctive of his office, so that they would have perceived that Rayḥāna, not to mention the other women in the house, knew exactly who he was. This would help account for the latter's intense mockery of him.

The early Ottoman period

I do not intend here to go into detail on the nature of prostitution in Egypt under Ottoman rule. However, I would like to mention the observations on this matter by several visitors to Egypt, above all Evliya Chelebi, in order to emphasize the continuity of practice after the extinction of the Mamlūk dynasty.

The first of these noteworthy travelers to Egypt was Leo Africanus, famous for his *History and Description of Africa*. He was born in Granada around 1494 and educated in Fez in modern-day Morocco. Afterward he led a remarkable life as a diplomat and traveler. He was in Egypt in 1517 at the time of the Ottoman conquest and was subsequently captured by corsairs. In 1520, after his release in Rome, he converted to Christianity. A few years later he completed his great work, but it was not published until 1550. He died around 1554. In his account of Cairo, he provides a colorful description of the area around Bāb al-Lūq.

> This large suburbe being distant from the wals of Cairo about the space of a mile, and containing almost three thousand families, is inhabited by merchants, and artisans of divers sorts as well as the former. Upon a certain large place of this suburbe standeth a great palace and a stately college built by a certain Mammaluck called Iazbach [that is, Azbak], counseller unto the Soldan of those times; and the place itself is called after his name Iazbachia [that is, Azbakiyya]. Hither after Mahumetan sermons and devotions, the common people of Cairo, together with the baudes and harlots, do usually resort; and many stage plaiers also, and such as teach camels, asses, and dogs, to daunce...[223]

Leo thus confirms Ibn Iyās' comments about the quarter of Bāb al-Lūq and also juxtaposes public women and other "entertainers" with merchants and artisans.

In 1615 the Italian Pietro Della Vale arrived in Egypt en route to the Holy Land. He was born in Rome in 1586 to a well-known and wealthy family. He received an excellent education and then, motivated by a failed romance and great curiosity, set out for the East. Between 1615 and 1626, when he returned to Rome, he traveled, traded, and had various adventures in much of the Middle East and India. He described his experiences in a long series of detailed letters that he sent back to friends and relatives. Only a few were published before his death in 1652. Writing from Cairo in 1616, Pietro says that outside Cairo were certain places which were designated as public brothels. These places were inhabited by women who, with no fear of chastisement, wished to practice openly the trade of the harlot.

> Women such as these petition the Pasha, and he grants them his favour, provided that they pay I do not know what sum of money daily to the chief constable, who in turn stations policemen there to exact the money every day and guard the women from being harmed. And they do not spend the night in that place, since it is in the country, but just the livelong day, waiting for the arrival of customers, whom, as they come along one by one, they satisfy most courteously and

> for very little payment, say for a *maidino*, which is worth little more than a few pieces of small change in Naples. And when satisfaction is being given in this way to some lecher or other, because (as I said) there are no houses there, nor anywhere to stay under cover, they retire behind some little mounds of stones, which they build for this purpose, where on the bare ground they are scarcely concealed from the eyes of any passers-by. But what is still more abominable about this place is that these whores are brazen enough sometimes to ply their trade so publicly that quite often—not behind the retreat of stones but outside on the open road, in the sight of everyone—they freely expose themselves, clothed or stripped, to whoever wishes it, especially when there is some prurient lout who, giving them two or three of those *maidini,* wants, as often happens, to derive pleasure from seeing their debaucheries.[224]

Even taking into account the likelihood that Pietro was exaggerating somewhat in an effort to entertain as well as inform his readers, his report reveals the continuity in the administration of prostitution and some additional information about the trade. Women who wished to sell their sexual favors openly continued to register with the authorities and they paid a daily fee to the chief constable, who provided security. The women charged a small amount for their services, which suggests that they had a lot of competition. Pietro gives the impression that the women were free and independent operators and not slaves. He does not mention pimping. He is vague on exactly where the prostitutes conducted business, saying that there were several quarters outside Cairo that were designated as places of public brothels. However, he also says they were in the country and that the women did not live there. Keeping in mind that the walls of Cairo were probably several kilometers east of the Nile, we might guess that the "country" refers to this area in between—perhaps to the districts of Azbakiyya and Bāb al-Lūq, which were outside the old walls, or to the banks of the Nile itself. It makes no sense for the women to have worked in the distant countryside because of the lack of customers, especially high-paying ones. His statement that the women did not live where they worked is reminiscent of the story of

Rayḥāna, who brought clients to an apartment house but lived elsewhere in the city. Pietro appears shocked at the brazenness of their approach, which may well have been aggressive. However, his assertion that in some cases they consummated their sales virtually in public is difficult to believe.

The last report that I will mention is that of the indefatigable Ottoman traveler Evliya Chelebi. He spent the last decade or so of his life in Egypt, mostly in Cairo, where he died around 1684. The last volume of his great *Book of Travels* contains the most detailed and vivid description of Egypt written between the fifteenth and nineteenth centuries—between al-Maqrīzī's composition of his *al-Khiṭaṭ* and the French publication of the enormous *Description de l'Égypte*, which appeared after their invasion of that country in 1798. Indeed, in certain respects Evliya's work surpasses them both. For our purposes he provides information not found elsewhere. He also confirms and helps to clarify some of Pietro's statements.

Evliya says that public women were concentrated in the area around Bāb al-Lūq, where there were many coffee shops and other drinking establishments. At Bāb al-Lūq was a guild of 800 prostitutes. They had huts among the rubbish heaps at the base of the gate. These were probably the shelters to which Pietro referred as "mounds of stones." In addition there was a guild of home-bound prostitutes. They were "covered and honorable" women, who had pimps but conducted their trade at home. There were 2,100 listed in the register of the chief of police, and they paid a tax. Furthermore, there were an incalculable number of public women under the control of the military groups whom the police could not touch (meaning that the women paid them no taxes). There were three men—one in Būlāq, one in Cairo, and one in al-Fusṭāṭ—each called *shaykh al-arasāt* (sheikh of marriages?), who recorded all male and female prostitutes in their registers and extracted taxes from them. There were 40 sergeants (s. *çavuş*) at Bāb al-Lūq, probably policemen, who knew the residence of each prostitute and whether or not she slept at home. Furthermore, there was a guild of pimps there. They would go "from house to house in the whore-house district with the *akçe* [a small silver coin] counting-boards in hand and wheel and deal as though trading in horses and mules." Even female panderers, 300 old hags, had a guild. They found the finest "fornicatresses" for would-be fornicators.

And there was a guild of jobbers composed of men who obtained for three *akçe* wine, kebabs, or whatever one wanted while visiting a sweetheart in one of the huts.[225]

Evliya's remarkable report concerning Bāb al-Lūq is the earliest that I have discovered that mentions guilds of prostitutes in Cairo. Presumably these guilds were found in other cities, such as Alexandria. Carsten Niebuhr (d. 1815), who reached Egypt in 1761 as a member of an ill-fated Danish expedition to the Middle East, wrote in his memoirs that at Cairo and other cities of the East:

> every trade has a head, who is entrusted with authority over them, knows every individual in the body to which he belongs and is in some means answerable for them to government. Those heads of the trades preserve order among the artisans. Even the women of the town and thieves have each a head in the same manner.[226]

Well-organized prostitution was therefore very much a part of the economic and social life of Cairo. There were different classes of public women who had their own guilds. Even "respectable" women, some of whom must have been married, worked in the trade. All they had to do was register and pay a tax, as had been the case in the eighth/fourteenth century. By working at home and using pimps, they could be quite discreet,[227] and this may also have been the safest way for women to engage in this trade. They were, perhaps, roughly the equivalent of today's call girls. Presumably they charged higher rates than the women at Bāb al-Lūq. Given the large number of women in the business, the tax accruing to the government must have been significant. Evliya says that when the Ottoman governor of Egypt Canpoladzade Hüseyn Pasha later decided to tear down the brothels at Bāb al-Lūq, he was warned that this would result in a considerable loss of revenue.[228] Evliya is also the first to mention the presence of a large number of prostitutes who worked directly under the control of various military groups. This was surely not a new practice, but we have no further details. Altogether, he shows us in this account that public women were well integrated with other classes and professions who were—to a greater or lesser degree—dependent on them, from panderers, policemen and the military establishment to wine and kebab sellers.

Elsewhere in the same volume, Evliya writes that nowhere in Egypt were there brothels like those at Bāb al-Lūq and that at Damietta, for example, prostitutes simply went around with a lantern at night and were not allowed to enter the markets.[229] Furthermore, he claims that because there were droves of public women at Bāb al-Lūq, syphilis (*Freng zahmeti* [Frankish affliction] or *Freng uyuzu* [Frankish itch]), which he believed was contagious, was common there.[230] He also refers to gonorrhea (*belsovukluğu*) in Egypt, asserting rather fancifully that some Arab tribesmen had sex with crocodiles in order to rid themselves of it. Those who were hesitant to take this cure could instead resort to black Ethiopian slave girls, who generated great heat, to the same effect.[231] Leo Africanus had seen the ravages of syphilis in Cairo in the early sixteenth century.[232] Later, after the French invaded, they found it among all classes and recorded that the Egyptians themselves said that it had always existed. In order to control the disease, the French proposed the creation of a hospital for women who had contracted it; they established in Cairo a favorably located *grande maison* for all women suspected of having had commerce with French soldiers.[233] In an oblique reference to slaves as customers of prositutes, Evliya says that a male slave (*oğlan*) of a chief captain (*baş bölükbaşı*) frequented Bāb al-Lūq, where he was afflicted by leprosy.[234] Evliya also provides the earliest reference to a method of birth control used by prostitutes in Egypt. He states that there was a "pied stone like a bead." A woman who tied it to her waist during intercourse would not conceive. It was commonly used by the prostitutes at Bāb al-Lūq.[235]

Finally, Evliya is perhaps the first to mention that the tomb of Aḥmad al-Badawī in the town of Ṭanṭā in the center of the Delta was a resort of public women. A contemporary of Sultan Baybars, al-Badawī became the most popular Sufi saint in Egypt. After his death in 675/1276, a mosque was built over his tomb. It became the most important pilgrimage site in Egypt. Visitors flocked to it, especially during three great festivals held there each year: his birthday, the vernal equinox, and another about a month after the summer solstice but before the dikes were cut on the canals.[236] These were tantamount to major fairs like those that Evliya described in the Balkans. As on other festive occasions in Egypt, there was always a huge crowd and a carnivalesque atmosphere, both of which provided excellent opportunities for prostitutes. Describing in great detail all the entertainment at the Saint's birthday celebration, Evliya relates: "Speaking of women, there is a special bazaar for them—over 1,000 tents and huts of fornication, where women's skirts are lifted and men's breeches are untied, and the women are auctioned off to the highest bidder."[237] No doubt both independent prostitutes and managers controlling others cashed in on the occasion. Their places of business were temporary, meaning, of course, that public women traveled as opportunities dictated. Several later writers, including Europeans, noted the public display of guilds of prostitutes at the shrines of Aḥmad al-Badawī and other saints in Egypt. The Egyptian historian al-Jabartī (d. 1825 or 1826) recorded that public women paid an annual fee to the keepers of Aḥmad al-Badawī's shrine.[238] Among other saints whose birthday festivities heightened the libido was the obscure Ismā'īl ibn Yūsuf al-Inbābī. Ibn al-Ṣayrafī reported in 790/1388 that his tomb in Giza became the site of exuberant fornication (*zinā'*) on his birthday.[239]

CONCLUSION

The chronological gaps in the sources, the different nature and frequent terseness or ambiguity of many references, and the lack of any voice from the women involved have inevitably resulted in an uneven account of the socioeconomic history of prostitution in Egypt under Muslim rule. Nevertheless, we can say with certainty that—despite many interruptions, which were usually short—this trade flourished in Egypt throughout the period in question.[240] Furthermore, we can reach certain conclusions about its practice at various times during this period.

Public women were native Egyptians and "foreigners." The Egyptians were probably Muslims and Christians. A few names that we know, such as Fāṭima, are Muslim. Others, such as Anas and Badriyya, are not specific to either religion, nor are the nicknames found in Ibn Dāniyāl's poem.

The foreign women were Christians from Europe who sold their services in Alexandria and other ports or who accompanied and served invading Crusaders. The foreigners who worked in the ports were either brought by European merchants or were itinerants. Prostitutes could be free and independent businesswomen, or they could be slaves. They could work alone or under management in brothels. Procurers and the keepers of brothels could be men or women. Some brothel-keepers were Armenian Christians. Prostitutes solicited customers in the street or customers visited (or were taken to) their place of work. Public women wore distinctive and often luxurious clothing, which made them easy to identify in the street for both potential customers and the authorities, who might want to make sure they paid their taxes. They were unveiled. There were different classes of prostitutes who charged different rates. The minimum charge for a visit could be the equivalent of the tax they paid, which could be a daily amount. Some women became quite wealthy. Some were singing girls or musicians; some were married.

Prostitutes worked in various establishments, above all apartment houses, which could be transformed into brothels, and caravanserais or inns (khans, *wakālas*, *funduqs*). They also worked at home or set up huts or tents at Muslim and Christian holidays and festivals, places of resort along the Nile, or at pilgrimage sites. Some entertained customers on boats in the river. Many must have solicited customers and entertained them in taverns, which included popular "cabarets" along the canals west of Cairo. Special housing may have been provided for those who served the troops. Some cities apparently had a quarter reserved for prostitutes. In Cairo they were somewhat dispersed,[241] although many came to be concentrated around Bāb al-Lūq. Their favorite places of work, apart from festivals, resorts, pilgrimage sites, and taverns, were the commercial districts. At ports, markets, and clusters of warehouses and inns they catered to merchants and traders who could have been "foreigners," local city dwellers, or farmers from the countryside. These were also the places through which travelers, such as pilgrims or students, would have passed.

From time to time the authorities attempted to ban prostitution. This was especially the case with new rulers who sought legitimacy in part by "commanding right and forbidding wrong" or by rulers who sought relief from natural disasters, chiefly a low flooding of the Nile or plague, which the Muslim religious class interpreted as God's punishment for the popular indulgence in certain vices. All bans were short-lived. There is almost nothing in the sources about punishment for prostitution. The execution of the brothel-keepers Anas (who was held symbolically responsible for a low Nile) and Badriyya, and the amputation of the hand of a woman who worked the bathhouses were highly exceptional. For ordinary public women the worst punishment, if any, seems to have been public scorn while being paraded through the streets on a donkey, banishment, and perhaps temporary imprisonment.[242] Public shaming or banishment was meant to force the women to keep a low profile, not to give up the trade. Pimps could be caned and paraded. Given the examples of Anas and Badriyya, if a prostitute had ever been punished by stoning for an act of fornication, our sources would surely have mentioned it. The continuity and ubiquity of the trade are solid evidence, however, that this punishment was not inflicted on prostitutes. Indeed, Baybars and Barsbay tried, during bouts of religious piety, to eliminate or "deter" prostitution not by punishment but simply by forcing the women to marry! Their work was therefore accepted and considered to be legitimate. It was not a crime. Some people, especially members of the religious class, may have considered the sale of sexual favors to be morally reprehensible, but as we discussed earlier, legality and morality were not necessarily the same thing.[243] If one did not want public women in his neighborhood, he could complain to the authorities, who could force them to move on. Neither the ruling authorities nor the populace as a whole considered public women to be criminals.

Most important, the ruling authorities' recognition and institutionalization of prostitution confirmed its legitimacy as a trade in Egypt. Perhaps as early as the Fāṭimid period, the state taxed public women. If they were taxed, there was certainly no point in imprisoning them. Agents, such as a *muḥtasib* or *wālī*, monitored them and even provided security. Prostitutes registered with a special office in order to conduct their business and to ensure that they paid their taxes. It was a simple process, and supposedly even "respectable" women did so. Prostitution may have been an acceptable full-time or part-time job for respectable women who worked from their homes. The potential revenue that the state could earn from taxing prostitutes was considerable. The police collected the taxes or the government farmed them out to both men and women, or the state granted the collection of these taxes to a high-ranking military officer in return for military services (as an *iqṭāʿ*). Funds derived from prostitution thus helped pay for military units. At some point prostitutes, like other tradesmen and artisans, formed guilds which the state also recognized.

Prostitution was fully integrated into economic and social life. Although it was mostly an urban phenomenon, it was found wherever large groups of men worked, celebrated, played, or prayed. Moreover, not only the state but also people from various classes had an economic stake in it. We have seen how public women had a symbiotic relationship with many professions. Furthermore, many landlords—mainly wealthy and powerful families and government and military officials—profited from their trade; this must have extended to properties included in endowments (*waqfs*) for pious or family purposes. Consequently, even religious institutions may have derived, at least indirectly, income from their business through endowments. Rooms rented out to public women in taverns or inns, not to mention apartment houses transformed into brothels, were good investments. They provided a guaranteed and almost continuous stream of income. Indeed, prostitution as an institution was to some extent immune even to natural disasters such as famine and plague. Although many women (and men) fell victim to these catastrophes, such events would have forced others into the trade. The abolition of the tax on prostitution at such times would have been a further inducement. Under these circumstances prostitution can be seen as a safety valve for survival as much as a stable source of income. Altogether, prostitution was an important part of society, and public women helped bind it together. They were far too valuable to eliminate.

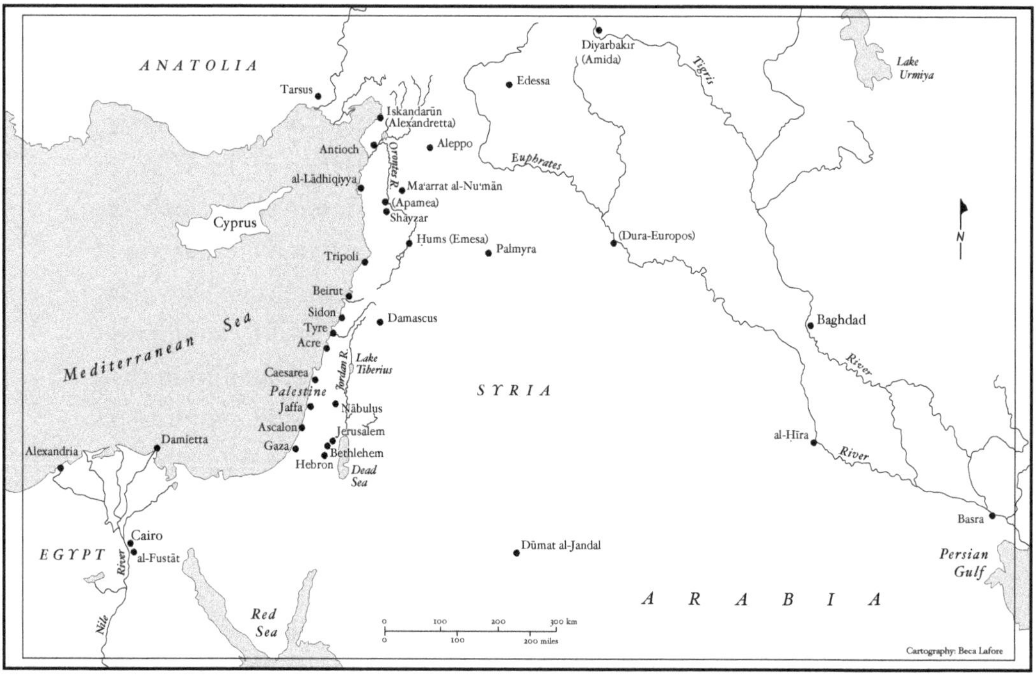

MAP 3

Syria at the time of the Crusades

FOUR

Public Women in Medieval Syria

POLITICAL AND SOCIAL CONTEXT

Syria, or Bilād al-Shām as it was known in Arabic, extended from the eastern shore of the Mediterranean to the Euphrates River. It was also often closely connected with the region lying further east between the upper Euphrates and Tigris rivers. Its natural border in the north was created by the Taurus Mountains. In the south it reached the Sinai Peninsula and elsewhere faded into the Arabian Desert. Like Arabia it was characterized by great geographical diversity, from well-watered mountain ranges to extensive desert, and lacked any unifying topographical feature.

The great majority of the population lived in the cities and towns along the sea or in the parallel string of cities and towns a short distance inland beyond the mountain ranges. On the eve of the Arab conquest, Syria had a diverse population of many cultures, but it had been strongly Hellenized and Greek was the dominant language. Most people were Christians of various confessions, but mainly that adopted by the sees of Alexandria and Antioch, while Jews were also found in many places. The ports, which had been magnets for commercial exchange since ancient times and were connected to several trade routes stretching far into Asia, created considerable wealth, and agriculture flourished in much of the immediate hinterland.

Syria had suffered, however, as a battleground in the long war between Byzantium and Persia from 572 to 629. Exhausted after its triumph, Byzantium yielded Syria to the Arabs with little resistance. The onslaught of the Arabs began under the second caliph, 'Umar (r. 13–23/634–44). Damascus fell in 14/635. The next year the Arabs defeated the Byzantines at the Yarmuk River, a tributary of the Jordan. This sealed the fate of Syria. Byzantine forces withdrew to the north and by 19/640 all cities and towns had surrendered. The Arab conquest was then complete.

The assassination of 'Umar's successor, 'Uthmān (r. 23–35/644–56), began a long period of strife among the Arabs which stalled the consolidation of their control of Syria. Eventually a kinsman of 'Uthmān, Mu'āwiya, who had been governor of Syria for 20 years, emerged from this strife to proclaim himself caliph and establish the Umayyad dynasty (41–132/661–750). Under the Umayyads, Syria became the capital of an Arab empire, with Damascus as its capital. This empire eventually extended to Central Asia and South Asia in the east, Iberia in the west, Armenia in the north, and Yemen in the south. And great wealth flowed into Damascus as a result.

Initially there was a strict division in Syria between the conquerors and the conquered, who were subjects to be exploited. Conversion was slow despite the settlement of increasing numbers of Arabs from Arabia. Some four centuries passed before the majority of the population became Muslim. Arabic took root much sooner, however, and Greek largely disappeared by the end of the second/eighth century. This roughly coincided, somewhat ironically, with the demise of the Umayyad caliphate. Growing social tensions between the ruling Arabs and non-Arab converts and rejection of the legitimacy of Umayyad rule by different parties—in particular the supporters of the fourth caliph 'Alī and his descendants—eventually coalesced into a movement of opposition that arose in the east of the empire. Supposedly instigated by descendants of the Prophet's uncle al-'Abbās, this movement culminated in the overthrow of the Umayyad caliphate in 132/750. It was replaced by that of the 'Abbāsids who established a new capital, Baghdad, on the Tigris. Syria thus lost its position as the center of a great empire.

The 'Abbāsids not only took over but also expanded the empire established by the Umayyads. One consequence of this was that from Central Asia they brought many Turkish slaves to Baghdad, where they were trained as elite troops. A descendant of one of them was the soldier Ibn Ṭūlūn, who, as we have seen, was appointed to serve as the ʿAbbāsid governor of Egypt and subsequently founded his own dynasty there in 254/868. In 264/877 he invaded Syria and ruled it as an autonomous province of his own empire. From then until the Ottoman conquest of Syria in 1516, it was ruled wholly or partially as part of empires based on Egypt.

During this period, life in Syria was often tumultuous. The Carmathians devastated the region after the Ṭūlūnid intervention and helped sow the seeds of Ismāʿīlī Shīʿism. The Fāṭimids further encouraged it but also added to the diversity of Shīʿism there by spawning new branches, namely the Druze, Nuṣayrīs, and Imāmīs. Nevertheless, most Muslims remained Sunnis. Furthermore, the social policies devised by the Fāṭimids in Egypt also affected Syria. When Caliph al-Ḥākim turned to persecuting Christians and Jews, for example, he burned the Church of the Holy Sepulcher in Jerusalem. Indeed, the Fāṭimids (and later Egyptian dynasties) adopted administrative and fiscal policies as well as social policies that they also applied to Syria, but distance and local conditions often made the results uneven.

Among the dynasties that arose in Syria, the most noteworthy were those of the Ḥamdānids and their successors, the Mirdāsids. They both ruled Northern Syria, the former in the second half of the fourth/tenth century and the latter late into the fifth/eleventh century. And they both had to contend with the Fāṭimids and a resurgent Byzantium which invaded Syria several times. Moreover, the Mirdāsids had to face another threat. By 457/1065, troops of the Seljuk Turks had begun to penetrate Syria after marching into Baghdad ten years earlier. In 463/1071 Sultan Alp Arslan turned from besieging Aleppo to face the Byzantine army at Manzikert in Eastern Anatolia. There he defeated and captured the Byzantine emperor. Immediately afterward, other Seljuk forces took Jerusalem from the Fāṭimids. Damascus fell in 467/1075 and Aleppo in 472/1079.

Responding to a subsequent plea for help from Byzantium, and hoping to reunify Christendom and conquer Jerusalem from the Muslims, Pope Urban II preached the First Crusade in 1095. The armies that responded appeared before Antioch in 1097 and proceeded to take control of Edessa and then conquer the entire coast of Syria, storming Jerusalem, which the Fāṭimids had reoccupied, in 1099. They thus added to the political fragmentation of the region. All or part of the Syrian coast remained in Crusader hands until 1291 when Acre, their last stronghold, fell to the Mamlūks.

The Crusaders left the Fāṭimids with little more than a foothold at Ascalon. Muslim opposition to these new invaders first galvanized around ʻImād al-Dīn Zangī (d. 541/1146), the founder of a Turkmen dynasty based on Mosul. He took Edessa from them in 539/1144. His son Nūr al-Dīn (d. 569/1174), who took Damascus in 549/1154 and managed to unify most of Muslim Syria, inspired further zeal against them. The resurgence of Egyptian power in Syria began with Saladin, who spent most of his time there. He took over Zangid-held territory and put relentless pressure on the Franks, defeating their forces at Ḥattīn and liberating Jerusalem in 583/1187. His dynastic successors, the Ayyūbids, and then the Mamlūks, generally managed to maintain Muslim unity in Syria and little by little expunge the Crusaders from the region. The Egyptian hold on Syria was briefly interrupted by the Mongol invasion in 658/1260 and was challenged by the Mongol Il-Khānids of Persia in the early eighth/fourteenth century. Tīmūr scourged Syria in 803/1400–1 and sacked both Aleppo and Damascus. But Egyptian control of Syria was not completely lost until the Ottoman sultan, Selim I, conquered it in 1516. Afterward it was divided into several governorates of the Ottoman Empire.[1]

OPPORTUNITIES FOR PUBLIC WOMEN

From the Arab invasion to the Crusades

I have not discovered any literary references to prostitution in Syria during the early centuries of Muslim rule. However, it must have continued to flourish there as it had under Christian rule of Late Antiquity. It would thus have generally followed the same pattern and have been practiced at many of the same locations as described in our account of that period, including ports, commercial centers, pilgrimage sites, taverns, inns, baths, and caravan stations. Syrian ports and inland cities such as Aleppo and Damascus thrived under the Umayyads, benefiting in particular from the wealth flowing in from the expanding empire. And, as we have seen in previous chapters, public women would have responded to the demands of large numbers of men with money to spend. In addition to merchants, these men would have included significant concentrations of administrators and soldiers at the center of the state.

Furthermore, Syria was full of holy sites, venerated tombs, and historical places. In Damascus were the head of John the Baptist and the grave of Sitt al-Zaynab, 'Alī's daughter. In Hebron were the tombs of Abraham, Isaac, Jacob, Sarah, Adam and Eve, Solomon, and Zachariah. In Jerusalem were, of course, the Wailing Wall, the places of Christ's Passion, the Holy Sepulcher, and the Muslim shrine of the Dome of the Rock. On the road to Jericho was the grave of Moses. In Gaza was the tomb of the great-grandfather of the Prophet. In Ascalon was one of the alleged burial places of the head of al-Ḥusayn, a son of 'Alī, beloved grandson of Muhammad, and the most venerated of the Shi'i martyrs. Later, Syria was sprinkled with the tombs of numerous Muslim saints, such as that of Ibn al-'Arabī (d. 638/1240) in Damascus. Many of these places, such as Hebron, also held annual fairs or festivals. There was a great Easter bazaar in Ramla. These and other locations attracted visitors—Muslims, Christians, and Jews—from great distances.[2]

Because Syria was overwhelmingly Christian in the first centuries of Muslim rule, prostitution would have been chiefly in Christian hands. However, as far as I can determine, contemporary Christian sources, only a few of which have survived, do not comment on this matter. Muslim writers, of course, would have had no interest in the sex trade among Christians. Moreover, Muslims would have had no reason to interfere in the practice of prostitution by non-Muslims, who in any case were subjects to be exploited. All this helps to explain our lack of information on public women in this period. Meanwhile, it should be noted that after the Arabs conquered Syria they adopted many Byzantine administrative and fiscal practices, including taxation, and many non-Muslims, chiefly Christians, continued to be subject to these practices. In addition, non-Muslims were allowed to manage their own affairs. Under such political circumstances it is reasonable to assume that prostitutes in Syria, who would have been overwhelmingly Christian, continued in fact to do business under Muslim rule just as they had under Christian rule.

A possible non-literary source confirming the presence of upper-class prostitutes or courtesans in Umayyad Syria might be found on the walls of one of several retreats for relaxation and pleasure built by members of the ruling class in the Syrian Desert. The retreat in question, Quṣayr ʿAmra, is today located 100 kilometers east of Amman, Jordan. It may have been built by Caliph al-Walīd II (r. 125–6/743–4), who lived in the desert and was given to wine, poetry, and music. This retreat, which included a bath, is remarkable because of its colorful wall frescoes depicting the good life. Among them are images of voluptuous women, many of whom are in various stages of undress (see Figure 4.1). Some of the women are musicians,

FIGURE 4.1
Fresco of a dancing girl in Quṣayr ʿAmra, Syrian Desert, first/seventh century.

dancers, and probably singers. These frescoes have generally been interpreted to derive from the classical cultural heritage and to be symbolic of a cycle of courtly pleasures.[3] If female musicians, dancers, and singers were in fact present in this retreat or elsewhere at the Umayyad court, some may have doubled as courtesans. Such women, who were musicians, singers, and poets and engaged in repartee, were later a common feature of the ʿAbbāsid court at Baghdad.[4]

The earliest literary reference to prostitution in Syria that I have come across is found in the geography of al-Muqaddasī (d. ca. 381/990), whom we met earlier. In describing Jerusalem when it was under Fāṭimid control, he states that "there are no people more respectable than those of Jerusalem [...] there, you find no brothel (*dūr fisq*), either secret or public."[5] We must take this with a grain of salt, however, because Jerusalem was his hometown and he was not about to say anything unflattering about it. He also states in general, as we have recorded above, that every town located on the seacoast or by a river seethed with fornication.[6] Presumably this generalization would have included the ports of Syria.

A more specific reference to the presence of public women appears somewhat later and concerns the large town of Maʿarrat al-Nuʿmān. It was an important crossroads and economic center located a two-day journey south of Aleppo and a day's journey east of al-Lādhiqiyya, which was the largest port on the northern coast of Syria. The practice of prostitution there comes to light in an incident that occurred in 417/1026–7 when that region was ruled by Ṣāliḥ ibn Mirdās, the founder of the Mirdāsid dynasty. His vizier was a Christian whose forceful policies created tensions between the Christian and Muslim communities in Aleppo and its surrounding districts. On a Friday of the aforesaid year a woman entered the congregational mosque of Maʿarrat al-Nuʿmān and shouted that the Christian proprietor of a wine house and brothel (*mākhūr*) had attempted to molest her. Thereupon all those assembled, except the qadi and notables (*mashāyikh*), rushed out and destroyed the house. At the instigation of his vizier, Ṣāliḥ arrested a number of notables including the brother of the famed poet Abū ʾl-ʿAlāʾ al-Maʿarrī (d. 449/1058), who was then in his hometown of Maʿarrat al-Nuʿmān. Afterward, al-Maʿarrī interceded with

Ṣāliḥ on behalf of his brother. Later al-Maʿarrī referred to this incident in several of his poems.[7]

An often cited description of how the sex trade was actually practiced is found shortly thereafter in the biography of the Christian doctor Ibn Buṭlān (d. 458/1066) who was at al-Maʿarrī's deathbed. His biography is included in Ibn al-Qifṭī's (d. 646/1248) *Ta'rīkh al-ḥukamā'*, a biographical dictionary of physicians. In his entry on Ibn Buṭlān, Ibn al-Qifṭī cites the report that he sent to the secretary and writer Hilāl al-Ṣābi' (d. 448/1056) in Baghdad recounting his journey from that city to Cairo. According to this report, Ibn Buṭlān departed Baghdad in Ramadan 440/January 1049 and reached Aleppo in Jumada al-Thani/November, where he was honored by the Mirdāsid governor. From there he continued west on the commercial highway to Antioch, which was then in Byzantine hands. En route he spent the night in a town called ʿAmm (pronunciation conjectural), which belonged to the Byzantines (*al-Rūm*). It appears to have been a border town or village, probably a caravan stop, for he says it had four churches and a mosque. Moreover, "In it were pigs and whores (*al-nisā' al-ʿawāhir*) and fornication (*zinā'*) and wine in abundance."[8] But for Ibn Buṭlān a worse example of immorality was yet to come.

After reaching Antioch, he turned south for al-Lādhiqiyya. It too was controlled by Byzantium. He says it was a Greek city (*madīna yūnāniyya*) with a hippodrome and a "house for idols," which in his time was a church but had been a mosque in the early period of Islam. He goes on to relate that, for Muslims, the city currently had a qadi and a mosque where the call to prayer was made five times a day, but when this occurred the Greeks would usually ring church bells. Something else, however, riveted his attention:

> Among the strange things in this town is that the *muḥtasib* gathers together in a circle the prostitutes (*qiḥāb*) and the foreigners (*ghurabā'*) who indulge in corruption among the Greeks (*al-rūm*). He calls out each one of the women; and the dissolute ones are auctioned off for that night and then they are taken[9] to the hostels (*fanādiq*), which are the inns (*khānāt*) where the foreigners reside,

> after each one of them takes a stamp (*khātim*),[10] which is the stamp of the metropolitan, as proof in her hand in case the *wālī* should investigate her. If he finds a male sinner with a female sinner without the certification (*khatam*) of the metropolitan, the man is charged with a crime.[11]

This report is somewhat garbled and confusing. A slightly different version of it is found in the entry on al-Lādhiqiyya in Yāqūt's famous geographical dictionary, *Muʿjam al-buldān*. The first draft of it was completed at Aleppo in 621/1224, although the final draft remained unfinished at his death in 626/1229. Ibn al-Qifṭī was actually his patron and assisted him in this project. Yāqūt's version of the aforesaid report may have been composed a bit earlier than that of Ibn al-Qifṭī, but it ultimately came from the same source. It reads:

> Al-Maʿarrī al-Mujallid[12] said, "al-Lādhiqiyya was in the hands of the Greeks (*al-rūm*). It had a *qāḍī*, a *khaṭīb*, and a mosque for Muslim worshippers. When they made the call to prayer, the Greeks would ring their church bells as an artful strategy [to drown out the call]." Then he said, "al-Lādhiqiyya is a place of contention between the Muslims and Christians..."
>
> Ibn Faḍlān[13] said, "al-Lādhiqiyya is an ancient city. It was named after its builder. In 442/1050–1 I witnessed there an unheard-of thing. This was that the *muḥtasib* gathers together in a circle the prostitutes (*qiḥāb*) and foreigners (*ghurabā'*) who indulged in corruption among the Greeks. He calls out to each one of the men[14] and they bid for the women[15] in dirhams. The successful bidder has her for the night. They take them[16] to the hostels (*fanādiq*) where the foreigners reside after each one of the men[17] takes from the *muḥtasib* the stamp (*khātim*) of the metropolitan as proof [of being the successful bidder]. The *wālī* checks on him and if he should find someone with a female sinner and he lacks the stamp of the metropolitan, he is charged with fraud (*khānahu*, perhaps a mistake for *khiyāna*).[18]

As can be seen, Yāqūt helps to clarify Ibn al-Qifṭī. First of all, we should note that al-Lādhiqiyya had been in Byzantine hands since 359/970, so it is highly unlikely that the officials in this port would have been called by such Muslim titles as *muḥtasib* (supervisor of the marketplace and public behavior) or *wālī* (chief of police). Ibn Buṭlān must be giving what he believed were the Arabic equivalents of certain Greek positions. Therefore an official, perhaps the *agoranomos*, would periodically (daily?) call together the prostitutes in the town and the "foreigners who indulged in corruption among the Greeks." It is difficult to know what he means by "foreigners." They appear to be pimps or operators of brothels. It makes no sense for them to be customers of the women. Then the official supposedly auctioned off each woman to these foreigners. The "auction" must actually have been a method of taxation of the women and their managers. Perhaps some women were more popular than others or earned more for their services. Thus they may have been required to pay different rates of taxation.[19] After the auction, each woman (or pimp, depending on the version) was given a receipt or license bearing the stamp of the metropolitan (*al-maṭrān*). In the Eastern Churches of Constantinople and Antioch, a metropolitan ranked above an archbishop and below the patriarch. Even if the population of al-Lādhiqiyya and its surrounding area would have been large enough to have justified its own metropolitan, the idea that such an ecclesiastical figure would certify the licenses of prostitutes seems incredible. As we have seen in Egypt, this was the job of low-level civil officials. Ibn Buṭlān was a Christian and presumably understood the organization of these churches. Thus, *al-maṭrān* may be a mistake for another word. After being licensed the women were taken to the inns where the foreigners lodged—that is, to the brothels. There they sold their favors. If later an inspector discovered that a woman was being pimped without a license, the pimp was charged with a crime because the tax had not been paid. Problematic words and phrases aside, this passage from Ibn Buṭlān, as well has his short account of the town of ʿAmm, provide confirmation that prostitution thrived along the trade routes of Syria. It also reveals, of course, that prostitution was a legal profession regulated by the authorities.

Prostitution and the Crusades

We have seen in the previous chapter that prostitutes accompanied the Crusaders on their invasions of Egypt. This was also true of the repeated Crusader invasions of Syria. In fact, public women arrived with the First Crusade and were a common feature of life in the Frankish-held ports and cities on the Syrian coast for the entire 200 years of the Crusading enterprise.[20] During this period I have found more references to prostitution in the Christian-controlled territories of Syria than in those parts of the region that were under Muslim control. This is because prostitutes arrived from Europe in large numbers and their presence could not be ignored by Christian writers, for various reasons. Moreover, the most populous part of Syria had long been held by the Franks and thus business opportunities for prostitutes in the part of Syria ruled by Muslims would have been reduced. Furthermore, the Muslim writers from this time were more concerned with the struggle against the invaders than anything else. Under these circumstances, prostitution was hardly an issue of concern to them.

In 490/late October 1097, after marching across Anatolia, the armies of the First Crusade arrived before the walls of Antioch, which had been captured by the Seljuks in 477/1084. They laid siege to the city, but it did not go well. While the defenders held out during a bitter winter and into the following spring, many Christian troops drifted away. Some began to ask why God had not granted them victory, especially in light of their suffering. Fulcher of Chartres (b. 1059, d. after 1127), a cleric who had accompanied the Crusaders, states in his chronicle of their campaign, *Historia Hierosolymitana*:

> [w]e believed that these misfortunes befell the Franks, and that they were not able for so long a time to take the city because of their sins. Not only dissipation, but also avarice or pride or rapaciousness corrupted them.
>
> After holding council, they drove out the women from the army, both married and unmarried, lest they, stained by the defilement of

> dissipation, displease the Lord. Those women then found places to live in the neighboring camps.[21]

In June, the Crusaders managed to take the city by stealth, but almost immediately found themselves besieged in turn by a Turkish army sent to relieve the defenders. Once more the Crusaders found themselves in dire straits. According to the *Gesta Francorum* (The Deeds of the Franks), composed by an anonymous participant in this Crusade, Christ appeared to a Frankish priest and said to him,

> Behold, I gave you timely help, and put you safe and sound into the city of Antioch; but you are satisfying your filthy lusts both with Christians and with loose pagan women, so that a great stench goes up to Heaven.[22]

Christ then promised that if the army would repent its sins he would give them a sign of his favor in a few days. Adhemar, the papal legate, accepted this vision as genuine and used it to humble the Crusader leaders.[23] This vision had followed on the heels of another in which St. Andrew appeared to a certain servant named Peter Bartholomew and told him where the lance that had pierced Christ's side was hidden in the city; sure enough, a piece of iron was subsequently discovered at the place Peter had indicated.

These events helped give the besieged a psychological boost. They then emerged from Antioch and attacked and defeated the Turkish army. Upon overrunning the Turkish camp, the Franks plundered it and seized the Muslim women. As Fulcher reports rather indifferently, "When their women were found in the tents, the Franks did nothing evil to them except pierce their bellies with their lances."[24] Repentance of "satisfying one's filthy lusts" clearly had its limits. It is worthy of note, as James Brundage has pointed out, that the chroniclers of the First Crusade blamed every reversal of the Christian soldiers on their sexual excesses. Indeed, this pattern continued after that invasion ended.[25] For example, the destruction in Anatolia of the armies of the Crusade of 1101, which were accompanied by many women "of varying degrees of honesty," was attributed to God's punishment for (among other things) the wantonness of the soldiers.[26] There is certainly great irony in the fact that these men went on Crusade in part to purge themselves of the penance that their sins—many of which were undoubtedly sexual offenses—merited. In contrast to the Christian chroniclers of the Crusades, their Muslim counterparts never attributed their tribulations in the field or defeats in battle to the sexual turpitude of their troops. Even if an expected victory suddenly turned to a defeat, the Muslims simply attributed it to the inscrutable will of God, or fate.[27] The closest exception to this was Nūr al-Dīn's decision to refrain personally from sexual relations as penance following two setbacks at the hands of the Franks between 557/1162 and 558/1163. More will be said about his actions below. Furthermore, Muslim historians do not link the military successes of the likes of Saladin or Baybars against the Crusaders to their intolerance of vice in the cities of their realm. As we have seen in the previous chapter, if God wished to punish Muslims for their sins—only one of which was fornication—He would do so by inflicting a natural, not a human, disaster.

The public women who joined the Crusaders must have been a critical element in the entire enterprise, despite their denunciation in the Christian sources. They joined other women in cooking, doing laundry, keeping the camp tidy, and tending the wounded. Some may even have taken up arms. Moreover, their very presence (or should we say their availability?) on the long and dangerous journey to Syria must have helped convince some men to take the cross, because they would not have had to give up an important home comfort. The ubiquity of prostitutes in the Crusading armies later led the Italian canonist Cardinal Hostiensis (Henry of Segusio, d. 1271) to pose the question, in fact, of the Crusading harlot:

> What would the legal situation be if a whore took the cross? She would surely be followed by many men, since nothing is stronger than love, and this would clearly bolster the defensive forces of the Holy Land. Should the Crusading harlot therefore be obliged to fulfill a crusading vow?"[28]

Hostiensis thought not, because her followers would not have been spiritually motivated. But surely she would have lifted their "spirits" in other ways.

Prostitutes flocked to the Crusading armies. They seem to have been undaunted by the long journey and its potential hazards; indeed, there was a precedent of sorts. Even before the First Crusade, women "pilgrims" from Europe were said to support themselves by selling sex along the route to Palestine. Sometimes they traveled disguised as men.[29] And, of course, public women were long a common feature of European armies that did not go on Crusade. In 1158, three decades before he joined the movement known as the Third Crusade, the Holy Roman Emperor Frederick I Barbarossa (d. 1190) was taken aback by the large number of prostitutes traveling with his army. He tried to purge them by punishing the women and their customers, but his effort failed and was not repeated.[30] Moreover, once the popes granted the remission of penance for sin, or a plenary indulgence (a full pardon for temporal punishment for sin, in return for going on Crusade or making the pilgrimage), accompanying the Crusader armies may have become doubly attractive for public women.[31] They could do a brisk business en route and then, once they had reached Jerusalem, repent—and the penance for conducting their business would be remitted!

As mentioned above, the first concerted Muslim effort against the Crusaders was carried out by Zangī. In 539/1144 he captured Edessa, which was the first Crusader capital to fall to the Muslims. This event subsequently provoked the Second Crusade. The leaders of its two major armies were Conrad III, the Holy Roman Emperor, and Louis VII of France. This Crusade culminated in 543/1148 in a failed attack on Damascus. Zangī's most renowned descendant was his son Nūr al-Dīn (d. 569/1174), in whom he inspired zeal against the Crusaders and the Shiʿis. Nūr al-Dīn captured Damascus in 549/1154 and went on to unite most of Syria against the Franks. And it was he who sent Saladin to Egypt in 564/1169, where he soon overthrew the Fāṭimids.

The presence of European prostitutes in Frankish-held territory after the Second Crusade seems to be reflected in a "mirror for princes," or book of advice for rulers, that was composed during the reign of Nūr al-Dīn in Aleppo. The author of this work, *Baḥr al-favāʾid* (The Sea of Precious

Virtues), is unknown. Written in Persian and dedicated to an *atabeg* (or tutor of princes) named Arslan Aba ibn Āq Sunqur, who spent his career in Northeastern Iran, it nevertheless reflects certain local attitudes and conditions.

In the second half of his book, the writer goes into some remarkable detail on the sexual iniquities of Christians, by whom he means the Franks. As he relates:

> They allow fornication [to a woman] who has no husband, saying, "A woman knows best about her own affairs; her private parts are hers; if she wishes she can guard them, and if she wishes she can bestow them." Their king does not fix the rate for copulation and lust; the judges do so, four *fils* [copper coins] for each act of coition and one *fils* for each ejaculation. If there is a dispute between them the woman and the man go before a judge and say, "This man performed an obscene act with her and gave her nothing." The judge asks, "Why do you not give her her wages?" If he replies, "I am poor, I have nothing," then the judge tells (her), "Give it to him in charity; your wages and recompense are with the Lord." If any of these fornicators bears a child, she takes him to the church, [saying,] "I give him to the Lord, that he may serve Him." The priests say, "You have done well, O pious woman; rejoice in the pleasure of Christ and his reward."
>
> Another iniquity is that these women go to the priests in the church at night to keep company and fornicate with them; they consider this piety, and (worthy of) recompense. Their women do not cover their faces; they say, "We are not stingy, like the Muslims."[32]

Here the author seems to be telling us that among the Franks an unmarried woman was allowed to sell her favors if she chose to do so. In other words, prostitution was completely acceptable. The sale of her favors was regulated by the act, meaning there was some kind of official oversight, probably for the purpose of taxation. If there were a dispute between a public woman and her customer over the charge for her services, it would be resolved by a "judge," perhaps some kind of administrative or policing official. If a child were born from such a liaison, it could be given up to the Church. Finally, if the author is not indulging in a common form of polemic against Christians, prostitutes did not hesitate to provide comfort to priests, considering this an act of piety.[33] Thus, all was forgiven. The source of this information about the behavior of the Franks is not stated. At the time of the composition of this work, trade relations between Aleppo and the Crusader-held cities along the northern coast, especially Antioch, were close. Consequently, the author could have had a variety of informants. He may even have seen this behavior for himself.

After Nūr al-Dīn's death, Saladin took up the mantle of defender of Islam against the Christian invaders. In 583/1187, after a terrific siege, he forced the Crusaders to surrender Jerusalem. On hand was his secretary 'Imād al-Dīn al-Iṣfahānī (d. 597/1201), who wrote an account of the conquest of the city called *al-Fatḥ al-qussī*. He states that, among the prisoners,

> Women and children together came to 8,000 and were quickly divided up among us, bringing a smile to Muslim faces at their lamentations. How many well-guarded women were profaned, how many queens were ruled, and nubile girls married, and noble women given away, and miserly women forced to yield themselves, and women who had been kept hidden stripped of their modesty, and serious women made ridiculous, and women kept in private now set in public, and free women occupied, and precious ones used for hard work, and pretty things put to the test, and virgins dishonoured and proud women deflowered, and lovely women's red lips kissed and dark women prostrated, and untamed ones tamed, and happy ones made to weep! How many noblemen took them as concubines, how many ardent men blazed for one of them, and celibates were satisfied by them, and thirsty men sated by them, and turbulent men able to give vent to their passion. How many lovely women were the exclusive property of one man, how many great ladies were sold at low prices, and close ones set at a distance, and lofty ones abased, and savage ones captured, and those accustomed to thrones dragged down![34]

In so many words, we learn that many of the captured women, some of whom must have been prostitutes, were raped. And it is highly likely that many of the women captives, whether kept as booty or sold as slaves, were subsequently prostituted.

The plentitude of prostitutes in Crusader-held cities is, in fact, confirmed by ʿImād al-Dīn. He goes on to report that—apparently at the end of 585/ end of 1189 or beginning of 1190—a shipload of them arrived to comfort the troops. He does not say where they disembarked, but it was probably Tripoli or Tyre, both of which were still in Christian hands after Saladin's offensives. Pitching tents in which to assist the Crusaders in their attempt to fulfill the will of God, they were brazen, seductive, and spectacularly adorned. Word of them spread rapidly, even reaching the Muslim troops nearby. These women proved to be so enticing that some Muslim soldiers yielded to temptation and slipped through enemy lines to enjoy their favors. This time writing in an even more ornate and exaggerated style full of wordplay, ʿImād al-Dīn provides the following long account, described by his translator Gabrieli as an example of "baroque pornography," of the affair of these prostitutes:

> There arrived by ship three hundred lovely Frankish women, full of youth and beauty, assembled from beyond the sea and offering themselves for sin. They were expatriates come to help expatriates, ready to cheer the fallen and sustained in turn to give support and assistance, and they glowed with ardour for carnal intercourse. They were all licentious harlots (*zāniyya*), proud and scornful, who took and gave, foul-fleshed and sinful, singers and coquettes, appearing proudly in public, ardent and inflamed, tinted and painted, desirable and appetizing, exquisite and graceful, who ripped open and patched up, lacerated and mended, erred and ogled, urged and seduced, consoled and solicited, seductive and languid, desired and desiring, amused and amusing, versatile and cunning, like tipsy adolescents, making love and selling themselves for gold, bold and ardent, loving and passionate, pink-faced and unblushing, black-eyed and bullying, callipygian [having well-shaped buttocks] and graceful, with nasal

voices and fleshy thighs, blue-eyed and grey-eyed, broken-down little fools. Each one trailed the train of her robe behind her and bewitched the beholder with her effulgence. She swayed like a sapling, revealed herself like a strong castle, quivered like a small branch, walked proudly with a cross on her breast, sold her graces for gratitude, and longed to lose her robe and her honour. They arrived after consecrating their persons as if to works of piety, and offered and prostituted the most chaste and precious among them. They said that they set out with the intention of consecrating their charms, that they did not intend to refuse themselves to bachelors, and they maintained that they could make themselves acceptable to God by no better sacrifice than this. So they set themselves up each in a pavilion or tent erected for her use, together with other lovely young girls of their age, and opened the gates of pleasure. They dedicated as a holy offering what they kept between their thighs; they were openly licentious and devoted themselves to relaxation; they removed every obstacle to making of themselves free offerings. They plied a brisk trade in dissoluteness, adorned the patched-up fissures, poured themselves into the springs of libertinage, shut themselves up in private under the amorous transports of men, offered their wares for enjoyment, invited the shameless into their embrace, mounted breasts on backs, bestowed their wares on the poor, brought their silver anklets up to touch their golden ear-rings,[35] and were willingly spread out on the carpet of amorous sport. They made themselves targets for men's darts, they were permitted territory for forbidden acts, they offered themselves to the lances' blows and humiliated themselves to their lovers. They put up the tent and loosed the girdle after agreement had been reached. They were the places where tent-pegs are driven in, they invited swords to enter their sheaths, they razed their terrain for planting, they made javelins rise toward shields, excited the plough to plough, gave the birds a place to peck with their beaks, allowed heads to enter their ante-chambers and raced under whoever bestrode them at the spur's blow. They took the parched man's sinews to the well, fitted arrows to the bow's handle, cut off sword-belts, engraved

> coins, welcomed birds into the nest of their thighs, caught in their nets the horns of butting rams, removed the interdict from what is protected, withdrew the veil from what is hidden. They interwove leg with leg, slaked their lovers' thirsts, caught lizard after lizard in their holes, disregarded the wickedness of their intimacies, guided pens to inkwells, torrents to the valley bottom, streams to pools, swords to scabbards, gold ingots to crucibles, infidel girdles to women's zones, firewood to the stove, guilty men to low dungeons, money-changers to *dīnār*, necks to bellies, notes to eyes. They contested for tree-trunks, wandered far and wide to collect fruit, and maintained that this was an act of piety without equal, especially to those who were far from home and wives. They mixed wine, and with the eye of sin they begged for its hire.[36] The men of our army heard tell of them, and were at a loss to know how such women could perform acts of piety by abandoning all decency and shame. However, a few foolish *mamlūks* and ignorant wretches slipped away, under the fierce goad of lust, and followed the people of error. And there were those who allowed themselves to buy pleasure with degradation, and those who repented of their sin and found devious ways of retracing their steps, for the hand of any man who shrinks from (absolute) apostasy dares not stretch out, and it is the nature of him who arrives there to steal away from them, suspecting that what is serious, is serious, and the door of pleasure closes in his face. Now among the Franks a woman who gives herself to a celibate man commits no sin, and her justification is even greater in the case of a priest, if chaste men in dire need find relief in enjoying her.[37]

Well, as loquacious and entertaining as this passage is—and meant to demonstrate, above all, the author's literary virtuosity to an intellectual elite—it tends to corroborate what we learned from the *Baḥr al-favā'id.* And like that work it raises the question of the author's source of information. On the reasonable assumption that 'Imād al-Dīn was not giving personal testimony in any respect, we may guess that he learned of these Frankish women from Muslim traders who visited their place of business during one of the many peaceful interludes between the clash of Christian and Muslim arms. Or perhaps some Muslim troops who actually reached their tents by stealth told him of their escapades. This is not impossible. Ibn Shaddād (d. 632/1234), who entered the service of Saladin right after the fall of Jerusalem and was given judicial and administrative responsibilities in that city, states in his biography of the sultan that from time to time Muslim thieves would slip across Frankish lines and abduct people.[38] Whoever may have informed ʻImād al-Dīn of the European beauties, it is clear that these women did not hesitate to sell their favors to Muslims as well as Christians if an opportunity arose. Thus their allegiance to the faith and the cause went only so far. These women had to earn a living and, as we will see below, could be aggressive in doing so. Furthermore, this feature of their profession may be related to what ʻImād al-Dīn says at the end of his report, namely that Frankish women provided comfort to the clergy. Although this was (as already mentioned) a common accusation in Muslim polemics against Christians, we have a Christian source, James of Vitry, who, as we will see shortly, at least confirms that some clergy rented lodgings to prostitutes in Syria. In other words, these public women carried out their trade truly without discrimination among potential customers, and their earnings were significant enough to encourage many people to profit from them.

The fall of Jerusalem sparked the Third Crusade. This was led by Frederick Barbarossa, Richard I of England (the Lionheart), and Philip II of France. Frederick went overland and died en route near Antioch, while Richard and Philip went by sea. The armies of all three rulers attracted large numbers of women. At Vienna, Frederick had to send some 500 prostitutes and other disreputable people back to Germany, although others certainly joined his host later.[39] On leaving the port of Messina in the spring of 1191, Richard and Philip issued an ordinance forbidding women to board their ships.[40] Nevertheless, a significant number of prostitutes managed to accompany Richard's troops in particular and did good business. Richard of Devizes, who was a monk of St. Swithun's at Winchester, participated in this Crusade and composed a short history of it. Taking every opportunity to mock the French, he says at one point, under the year 1191, "It became a perpetual torment to his (Philip's) conscience that a camp-follower of the king of the English lived more splendidly than the butler of the king of the French."[41]

Richard and Philip laid siege to the port of Acre, which had fallen to Saladin after Jerusalem, along with almost all other territory belonging to the Frankish states.[42] The possession of Acre was vital to maintaining a Christian military presence in Syria and any hope of reconquering Jerusalem. The siege was successful and Richard remained to campaign for another year, while Philip immediately returned to France. After the fall of Acre, its fleshpots became a major distraction for the troops, who sometimes had to be dragged away to the front.[43] By the end of 1192 the Franks controlled pockets around Antioch and Tripoli and a coastal strip between Tyre and Jaffa with Acre in the middle. The Fourth Crusade was intended to expand these beachheads and recover Jerusalem, but it was diverted from its original purpose and resulted instead in the 1204 conquest of Constantinople, the greatest city of Christendom, and the excommunication of its participants. As we will see in the next chapter, public women also accompanied this invasion force.

Despite the disillusionment with the Crusading movement that inevitably followed in Europe, the idea of recapturing the Holy Land still had considerable appeal. The popes were therefore able to organize the Fifth Crusade, which was directed against Egypt in the belief that it was the major source of Muslim power and the chief obstacle to the success of Christian arms in Syria. As we saw in the previous chapter, one of the leading preachers of this Crusade, which captured Damietta, was James of Vitry. He arrived in Acre in 1216 with the mission of helping to raise troops and "support personnel" (camp followers) for this endeavor. He was shocked by what he found in Acre. The Franks who lived there had become corrupt traitors. Spending their lives in effect among Muslims, they had conformed to the "debased morals" of the natives. The situation was so bad that their daughters only went out veiled so that no one could see what they looked like, not even their future husbands. Moreover, these Franks did not believe that fornication was a mortal sin. They were, in fact, raised in laxity from infancy and were entirely given over to the pleasures of the flesh.[44] "Furthermore," he says, Acre

> "was full of widespread prostitution wherever one looked (*Cette ville était en outre pleine de prostituées répandues de tous côtés*). Now, these courtesans paid higher rents than others for lodging; thus, throughout the town many laymen, but also some clergymen, and certain regulars (*réguliers*, monks, soldiers of lower rank) rented lodgings to public women."[45] He adds, "Once having entered this horrid town, I found it full of depravity and iniquity."[46]

It was, in short, a new Babylon. Nevertheless, this did not stop the good preacher from recruiting women and men from the demimonde for the Fifth Crusade.

Word of "sexual liberality" among the Franks in Syria must have spread quickly to Europe. It may well have become an incentive in attracting men to the East. It certainly would have contributed to the Western fantasy of the "sensuous Orient." In any case, there is no doubt that reports of this lasciviousness reached the European pulpit. There, Frankish prostitutes in Syria became the archetypes of infamy and the objects of thunderous sermons. The summary of a kind of standard sermon in this respect has luckily come down to us from France from around the middle of the thirteenth century. The composer of the text says it should state the following:

> In the Orient, pilgrims, Crusaders, and sailors were entrapped by women of ill repute who went so far as to slip in under the tents next to those of the saintly king. These birds of prey were so rapacious that to leave their victims with a single piece of clothing gave them remorse. This is a sad commentary on morality over the centuries. Happy is the era when religion arrives to raise from the depths of degradation the vilest beings and when the houses of the repentant are filled with its voice.[47]

If the "pilgrims" included the clergy, this may be subtle evidence that, as 'Imād al-Dīn claims, some members of the religious class succumbed to the charms of public women. The reference to prostitutes slipping under tents next to those of the "saintly king" is an allusion, of course, to the passage in Joinville's *Life of St. Louis* in which he says that prostitutes set up their tents of business near those of Louis IX in the midst of the Seventh Crusade. As we discussed in the previous chapter, this campaign consisted of Louis' assault on Egypt in 1248. The allegation that these harlots were so rapacious that a client was lucky to escape with the shirt on his back is reminiscent of "The Third Constable's Story" in the *Arabian Nights*, discussed in Chapter 3, in which the protagonist loses both his money and his clothes to a shrewd public woman.

The Sixth Crusade (1228–9) was led by the Holy Roman Emperor Frederick II. He made a peaceful visit to Syria and negotiated a treaty with the Muslims for the partial surrender of Jerusalem and other holy places. In 1244, however, Jerusalem fell once more into Muslim hands. This event prompted Louis to embark on the Seventh Crusade. Despite his failure in Egypt, he subsequently undertook another invasion, the Eighth Crusade, in 1270. This time he landed in Tunisia, where he died. The Ninth Crusade (1271–2) was a modest effort by Prince Edward of England in which he reinforced Acre. Prostitutes probably accompanied or later joined Frederick, Louis, and Edward in their missions, but I have not discovered references to this. The Crusading era in Syria finally ended in 1291 when the Mamlūks captured Acre, the last Frankish stronghold in the region. Its fall also ended a stream of enterprising European women to the East, women who had certainly contributed much to the color of life in the Frankish states. Indeed, the Mamlūks went so far as to destroy Acre and the other leading ports on the Syrian coast, including Tyre and Tripoli, to make sure the Franks would not return. This action contributed to the economic stagnation of Syria for a century until they were rebuilt.

Public women outside the Crusader states

While prostitution was flourishing in the cities held by the Crusaders along the coast of Syria, the situation in the rest of the country beyond the coastal ranges is less clear. Evidence for this trade there is extremely spotty. Among the extant illustrations of the renowned *Maqāmāt* (Sessions or Assemblies) of the poet al-Ḥarīrī (d. 516/1122) is an image that may demonstrate its presence. The *maqāma* (s.) was a literary genre in rhymed prose characterized by a description of the adventures and speeches of a hero. In the case of al-Ḥarīrī, this was a bohemian named Abū Zayd al-Sarūjī, who was a real person. He was associated with the town of Sarūj, near Edessa, which fell to the Crusaders in 494/1100. Al-Ḥarīrī's *Maqāmāt* proved to be very popular, and many copies were made. Some of them included colorful paintings that illuminated various scenes. In an analysis of these paintings, from different manuscripts which were made in Syria and Iraq in the sixth/twelfth century, Oleg Grabar has asserted that one depiction of the famous tavern scene in Damascus from the twelfth *maqāma* "shows a female companion of Abū Zayd in a tavern wearing clothes that probably signify the class of singer/prostitute."[48] This painting may, therefore, have given this tale a touch of local verisimilitude.

A possible implicit literary reference to prostitution around the same time concerns the policies of Zangī (d. 541/1146), the ruler of Mosul. He was often on campaign in Syria in an attempt to expand his territory. He occupied Aleppo in 522/1128 and later, as we have seen, went on to capture Edessa in 539/1144. Because Zangī was frequently in the field, Ibn al-Athīr states that he was extremely protective of the wives of the soldiers who were left behind. This historian quotes him as saying, "If we had not guarded the wives of our soldiers by the fear we inspire, they would have been corrupted because their husbands are so frequently absent on campaigns."[49] This statement may imply that the wives of soldiers who were on campaign might have been forced to sell their favors in order to support themselves. How the wives were guarded by fear is not specified. Nothing is said about the behavior of their husbands while they were away from home, of course.

In 558/1163 Zangī's son Nūr al-Dīn went through a period of self-doubt after the Crusaders had defeated him in several battles following his pilgrimage to Mecca in 556/1161. While he was in this state of gloom, the jurist Burhān al-Dīn al-Balkhī, who taught in the Ḥallāwiyya Madrasa in Aleppo, addressed him, saying, "Do you wish to be victorious while wine and [the sounds of] drums and fifes are found among your troops? No, by God!"[50] Burhān al-Dīn was obviously castigating Nūr al-Dīn for laxity in his army, which had an apparent preoccupation with drinking, dancing, and—no doubt—female companionship. When he heard this, Nūr al-Dīn promised God that he would repent. He put aside his costly clothing and wore only coarse garments. He also abolished the non-canonical tithes, taxes, and imposts in all the territory under his rule and forbade the commission of all indecencies (*al-fawāḥish*). Furthermore, he stressed the need for asceticism and piety above all else and personally refrained from sexual intercourse and all carnal pleasures.[51] It is not stated if he tried to impose such extreme self-denial on his army. He certainly would have failed. Indeed, in 567/1171–2, two years before he died, he once again abolished iniquitous taxes and "all traces of reprehensible acts and indecencies," which would have included prostitution. The historian Ibn al-'Adīm (d. 660/1262) reports that after this was done the state lost an enormous amount of revenue.[52] This is virtual acknowledgment that public women were plentiful and that the authorities taxed them.

At one point the contemporary anonymous author of the *Baḥr al-favā'id* speaks of prostitution among Muslims, presumably with reference to Syria. He comments on what the Qur'an says about fornication and asserts that women are more inclined to it than men. Then he gives examples of legendary women who sold themselves.[53] Such a view of women would, naturally, make it easier to rationalize prostitution. In a more interesting passage concerning unlawful trades, he says that contraceptive measures should *not* be used for the purpose of the prostitution of male and female slaves.[54] But it would seem that with respect to men the author means homosexual prostitution, in which case contraception would be meaningless. And as for women, the lack of contraception would only be desirable if their owners intended to sell their children.[55] I have encountered no confirmation of such a practice. A few sentences later in the same passage, the author repeats the old injunction against pimping. However, this does not seem to be in accord with what he previously said about prostituting male and female slaves. Altogether, there seems to be considerable vagueness here on the status of prostitution. Still, this work does show that it existed at that time, that some public women were slaves and were pimped, and that a means of contraception was available, although of unknown effectiveness.

We have seen in the previous chapter that when Saladin became the Fāṭimid vizier in 564/1168 he denounced the usual vices, and he continued to oppose them officially after he overthrew the Fāṭimid dynasty three years later. Furthermore, as he expanded his military and political power into Syria, he extended his authority over public morality there as well. Thus, when he was in Damascus in 570/1174, he declared that "the outrages, abominations, and imposts that had reappeared on the death of Nūr al-Dīn would cease."[56] These were the usual code words for a crackdown on prostitution, among other things. Nevertheless, as was the case in Egypt, the abolition of wrongful behavior in Syria was not consistently enforced. It is also difficult to guess how effective bans issued in Egypt would have been in Syria. Saladin's modifications (or reinstitutions) of his original ban on prostitution and other reprehensible acts in Egypt may have been more readily applied to Syria while he was on the march in that country in 567/1171, 574/1178, and 580/1184. But bans intended to propitiate God when he punished Egyptians with a low Nile or other natural disaster would certainly have been irrelevant to Syria.

We know that some Syrian jurists addressed the issue of prostitution. A contemporary of Saladin, 'Abd al-Raḥmān ibn Naṣr al-Shayzarī (d. 589/1193), who spent time in the town of Shayzar in Northern Syria, composed a treatise on the duties of the *muḥtasib* called *Nihāyat al-rutba fī ṭalab al-ḥisba*. In this work, which he may have written on Saladin's request, he declares, "Whenever the *muḥtasib* hears of a woman who is a harlot or a singer, he should call her to repent of her sin. But if she returns to it, he must chastise her and banish her from the town."[57] This suggests that public women continued to be a significant presence in the marketplaces regardless of the will of the sultan or his relatives who were given various principalities in Syria.

This is confirmed, in fact, by Sibṭ ibn al-Jawzī (d. 654/1256), whose *Mir'āt al-zamān* is one of the most important sources for the history of Ayyūbid Syria. He was in the service of al-Mu'aẓẓam 'Īsā, the second of the many sons of Saladin's brother and successor, al-'Ādil (r. 596–615/1200–18), in Damascus. In his obituary of al-'Ādil, Sibṭ states that, once he became sultan, he commanded right and forbade wrong. As we saw earlier, he had attempted to do this when he ruled Egypt during Saladin's absence in Syria. Thus, upon assuming the throne:

> He purified all his realm of wine, sinners (*khawāṭi'*, harlots), gambling, the effeminate (*makhānīth*), non-canonical taxes and [other] iniquities. The income from all these activities in Damascus alone amounted to 100,000 *dīnārs*. He banned them all for the sake of God. His governor (*wālī*) [of Damascus], the late al-Mubāriz al-Mu'tamid, assisted him in this. He assigned men to the routes over Mt. Qāsyūn [north of Damascus] and Jabal al-Thalj [Mt. Hermon] and to the environs of Damascus and paid them [good] salaries [so they wouldn't take bribes] and they prevented anyone who would do wrong (*munkar*) from entering Damascus. Still, the people of corruption were clever and put wineskins inside drums and by this means brought them into Damascus, but he put a stop to it.[58]

Sibṭ then goes on to say:

> I learned that some female singers went up to al-'Ādil at a wedding and he said to them, "Where were you?" and they said, "We were not able to come until we paid what the *ḍāmin* (tax farmer) required." And he said, "What *ḍāmin*?" They replied, "The *ḍāmin* of the *qiyān* (singing slave girls)." He became angry and summoned al-Mu'tamid and rebuked him.[59]

Sibṭ seems to be telling us that, at least in the later years of Saladin's reign and at the beginning of that of al-'Ādil, the usual vices were thriving in Damascus (and probably in other places in Syria); indeed, they were taxed, resulting in a large income for the state. The effectiveness of al-'Ādil's bans is difficult to determine. His attempt to set up roadblocks as far away as Mt. Hermon—some 40 kilometers southwest of Damascus—to prevent undesirables from entering the city is remarkable and (so far as I know) unique in the Eastern Mediterranean world. Nevertheless, he seems to have expected the *qiyān* to perform at the wedding he had attended. There is some ambiguity here.

There was no ambiguity, however, with respect to al-Mu'aẓẓam 'Īsā's policy in this matter. When his father became sultan, he was made prince of Damascus (597–615/1201–18). As soon as his father died, he became its independent ruler (615–24/1218–27). Among al-Mu'aẓẓam's first actions as sovereign were to revoke his father's bans on non-canonical taxes in general and on vice, which was to be taxed, and to dismiss al-Mu'tamid.[60] The historian al-Dhahabī, who was born in Damascus and died there in 748/1348 or 753/1352–3, reports that he farmed out (*ḍammana*) the tax on wine and prostitution (*al-khanā*) in Damascus and that the revenue from all this amounted to 300,000 dirhams.[61] He justified this action because of his lack of income and the need to defend his realm against the Crusaders.[62]

Sibṭ provides evidence of the continued practice of prostitution in Damascus in the details that he gives about the life of al-Ashraf Mūsā, who ruled that city shortly after al-Mu'aẓẓam 'Īsā (that is, 626–35/1229–37). Sibṭ, who also served al-Ashraf, says that in 632/1234–5 he began to transform the Khan of Ibn al-Zanjārī, which was in al-'Aqība (near Damascus), into a mosque (*masjid*). This khan had been notorious as a place of debauchery (*al-fujūr*), sinners (*khawāṭi'*), and drinking wine.[63] Writing a little later, the famous biographer Ibn Khallikān (d. 681/1282) has a bit more to say about this in his entry on al-Ashraf. Here he states:

> There was at a place called al-'Aqība on the outskirts of Damascus a caravanserai called the Khān of Ibn al-Zanjārī. Every sort of amusement was to be found in that establishment; and the unbounded lewdness (*al-fusūq)* and debauchery (*al-fujūr*) which prevailed there surpassed description. Al-Ashraf, being told that such doings should not be tolerated in a Muslim country, ordered it to be demolished and replaced by a mosque for the building of which he got indebted to a great amount. The people named it the Mosque of Repentance (*Jāmi' al-Tawba*), as if to say that it [the edifice] had repented and turned to God.[64]

Clearly, prostitution continued to flourish with or without the permission of the Syrian authorities.

Like Saladin, Baybars, who established the succeeding Mamlūk dynasty in Egypt on a firm footing, had to repeatedly enforce his own ban on public women. In 661/1263 and again in 664/1266, he attempted to curb prostitution in Egypt. In the second case, al-Maqrīzī specifically states that this attempt applied to both Egypt and Syria.[65] The sultan tried again in 667/1269 and 670/1271. In these instances only Egypt is mentioned. In 668/1269–70, Shaykh Khiḍr al-Kurdī, the "sheikh of the sultan," carried out a violent attack on wine drinking in Damascus, threatening wine producers with death and raiding the homes of Christians and Jews.[66] This must have been part of a campaign against vice in general.

As we have seen, al-Maqrīzī also reports that as a result of the measures putting public women out of business, the *muqṭaʿīn* in Egypt suffered a loss of revenue, thus showing that income generated by prostitution was farmed out and granted as an *iqṭāʿ*, like that for land, to military officers. This practice was already well established in Egypt in the Ayyūbid period. Under both the Ayyūbids and Mamlūks, Syria was generally administered along the same lines as Egypt, although there were some local variations in government structure and taxation. The *iqṭāʿ* system was in place there under both the Ayyūbids and Mamlūks as a means of raising military forces. Consequently, as in Egypt, it may also have been used in Syria to raise funds from prostitution.[67]

After Baybars, the ban on prostitution in Egypt frequently lapsed, and a number of sultans reimposed it. As we have seen, Lājīn did so sometime during his reign of 696–8/1296–9. Al-Nāṣir and al-Ashraf did the same in 715/1315 and 778/1376 respectively, the former's action even demolishing the state apparatus of the tax farming of prostitution, and Barsbay tried to eliminate prostitution by forcing those in the trade to marry during his reign of 825–41/1422–38. Presumably these measures also applied to Syria. Al-Dhahabī records that in 690/1291, as Baybars had done earlier in Egypt, the governor of Damascus, al-Shujāʿī, banned women from wearing turbans. They were to wear no more than the veil on their heads. He also banned the *ṣibāghāt* of women.[68] The meaning of this term is not clear. It could, for example, mean the craft of dyeing or staining cloth, which would seem odd, although perhaps here it means the coloring of women's skin. Altogether this might be a reference to cross-dressing and painted ladies. In any case, we don't know if Mamlūk Syria had the same lapses as Egypt!

Prostitution after the Crusades

After the Crusading phenomenon faded in the last half of the seventh/thirteenth century, Syria was spared further violence from the West. Unfortunately, this was not true from the East. As mentioned, the Mongols invaded Syria in 658/1260. They brutally sacked Aleppo in that year and occupied Damascus. Although the Mamlūks drove them from the country, Syria became a marchland between the Mamlūks and the Mongol Il-Khānid rulers of Iran for almost 50 years. This compounded the economic distress of the country, which resulted in particular from the destruction of Syria's major ports in the aftermath of the Crusades.

Carl Petry has brought to light the earliest known reference to prostitution in Syria after the Mongol depredations. It is found in the chronicle of al-Jazarī (d. 739/1338), who spent much of his life in Damascus. Under the year 737/1337, he records the modus operandi of a procuress (*qawwāda*) in Damascus. She attended wedding festivals, where she tried to recruit women by their jewelry, clothing, and general appeal; this suggests that they were free and well-to-do. The procuress offered them 50 dirhams to start and 100 later for giving pleasure to handsome young men. She would lure the women to a safe place outside town, where her husband served as pimp, and ran a successful business until the female slave of a bridal guide and a co-conspirator informed on her and her husband. Arrested by the *wālī*, she was interrogated under torture, confessed eventually, and was strangled. Her husband fled and apparently was never heard of again.[69] Her execution is an extremely rare instance known of such punishment, after that of Anas and Badriyya in Egypt. In each case it was for procuring rather than for prostitution as such. The execution of a fourth woman, described below, may also have been for procuring.

Shortly after our procuress met her end, the Black Death arrived from Egypt in 749/1348, striking Damascus and Aleppo with perhaps as much ferocity as the Mongols. A great human toll was also taken by Tīmūr (also known as Tamerlane). In 803/1400 his hordes entered Syria and brutally sacked Aleppo. They did the same to Damascus the following year.

Women in all walks of life—including prostitutes, of course—suffered greatly from all of these events. The behavior of marauding soldiers toward women was especially savage. Ibn Taghrībirdī gives a dramatic description of the cruelty of Tīmūr's troops in Aleppo, saying:

> The women and children fled to the great mosque of Aleppo and to the smaller mosques, but Tamerlane's men turned to follow them, bound the women with ropes as prisoners, and put the children to the sword, killing every one of them. They committed the shameful deeds to which they were accustomed; virgins were violated without concealment; gentlewomen were outraged without any restraints of modesty; a Tatar would seize a woman and ravage her in the great mosque or one of the smaller mosques in sight of the vast multitude of his companions and the people of the city; her father and brother and husband would see her plight and be unable to defend her because of their lack of means to do so and because they were distracted by the torture and torments which they themselves were suffering; the Tatar would then leave the woman and another go to her, her body still uncovered.[70]

The women in Damascus met a similar fate.[71]

Apart from the general policies that certain Mamlūk sultans explicitly or implicitly adopted regarding prostitution in Syria, I have not encountered any specific reference to it again in that region until well into the ninth/fifteenth century, and then associated with another plague. The Black Plague was not the first or last pandemic to spread throughout the lands encompassing the Eastern Mediterranean, although it may have been the most disastrous. Other forms of plague appeared periodically, sometimes with cyclical recurrence. Al-Maqrīzī reports that a plague struck Egypt and

Syria in 841/1438. Interpreting this as punishment from God for the usual sins, the civil authorities in Aleppo closed all wine shops and restrained prostitutes from carrying on their business (*al-baghāyā al-wāqifāt li-l-bighā'*) and youths (*al-shabāb*) from procuring indecent acts by imposing taxes on them. After the plague subsided, the people of Aleppo rejoiced and reopened the taverns. Prostitutes and youths (*al-aḥdāth*), however, had to continue to pay specific taxes in order to practice their despicable trades.[72] This obviously shows that prostitution was a legitimate (if despised) occupation, and that it was recognized and regulated by the government.

For the remainder of the Mamlūk period, the sources containing references to prostitution in Syria are again sparse. Virtually all that have come to light concern Damascus. Bernadette Martel-Thoumian has made a careful examination of them and has shown that (as far as can be determined), from the late ninth/fifteenth to the early tenth/sixteenth century, the sex trade there seems to a certain extent to have paralleled that in Cairo.[73] Some of the material that she has uncovered is ambiguous, as would be expected. This is true of the affair of a certain jurist (*faqīh*) described in the *Ta'rīkh* of al-Buṣrawī (d. 905/1499–1500). In 879/1474 he was arrested in Damascus for indulging in wine and hashish and frequenting dissolute people (*al-fussāq*). His case was turned over to the religious authorities, who had him beaten, paraded through Damascus in shame, and then imprisoned. The dissolute people in question may have been homosexuals.[74] Later, in 886/1481, another historian, Ibn Ṭawq (d. 915/1509), related a personal experience in his *al-Ta'līq*. In his report, he and some companions encountered two male acquaintances—Ilyās, the *mamlūk* of the Ḥanafī judge, and 'Īsā, the agent of the North African Mālikīs—in the company of a "foreign" woman in the garden of the sultan in al-Nayrab, which was a verdant village northwest of Damascus.[75] All three were drinking wine. Ilyās fled, but the woman was arrested and 'Īsā was seized and given 40 lashes. Martel-Thoumian suspects the woman was a prostitute, perhaps a Turk if not from another region or country.[76]

Ibn Ṭawq also suggests a questionable mixing of the sexes with respect to the Bādharā'iyya Madrasa. This law school was located just inside the gate called Bāb al-Farādīs, which was in the northern wall of Damascus and a short walk northeast of the great Umayyad Mosque.[77] By the end of the ninth/fifteenth century it had become a place of lodging for merchants and artisans. It functioned, in fact, as a khan, or inn. Our author reports that one evening in 891/1486, while the attendant of a certain Ibn Muzhir was staying in one of its rooms, a group of tipsy men returned to it in the company of women.[78] Both the same writer and the well-known Damascene polymath Ibn Ṭūlūn (d. 953/1546), in his chronicle *Mufākahat*, recount more specifically (albeit rather sketchily) an incident concerning prostitution in 893/1488. On a day in May two men—Ibn al-Jaramūsh and Ṣadr al-Dīn Ibn al-Mawṣilī—met southwest of the city in the quarter called Maydān al-Ḥaṣā, where they were joined by three others, one of whom organized an evening's entertainment. They went to a place to drink, where a daughter of joy (*ṣabiyya*) joined them. Afterward they refused to pay her, and the woman who kept the house (*dammāra*) was called.[79] What then transpired is not reported. Indeed, it is not clear if the establishment was a private home, cabaret, or brothel. At that time Maydān al-Ḥaṣā was dominated by a hippodrome, and a powerful gang which may have been involved in prostitution.[80] Finally, we can mention that in nights 28 and 29 of the *Arabian Nights*, a leading character is a street prostitute and procuress in Damascus who learned her evil ways in Cairo.[81] We can infer from this, of course, that she might have been itinerant.

The sources do not indicate if there was a particular part of Damascus where women sold their favors. But, as in other cities, the residents certainly knew where to go if they sought these favors. Ibn Ṭūlūn briefly mentions that in 885/1480 a large crowd gathered at the *mashhad* of the Umayyad Mosque to discuss places of debauchery.[82] This suggests that the usual vices (including prostitution) had either become especially prevalent or they were encroaching on "respectable" neighborhoods or religious institutions, resulting in a rising number of complaints. Ibn Ṭūlūn also says that, in the same month that this meeting was held, the authorities destroyed the brothels in the Bughayl Quarter between the Mosque of al-Tawba and the New Mosque (al-Jāmiʿ al-Jadīd).[83] As noted above, the Mosque of al-Tawba was built on the site of an establishment devoted to lewdness and debauchery that was demolished in the late Ayyūbid period. It was in the al-'Uqayba quarter, which was outside the northern wall of Damascus and across the Baradā River.[84] It was a very short walk from the Umayyad Mosque. The New Mosque was in the suburb of al-Ṣāliḥiyya, further to the north at the foot of Mt. Qāsyūn.[85] The houses were demolished after some women there had purchased a complex called the Qaysāriyya of Ibn Saqr as a place of business. A *qaysāriyya* was a cluster of buildings, including shops, workshops, and living rooms. It was characterized by having several galleries around an open court, and was essentially a market. In this case it must have been small, because the women bought it for only 30 gold *ashrafī* dinars. The fact that a group of women pooled their resources to purchase this place implies that they were organized. Afterward, however, on the order of the *sharabdār*[86] Ibn al-Dawādārī and the *wālī* Ibn al-Khayyāṭa, the women had to move to a place near the al-Yūnusiyya Madrasa[87] in the Sharaf al-A'lā' quarter. The latter was an area west of Damascus and was next to the al-Maydān al-Akhḍar, another quarter with a hippodrome and dominated by a powerful gang.[88] There, some distance from the city, they opened brothels in some abandoned houses.[89] Later, in 890/1485, Ibn Ṭūlūn mentions the presence of libertines at the village of al-Qābūn northeast of Damascus and in 893/1488 at the village of al-Rabwa, west of the city.[90] It appears that the authorities attempted to keep part of the sex trade outside the city.

Nevertheless, it seems that public women continued to serve customers in Damascus. Evidence for this again comes from Ibn Ṭūlūn, this time in his account of the affair of the *khawāja* Ibn al-Zaqīq. *Khawāja* was a title applied to men in a number of capacities, including teacher, merchant, rich man, and even civil official or minister. In this case we can't be sure of Ibn al-Zaqīq's status, but he must have been a man of some respect. In 894/1489 he was caught at night in the company of a prostitute of color. He was taken before the *nā'ib al-ghayba* (the lieutenant governor, the person in charge during the ruler's absence) and forced to pay a fine of 500 dinars, thus avoiding any punishment. Nothing is said of the fate of the woman.[91] We cannot know for certain why Ibn al-Zaqīq was fined—as we have seen, prostitution was regulated. It is unlikely that he was a pimp, and also unlikely that the fine was meant to discourage prostitution within the city. The large size of the fine suggests that Ibn al-Zaqīq was rich. Indeed, it was probably simply a form of extortion, a way of allowing a prominent person to avoid public humiliation. We will see an account below of this method of extortion in the Ottoman period. Still, if fines associated with regulating prostitution were common, this would, of course, be additional confirmation that this trade was legal and fully institutionalized. Judging from the experience of Ibn al-Zaqīq, the government stood to gain handsomely from such fines, not to mention from the taxation of public women themselves.

Finally, Ibn Ṭūlūn records the death of Jān Suwār ("Troops' Delight"), whom he describes as the greatest prostitute in Damascus (*kānat aʿẓam bint khaṭā' bi-Dimashq*). He says that in 904/1498 she was executed on the order of the governor (*nā'ib*) of Damascus.[92] Ibn Ṭūlūn does not give a reason for this action. Was she a brothel-keeper? Was the governor trying to make an example of her? Was this meant to deter public women from doing business in the city? Did she compromise men in high places? Did she have too much influence? If she were indeed the greatest prostitute in Damascus, we would expect her to have accumulated considerable wealth; was her execution the governor's way of confiscating her riches? We don't have an answer to any of these questions. Adding to the puzzle is Ibn Ṭūlūn's statement that Jān Suwār was a white slave. Perhaps he means she was a freed slave who had turned to the sex trade. If not, then money would not have been an issue because her earnings would have gone to her owner. She had clearly given the governor some cause to take drastic action against her.[93]

We might get the impression that Damascus was more puritanical in the late Mamlūk period with respect to the usual pleasures than, say, Cairo. Except for certain periods, this would be difficult to prove. In general the Damascenes could resort to the same kinds of places of entertainment as the people of Cairo. Whatever effect the death of Jān Suwār might have had on their behavior, it was short-lived. In 910/1505 Arikmās, the governor of Damascus, proclaimed again the suppression of houses of debauchery.[94] In fact, the sources for the late Mamlūk period frequently mention inns and cabarets, which were the haunts of public women, in Damascus, but don't give their location.[95] Furthermore, the Muslims of Damascus celebrated the same holidays as those in Cairo; these festive occasions, such as Ramadan and the birthday of the Prophet, brought out the crowds and, no doubt, public women. In addition, writing in the late seventeenth century, el-Dimeşkî states that every spring after Nawrūz (March 22, the vernal equinox), one of the Sufi sheikhs of Damascus led pilgrims from that city to Jerusalem. On their arrival in the holy city, "merchants began to buy and sell." These pilgrims also made side trips to Hebron and the tomb of Moses near Jericho.[96] An even greater cause for celebration, of course, was the annual departure of the pilgrimage caravan from Damascus to Mecca, for which preparations were made weeks in advance. Afterward, there was a great parade through the city and then the cavalcade departed. It was led by the Damascenes' own palanquin, which was kept in the citadel.[97]

Elsewhere, Gaza was especially famous for its celebration of the Prophet's birthday. Its residents also enjoyed a promenade along the coast every Saturday.[98] Lydda (modern-day Lod) and Ramla each had a weekly market, and the latter had a noteworthily large fair on "red egg" day (Easter).[99] In addition, Hebron also had an annual great fair.[100] There were therefore many occasions that brought out the crowds in Damascus and other cities and created opportunities for prostitutes.

Finally, before saying a few words about the sex trade in Syria under the Ottomans, we can note the possibility that, as in Egypt, some of the endowed properties of Muslim charitable foundations may have generated income from public women. There are far fewer surviving endowment documents from Syria than from Egypt, but they generally follow the same format and provide the same kinds of information. Thus they too hint that, because some endowed properties would have been ideal places in which to conduct the business of prostitution, they may have been rented for that purpose. It suffices here to give as examples three of the properties included in the endowment of the al-Ẓāhiriyya in Damascus. This structure was a complex comprising two *madrasas*, a school for teaching the Tradition of the Prophet (*dār al-ḥadīth*), and the tomb of Sultan Baybars. It was established in 676/1277, the year in which the sultan died in Damascus, but it took several years to finish. The original endowment had to be supplemented twice because it did not produce enough revenue for the expenses of the institution. One of the supplements included a khan in a place called Bayt Ḥannā, another known as al-Iṣṭabl (the stable), outside Damascus, and the entire ground floor of the al-Sharab marketplace, which was part of the Street Called Straight.[101]

The Ottoman period

As with my discussion of prostitution in Egypt, I do not intend to go into detail here on the nature of this trade in Syria under Ottoman rule. I would only like to mention the observations on this matter by several visitors to that country in order to show once more the continuity in practice after the fall of the Mamlūks.

First is the remarkable French traveler Jean-Baptiste Tavernier (d. 1689), who played a major role in opening French trade with India. In 1638, on the second of six voyages to the East which he described in some detail, he sailed from Marseille to Alexandretta (Iskandarūn; İskenderun in modern Turkey). He found this port town, located on the coast north of Antioch, to be a mass of disreputable (*méchante*) houses inhabited by Greeks who operated cabarets for sailors and other humble folk (*petits gens*).[102] The implication, of course, is that public women could be found there. These comments on Alexandretta are somewhat reminiscent of Ibn Buṭlān's depiction of the border town of 'Amm, cited above.

Next is again the intrepid Evliya Chelebi. At the end of 1671 he was on his way south through Syria on a journey that eventually took him to Egypt, where he spent the rest of his life. In the coastal town of Jabala, a short distance south of al-Lādhiqiyya, he visited the reputed tomb of the renowned Sufi Ibrāhīm ibn Adham (d. 161/777–8). He tells us that prostitutes, Jews, and infidels did not live there because of the presence of the tomb. If they came to the town, they did not live a long life.[103] This suggests that there were public women in the region, but they did not serve pilgrims here as they did at the tomb of Aḥmad al-Badawī in Egypt. Curiously, Evliya says nothing about prostitutes in large cities like Aleppo and Damascus.

A later traveler, however, reports on public women in Jerusalem. The Englishman Henry Maundrell (d. 1701), who was the chaplain to the English factory (the Levant Company) at Aleppo, wrote a brief but accurate description of the Holy Land entitled "A journey from Aleppo to Jerusalem at Easter, A.D. 1697". He records that on April 10 of that year:

> We went to take our leaves of the holy sepulcher, this being the last time it was to be opened this festival. Upon this finishing day, and the night following, the Turks allow free admittance for all people, without demanding any fee for entrance as at other times, calling it a day of charity. By this promiscuous licence they let in not only the poor, but, as I was told, the lewd and vicious also, who come thither to get convenient opportunity for prostitution, profaning the holy places in such manner (as it is said) that they were not worse defiled even when the heathens here celebrated their aphrodisia.[104]

It appears, therefore, that prostitutes had continued to seek customers among pilgrims to Jerusalem since the time of Mary of Egypt.

Also attached to the factory were the brothers Alexander and Patrick Russell, who were the keenest observers of life in any part of Syria before modern times. They both served as physicians to the Levant Company. Alexander lived in Aleppo from 1740 to 1753 and Patrick from 1750 to 1768. Their long residence, knowledge of Arabic, and profession—all of which gave them entrée to places denied to other Europeans—allowed them to accumulate a vast amount of knowledge about all aspects of life in that city. They published the fruit of that knowledge as *The Natural History of Aleppo*. In it they provide a description of local public women, saying:

> The youth of distinction, without the precincts of the Harem, have little or no opportunity to indulging in illicit pleasures, for they are not only never permitted to go abroad unattended, but there are no private places of resort where the sexes can meet. The common prostitutes (who are chiefly attached to the soldiery) are of the lowest order, and lodge in such obscure places of the town, that no person of character can have any decent pretence to approach them. These prostitutes are licensed by the Bashaw's Tufinkgi Bashee,[105] whom they pay for his protection. Some are natives of Aleppo, but many

> come from other places. They parade in the streets, and the outskirts of the town, dressed in a flaunting manner, their veil flying loosely from the face, their cheeks painted, bunches of flowers stuck gaudily on the temples, and their bosom exposed; their gait is masculine, and full of affectation, and they are in the highest degree impudent and profligate. There are perhaps a few courtesans of somewhat higher class, who entertain visitors in more suitable lodgings; but the risk which people of property run, when detected, of being forced to submit to arbitrary extortion, or to be exposed to public ridicule, confines this mode of gallantry to the inferior class of Osmanli, and the Janizaries.[106]

In other comments, the Russells state that the chief eunuch of one of the governors used to go out of the palace at night, after his master had retired, and pass his time until morning in the company of two or three prostitutes at a house nearby.[107] The nature of the accompaniment is, of course, not mentioned. They also report that there were Christian as well as Muslim prostitutes who were well known to the police.[108] As for illicit Jewish amours, the brothers simply say they appeared to be confined to their own community. They note that venereal disease was common among the Muslims and Christians but was seldom encountered among the Jews.[109] Finally they tell us that, with the exception of some Jewish brides who sometimes painted their faces on their wedding night, only women of ill fame among the Muslims and Christians used rouge, which was considered a mark of their profession.[110] From the Russells' account it is clear that prostitution continued to be a legal trade and that it was regulated by the authorities.

Indeed, their account of the status of prostitution in Aleppo is echoed to some extent in Damascus in the contemporary chronicle of Aḥmad Budayrī, a local barber. His work covers the period 1741–63. In his remarks on popular culture, he says that public women brazenly strolled in the streets of the city and gathered at its marketplaces. They would parade in honor of a local saint, or on other occasions "staged public celebrations and walked unveiled while chanting and dancing." The governors of Damascus tried several times to ban them but their efforts failed, in part because they had the support of the soldiers in the city. Finally, the authorities simply resorted to taxing them. Prostitutes were thus such a common feature of life that the treasurer of Damascus invited some of them to his daughter's wedding, at which they undoubtedly sang and danced, and he gave them gifts.[111]

A contemporary of the Russells was the French army officer François Baron de Tott (d. 1793), who arrived in Constantinople in 1755 as the secretary of his uncle, the French ambassador. His task was to learn Turkish and make an inspection of the Ottoman Empire. He remained there until 1763. Returning once more to Constantinople after 1768, he played a role in helping to reform the Ottoman military. In the course of his duties, he visited the cities and towns around the Eastern Mediterranean coast. In his memoirs, he mentions lodging in the village of Martavan, on the main road just north of Aleppo, and says that it and another village nearby had a certain notoriety. Both settlements were owned by a rich man in Aleppo to whom they paid rent. The men of the villages were engaged in agriculture while the women, who were generally handsome, entertained visitors. An agent, apparently a tax farmer, took orders from the guests and provided them with the female company that they desired. He then distributed a portion of the profits to the women.[112]

Our final traveler was another Frenchman, Constantin-François de Volney (d. 1820), who generally confirmed de Tott's observations, although a little later. Volney spent two years in Syria and learned Arabic, later composing a long account of his experiences there and afterward in Egypt. This work also served in part as a kind of intelligence report, and was one of the books that Napoleon took with him on his invasion of Egypt in 1798. In 1785 Volney set out on the road from Alexandretta to Aleppo. He describes the last stage before reaching his destination as follows:

> at the last place travelers sleep at, is the village of Martawan, celebrated among the Turks and Europeans on account of an extraordinary practice of the inhabitants who let out their wives and daughters for a trifling sum. This prostitution, held in abhorrence by the Arabs, seems to me to have originated in some religious custom, which ought perhaps to be sought for in the ancient worship of the goddess

> Venus, or to be attributed to the community of women permitted by the Ansarians,[113] to which tribe the inhabitants of Martawan belong. The Franks pretend that the women are pretty. But it is probable that long abstinence at sea, and the vanity of intrigue, constitute all their merit; for their exterior announces nothing but the disgusting uncleanliness of misery.[114]

Again, these reports are similar to Ibn Buṭlān's observations about the border town of ʿAmm.

CONCLUSION

Despite many gaps in time and place in our sources, it is fairly clear that prostitution in Syria thrived under many of the same circumstances as it did in Egypt. Initially it was in Christian hands, but as conversion progressed it became dominated by Muslims. The pattern set in Late Antiquity continued for some time. Public women conducted their trade at Syria's many commercial ports and inland emporia. In addition they sought customers at hostels, inns, and caravanserais along trade routes as well as in the cities. Between the first/seventh and second/eighth centuries, the creation of a vast Arab empire by the Umayyads, with Damascus as the capital, brought Syria great wealth and an increase in potential clients for prostitutes. These clients were supplemented by a continuous stream of visitors to Syria's numerous holy and historical sites.

Between the third/ninth and tenth/sixteenth centuries—from the time of Ibn Ṭūlūn until the Ottoman conquest—Syria was usually ruled wholly or partly from Egypt, and thus Egyptian policies toward vice were often also applied (although inconsistently) to Syria. Attempts to ban it from Egypt inevitably failed. Perhaps as early as Fāṭimid times, Syrian public women were taxed; this was certainly true by the reign of Zangī. Their trade was supervised by the same kinds of officials, such as the *muḥtasib*, and by Ayyūbid times the tax was probably farmed out and granted as an *iqṭāʿ*. As in Egypt, the authorities attempted to ban prostitution during natural disasters, such as plague. Although the sex trade generally flourished in Syria, there seems to have been an effort, at least under late Mamlūk rule, to restrict it to the suburbs of Damascus and keep it out of the city proper.

The little that we can glean from the sources about prostitutes in Syria is that they were free women or slaves and were pimped. They were of diverse backgrounds and religions, and were aware of methods of contraception. Some became quite notorious. There are cases where prostitutes pooled their resources to purchase and operate their own establishments, and some may have been organized into guilds. Virtually all the women and their customers are faceless. Except for the cases of an anonymous procuress and of Jān Suwār, no mention of punishment of prostitutes, not even banishment, has yet turned up in the sources for Syria until the late Ottoman period. Several of their customers, especially those who were identified, were subjected to public humiliation or extortion. Public women were present at all major public gatherings, such as fairs, festivals, and holidays; they were even invited to the homes of prominent people on special occasions in order to provide entertainment. In short, they were an accepted and legitimate part of urban and commercial life. And as in Egypt, *waqf* documents hint at the possibility that some endowed properties of religious and charitable institutions generated income from their earnings.

Without question, the most remarkable aspect of prostitution in Syria was the noticeable increase in this business as a result of the Crusades, which were carried out between the late fifth/eleventh and late seventh/thirteenth centuries. Each Crusade, each invasion force, was accompanied by a significant number of public women. As camp followers, they assisted the troops in many ways, but their sexual services were paramount. Other daughters of joy arrived separately by ship from Europe. Because they were such a prominent feature of the Crusader armies (even, it seems, accompanying soldiers into battle), and of life in the Crusader-held ports of Syria, they frequently appeared in the Christian sources. Word of them quickly spread beyond the Crusader lines, and even Muslim troops were tempted to visit them. As in Muslim-ruled Syria, the prostitutes in Christian-controlled Syria carried on a legitimate trade. They were supervised and taxed by the authorities, and many people, including men of the cloth, profited from them. There were no bans on these women except when the Crusaders encountered difficulties on campaign and the clergy blamed their setbacks on sexual excesses; no such phenomenon occurred, however, among Muslim forces. Many tantalizing questions remain unanswered about the European public women, who in their own way took the cross and went to Syria. What was their background, and where exactly did they come from? Were they predominantly free women, or recruited and managed? Did they sell their favors in the usual places in the Syrian ports? Were they organized? Did they usually return to Europe, or stay in Syria? And, of course, what happened to them when they were captured by Muslim troops?

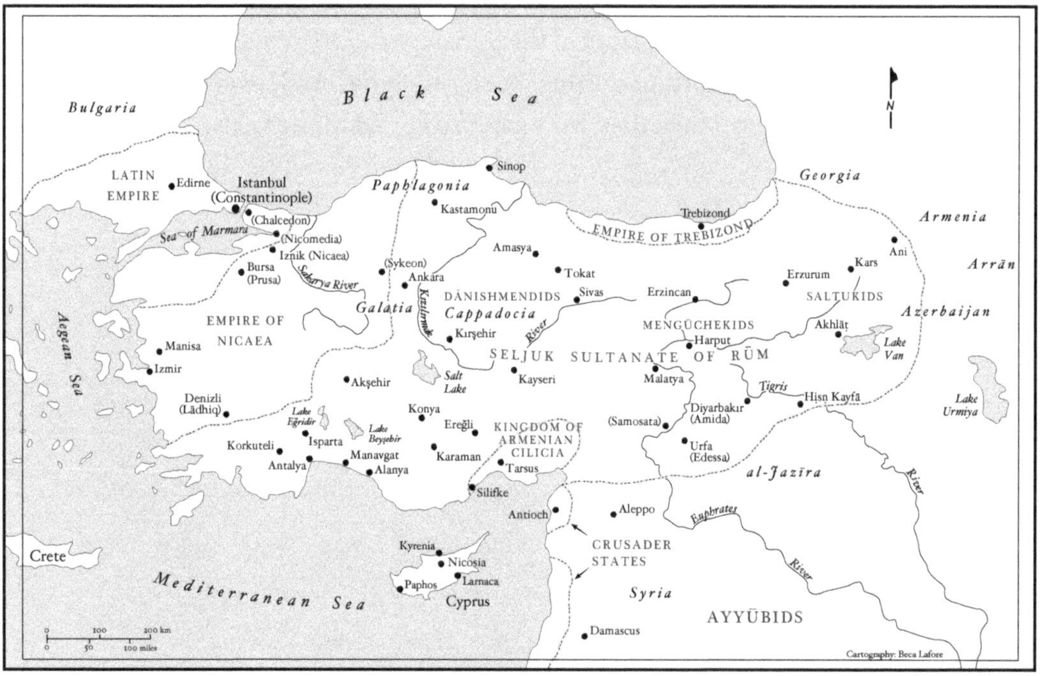

MAP 4

Anatolia in the early seventh/thirteenth century (classical names are in parentheses)

FIVE

Public Women in Medieval Anatolia

POLITICAL AND SOCIAL CONTEXT

At the beginning of the fifth/eleventh century, Anatolia (roughly the present area of Turkey in Asia) was the heartland of the Byzantine Empire. Essentially a high plateau surrounded by mountains, it had a wealth of natural resources, many well-watered fertile valleys, and several natural harbors on the Black Sea, the Aegean, and the Mediterranean. It was a land of countless villages and small towns as well as many large cities, most of which were connected to the major trade routes of Southwest Asia and beyond. It was the richest and most populous part of Byzantium.

Long familiar with the Arabs and Islam, the Byzantine Empire faced a new Muslim people in the late eleventh century who would determine its fate: the Turks. As early as the second/eighth century, the 'Abbāsid caliphs had recruited Turks from Central Asia as soldiers, and eventually these soldiers constituted the major element in the 'Abbāsid army. It was not until the middle of the fifth/eleventh century, however, that large Turkish tribes began to move from Central Asia to Southwest Asia, with major demographic, political, and cultural consequences. In 447/1055, Toghril, the leader of the Seljuks, the most important confederation of Turkish tribes, entered Baghdad, proclaiming himself the protector of the 'Abbāsid caliph and of Sunni Islam. While keeping the caliph under tight control, he sent various family members to carry out further conquests. Thus, he laid the foundation of the Great Seljuk Empire, centered primarily on Iran and Iraq. Toghril's nephew, Alp Arslan, succeeded him in 455/1063. Continuously in the field suppressing revolts and campaigning on the frontiers, in 462/1070 he marched into Northern Syria and unsuccessfully besieged Edessa and Aleppo. Afterward, he learned of the approach of the Byzantine emperor, Romanus IV Diogenes, who had set out to put an end to the growing Turkish danger. In 463/1071 the two armies met at Manzikert in Eastern Anatolia. Alp Arslan was victorious, and Byzantine defenses in the east collapsed.

It seems that Alp Arslan did not order a systematic conquest of Anatolia, but the routes into that region were now open and Turkish tribes surged along them. The most important Turkish chief to appear in Anatolia after Manzikert was Sulaymān ibn Quṭulmush, a member of the Seljuk family. He managed to seize Nicaea (Iznik) and its environs as early as 467/1075, and the Byzantine emperor Alexius I Comnenus acknowledged his suzerainty over the territory under his control. His son Qılıj Arslan I (r. 485–500/1092–1107) expanded his territory to the Aegean and toward the east, guaranteeing the establishment of the Seljuk Sultanate of Anatolia (or Rūm)—that is, of "Rome" or Byzantium. Other Turkish leaders founded additional principalities in Eastern Anatolia. The most powerful of them was that of the Dānishmendids, centered around Tokat, Amasya, and Sivas.

A major clash between the Seljuks and Dānishmendids was averted by the sudden appearance of the First Crusade in 489/1096, which made allies of the rivals. This crusade had resulted from the Byzantine emperor's plea to the West for help after the disaster of Manzikert and the fall of Jerusalem to another Turkish army in the same year. Despite the temporary alliance of the Seljuks and Dānishmendids, the Crusaders were able to cross Anatolia and reach the Holy Land. The long reign of Qılıj Arslan's son Mas'ūd (r. 510–51/1116–56), who seized the throne from his brother Shāhanshāh, laid the basis for the survival of the Seljuk Sultanate. He developed Konya as the capital, staved off the Second Crusade by forcing it to avoid his territory, and expanded his realm to the east at the expense of the Dānishmendids. His son, Qılıj Arslan II (r. 551–88/1156–92), captured almost all of Dānishmendid territory, and in 572/1176 at the Battle of Myriokephalon in Southwestern Anatolia ended the Byzantine hope of retaking Anatolia. Henceforth, the Greeks referred to it as "Turcia." He subsequently united all of Central Anatolia in one Turkish state. The army of Frederick Barbarossa marched across Anatolia in 586/1190 as part of the Third Crusade and plundered Konya, but this was only a temporary setback to the sultanate.

Following the death of Qılıj Arslan, there was a struggle among his many sons for the throne, but the weakness of the Seljuks' enemies prevented them from taking advantage of this. In fact, during this time the Fourth Crusade stormed Constantinople in 1204, a blow from which Byzantium never fully recovered. During the struggle for succession, Kaykhusraw I (r. 588–93/1192–7, 601–8/1205–11) ultimately triumphed. In 603/1207 he captured Antalya on the Mediterranean, acquiring the sultanate's first major port. In 611/1214, his successor Kaykā'ūs I (r. 608–16/1211–20) seized Sinop on the Black Sea and opened Seljuk commerce with Crimea. In 613/1216 he recaptured Antalya after it had revolted. The opening of trade between the ports of Sinop and Antalya gave the sultanate indisputable dominance in Anatolian commerce and politics. This set the stage for the growth of Muslim urban life that occurred under his brother, the renowned 'Alā' al-Dīn Kayqubād I (r. 616–34/1220–37).

Under 'Alā' al-Dīn, the sultanate reached the height of its power and glory. He expanded its frontiers to their greatest extent, uniting all of Anatolia (with the exception of the remnants of Byzantium, centered on Nicaea in the west and Trebizond on the Black Sea coast, and Cilician Armenia). He even seized Sughdaq in the Crimea, which made the sultanate the chief transit center for trade between the steppes of Russia and Alexandria. The wealth that flowed to the sultanate resulted in much building activity and a great flowering of Muslim culture. It is worthy of note that the largest building projects undertaken by the Seljuks, apart from the fortifications of a few cities, were caravanserais along the major trade routes. 'Alā' al-Dīn's court attracted luminaries from beyond his borders, including the family of Jalāl al-Dīn al-Rūmī, whose Persian mystical poetry later won undying fame.

The power and glory of the sultanate under 'Alā' al-Dīn proved, however, to be short-lived. His successor, Kaykhusraw II (r. 634–44/1237–46), who was often preoccupied with political intrigue, had first to crush a revolt of the Khwārazmians, who had been driven into Anatolia from Central Asia by the Mongols, and then a large-scale uprising among the Turkish tribes in South-Central Anatolia. In no condition to face the Mongols when they finally appeared, his army was annihilated in 641/1243. At first the Mongols turned the sultanate into a puppet state and appointed the sultan at will. Later on, in 676/1277, they took direct control.

Meanwhile, in regions of Anatolia outside the direct control of the Mongols, various Turkish principalities began to take root. By the early eighth/fourteenth century, as Mongol influence waned, the Seljuk Sultanate had vanished and in its place some 20 principalities had appeared. One of them was that of the Ottomans, which crystallized in the far northwestern corner of Anatolia. Its founder, Osman, who gave his name to the dynasty, captured Bursa in 726/1326 and made it his capital. In 755/1354 the Ottomans occupied Ankara and crossed the Dardanelles to take Gallipoli, which became their base for expansion into Europe. In 773/1369 they moved their capital to Adrianople (modern-day Edirne). For the remainder of the eighth/fourteenth century the Ottomans expanded into both Europe and Anatolia, gradually reducing Byzantium to little more than Constantinople. Ottoman expansion in the east was briefly checked by Tamerlane at the Battle of Ankara in 804/1402, but the Ottomans quickly recovered and firmly established themselves in the Balkans and Anatolia. Then, in 1453, Mehmet II (r. 1451–81) conquered Constantinople and the great city became the capital of the Ottoman Empire.[1]

During the roughly 200 years during which the Seljuks and contemporary Turkish dynasties (such as the Dānishmendids) held political sway over Anatolia to a greater or lesser degree, the Turkish element of the population remained a distinct minority. With the coming of the Turks, the process of the transformation of Anatolia from a predominantly Greek and Christian region into a predominantly Turkish and Muslim region began, but it took many centuries to complete. This process was similar in some respects to what occurred in Syria after the Arabs conquered it from Byzantium. The Christians were sedentary, living in both villages and cities. The Turks were mainly nomadic with (initially) a somewhat superficial attachment to

Islam, and they founded no new cities. During the Seljuk period, the most important language for the population as a whole was Greek. Even many of the Seljuk sultans were the products of mixed marriages and spoke Greek, and Greeks and other Christians served in the Seljuk government. Turkish was not yet a literary language. For this purpose Persian was used, but it was not widely understood outside the court. Therefore, in the Seljuk period, Anatolia, as a mostly Christian region within Islamdom, was an anomaly.[2]

Opportunities for public women

In light of the relatively short existence of the Seljuk Sultanate and its contemporary Turkish principalities, and the demographic and linguistic nature of Anatolia at that time, few Muslim literary works from that era were produced. We are compensated to some degree for this paucity of sources by Christian works in various languages. Nevertheless, their combined coverage of the social and economic history of that period is (as one might expect) uneven. And it must be kept in mind that, because the population was overwhelmingly Christian, it is reasonable to assume—as we did under similar circumstances earlier—that prostitution was practiced primarily by Christians and that Muslim writers would have had no interest in it as a Christian trade. Christian sources themselves are almost silent on this business among their coreligionists. This said, however, our combined sources do provide a few glimpses of the lives of contemporary public women. As far as we can tell, they practiced their trade under the same conditions as women did elsewhere around the Eastern Mediterranean.

The earliest apparent reference to prostitution that I have come across in Seljuk Anatolia is found in Ibn al-Athīr's renowned thirteenth-century chronicle *al-Kāmil*, which is cited in earlier chapters. Although Anatolia was on the periphery of his interests, he records a very brief story of the rise to prominence there of a woman whose career was vaguely reminiscent of that of Theodora. After Saladin consolidated his power in Syria, he began to contend with the Seljuks for control of Southeastern Anatolia, above all the region around Āmid (modern-day Diyarbakır) and Ḥiṣn Kayfā (modern-day

Hasankeyf) on the Upper Tigris. These towns were then at the center of the Turkish principality of the Artuqids, who found themselves caught between the rival powers of the Seljuks and Ayyūbids.

Qılıj Arslan II had formed an alliance with Nūr al-Dīn Muḥammad ibn Qara Arslan (r. 562–81/1167–85), who ruled from Ḥiṣn Kayfā, by marrying his daughter to him, probably between 570/1175 and 575/1180. Shortly after Muḥammad married her, however, he fell in love with a singing girl. He then married her as well, and she exercised "authority over his land and his treasury" while he neglected the daughter of Qılıj Arslan, leaving her "forgotten and abandoned." This was an affront to Qılıj Arslan, who threatened to attack Muḥammad; the latter in turn asked Saladin for help. Saladin marched to his assistance in 576/1180–1, but changed his mind during negotiations with an envoy from Qılıj Arslan when told he would be taunted for gathering troops from far and near and taking the field and spending vast sums "for the sake of a harlot singing girl."[3] Saladin then forced Muḥammad to dismiss her in a year's time, and she went to Baghdad.[4]

Another incident of political import concerning a singing girl occurred during the reign of Kaykhusraw II. It is recorded in the Persian memoirs of Ibn Bībī (d. ca. 684/1285), who was head of the Seljuk chancellery. He reports that after the death of 'Alā' al-Dīn Kayqubād I, his son Kaykhusraw was brought to the sultanate by a group of powerful *amīrs* who preferred him to his brothers. No sooner did he take the throne in 634/1237 than these *amīrs* began a bloody rivalry for dominance. The most ambitious of them and the most influential with Kaykhusraw was Sa'd al-Dīn Köpek, who managed to eliminate his rivals, one of whom was Tāj al-Dīn Pervāne. Shortly after Kaykhusraw became sultan, it was rumored that while on the way from Antalya to Ankara to meet with Köpek, Tāj al-Dīn passed through Akşehir, where he had illicit (*ghayr-i mashrū'*) sexual relations with a singing girl who belonged to the ruler of the town of Harput (Khartpert), far to the east of Akşehir. Köpek seized this opportunity to have some legal authorities (qadis and imams) whom he knew issue opinions (fatwas) declaring him to be guilty and requiring him to be stoned. With the compliance of the sultan, Tāj al-Dīn was brought to the main square of Ankara, where he was buried up to the waist before the local people were forced to carry out the sentence.[5]

Unfortunately we are not told the nature of the "illicit" relations, but they must have been "unusual" or scandalous in some way. It is puzzling that the alleged offense had occurred in Akşehir and not in Harput. This may mean that Tāj al-Dīn had stolen the girl or that other factors were involved. In the event, this report of the execution of a powerful *amīr* by stoning for a sexual offense may be unique in medieval Muslim sources. Nothing is said about the fate of the singing girl.

Prostitution and the Crusades

As we have seen in the previous two chapters, public women accompanied the Crusaders on their invasions of the Eastern Mediterranean world, and the armies of the First Crusade and the Crusade of 1101 marched across Central Anatolia to Syria. We noted that a significant number of prostitutes accompanied the latter; its destruction by the Turks in Anatolia was attributed in part to the wantonness of the Christian troops. Many—perhaps most—of the prostitutes were captured by the Turks; their subsequent fate is unknown.

Between 1147 and 1148, the two largest armies of the Second Crusade, led by the Holy Roman Emperor Conrad III and Louis VII of France, marched around Western Anatolia and then took ship from Adalia (modern-day Antalya) to Tarsus and Antioch. This was the largest of all the Crusades in scope and was accompanied by a huge number of camp followers and pilgrims, which included large groups of thieves and criminals who had supposedly repented their sins and sought remission of the penance for those sins by making the pilgrimage to the Holy Land. This suggests, of course, that many public women did the same. In any case, Conrad was defeated near Dorylaeum (near modern-day Eskişehir) and Louis near Cadmus (Khonaz/Honaz), and most of the remaining camp followers and pilgrims were abandoned at Adalia. Consequently, many of the public women among them must once again have fallen into the hands of the Turks.[6]

As part of the Third Crusade, the army of Frederick Barbarossa also marched across Anatolia. It stormed the Seljuk capital of Konya on the way, but disintegrated in 1190 after Frederick drowned in Cilicia, just short of Antioch. There must have been many public women in its train who were, no doubt, also taken by the Turks.

The Fourth Crusade was diverted to the conquest of the great Christian city of Constantinople in 1204. In the aftermath of plundering the city, the Crusaders made no attempt to continue to the Holy Land by traversing Anatolia. We know, however, that prostitutes were with them. Recounting the horrors inflicted on the city by the Crusaders, the Greek historian Nicetas Choniates (d. 1215 or 1216), an eyewitness, says of their desecration of St. Sophia,

> Nay more, a certain harlot, a sharer in their guilt, a minister of the furies, a servant of the demons, a worker of incantations and poisonings, insulting Christ, sat in the patriarch's seat singing an obscene song and dancing frequently.[7]

It seems that she was singing in French, which would tend to confirm that she had traveled with the troops.[8]

Public women on the fringes of the sultanate

As a result of the Fourth Crusade, Constantinople became the capital of a small Latin "empire" composed of little more than a slice of the Balkans. The remainder of Byzantium in Europe was parceled out into various Latin kingdoms. In Anatolia, two rump Byzantine states emerged. The larger, on the western edge of Anatolia, was that of the Empire of Nicaea, founded by members of the aristocratic Lascaris family. The smaller, stretching along the eastern Black Sea coast of Anatolia, was the Empire of Trebizond, founded by members of the royal Comnenus family. The splintering of Byzantium helped the Seljuks to consolidate their power and expand their territory, taking Sinop in 611/1214 and Antalya once and for all in 613/1216.

A few years later the Seljuks besieged Trebizond. John Lazaropoulos, who became metropolitan of that city in 1363, provides the longest and most reliable account of this siege. His account has traditionally been interpreted to date this event to the winter of 1222–3.[9] More recently, however, because of certain ambiguities in the text and other factors, it has been suggested that this event occurred in the fall of 1230.[10] Lazaropoulos says that the Seljuk army, under the command of "Melik" (king), attacked Trebizond but encountered strong resistance. Consequently, he decided to undermine the morale of its defenders by profaning the monastery of their patron saint, Eugenius, which was outside the city. Melik had the relics and offerings removed from the chapel and had horses placed in lines outside. Then, in view of the city, our cleric states, "O, what a horrendous, what a monstrous and unspeakable sight! He told several immoral and lascivious women, who were in a frantic condition, to enter the church!"[11] This is, of course, reminiscent of what Choniates had to say about the desecration of St. Sophia. We are not told who these women were or whether they were Muslim or Christian. Trebizond was a major port and center of trade and must have attracted public women from many places. It is noteworthy that Lazaropoulos and Choniates considered the presence of a prostitute in a church to be a desecration.

There is disagreement over Melik's identity. Claude Cahen thought he was probably Mughīth al-Dīn Toghrıl Shāh, a son of Qılıj Arslan II and the *amīr* of Erzurum.[12] This city, to the southeast of Trebizond, had been the capital of the Turkish principality of the Saltuqids, which was annexed by the Seljuks in 598/1202 and became the seat of a prince (*malik*). It was predominantly an Armenian city and one of the most important centers of trade in Anatolia. Alexis Savvides believes the man in question was Toghrıl Shāh's nephew, Sultan 'Alā' al-Dīn Kayqubād I.[13] Rustam Shukurov says he was probably Kayqubād's son (and crown prince) Ghiyāth al-Dīn Kaykhusraw, who had been vicegerent of nearby Erzincan and the entire region, including Erzurum, bordering the Empire of Trebizond.[14] Whatever the case, it is worth mentioning that Yāqūt—who wrote the first draft of his great geography in Aleppo in 621/1224—says that the independent "sultan" of Erzurum, "whose inhabitants were Armenians," was a just man, but "dissoluteness, drinking wine, and the perpetration of sinful activity there were well known; no one denied it and no one was distressed about it."[15] This was certainly a reflection of Erzurum's significance as a commercial hub and must also have been true of the port of Trebizond, with which it was connected.

The sex trade in the sultanate

In general, the Seljuk sultans seem to have tolerated prostitution. Al-Dhahabī characterized Kaykā'ūs I as licentious (*fāsiq*), which suggests that he would not have taken measures against it.[16] Most of what we know concerning the practice of prostitution in the sultanate, mainly in and around its capital of Konya, revolves about the famous mystic Jalāl al-Dīn al-Rūmī. He was born in Balkh in present-day Afghanistan in 604/1207. His family emigrated west and by 614/1217, just before the death of Kaykā'ūs I, had reached Anatolia. They arrived in Konya in 626/1228, where al-Rūmī spent most of the rest of his life and died in 672/1273. Apart from his renowned *Mathnawī*, a didactic Persian poetical work, his greatest literary achievement was his *Dīwān-i kabīr*, a great anthology of verse.[17] The latter, also in Persian, sometimes reflects on the life of the common people, and Erdoğan Merçil has tabulated references to public women in the *Dīwān*, using a somewhat abbreviated version of the published Persian text and comparing it with the published Turkish translation of the full text. The latter was based on a Persian manuscript that does not always correspond to the published Persian text.[18] As a result, he says, it was sometimes difficult to find the Persian equivalents of the Turkish names of professions found in the translation.

In the *Dīwān*, al-Rūmī mentions prostitutes (*rūspī* in Persian) only in a few places and in passing, usually in a negative metaphorical sense.[19] He also refers to public singers (*lūlī* in Persian) who were also dancers, and, by extension, courtesans,[20] but gives no details about their trade. These references simply show that prostitutes were present in the poet's world and were probably common.

In fact, public women were among al-Rūmī's followers. His well-known toleration of people of all religions carried over to people of all ethnicities

FIGURE 5.1
Caravanserai. The Sultan Hanı, 100 kilometers east of Konya.

FIGURE 5.2
Interior of the Sultan Hanı.

and professions. His biographer Shams al-Dīn Aflākī (d. 761/1360), who was a disciple of al-Rūmī's grandson, has left us two stories of al-Rūmī's encounters with women in the sex trade. In the first, he records the following:

> Likewise, it is transmitted from the great among the men of poverty [the Sufis] that in the Vizier Ḍiyā' al-Dīn Caravanserai there was a lady by the name of Ṭā'us (Peacock) who played the harp. She had a delightful voice, played sweetly and soothed the heart, and wore elegant clothes. She was a heart-ravishing beauty and unique in the world. Due to the refinement of the harp (*chang*), all lovers [Sufis] had become a prisoner in her grip (*chang*). As it happened, one day Mawlānā [our master, i.e., al-Rūmī] entered the caravanserai and sat down opposite her room. Ṭā'us the Harpist came forth in her radiance. Lowering her head, she fixed her grip on Mawlānā's skirts and invited him into her room. Mawlānā consented. Then from the beginning of the day until the hour of evening prayers he prayed and raised up supplications. He cut off a cubit of cloth from his blessed turban and gave it to her, and bestowed gold dinars on her slave girls. Then he left.[21]

This story is noteworthy on several counts. First we learn that a beautiful woman named "Peacock" (a pet name), who was an excellent musician and singer, employed slave girls in a brothel in a caravanserai. "Peacock" was not specific to any religious or ethnic group, so she symbolized prostitutes in general.[22] Second, she wore elegant clothes, which is evidence of the wealth she earned from her business. Third, the brothel was in the caravanserai of none other than Vizier Ḍiyā' al-Dīn, that is, Ḍiyā' al-Dīn Kara Arslan, who served as a vizier from at least 625/1228 under 'Alā' al-Dīn Kayqubād I until the end of the reign of his successor Kaykhusraw II in 644/1246. Because he was one of the most powerful men in the sultanate, his caravanserai must have been an imposing building. None of the surviving Seljuk caravanserais bears his name, but many of them lack inscriptions or no longer retain their original names.[23] It is also possible that he may actually have been responsible for one of the caravanserais built in the name of Kayqubād or

Kaykhusraw but referred to as that of Ḍiyā' al-Dīn in common parlance. In any case, his caravanserai was probably in or near Konya. The fact that public women sold their favors in the caravanserai of such an important figure suggests, of course, that they could do so unhindered in any caravanserai; they were simply part of the establishment. Fourth, Peacock was so enticing that even Sufis became her clients. And fifth, ultimately al-Rūmī himself visited her. She invited him to her chambers, where he spent his time in prayer. Afterward, he distributed gold to her girls, which clearly indicates his acceptance of their profession.[24]

Aflākī goes on to say that immediately afterward the sultan's treasurer, a certain Sharaf al-Dīn, happened to "walk by" Peacock. Smitten, he had her sent to a bathhouse and married her, bestowing on her a nuptial gift of 50,000 gold dinars. He noted in particular the new radiance she had acquired after al-Rūmī honored her with a visit. Subsequently, she led a saintly life, attracting the beauties of Konya and others who became her disciples. She performed miracles, freed her slave girls and found them husbands.[25] The profession of prostitute thus proved to be no obstacle to a respectable marriage, even in the highest circles. This story is clearly similar to the accounts of some of the early Christian monks, such as that of Vitalios, who ministered to public women. It even has a few parallels with the story of "Hārūn al-Rashīd and Abū 'l-Ḥasan the Merchant of Oman" in the *Arabian Nights*.

In his second story of an encounter of al-Rūmī with prostitutes, Aflākī provides a much more specific and vivid description of the master's view of the sex trade. He says:

> It is also transmitted from Shaykh Maḥmūd Ṣāḥib Qirān that in the Ṣāḥib Iṣfahānī Caravanserai there was a prostitute who was extremely beautiful. And she had many slave girls working for her [as prostitutes]. One day Mawlānā passed by there. This woman came running toward him and, lowering her head, she fell at Khudāvandgār's [the divine one's] feet and displayed humility and self-abasement. Mawlānā exclaimed: "Oh Rābi'a, Rābi'a, Rābi'a!" Her slave girls were informed of this and they all came forth together and placed their heads at his

> feet. Mawlānā said: "Bravo, oh champions! If it were not for your bearing the burden, who would have subdued so many censorious, headstrong carnal souls, and how would the chaste chastity of women ever have appeared?"
>
> It then happened that an eminent man of the time said: "It is not proper for so great a person to be this involved with prostitutes of the tavern and to show them these kindnesses." Mawlānā replied: "That woman presently goes about with a single color and she displays herself as she is without deception. If you're a man, you also do the same and abandon the quality of possessing two colors (hypocrisy) so that your exterior becomes the same color as your interior. If your exterior and interior do not become the same, whatever you do is false and vain."
>
> In the end, this beautiful lady repented in the manner of Rābiʻa and freed her slave girls. She gave over her house to be plundered and became one of the people of good fortune in the hereafter. She experienced devotion for Mawlānā and rendered many services.[26]

Like the previous story, this one is striking in many respects. First, al-Rūmī speaks of prostitutes as playing an acceptable—indeed, critical—role in society. In words echoing St. Augustine's justification of prostitution, he says public women were "champions" who tamed the male libido and ensured the chastity of other women; that is, they protected them.[27] Second, he goes so far as to call the woman operating the brothel "Rābiʻa." This is a reference to Rābiʻa al-ʻAdawiyya al-Ḳaysiyya (d. 185/801) of Basra, the most famous female mystic and saint in Islam. Stolen as a child and sold into slavery, she may, according to some accounts, have been a courtesan (*qayna*).[28] In any case, she refused to marry and, abandoning worldly life to practice extreme asceticism, became a paragon of virtue and piety. Likening the brothel-keeper to Rābiʻa gave her the status of sainthood! Also, like Peacock, she can also easily symbolize all women in the sex trade because she is anonymous. The story of her decision to repent and abandon her profession as well as the comforts of this world to follow al-Rūmī is also reminiscent of some of the stories of the holy Christian harlots which were examined earlier in this study, and it is also the closest example of such stories that I have discovered in an Islamic context. Presumably this woman was Muslim, because al-Rūmī referred to her as Rābiʿa. If so, she might even be interpreted as al-Rūmī's Mary Magdalene.[29] Third, the brothel-keeper is a woman who owns slave girls whom she prostitutes. Like her, they are anonymous, and nothing is said of their religion or ethnicity. Fourth, the brothel is also operated in a caravanserai. This one was built by another powerful Seljuk official, Ṣāḥib Shams al-Dīn Iṣfahānī. He had been the very influential *nā'ib* (vicegerent) and then vizier of Kaykhusraw II. He became *nā'ib* after the assassination of Köpek in 637/1240 and held the post of vizier from 642/1244 until 646/1249, when he was executed. During this time, Shams al-Dīn was one of the most powerful men in the sultanate. His caravanserai, therefore, like that of Ḍiyā' al-Dīn, must have been a monumental building. Still, no surviving Seljuk caravanserai bears his name and we are faced with the same problem that we encountered with the caravanserai of Ḍiyā' al-Dīn. Again, also, his caravanserai was probably in or near Konya. The fact that public women went about their business in the caravanserai of another powerful figure is further confirmation that they could freely do so in any caravanserai. Finally, in this story al-Rūmī praises prostitutes for being honest about what they do and criticizes the hypocrisy of those men who take advantage of their services while denouncing them. This is quite remarkable and may be unique in the medieval literature of the Eastern Mediterranean world.

At the end of his story about Peacock, Aflākī says that the "blessed" caravanserai which had been her place of business became a bathhouse for Muslims.[30] In his time it was called the Nakışlı ("Ornamented") Bathhouse. I have never come across another reference to such a transformation. Here it seems to mean that the part of the building that functioned as a brothel, rather than the entire structure, became a bath, or that one was added to the facility. In addition to having many rooms that could be used for different purposes, most caravanserais, especially the largest ones, had interior baths, or there were baths nearby.[31] Eating, drinking, amusement, and relaxation were all associated with the baths in seventh/thirteenth and eighth/fourteenth-century Anatolia.[32] Perhaps Aflākī is simply telling us that the blessed caravanserai increased its amenities as a center of pleasure after Peacock departed.[33]

One of Aflākī's contemporaries, the renowned traveler Ibn Battuta (d. 770/1368–9 or 779/1377), confirms that prostitutes provided their services in the public baths. In 731/1331 he was in the city of Lādhiq (Laodicia, modern Denizli) in Southwestern Anatolia. In a well-known passage in his book of travels, he says:

> The inhabitants of this city make no effort to stamp out immorality—indeed, the same applies to the whole population of these regions. They buy beautiful Greek slave-girls and put them out to prostitution, and each girl has to pay a regular due to her master. I heard it said there that the girls go into the bath-houses along with the men, and anyone who wishes to indulge in depravity does so in the bath-house and nobody tries to stop him. I was told that the *qāḍī* in this city himself owns slave-girls [employed] in this way.[34]

It is curious that Ibn Battuta speaks of the widespread immorality "of these regions." He probably means Western Anatolia rather than all of Anatolia. Writing a few decades before him, the encyclopedist Ibn Faḍl Allāh al-'Umarī (d. 749/1349), who served in the Mamlūk chancery, says (on the authority of a Genoese prisoner) that the people of the "principality of Denizli" were extremely given to drink and the pleasures of love.[35] In any case, Ibn Battuta does not distinguish between Christian and Muslim in his generalization, but the example that he gives of immorality definitely concerns a Muslim. As we have seen, the Qur'an forbade the prostituting of slave girls, yet here the qadi of Lādhiq had supposedly taken up this practice without any qualm. Perhaps he had few scruples about this because the girls were not Muslims. The fact that they were Christians should not be surprising; Christians were the majority, and girls would have been included in the booty taken in continuous Muslim raids and conquests.

In one of the anonymous Ottoman chronicles written in the fifteenth century, it is recorded that a certain dervish or mystic named Ak Bıyık Dede (White Mustache Grandfather [in the sense of an elder of a mystical order]), who lived near Yenişehir in Northwestern Anatolia in the reign of Murad I (761–91/1360–89), preached against the "fornication" and pederasty that prevailed among the Muslim religious leaders of Bursa, the main Ottoman capital from 726/1326 to 805/1402.[36] Meanwhile, the Byzantine emperor John VI Cantacuzene (d. 1383) had given up his throne and retired to a monastery, where he wrote his *History* concerning the years 1320–56. In it he described—in somewhat classic Christian polemical form—the unrestrained hedonism of Muslim life, which included the custom of prostitution.[37] On the other hand, another eighth/fourteenth-century writer, Qāḍī Aḥmad of Niğde in South-Central Anatolia, mentions a certain Turkish sheikh named Taptuk whose followers supposedly practiced sexual hospitality, offering their daughters, sisters, and wives to guests. Taptuk was apparently a Kızılbaş Shīʿī; this is therefore the earliest Sunni accusation of such a practice against the Kızılbaş, who were then found in Anatolia, and is among the evidence that at least some Turks, from Central Asia to Anatolia, had practiced sexual hospitality.[38] It is difficult to know what to make of all these assertions, although they do suggest that in the social and sexual atmosphere of the time men and women mixed rather freely and prostitution would have been easily accommodated.

Following the death of al-Rūmī in 672/1273, his tomb in Konya became a place of pilgrimage which attracted people from all religious backgrounds and walks of life. I have not, however, discovered any reference to public women who offered their services to visitors. By then there were also many other places in Anatolia that attracted Muslim and Christian pilgrims, but again I have found no references to prostitutes at these sites.[39]

Crowds, especially of men, were also drawn to periodic fairs that were held in various places in Anatolia. One of the most important was an international market called Yabanlu Pazarı at present-day Pazar Ören, about 100 kilometers east of Kayseri. We know it was functioning in the latter part of the seventh/thirteenth century, but we have no references to women engaged in the sex trade there.[40] About 20 kilometers (less than a day's march) west of Yabanlu Pazarı was a great caravanserai, Karatay Hanı, which included a bath. During the fair, prostitutes may have used it as a major place of business.

As their presence in caravanserais indicates, public women must have been omnipresent in commercial centers, and it is highly likely that they were taxed. This must have been the case from Byzantine times through the end of the Seljuk period. The Mongol Il-Khānids, who turned the sultanate into a puppet state, had introduced a tax (*tamgha*, a word of Turkish origin) on commercial services, including prostitution, into Southwest Asia during the reign of Hülegü (654–63/1256–65). This tax may have been as high as 10 percent before Ghazan (r. 694–703/1295–1304) reduced it by half.[41] Presumably the Il-Khānids extended this tax into the part of Anatolia that fell under their control. As we will see, prostitution was taxed by the Ottomans.

Before passing on to the continuity of the sex trade under the Ottomans, a few words are in order about prostitution and the properties included in pious endowments (*waqfs*) in the sultanate. We are fortunate to have a large number of *waqf* documents dating from seventh/thirteenth- and eighth/fourteenth-century Anatolia, although unfortunately most have not been published. Those that are accessible indicate that the *waqfs* of the Seljuk period contained large numbers of "shops" and frequently caravanserais, some with many residences, and public baths. It is difficult to believe that some of these shops and—in light of how they functioned—caravanserais did not house places of prostitution that generated funds for the institutions supported by the endowments.

The richest and most extensive endowment document known to us so far from the Seljuk period is that of Nūr al-Dīn Ibn Jājā. He first appears around the middle of the seventh/thirteenth century as the *amīr* of Sultanyüği (Eskişehir) in Western Anatolia. In 659/1261 he was appointed *amīr* of Kırşehir in Central Anatolia. He was on good terms with al-Rūmī, who mentions him in his writings. In 675/1277, the Mamlūk sultan Baybars invaded Anatolia in anticipation of an uprising there against the Mongols. This uprising failed to materialize, but Baybars defeated the Mongols and their Seljuk allies.[42] In the course of this action, he captured Ibn Jājā, who was collaborating with the Mongols. The *amīr* was later released, and disappears from the sources after 667/1278.[43] Ibn Jājā acquired enormous wealth. He used it to endow many institutions, including mosques and *madrasas* in various cities. One of the properties in his *waqf* was all the houses called

"Arman Khān" (the Khan of the Armenians) located next to the public bath built by the sultan outside the Laranda Gate of Konya.[44] This would have been an ideal location for a brothel. It is interesting to see that some of the endowments from the Seljuk period were used to support caravanserais.[45] Thus, if these facilities were also used as places of prostitution—which was common practice, as we have seen—they would have been at least in part tantamount to purpose-built brothels. In other words, one of the "charitable" institutions established or supported for the public good, along with mosques, *madrasas*, and hospitals, would have been houses of prostitution!

The early Ottoman period

As with my discussion of prostitution in Egypt and Syria, I would like to say a few words about this trade under Ottoman rule until around the end of the seventeenth century. Again, this will make it possible to highlight continuity of practice. Here the focus will have to be on the Ottoman capital, Istanbul, and some parts of Ottoman Europe, because I have not yet discovered any references to the sex trade in Anatolia in the early centuries of Ottoman rule (the fifteenth through seventeenth centuries).[46] Presumably the attitudes and official regulations concerning prostitution in the capital would also have been reflected in the regions of Anatolia that were nearby. In any case, documentation of this trade is not especially forthcoming until the eighteenth century. It is found mainly in the Ottoman archives and once again concerns, above all, Istanbul.[47]

The official Ottoman position on the sex trade from at least the early sixteenth century can be found in contemporary legal texts. In an important article, Colin Imber has studied the status of prostitution in Ottoman secular law (*qānūn*), as embodied in the Ottoman Criminal Code of *c.* 1540, and compared it with that in the sharia, specifically Ḥanafī law, which the Ottomans followed. He notes that the two forms of law overlapped to some degree, and determines that by the sixteenth century most Ottoman jurists considered prostitution to be legal, "probably on the grounds that it is pointless to legislate against the inevitable." While accepting the legality of this business, the *qānūn*, like the sharia, made procuring an offense. A woman procurer was to be whipped and fined one *akçe* (a small silver coin) per stroke; or a "person" who procured was subject to the same penalty and exposure to public scorn; or the procuress or procurer, and perhaps the woman on whose behalf they acted, could be branded on the forehead. There is clearly some equivocation here. A judge (qadi) could banish a public woman from her district or village if her neighbors complained of her activities. This was the most common reaction by officials to the complaints of neighbors, and was not intended to be punishment so much as maintaining public decency in accordance with public opinion.[48] In short, the legal status of prostitution under the Ottomans generally conformed to that under earlier Muslim dynasties in the regions that we have examined. Furthermore, it was standard practice of the Ottoman state, like others, to tax any activity that generated income. Thus the sale of sexual favors was simply regarded as another source of taxation. In some instances the amount might be called a "fine," but the effect was the same.[49]

Although prostitution was legal, this did not necessarily stop officials from taking severe measures against public women on their own account. A brutal example of this was reported by the leading Ottoman historian of the sixteenth century, Mustafa Âli (d. 1600), a secretary in the Ottoman inner circle. The fact that he mentions it at all in his great history *Kunh al-akhbār* is probably an indication that such measures were unusual. Under circumstances that are not clearly explained, he says that the grand vizier Lütfi Pasha, who took office in 1539, had the vulva of a prostitute cut out in the sultan's council chamber (*dîvân-ı pâdişâhî*). This action outraged Lütfi's wife, Şah Sultan, who was the sister of Sultan Süleyman the Magnificent. When she protested, he insisted that he would continue to inflict this punishment on prostitutes, and beat her when she lost her temper at him. Şah Sultan then complained to her brother, who had apparently been in Edirne at the time, and demanded a divorce. Süleyman granted her request and dismissed Lütfi from office. This occurred in 1541.[50]

We have mentioned several times that one rationalization for prostitution, both Christian and Muslim, was that public women helped to protect respectable women. This is the earliest reference to come to light in this study in which we get a glimpse of how respectable women might view their "protectors." It is obvious that Şah Sultan did not believe that prostitutes should be subjected to brutal punishment, but we cannot be sure if she felt they should be left alone. This does seem to be the case, however, in another somewhat similar incident that occurred a few decades later. It was reported by John Sanderson, who arrived in Istanbul in 1584 and served as the secretary of the English embassy, and concerned Safiye, the mother of Sultan Mehmed III (r. 1595–1603). One day, according to Sanderson,

> The queene Mother, with the Grand Sultana and other of the Grand Signiors women, walking in their seraglio espied a number of boates upon the river [the Bosphorus] hurrying together. The Queene Mother sent to enquire of the matter; who was told that the Vizier did justice upon certain chabies (*kahpe*), that is, whoores. Shee, taking displeasure, went word and advised the eunuch Bassa that her sonne [absent on campaign] had left him to govern the citie and not to devoure the women, commanding him to looke well to the other business and not to meddle any more with the women till his masters return.[51]

The vizier and eunuch "Bassa" (Pasha) here were the same person, the grand vizier and eunuch Hadım Hasan Pasha. Sanderson seems to be saying that Safiye, the sultan's wife, and other important women in the palace, noticed a large commotion of boats on the Bosphorus. When Safiye asked what was happening, she was told that the vizier had drowned some prostitutes.[52] Angered at this, she rebuked him, saying this was none of his business, and demanded that he return to his proper task of governing the capital. Like Lütfi Pasha, Hadım Hasan Pasha was acting on his own authority. The compassion here for women in the sex trade by women at the top of the social and political pyramid is certainly remarkable.

For the seventeenth century, most of the information that we have so far on prostitution in Istanbul and nearby regions comes from the great traveler Evliya Chelebi, whom we have encountered above on several occasions. Before mentioning his observations, however, it is curious to note another writer's experience. Louis Gédoyun, who spent the years 1605–10 with the French ambassador Salignac in Istanbul and who in 1623–4 served as the French consul in Aleppo, gives a brief account of the Turkish legal system in his *Journal et correspondence,* and says that it provided for temporary marriage. He states in fact that he and many other Christians availed themselves of it and he highly approved of it. Gédoyun writes in his correspondence that he is inserting a contract for such a marriage, but it is unfortunately lacking.[53]

As for Evliya, despite his great powers of observation, curiosity, and detailed treatment of countless subjects, he is tight-lipped about the sex trade in Istanbul, his hometown. While describing the capital in the 1630s, he limits his account of public women to only a few lines. Speaking of the city of Galata, which was on the north side of the Golden Horn and opposite Istanbul proper, he says:

> Along the edge of the sea and at Ortahisar are two hundred multi-storied taverns for the dissolute. Each one caters to five or six hundred depraved people devoted to pleasure and drinking. There is such a tumult with singing and music that it defies description."[54]

Galata was the main harbor for Istanbul and was teeming with sailors, soldiers, and merchants.[55] It was also where the European community resided. The city was surrounded by walls; Ortahisar, or "Middle Castle," may refer to one of the towers along these walls.[56] Presumably prostitutes sold their favors in these taverns for the "depraved." A few paragraphs later, Evliya remarks that Greeks operated the taverns while Jews were the "go-betweens in the market of love."[57] This is his way of saying they served as procurers.

About four kilometers north of Galata on the European shore of the Bosphorus was the village of Ortaköy. It was, as now, a popular resort. Evliya states that the public bath of Ortaköy was for prostitutes. They had their own bath just like members of other professions and groups both inside and outside the walls of Istanbul. Moreover, he says that this bath was built by one Hüsrev Kethüda, the steward of Kara Ahmed Pasha (d. 1555), who was a grand vizier under Süleyman. The architect was none other than Sinan (d. 1588), the greatest of all Ottoman architects. Evliya remarks that it was a delightful building and the bath attendants were "beloved" (*mahbûb*, a term also used for catamites).[58] This building is still standing today.[59] It is not clear from Evliya whether public women went to this bath for their own relaxation, or to entertain clients, or both. His reference to it in a list of baths specific to various professions and groups seems to imply the former, although this would mean that women in the sex trade had their own resort. Included in his list are baths for drunks, thieves, and beloveds (here no doubt meaning catamites).

It is difficult to know how much to deduce or infer from the fact that public women relaxed or carried on their business in such an elegant structure. Because this place was set aside for them, we can certainly claim that this is evidence that they were accepted, legally and socially, as part of the fabric of society. This may also be an indication that at least some prostitutes had considerable wealth and influence. Was Ortaköy a place where the rich and powerful in Istanbul could dally with them away from prying eyes? Many of the professions which had their own baths were organized into guilds. Evliya does not, however, include prostitutes in his description of these organizations.

It is worth mentioning that Evliya classifies one group of khans as *bekârhâne* ("bachelor quarters"), of which there were dozens in various places in Istanbul, and claims they could accommodate thousands of men. He says that their residents could be non-bachelors as well as bachelors. They were tradesmen, merchants (especially those who came from afar), and even the unemployed. In short, these men could be from almost any background, but these particular khans appear to have been connected with market life and transit trade. The doors were chained at night and there were doormen in charge of the rooms.[60] Such large concentrations of men, above all single men, would have obviously provided ideal business opportunities for public women. No reference to prostitutes catering directly to the men in these quarters has yet come to light.

On the western edge of Istanbul, Evliya describes the meadow of Kağıthane, through which a pleasant stream flowed into the Golden Horn, as a place of excursion and merrymaking reminiscent of al-Maqrīzī's account of the islands in the Nile opposite Cairo. Every form of entertainment was found there. When Evliya speaks of it as a favorite meeting place for lovers, he only refers to young men, whom he admired, but public women must certainly have been available there as well.[61]

Evliya made a number of extensive journeys into Anatolia and spent many years there altogether. In the course of these travels, he wrote detailed accounts of many cities and their inhabitants, chiefly in Eastern and Central Anatolia. Nevertheless, he mentions nothing about the sex trade. As was the case in Istanbul, he says there were many *bekârhânes* (*hân-ı mücerredân*) in Bursa, but again he makes no connection between them and public women.[62] We only find prostitutes in connection with his account of the battle between Âbaza Hasan Pasha and Murtazâ Pasha. The former was the governor of Diyarbakır in the east, who in 1658 revolted on the pretext of demanding the dismissal of the grand vizier and marched on Bursa, and the latter was head of the army sent against him. Hasan Pasha defeated Murtazâ Pasha at the end of 1658. Afterward, 70 slave girls in the retinue of Murtazâ Pasha fell into the hands of the rabble in Hasan Pasha's army. When they were brought before him, he said, "Isn't Murtazâ Pasha a disgrace? What a brave man he is! He should be the object of universal scorn for having so many prostitutes in the army of Islam in order to satisfy the evil of the flesh."[63] During his life, Evliya accompanied many armies and participated in many battles, but this seems to be his only reference of any kind to prostitutes in the Ottoman army while on the march. Certainly they accompanied it, which would be further evidence for the legitimacy of their trade.

Evliya's other references to prostitution concern places in the Ottoman Empire in Europe. His most detailed account of public women relates to Sofia, the capital of the province of Rumeli, which included all of modern-day Greece, Bulgaria, and other territory. It was the largest and most important Ottoman province in Europe. In 1652 Evliya was in Sofia in the service of his distant cousin and patron Melek Ahmed Pasha, who had been made governor of Rumeli. He prefaces his words about prostitutes in that city with the salacious story of an outlaw and rogue named Uşkurta

Debbağ-oğlu. When a bit drunk, the scoundrel went to see a married lady friend. As Evliya states in typical euphemistic fashion, "Just as he was shuttling on her loom like a master weaver, the lady's husband suddenly entered and saw that the workshop was in full swing."[64] The husband then attacked them with a sword and dragged them outside. They reached a place called Bana-başı, the gathering place of Sofia's mystics, where some janissaries were arguing over a woman. This woman was "the original whore" of Debbağ-oğlu. Freeing himself from his captor, Debbağ-oğlu tried to rescue her, but the janissaries then drew their swords and killed them both.[65] Apart from confirming the presence of public women in Sofia, this tale shows that they provided their services to troops in garrison, again a necessity that ensured the legality of their trade.

Immediately after the death of Debbağ-oğlu, Melek Ahmed Pasha banished all the prostitutes of Sofia from town. Furthermore, Evliya says,

> A few of them, by leave of the *Sharia* and for the reform of the world, were strung up like chandeliers to adorn the town at the street corners in the silk market. The notables of the province were grateful that their town was now tranquil and free of prostitutes. But the rogues and the brigands, for the sake of their carnal pleasures, bruited it about that the town's resources had grown scarce, and there would now be famine and dearth, even plague. And indeed—by God's wisdom—the plague did begin to spread in the city from day to day.[66]

Why Melek Ahmed Pasha decided to execute a few women is not stated. He did not do so because prostitution was illegal, and even if he justified his action based on sacred law, he was still acting on his own authority. Moreover, a man in his position could have easily found a qadi willing to justify his action by issuing a fatwa authorizing it on religious grounds. Perhaps he meant to frighten public women into leaving town in response to complaints, which may in fact have been based on concerns that the women were attracting too many ruffians. The women who were hanged supposedly on the basis of sacred law were presumably Muslims, because Islamic law would not have applied to Christians. The great majority of the population of Sofia, however, was Christian; perhaps only Christian prostitutes were banned.

Before relating the Debbağ-oğlu affair and its consequences, Evliya had claimed that, according to a certain "innovation," in Sofia there were

> several thousand loose women[67] who do go out every night to "wash themselves" or "do their laundry." They put their clothes in a bundle, get permission from their so-called husbands, take lanterns and go to the *bana* [hot springs] or some other house and "wash their soiled clothes." It is a disgraceful practice, peculiar to this city. Our lord Melek Ahmed Pasha wanted to put an end to the practice but the notables of the province would not let him. So every night women of this sort gad about in groups until morning.[68]

Here Evliya must be speaking of Christians. Moreover, the "notables of the province" must have included members of the Christian elite.

A few years later in 1657, Evliya headed south with Melek Ahmed Pasha from Aq Kirman, on the west bank of the Dniester estuary on the Black Sea, to repair the fortress of Kili on the north side of the Danube Delta. Within the delta they came to Snake Island, which was swarming with insects. There, on the road, they encountered three naked prostitutes who had been abandoned by the ruler of Kili. Two had died from mosquito bites and the third was barely alive. Saying, "they got what they deserved" (*Aleyhi mâ-yestahik*), Evliya continued his journey.[69] He does not tell us how he came by his information about these women; perhaps the one who was barely alive told him of their fate. Whatever the case, he seems to have had no pity for them.

At the end of 1659, Evliya participated in an Ottoman campaign in Moldavia, then an Ottoman vassal state. In the course of describing his adventures, he says that in the city of Jassy, in the central part of the country, prostitutes (who were called *kazda* in the local language) took up residence in the taverns. They wore a kind of satin, velvet, *kâmhâ* (?), and silk skirts and certain high-heeled shoes. The *kazda* showed their beautiful faces, and kept their heads bare and their black locks disheveled. Each one earned six purses a year for the ruler of Moldavia, a Christian appointed by the sultan. Evliya adds that other women from Jassy visited Istanbul but they wore different clothes, notably blue silk waistbands around silk skirts; thus their dress indicated that they were not prostitutes.[70] The public women were, of course, Christians, and their business was taxed.

In 1665 Evliya visited Bucharest. Among other things, he says there was a caravanserai outside town for Muslims. Right afterward he states that the city had many attractive men and women. The "chaste" girls in particular dyed their locks black with henna, had a seductive gait, and wore yellow shoes. Most girls, he claimed, were prostitutes.[71] He is speaking once more of Christians.

As we saw in the second chapter, Evliya also mentioned that public women flocked to major fairs in the Balkans, notably the one at Fohşan which was held every summer on the border between Wallacia and Moldavia, and at Doyran in the district of Strumitza in Macedonia. He also records this under the year 1665. These prostitutes could have been from any religious or ethnic background and may have been itinerant or traveled seasonally according to the cycle of the fairs.

In the same year Evliya traveled from Moldavia east to the territory of the Khan of the Crimean Tatars. After crossing the Prut, he came to the town of Kishinev. He says it had 17 churches. Scattered about it in vineyards and gardens were mansions (*kasır*) made of logs. Prostitutes came to these places and "sat on the laps of men."[72]

In 1668, our traveler was in Kavala on the north coast of the Aegean. Here too he came across a prostitute in the company of a soldier. In this instance she may have been a gypsy.[73] Later, Evliya took passage to Crete and was there during the Ottoman siege and conquest of Candia (Herakleion) in 1669. Afterward he roamed about the island and reports that there were many public women in the large port of Suda on the north coast.[74] Altogether, Evliya gives us a kind of small random sample of the presence of prostitutes in Ottoman Europe. He must have encountered them in many other places there but not have thought they were worth mentioning. The impression that he gives us, therefore, is that they were a common feature of life.

CONCLUSION

Despite the relatively short period covered in Anatolia and the paucity of sources for this period, what we have learned about the sex trade there parallels that in the other regions examined. We have seen that singing girls worked as prostitutes, and that they could also reach positions of power. Prostitutes were with the armies of the Crusaders who crossed Anatolia, and many were captured by Turks. They also accompanied the Ottoman army. Women sold their favors in ports like Trebizond and in commercial centers like Erzurum. They were available at public baths, and above all caravanserais, where they served the needs of travelers and merchants. Indeed, it is for Anatolia that we have the clearest and most detailed accounts of prostitution in these facilities. Prostitutes worked in caravanserais built by the most powerful figures of state, and they were blessed in their work by none other than the great mystic al-Rūmī. This indicates that they were not only accepted in society but also had an important role in it. Their business was not illegal; late references to the punishment of public women concern officials acting on their own authority. Moreover, the seemingly relaxed sexual ambiance of Anatolia would have been conducive to the sex trade. In other words, prostitution was ubiquitous and people were generally indifferent to it. The surviving *waqf* documents again suggest, with some ambiguity, that prostitutes may have worked from endowed properties and generated revenue for pious purposes. Their business was surely taxed, as was the case by the time of the Ottomans. Unfortunately, we are told little about the women in the trade, who are mostly anonymous, but we know that many were slave girls who were owned and managed by other women. Ibn Battuta tells us specifically that it was a common practice to prostitute Greek slave girls. Because the great majority of the population was Christian, most prostitutes were probably Christian as well. Finally, we have remarkable evidence that respectable ladies at the highest level of society, in the Ottoman court itself, viewed public women sympathetically.

EXCURSUS

Prostitution as an Incentive to Long-Distance Trade

We have seen earlier that prostitution was practiced in caravanserais and inns along the major overland trade routes in the regions that we have studied. Frequently located a day's march apart, these institutions were oases of security, provisioning, lodging, relaxation, and entertainment for travelers, merchants, and caravan conductors, who could be away from home for months or years. The hardships and dangers they faced on the road could be many, including harsh weather, bandits, and marauding armies. Knowing that female comfort awaited them in caravanserais and inns along their routes would certainly have made their journeys easier to bear. Thus it could be said that prostitution in caravanserais and inns provided an incentive to long-distance overland trade.

This sexual incentive would have been even more important with respect to long-distance trade by sea. As shown in this study, the sex trade was commonly practiced in the major ports of the Eastern Mediterranean coasts. In fact, public women sold their services in ports all around the Mediterranean, and the same was true in the ports of Arabia, India, and beyond to China. Travel on the open waters of the Mediterranean was slow, and more dangerous than travel by land. Ships tended to stay close to the shore, where they could seek shelter when necessary. Although the lateen sail, which allowed tacking (and therefore sailing against the wind), had been introduced to the Mediterranean from the Indian Ocean by the third/ninth century,[1] convoys still tended to sail with the prevailing winds of the monsoons, going west in the spring and east in the fall. It could take months to sail from one end of the Mediterranean to the other.

Sailing from Red Sea, Arabian, East African, or Persian Gulf ports to India and on to China was just as slow and dangerous.[2] Even with the help of the prevailing monsoon winds, it could take six months for a ship departing Arabia to reach Canton, the primary destination of the sea trade to China.[3] Travelers, merchants, and sailors could therefore be away from home and out of touch for more than a year. For these men, like those traveling with caravans, the lack of female companionship for such long periods would have been a hardship compounded by all the potential hazards of the voyage: insufficient provisions, bad weather, shipwrecks, getting lost in unfamiliar waters, pirates, and so forth. These intrepid voyagers risked their lives in the pursuit of profit from trade, more so than men traveling by land. It is therefore easy to posit that the knowledge that feminine comfort was available at ports along—and at the end of—their trade routes helped them to tolerate the many hardships that they endured. Indeed, the prospect of finding women during a voyage must have been an important lure, and may even have been regarded as a form of compensation.

Furthermore, it would have been in the interests of the rulers of the major ports to encourage local prostitution. On the one hand, the presence of public women at the ports would have attracted merchants with their rich trade goods; on the other, by encouraging the merchants (not to mention the sailors) to spend freely on sexual favors, the prostitutes would have relieved the visitors of additional hard currency. This would have given an additional boost to the local economy, and no doubt to the tax revenue of the rulers as well.[4] Altogether, prostitution was a business that was good for business, in particular as an important incentive for—or stimulus to—"international" or "global" trade. In this respect, women played a significant role in economic history, and one which has not been fully appreciated until now.

THE SEXUAL ATTRACTIONS OF THE INDIES

With reference to India and the Far East, the earliest—and in some ways the most intriguing—travel accounts are *Akhbār al-Ṣīn wa 'l-Hind* (Tales of China and India) and *Kitāb 'Ajā'ib al-Hind* (The Book of the Marvels of India). The first is a modern conventional title designating two untitled narratives, a primary text and a sequel. Both are recollections of voyages to the East and concern China and India. The primary text, often ascribed to a certain Sulaymān the Merchant, was composed in 237/851. The sequel was written by one Abū Zayd al-Ḥasan ibn Yazīd, from the port of Sīrāf on the Iranian coast of the Persian Gulf, around 303/916.[5] Whereas Sulaymān has nothing to say about the attractions of women in the Indies, Abū Zayd, who gives much space to sailors' stories, makes the following remarks about Ceylon:

> A great [sexual] corruption (*fasād*) reigns unchecked in this country among both women and men. This is to the extent that sometimes a foreign merchant makes demands on one of the women of the country and even on the daughter of the king; and she, giving her consent and with her father's knowledge, goes to meet the merchant in a wooded place. The elderly men among the merchants of Sīrāf avoid sending their ships to this country especially when they have young sailors aboard.[6]

The second travel account, *Kitāb 'Ajā'ib al-Hind*, was written by Buzurg ibn Shahriyār, a Persian ship captain. It is a collection of stories and anecdotes in Arabic taken from traders and seafarers who sailed the Indian Ocean. Most are of the nature of sailors' yarns, with some reliable information included here and there, and sometimes the year for the event under discussion is given, the latest being 342/953. The narrators were especially interested in the marvels of the natural world, but they do make a few references to the exotic women that they encountered. Perhaps the most provocative is the description of the mysterious island of women somewhere beyond India. There, throngs of women fell upon any men who came ashore and carried them off to the mountains, where they had their way with them.[7] One wonders if this is a vague allusion to hordes of public women who met the ships that dropped anchor in the ports of India and beyond.[8] At the very least, such stories would certainly have stimulated a desire for adventure among many men who traveled by sea.

Not until the eighth/fourteenth century do we find more accurate and detailed information from Muslim sources on the sexual attractions of the Indies. The most important of these sources is Ibn Battuta, who went all the way to China and who, it must be stated, acquired various wives and slave girls along the way. In 742/1341, after spending some time in Delhi, he departed for China. Heading southeast, he passed through the large town of Marh, where the Hindu women were "exceedingly beautiful and famous for their charms in intercourse and the amount of pleasure that they give. So also are the women of the Marhata and of the Maldive Islands."[9] He went on to reach the port of Cambay on the Gulf of Khambhat on the northwest coast of India, then traveled south along the coast. From Southern India he went to the Maldive Islands, which by his time had become Muslim, arriving around the end of 744/1343. Here, he reiterates the charms of the native women, remarking that the diet of the natives had "an amazing and unparalleled effect in sexual intercourse, and the people of these islands perform wonders in this respect." He adds,

> I had there myself four wives, and concubines as well, and I used to visit all of them every day and pass the night with the wife whose turn it was, and this I continued to do the whole year and a half that I was there.[10]

If a visitor wished to marry a local woman, he could do so, but he had to divorce her when he left.[11] In Ibn Battuta's view, when ships arrived the crews simply arranged temporary marriages. Indeed, it was easy to "marry" because of the smallness of the dowries and the "pleasure of their women's society."[12]

Apart from these travel accounts, only a few other references or possible allusions to the sex trade in the Indies during our period can be found in Muslim sources.[13] For example, the well-known Arab *littérateur* al-Jāḥiẓ of

Basra reports in his *Kitāb al-Ḥayawān* (Book of Animals), written before 233/847, that if a woman used a suppository of elephant dung after mixing it with some honey, she would not conceive, and that the prostitutes in India did this in order to keep their customers.[14] The extent to which this practice was common to India is not stated, and al-Jāḥiẓ may have learned this from someone who had sailed from Basra to India. One of the earliest geographers to write in Arabic, Ibn Khurradādhbih (d. 309/911), a contemporary of al-Jāḥiẓ who grew up in Baghdad, says in his *Kitāb al-Masālik wa 'l-mamālik* (Book of Itineraries and Kingdoms), "The kings of India and its people permit fornication (*zinā'*) [...] except for the king of Qumār who forbids fornication."[15] Such a broad assertion is difficult to interpret, but presumably "fornication" here includes prostitution. In the first part of his *Murūj al-dhahab*, composed in 332/943, al-Mas'ūdī has an interesting comment on the women of the kingdom of al-Ṭāfin, which was on the Bay of Bengal and next to the kingdom of Rahmā (Pegu, near modern Rangoon). He says they were the whitest and most beautiful and gracious women of India. They were mentioned in the books on sexual desire (*kutub al-bāh*) and sailors contended with each other in "purchasing them."[16] Another geographer, the Persian Ḥamd Allāh al-Mustawfī al-Qazwīnī (d. after 740/1339–40), who was a financial director for the Il-Khānids in Iran, gives a curious account of the island of Niyās, which was off the northwest coast of Sumatra, in his *Nuzhat al-qulūb* (Hearts' Bliss). He says it was densely populated by a handsome people. Because of their attractiveness, "our folk often catch the women here and keep them in bonds, begetting children from them; but when occasion befalls, most of these women, having no true affection for their offspring, escape and flee away."[17] One wonders if Ḥamd Allāh is saying that men, traders and sailors from the Il Khānid state captured and prostituted the women?

THE SEXUAL ATTRACTIONS OF CHINA

As for China, Sulaymān the Merchant simply says "the Chinese are debauched."[18] Presumably this claim is based on experience in (or reports from) Chinese ports. Abū Zayd, however, is rather prolific in his account of institutionalized prostitution in China. He states:

> In China there are women who do not want to lead virtuous lives and who prefer to devote themselves to prostitution (*zinā'*). According to the custom, they apply to the chief of police and declare to him that they do not have any desire for the life of a virtuous woman and that they prefer to be registered as a prostitute (*zānī*), undertaking to follow the legal regulations that apply to such registered women. The regulations that apply to such registered women are the following: she is registered in writing by her origin, her sign [description], and her place of residence; and she is recorded in the bureau of prostitutes. Around her neck is placed a cord from which hangs a copper seal bearing the imprint of the royal seal. She is also given a certificate testifying that the person named in it is a registered prostitute, that she will pay annually to the royal treasure a specified sum in copper, and that whoever would marry her would be put to death. [Afterward,] the woman pays annually the agreed amount and she is free, without danger, to engage in prostitution.[19]

Again, Abū Zayd's account must be based on contacts with Chinese ports. His description of the availability of sensual delights in China is confirmed by a later and distinctly non-Muslim source, the renowned Venetian Marco Polo (d. 1324). He made two trips to China, in 1266 and 1275. On the second, he remained in the country many years and became a favorite of the Mongol emperor Kublai Khan, who ruled from Khan Balik (Beijing). Despite the huge gap in time between Abū Zayd and Marco Polo, their accounts of prostitution in China have much in common. Speaking of Khan Balik, which was not far from the coast, Polo says,

> Let me tell you also that no sinful woman dares live within the city, unless it be in secret—no woman of the world, that is, who prostitutes her body for money. But they all live in the suburbs, and there are so many of them that no one could believe it. For I assure you

> that there are fully 20,000 of them, all serving the needs of men for money. They have a captain general, and there are chiefs of hundreds and of thousands responsible to the captain. This is because, whenever ambassadors come to the Great Khan on his business and are maintained at his expense, which is done on a lavish scale, the captain is called upon to provide one of these women every night for the ambassador and one for each of his attendants.[20] They are changed every night and receive no payment; for this is the tax they pay to the Great Khan. From the number of these prostitutes you may infer the number of traders and other visitors who are daily coming and going here about their business.[21]

Furthermore, describing the city of Kinsai, which he says meant "City of Heaven" and was located far to the south of Khan Balik on the coast near modern-day Shanghai, he says:

> Other streets are occupied by women of the town, whose number is such that I do not venture to state it. These are not confined to the neighbourhood of the squares—the quarter usually assigned to them—but are to be found throughout the city, attired with great magnificence, heavily perfumed, attended by many handmaids and lodged in highly ornamented apartments. These ladies are highly proficient and accomplished in the use of endearments and caresses, with words suited and adapted to every sort of person, so that foreigners who have once enjoyed them remain utterly beside themselves and so captivated by their sweetness and charm that they can never forget them. So it comes about that, when they return home, they say they have been in "Kinsai," that is to say, in the city of Heaven, and can scarcely wait for the time when they may go back there.[22]

From this report, it certainly appears that the sex trade was big business in this large port. Indeed, it is clear that public women catered to merchants in both Khan Balik and Kinsai. Needless to say, even if Abū Zayd and (above all) Marco Polo are exaggerating, one can imagine what effect mere rumors of such attractions would have had in the ports scattered between China and Europe.

Ibn Battuta, who reached China about a century later, is much more subdued than these two writers in his account of the availability of women for merchants and other visitors. He disembarked at Quanzhou (Zaitun) on the coast opposite Taiwan around the end of 746/1345. Speaking of the Chinese, he says:

> Slave-girls are cheap in price, but all the Chinese sell their sons and daughters, and it is not thought shameful among them. They do not all the same compel them to travel with their purchasers, nor do they prevent them if they wish to do so. So if the foreign merchant wants to marry, he gets married, but there is no way he can spend his money on debauchery. They say: "We do not want it said in the Muslim countries that they lose their money in our country, and that it is the land of debauchery and fleeting pleasure."[23]

In sharp contrast to Ibn Battuta, the merchant and traveler 'Alī Akbar Khiṭā'ī, who may have been Iranian or even a Chinese Muslim, later portrayed in detail the practice of prostitution in China on a scale surpassing that even found in Marco Polo. He traveled to China at the beginning of the sixteenth century and then, after going to Istanbul, wrote an account of his journey in 1516. This account, entitled *Khiṭāynāma* (The Book of China), was originally in Persian, but it was translated into Ottoman Turkish in 1582.[24] Later, Katib Chelebî incorporated extracts from it, including the description of prostitution, into the second version of his great geographical panorama of the world, *Kitâb-ı Cihânnümâ*, which he worked on between 1648 and his death in 1657.[25] It reads:

> *Law of prostitutes*: There are separate districts for prostitutes in every city of Khitay [China]. The smallest such district is 500 houses; districts of 1000 houses also exist. Most of the prostitutes are daughters of *beys* [lords] and notables who were found guilty of a crime, imprisoned and executed. Their sons become soldiers at a low rank.

Their wives and daughters are banished to the brothels and they never see each other again. Their lineage dies out. One such crime is to establish a relationship with the prostitutes in these brothels.

If there is a drought and the prayer for rain becomes necessary, these prostitutes do it. The amount of rain and snow that falls in every province and the amount of crops sown are presented to the Khaqan [ruler]. Wherever lack of rain is reported, a decree comes ordering the prayer for rain. Then these women bid farewell to their retainers and go to the temple (*kilise*—lit. "church") of the province where the prayer is to be performed. If rain does not fall after the prayer for rain, the governor of the province puts to death as many of these women as he wishes, on the grounds that they were previously condemned to death; because when they are banished to the brothels, it is on condition that they will be put to death if their prayer for rain is not accepted.

In the temple, the women are given a meatless diet from the pious endowment for a time, based on the belief that they are purified by this. Then the temple musicians and singers take their seats and strike up various songs and melodies. The temple dancers dance to exhaustion, then get up in groups and weep and lament before the idol; to such a degree that God[26] has mercy on those miserable ones and responds to their entreaties. At times so much rain falls that some places are flooded.

It is for this reason that the Khitay sages frighten the prostitutes with the death penalty, so that when they cry and lament and pray for rain out of fear for their lives, God[27] will overlook their sin committed out of ignorance and will grant rain. The Muslim jurists as well have permitted the prayer for rain of unbelievers, based on the abundance of divine mercy. So the sages have laid down the law in this manner. And sometimes if it does not rain and drought continues, they sacrifice some of those prostitutes.

Schools have been built for the children of those women in the brothels. They teach the girls musical instruments and singing and the boys dancing and various amusements and games.

> These women go about in the markets, playing music and singing, and dancing with wine glasses. Those who draw a salary from the Khaqan may not converse or drink with them; if caught, they are put to death. Most of those who go to them are craftsmen and merchants, and quite a few dissipate their wealth in those brothels. If they become impoverished and go begging, as a rebuke no one gives them a penny and they starve to death. And when one of that sort dies, they throw him into the sea.
>
> These prostitutes have strange and marvelous amusements. Their women are tightrope walkers. They put on strange garb and perform marvelous deeds.[28]

For travelers to China, prostitutes were therefore readily available and inexpensive.

THE SEXUAL ATTRACTIONS OF EUROPE

No less than those of Asia, the sexual attractions of European ports would also have been a spur to travelers, merchants, and sailors from the Eastern Mediterranean world. Moreover, they were much closer, more frequented, and better known.[29] We shall only note here two examples in passing. With regard to the great emporium of Constantinople, we have already mentioned the assertion of 'Abd al-Jabbār ibn Aḥmad (d. 415/1025) of Baghdad that the cities of Byzantium had many markets for prostitutes and Michael Psellus' (1018–ca.1078/96) statement that scattered all over Constantinople was a vast multitude of harlots.

Further west, the next great port was Venice, which had close trade relations with Alexandria by the third/ninth century. Prostitution thrived there throughout the Middle Ages. In fact, in 1358 the Grand Council of Venice declared that brothels were indispensable. Two years later the sex trade was further institutionalized when the brothel called the Castelletto was opened in a parish belonging to two patrician families.[30] At the beginning of the sixteenth century, one contemporary Italian chronicler recorded that there were precisely 11,654 prostitutes in Venice, which was about 10 percent of the population.[31] Furthermore, it is worthy of note that, around the same time, courtesans were forbidden to have commerce with infidels (that is, Jews, Muslims, and Moors), which means, of course, that this is exactly what was taking place. In 1507, three women were whipped in public for having slept with Turks.[32]

THE VIEW FROM THE SHIP

Unfortunately, no sources have come down to us from our period that give an idea of the kind of attractions travelers, merchants, caravan conductors, and sailors themselves imagined or expected to find at the end of long voyages. It seems certain, however, that sex was not far from the minds of many (perhaps most?) of them. This can easily be deduced from what we know about the behavior of the crews who sailed with none other than Columbus and Magellan, captains who set out for the Indies several centuries later but by quite different routes. Nevertheless, the situation of their crews was analogous to that of those who plied the seas between Southwest Asia and China.

In 1492 Columbus set out from Spain on the first of four voyages to the New World. From his first landfall until his death, he firmly believed that he had reached the Indies. On the first voyage, which was into the unknown and often frightening, he sailed for more than two months before reaching the Caribbean. By the time he returned to Spain, he had been gone more than six months. Initially the native Arawak people received him and his men favorably. The Europeans were able to trade trifles such as brass bells and bits of glass and pottery for provisions and small amounts of gold. It is clear from Columbus' logs and the reports of his officers that soon more than provisions and gold were being traded; the Europeans were sex-hungry.[33] There are hints of this in the records from the first voyage, and it is very clear in the accounts of the second voyage in late 1493. Michele de Cuneo, Columbus' boyhood friend who was on the second voyage, states the following:

> I captured a very beautiful woman, whom the Lord Admiral gave to me. When I had taken her to my cabin she was naked—as was their custom. I was filled with a desire to take my pleasure with her and attempted to satisfy my desire. She was unwilling, and so treated me with her nails that I wished I had never begun. I then took a piece of rope and whipped her soundly, and she let fourth such incredible screams that you would not have believed your ears. Eventually we came to such terms, I assure you, that you would have thought she had been brought up in a school for whores.[34]

The behavior of the men in Magellan's expedition was no different. He set out from Spain in 1519 on an even more dangerous adventure. This one resulted in the first circumnavigation of the globe by sailing around the southern tip of South America. After three years of traveling, only one of his five ships had survived, along with 18 of the 237 men who had begun the voyage. It took more than two months for his fleet to reach the coast of Brazil. Several weeks later he entered the bay of modern Rio de Janeiro and dropped anchor. Then, in the words of a recent biographer,

> As Magellan's ships came to rest, a throng of women—all of them naked and eager for contact with the sojourners—swam out to greet them. Deprived of the company of women for months, the sailors believed they had found an earthly paradise. [...] Discovering that the women of Verzin (Brazil) were for sale, the sailors gladly exchanged their cheap German knives for sexual favors. Night after night on the beach the sailors and the Indian women drank, danced, and exchanged partners in moonlit orgies.[35]

For many sailors, this was but a taste of what they imagined to find in the Indies. Some planned to desert their ships on arrival and live in luxury with their accumulated wealth and women. In Cervantes' words, the Indies served as

> the shelter and refuge of Spain's desperadoes, the church of the lawless, the safe haven of murderers, the native land and cover for cardsharps, the general lure for loose women, and the common deception of the many and the remedy of the particular few.[36]

In short, crews expected the availability of sex with native women along their route and regarded it as a form of compensation. They could obtain the favors of these women for objects that were of little or no value to the Europeans.[37] Each "long-term" encounter with such women along the journey was an occasion for sexual gratification. From time to time, such occasions seem to have gotten out of hand, and at Cebu in the heart of the Philippines Magellan attempted to establish certain rules of behavior toward native women. These rules were not, however, effective.[38]

THE VIEW FROM "HOME"

Despite the sexual attractions of the Far East, we should mention here that S. D. Goitein encountered almost no references to sex in any respect in his study of the Geniza documents, which date between the fourth/tenth and seventh/thirteenth centuries and include much correspondence of Jewish traders who had gone from Egypt to India and beyond. He says that the men who composed these documents would have been reluctant to put even the phrase "my wife" on paper.[39] Such extreme prudishness, combined with the commercial nature of the correspondence that arrived from the East, easily explains the lack of references in the Geniza to prostitution. Trysts with public women were not the kind of thing that one wrote home about. Pondering this virtual silence, Goitein wondered how Jewish merchants who could be gone for a year or more dealt with the demands of sexuality. Based on the silence of the Geniza, he concluded that they must have practiced abstinence. This is unconvincing. "Furthermore," he says,

> the rhythm of life was punctuated by the obligatory daily prayers, and for those educated merchants, by regular readings from the holy

> scriptures and sacred law. In other words, the little time left free from business was constantly occupied by religious activities normally pursued in company."[40]

But this is also difficult to believe, for it would have been true of merchants who stayed at home with their wives as well. It is inconceivable to me that many Jewish, Christian, or Muslim merchants who were far from home in a strange land for long periods and who were without their families and free of their usual domestic cultural and group pressures would *not* have enjoyed the services of prostitutes. Indeed, these women were available precisely because they expected these men to seek them. Furthermore, we must keep in mind that in many places in India, such as Kūlam (Quilon), a major port on the southern end of the Malabar coast, these merchants would have come in contact with large numbers of nearly naked women.[41] Goitein himself says he came across one documented case in which a man was suspected of visiting public women in Aden and another in which a man lived with a slave girl, probably an Indian, and then abandoned her in 'Aydhāb on the Red Sea.[42]

We met earlier in Egypt the Mālikī jurist Ibn al-Ḥājj, who was born in Cairo in 737/1336. We saw that in his moralistic work *al-Madkhal* (Introduction [to sacred law]) he described the proper dress for women lest they be taken for prostitutes. In the same book he has a fairly long chapter on the proper behavior of merchants who traded from region to region and from country to country, and their need for the favor of God.[43] He distinguishes between those who traveled by land and those who traveled by sea. With regard to merchants traveling overland, he describes their preparations for travel, such as how to select a riding animal and look after it, what to look for in traveling companions, the necessary pious sayings or prayers for departure and arrival, what to wear, the importance of traveling with a group, and the need for someone to be in charge. When a merchant arrived at a staging point, such as a caravanserai, he should say three times "*a'ūdhu bi-kalimāti 'llāhi 'l-tāmmāti min sharri mā khalaqa*" (I seek protection in God's perfect words from the evil that he [Satan] has created),[44] which certainly suggests that such places could be snares for the righteous.

As for those traveling by sea, they should first say a prayer to help ensure that they would not drown. Furthermore, they should not miss prayer times on ship, travel in bad weather, or be with seamen who were in the habit of showing their genitals. If travel to the lands of unbelievers was unavoidable, one should go in the company of other Muslims in order to avoid being led astray. It was also important to find privacy on the journey. One should avoid playing chess, shooting pellets at birds, or telling amusing stories to pass the time. Despite his obvious puritanical views, Ibn al-Ḥājj does not say anything specific about consorting with local women; perhaps he was too prudish to do so. He provides only a hint of probable disapproval when he says that one should not linger in the market because it is a place teeming with people one does not know and is the place of Satans.[45]

The sexual temptations that Muslim travelers could encounter abroad are reflected in a story from the *Arabian Nights* about a certain ʿAlī from Cairo, who found himself not in a land of unbelievers but in Baghdad. One day he met a splendidly dressed beautiful woman who was brazenly flaunting herself in the market. She rubbed herself against him and suggested that they have an affair, although she was married to a merchant. ʿAlī readily agreed, but as he walked behind her, he said to himself, "How can you do this in a strange city? The proverb has it that those who fornicate while abroad will have their hopes dashed by God."[46] As put in the mouth of ʿAlī, this proverb must have expressed behavior that was, in fact, quite common.

CONCLUSION

Despite the gaps in our sources in both chronology and the coverage of life along overland trade routes and in the major ports of the Indies and beyond, they suffice to suggest strongly, if not entirely prove, that the services of public women were always available in those regions to travelers, merchants, conductors of caravans, and sailors from Southwest Asia. Furthermore, the men concerned knew that female companionship could easily be found virtually everywhere they went. Rumors or exaggerated stories—certainly mixed with some facts—of the sensual delights to be found abroad must have been part of the lore of the staging points for overland trade and the scuttlebutt of all major ports. Needless to say, the same phenomenon would have been current for those traveling from, say, China to Southwest Asia as well as those traveling from Southwest Asia to China, or between the Eastern Mediterranean and Europe or the reverse. In other words, it would have been universal no matter what the direction of travel or origin of the traveler. And given the actual and potential hardships, dangers, and duration of such travel, the expectation of finding sexual satisfaction along and at the end of strenuous journeys must have been an incentive for the men who undertook them. Consequently, the women who served these men helped to promote and maintain long-distance trade and at the same time brought in hard currency to boost their local economies and to generate additional tax revenue for local rulers. Altogether prostitutes played a major role in global economic history, and one which has not yet been fully evaluated.

Summary

In the present study, we have examined the economic and social history of public women in the Eastern Mediterranean world—Arabia, Egypt, Syria, and Anatolia—between approximately 300 and 1500 CE. Public women were prostitutes, one of the few groups of women with a collective identity. They were women who constituted part of the service industry, selling their sexual favors to men, frequently and indiscriminately. A fairly clear account of this industry has emerged from our sources, although it is uneven because of various chronological and geographical gaps. The salient points in this account are the following:

1. In Late Antiquity prostitution was well established in the Eastern Mediterranean world. When that area was under Christian rule, the sale of sexual favors was a legal and institutionalized profession and the government taxed it. Procuring and the prostitution of slave girls, however, were illegal, but these proscriptions were largely ignored. The Church was ambivalent toward it, regarding the trade as immoral while tolerating it in practice.
2. Prostitution was primarily an urban phenomenon. It was practiced in all the large cities, especially in the ports and other commercial hubs.
3. Prostitution thrived where groups (especially large groups) of men gathered. Public women carried on their business in taverns, inns,

public baths, markets, circuses, and theaters. They also flocked to fairs, pilgrimage sites, and holiday locales in search of customers.

4. The clients of prostitutes could come from all walks of life: government officials, merchants, clergy, ascetics, soldiers, sailors, students, farmers, slaves, and travelers. Their ceaseless demand for sexual services was met by both women in need and women who were opportunistic. Prostitution could be a means of upward mobility, and was virtually the only business open to women who tried to live independently of their families.
5. Public women could come from all backgrounds. Some were free, others were slaves. Some worked under management in brothels, while others were independent or itinerant. Brothels were generally run by women. Prostitutes were sometimes married, or gave up the trade and then married. Marriage was a sign of social acceptance.
6. Public women wore distinctive clothing to distinguish them from "respectable" women and to attract customers.
7. When the Eastern Mediterranean world came under Muslim rule, all the aforesaid features of the profession continued to apply, although circuses and theaters disappeared. Indeed, during the first centuries of Muslim rule, when the majority of the population was Christian, the sex trade continued to be mainly in Christian hands.
8. There was no sacred prostitution in pre-Islamic Arabia, but there were numerous forms of cohabitation, of which prostitution was one, and this could take several forms.
9. Prostitution had essentially the same status in Islamic law as in Byzantine law, and was not illegal. Only procuring and prostituting slave girls were prohibited. Moreover, prostitution was distinguished from "fornication." Muslim public women were, in theory, freed from exploitation by men. They were allowed to go about their business on their own and keep their earnings. The execution of two or three procuresses is mentioned in the sources, but no record of punishment for prostitution per se has yet appeared except for the use of banishment and public shaming when neighbors complained. Over the centuries, this profession seems to have been regarded increasingly as

immoral. But what was immoral and what was illegal was not always the same thing.

10. Prostitution was not a threat to the social order. It reinforced it.
11. The coming of Islam brought new opportunities for public women. New places of pilgrimage, especially Mecca, holidays, and trade opportunities appeared. And women were allowed to have their own businesses.
12. Various Muslim states registered and taxed prostitution, which generated considerable income. The amount of the tax on each public woman seems to have been a daily charge equal to the price of her services to one customer. Taxes on prostitution were sometimes farmed out, often to women. In some cases the police collected these taxes, and they also monitored the trade along with the supervisor of the marketplace.
13. From time to time various Muslim rulers attempted to ban prostitution on their own authority, usually for political reasons, but all of these attempts failed. In a few instances an attempt was made to encourage or force public women to marry in order to have them give up their profession. Natural disasters, such as a low Nile or plague, were attributed to divine displeasure with immorality and gave some rulers cause to ban the sex trade, at least temporarily.
14. Prostitution was integrated with many trades and businesses, from dressmakers to the owners of large residential buildings. Many people profited from it directly or indirectly, and altogether public women were a significant component of the economy. This, combined with the continuous demand from men for sex, made its eradication impossible.
15. The rich and powerful, including prominent men in the government and military as well as merchants or entrepreneurs, invested in prostitution. They owned the apartment houses, inns, taverns, and other establishments where prostitutes worked.
16. There is a high likelihood—if not certainty—that some properties included in pious endowments, or *waqfs*, were rented by prostitutes or brothel operators. Thus some earnings from the sex trade would have gone to charitable purposes and such religious institutions as mosques and law schools. Prostitutes could certainly donate alms to the poor.

17. Prostitution was a common profession for women. Indeed, the general populace was indifferent to it. Even some respectable women engaged in it part-time from their homes. By the late Middle Ages, prostitutes may have been organized into guilds in the largest cities.
18. A significant number of prostitutes accompanied the Crusader armies that invaded the lands of the Eastern Mediterranean. Some traveled overland with the troops or arrived with them by ship, while others took passage by sea on their own or were imported by European merchant communities. As camp followers, they provided many services in addition to sexual comfort. The Crusaders sometimes attributed their tribulations or their defeat in battle to immorality with such women. When the Crusaders were defeated in battle, the Muslims sometimes captured prostitutes in their camps, and the reverse may also have been true.
19. Finally, prostitution was an incentive to long-distance trade either overland or by sea. Given the hardships, dangers, and duration of such trade, the knowledge that female comfort was available at major caravan stops and ports of call would have made it much easier to tolerate. The encouragement of prostitution would also have been in the interest of the owners and operators of caravanserais and the rulers of ports. Public women would have helped stimulate the local economy by attracting merchants and their rich goods on the one hand, and by relieving them of hard currency in exchange for their favors on the other.

Notes

List of Abbreviations

AI Annales Islamologiques
EI[2] *Encyclopaedia of Islam, 2nd edition*
EI[3] *Encyclopaedia of Islam, 3rd edition*

Chapter 1: Public Women in the Eastern Mediterranean World in Late Antiquity

1 See James Russell, 'The Persian invasions of Syria/Palestine and Asia Minor in the reign of Heraclius: archeological, numismatic and epigraphic evidence,' pp. 41–71.
2 See Averil Cameron, *The Mediterranean World in Late Antiquity, AD 395–600*, and Mark Whittow, 'The late Roman/early Byzantine Near East,' pp. 72–97.
3 The discussion that follows relies heavily on the material used in Stavroula Leontsini, *Die Prostitution im frühen Byzanz*, which is the only comprehensive study of this subject. For those who are not specialists in this period, her cryptic notes can sometimes be difficult to decipher. Furthermore, she frequently includes passages from original Greek sources without translating them. I have relied throughout on English translations of the original works. Earlier, Phaidon Koukoules had collected references to prostitution in Byzantium in his *Vizantinōn vios kai politismos*, but according to Cyril Mango, 'Daily life in Byzantium,' pp. 337–8, it lacks a sense of historical development.
4 *Dio Chrysostom* (Discourses), vol. 3, p. 207.
5 Christopher Haas, *Alexandria in Late Antiquity: Topography and Social Conflict*, p. 58.

6 *Dio Chrysostom* (Discourses), vol. 3, p. 203.
7 Mango, 'Daily life in Byzantium,' pp. 338, 345. Mango concentrates on the period after the seventh century, but his comments on circuses, theaters, and baths are also germane to earlier centuries. On the layout of Alexandria in our period, see Haas, *Alexandria in Late Antiquity*, pp. 19–44, and Annick Martin, 'Alexandrie à l'époque romaine tardive: l'impact du christianisme sur la topographie et les institutions,' vol. 1, pp. 9–21.
8 *Dio Chrysostom* (Discourses), vol. 3, p. 211.
9 Ibid., p. 217.
10 Ibid., vol. 1, p. 363.
11 Thomas McGinn, *Prostitution, Sexuality, and the Law in Ancient Rome*, pp. 248, 281.
12 Lionel Casson, *Travel in the Ancient World*, p. 155.
13 Sarah Pomeroy, *Goddesses, Whores, Wives, and Slaves: Women in Classical Antiquity*, p. 141.
14 McGinn, *Prostitution, Sexuality, and the Law*, pp. 281–2.
15 Roger Bagnall, 'A trick a day to keep the tax man at bay? The prostitute tax in Roman Egypt,' p. 8; Rebecca Flemming, '*Quae corpore quaestum facit*: the sexual economy of female prostitution in the Roman Empire,' p. 46.
16 Flemming, '*Quae corpore quaestum facit*,' pp. 55–6.
17 Cyril Mango and Roger Scott (trans.), *The Chronicle of Theophanes Confessor: Byzantine and Near Eastern History AD 284–813*, p. 109.
18 Flemming, '*Quae corpore quaestum facit*,' p. 41.
19 There would be a long tradition in the Church of clerics ministering to prostitutes. This is obvious evidence of the enduring demand for the services of these women and their availability—willingly or unwillingly—to provide them. In Byzantium, for example, the monk Nikodemos, who was born during the reign of Andronikos II (1282–1328) and later joined a monastery in Thessalonica, was obsessed with the fate of fallen women and devoted his life to their rehabilitation. He was so successful that some procurers, angry at losing money, murdered him. Nikodemos followed the example of St. Vitalios whom we will meet below. See Demetrios J. Constantelos, *Poverty, Society and Philanthropy in the Late Mediaeval Greek World*, p. 91.
20 See for example Vern Bullough, 'The prostitute in the early Middle Ages,' p. 40; and Sebastian P. Brock and Susan Ashbrook Harvey, *Holy Women of the Syrian Orient*, p. 24.
21 *The Lausiac History of Palladius*, pp. 106–7.
22 John Moschos, *The Spiritual Meadow*, pp. 185–7.
23 Later, Muslim ascetics or Sufis faced the same demon; see Annemarie Schimmel, 'Eros—heavenly and not so heavenly—in Sufi literature and life,' p. 124.
24 Moschos, *The Spiritual Meadow*, pp. 226–7.
25 Benedicta Ward (trans.), *The Sayings of the Desert Fathers: The Alphabetical Collection*, pp. xvii–xxi, xxix.
26 Ibid., pp. 59–60.
27 Ibid., pp. 88–9.
28 Ibid., pp. 93–4.
29 Ibid., p. 196.

30 Ibid., pp. 226–7.

31 Ibid., p. 237. Among other collections of sayings, the most famous in the West was the *Systematic Collection*, arranged by subject. It was translated into Latin in the fifth century by Pelagius and in the eighth century by John the Deacon. Here we find the tale of the old monk who, overcome with desire, runs as fast as he can to the prostitutes of Alexandria after mocking novices who had the same desire. See Aline Rousselle, *Porneia: On Desire and the Body in Antiquity*, pp. 138–9.

32 The account of her working life is in Procopius' well-known *The Secret History*, trans. Geoffrey Williamson, pp. 85–6. Procopius knew her personally. For a good overview of her early career, see Lynda Garland, *Byzantine Empresses: Woman and Power in Byzantium AD 527–1204*, pp. 11–14.

33 Sophronius' life of Mary, trans. in Benedicta Ward, *Harlots of the Desert*, p. 45.

34 Ibid., p. 46.

35 Ibid., pp. 46–9.

36 Dionysius' life of Thais, trans. ibid., p. 83.

37 Ibid., pp. 83–4.

38 The Greek text of the biography of St. John has been edited by Heinrich Gelzer as *Leontios' von Neapolis Leben des heiligen Johannes des Barmherzigen, Erzbischofs von Alexandrien.* I have relied on Harry Magoulias, 'Bathhouse, inn, tavern, prostitution and the stage as seen in the lives of the saints of the sixth and seventh centuries,' pp. 245–6.

39 John Wilkinson, 'Jerusalem under Rome and Byzantium 63 BC–637 AD,' p. 96.

40 Georges A. Barrois, trans. and ed. *The Fathers Speak: St Basil the Great, St Gregory Nazianzus, St Gregory of Nyssa*, pp. 43–4.

41 *The Lausiac History of Palladius*, p. 108.

42 Moschos, *The Spiritual Meadow*, pp. 35–6.

43 Ibid., pp. 78–9.

44 Ibid., p. 11.

45 Presumably this is a mistake for Syriac, because Hebrew was not then a spoken language. See Magoulias, 'Bathhouse, inn, and tavern,' p. 244.

46 Moschos, *The Spiritual Meadow*, pp. 111–12.

47 Claudine Dauphin, 'Brothels, baths and babes: prostitution in the Byzantine Holy Land,' no pagination. See under subheadings 'Brothels' and 'Prostitution, baths and illness.'

48 Moschos, *The Spiritual Meadow*, pp. 158–9.

49 Ibid.

50 Elizabeth Dawes and Norman H. Baynes, *Three Byzantine Saints: Contemporary Biographies translated from the Greek*, pp. 252–3.

51 Eusebius, *The History of the Church: From Christ to Constantine*, p. 361.

52 J. F. Matthews, 'The tax law of Palmyra: evidence for economic history in a city of the Roman East,' p. 177.

53 Derek Krueger, *Symeon the Holy Fool: Leontius's Life and the Late Antique City*, p. 150.

54 Ibid., p. 159.

55 Ibid., p. 160.

56 Ibid., pp. 6–7, 35.

57 Krueger argues that Emesa should not be taken as a real place, but as a generic Late Antique city (ibid., pp. 9–10, 21). He believes that Leontius' work reflects small-town life on Cyprus, where he composed Symeon's biography, not Syria. But this begs the question of why Leontius selected Emesa for his setting and not a more prominent city such as Edessa. Or, phrased another way, there is no reason why Emesa could not have been the setting. Moreover, Emesa had to be a believable location for Leontius' readers.

58 Michael I. Rostovtzeff et al., *The Excavations at Dura-Europos, Preliminary Report of the Ninth Season of Work 1935–36, Part I, The Agora and Bazaar*, pp. 117, 155, 157–61.

59 Theodore Nöldeke, 'Some Syrian saints,' in Theodore Nöldeke, *Sketches from Eastern History*, p.233.

60 Perhaps this means he had never bathed, which indicated he was an ascetic!

61 Translation of the Syriac text of Abraham's life in Brock and Harvey, *Holy Women of the Syrian Orient*, pp. 27–36. It differs considerably from the later translation into Latin. There, for example, the tavern becomes a brothel, the keeper is a woman, and Abraham's advances are more titillating; cf. the trans. of the Latin in Ward, *Harlots of the Desert*, pp. 92–101.

62 Procopius, *History of the Wars*, book II, p. 373.

63 Ibid., book I, p. 55.

64 For an overview of the history of Antioch in the sixth century, see Clive Foss' essay 'Late Antique Antioch,' pp. 23–7. The old standard work on the city is Glanville Downey, *Ancient Antioch*.

65 The Olympic Games, by the way, attracted a motley crowd including prostitutes (see Casson, *Travel in the Ancient World*, p. 78). The same may be true of major athletic contests today. The American football extravaganza Super Bowl XLIV in Miami, Florida in 2010 supposedly drew as many as 10,000 prostitutes, but this is difficult to confirm; see Amy Sullivan, 'Cracking down on the Super Bowl sex trade,' *Time*, February 6, 2011. See also Mary Pilon, 'Jump in prostitution arrests in Super Bowl week,' *New York Times*, January 29, 2014.

66 Glanville Downey, 'Libanius' oration in praise of Antioch (oration XI),' *Proceedings of the American Philosophical Society* vol. 103, no. 5 (October 15, 1959), p. 670. Downey provides a complete translation of the oration.

67 Ibid., p. 680. It is interesting that the Chinese, who only knew of the Asian part of the Roman Empire, considered Antioch to be its principal city; see Vasily V. Barthold, *La découverte de l'asie*, p. 78.

68 Procopius, *History of the Wars*, book I, pp. 155, 157.

69 It is worth mentioning that later, after Chosroes captured Antioch in 540, he visited the prosperous city of Apamea, about 100 kilometers to the south and near the Orontes, and watched chariot racing in its hippodrome or circus. This city, too, must have had all the usual professions (ibid., book II, pp. 359, 361). Laodicea, about the same distance down the coast from Antioch, had a hippodrome as well.

70 John Chrysostom, *The Homilies of John Chrysostom on the Gospel of St. Matthew*, vol. 2, pp. 544, 546.

71 Ibid., vol. 3, p. 1162.

72 John Chrystostom, *The Homilies of St. John Chrysostom on the Epistles of St. Paul the Apostle to Timothy, Titus, and Philemon*, pp. 64–5.
73 Ibid., pp. 65–6.
74 Jacob's life of Pelagia, trans. in Brock and Ashbrook, *Holy Women of the Syrian Orient*, pp. 42–3.
75 Ibid., p. 43.
76 Ibid., pp. 44–5, 55–7.
77 Mango and Scott, *The Chronicle of Theophanes Confessor*, p. 81.
78 *Dio Chrysostom* (Discourses), vol. 3, p. 319 on dress and p. 307 on snorting and brothels. See p. 273 for various uses of the term "snorting." Curiously, later in the Muslim world, sex manuals included "snorting" as one of the noises made during sex, *Encyclopaedia of the Qur'ān*, s.v. 'Sex and Sexuality' (Devin Stewart).
79 Moschos, *The Spiritual Meadow*, pp. 22–3.
80 Ibid., p. 23.
81 Strabo, *The Geography of Strabo*, vol. 5, p. 439.
82 See Mary Beard and John Henderson, 'With this body I thee worship: sacred prostitution in Antiquity,' p. 495, and especially Stephanie Budin, *The Myth of Sacred Prostitution in Antiquity*, pp. 179–84, for criticism of the notion of sacred prostitution and an explication of Strabo.
83 Strabo, *The Geography of Strabo*, vol. 5, p. 513.
84 Ibid., vol. 6, p. 299.
85 David Barchard, 'Sykeon rediscovered? A site at Kiliseler near Baypazarı,' pp. 175–9.
86 Even reputable inns provided prostitutes among their services. A late Roman inscription from southeastern Italy gives the tally for a night's lodging that included wine, bread, food, a girl, and hay for the mule. See Tönnes Kleberg, *Hôtels, restaurants et cabarets dans l'antiquité romaine*, p. 90, and Casson, *Travel in the Ancient World*, p. 207. John Moschos records a story, perhaps from the sixth century, in which a Syrian money dealer in Constantinople has a dream in which his brother, on the way to Syria, forces himself on a tavern keeper's wife, the implication being he considered her to be a public woman; see *The Spiritual Meadow*, pp. 160–1. On inns as places of prostitution in Late Antiquity, see Olivia Remie Constable, *Housing the Stranger in the Mediterranean World: Lodging, Trade, and Travel in Late Antiquity and the Middle Ages*, pp. 19–21, 28–9.
87 Dawes and Baynes, *Three Byzantine Saints*, p. 88.
88 Ibid., pp. 105, 185.
89 Procopius, *History of the Wars*, book II, p. 469.
90 On Helena's early life, see Jan Willem Drijvers, *Helena Augusta: The Mother of Constantine the Great and her Finding of the True Cross*, pp. 15–17.
91 McGinn, *Prostitution, Sexuality, and the Law*, p. 269; *Oxford Classical Dictionary*, 3rd ed., s.v. "collatio lustralis."
92 Steven Runciman, *Byzantine Civilization*, p. 150. Runciman seemed to believe that this was the only brothel in Constantinople. But this could only have been temporarily true.
93 Thomas McGinn, *The Economy of Prostitution in the Roman World: A Study of Social History and the Brothel*, p. 93.

94 *The Chronicle of John Malalas*, trans. Elizabeth Jeffreys et al., p. 187.

95 Clyde Pharr (trans.), *The Theodosian Code and Novels*, p. 435; McGinn, *Prostitution, Sexuality, and the Law*, p. 273. In one of his sermons in Antioch, John Chrysostom had thundered against men who compelled their domestics and slaves "to disgraceful services, to infamous love, to acts of rapine, and fraud, and violence," *The Homilies of St. John Chrysostom on the Epistles of St. Paul the Apostle to Timothy, Titus, and Philemon*, p. 341.

96 Dawes and Baynes, *Three Byzantine Saints*, pp. 29–30.

97 Ibid., p. 30.

98 Procopius, *The Secret History*, trans. Williamson, p. 91. We should note that some modern historians are skeptical of Procopius' description of Theodora as a prostitute. See for example Averil Cameron, *Procopius and the Sixth Century*, p. 77.

99 Procopius, *The Secret History*, trans. Williamson, pp. 82–3.

100 Ibid., pp. 84–5.

101 Ibid. pp. 86, 88–9. It does seem odd, as one can infer from Procopius, that Justinian would not have had a political marriage that allied him with a powerful family rather than one that brought him no advantage.

102 Ibid., p. 124.

103 *The Chronicle of John Malalas*, trans. Jeffreys et al., p. 255.

104 Procopius, *The Secret History*, trans. Williamson, p. 41.

105 As early as the fifth century BCE, the Athenian general Xenophon (ca. 430–354 BCE) mentions that many of the Greek soldiers who marched with him into Persia had their "mistresses" with them. When this army later retreated through Eastern Anatolia and along the southern coast of the Black Sea, it encountered the people called the Mossynocci, who lived on the coast west of Trebizond. Xenophon says "these people wanted to have sexual intercourse in public with the mistresses whom the Greeks brought with them" (see Xenophon, *The Persian Expedition*, pp. 189, 237). Apollonius of Rhodes (*fl.* third century BCE) later elaborates on the practice of public sex among the Mossynocci in *The Voyage of Argo*, p. 101.

106 George Dennis (ed. and trans.), *The Taktika of Leo VI*, p. 589.

107 Ibid., p. 615.

108 Steven Runciman, *The Emperor Romanus Lecapenus and his Reign: A Study of Tenth-Century Byzantium*, p. 60. As an aside, when Romanus became emperor (r. 920–44), he gave the prostitutes in Constantinople, who were "many thousands," a weekly dole of the equivalent of four British shillings (60 cents at the 1967 rate) per week. Romilly J. H. Jenkins concludes that this was meant to give them a possible alternative to their trade, but a beggar could earn more. See his 'Social life in the Byzantine Empire,' in Joan M. Hussey (ed.), *The Cambridge Medieval History*, vol. 4, *The Byzantine Empire*, part 2, *Government, Church and Civilization*, p. 87. Moreover, citing Koukoules, *Vizantinōn vios kai politismos*, Jenkins states that harlotry was rife in all ranks of society. He attributes it in part to the "rigorous seclusion of women in polite society." He adds, "No respectable woman ever appeared in the streets unveiled; and even in her house she never dined with a stranger, or entered his presence except silently and

with downcast eyes. This seclusion tended, as usual, to promote associations of a criminal character between the sexes" (ibid., pp. 88–9).

109 McGinn has studied the legal rules concerning prostitution from about 200 BCE to 250 CE in *Prostitution, Sexuality and the Law.*

110 Samuel Parsons Scott (trans. and ed.), *The Civil Law*, vol. 5, p. 251.

111 Ibid., vol. 5, p. 234.

112 Ibid., vol. 10, p. 316.

113 Ibid., vol. 3, p. 9.

114 Ibid., vol. 5, p. 251.

115 Ibid., vol. 11, p. 7.

116 Ibid., vol. 9, pp. 124–5; vol. 13, pp. 116–17.

117 On this subject, see the chapter 'Adultery and illicit love,' in Rousselle, *Porneia*, pp. 78–92. A double standard for men and women also came into effect with regard to members of the religious establishment. If a nun had intercourse, this would be considered adultery because she was married to Jesus, but if a monk did so it would be only a lewd act. See Leontsini, *Die Prostitution im frühen Byzanz*, p. 184. It seems to have been lost on medieval as well as modern Christian polemicists that, in theory, Christ has had far more wives than Muhammad.

118 Scott, *The Civil Law*, vol. 11, p. 34.

119 Ibid., vol. 16, p. 78.

120 Ibid.

121 Ibid., pp. 79–80.

122 Ibid., pp. 222–3.

123 Johannes Irmscher, 'Die Bewertung der Prostitution im byzantinischen Recht,' pp. 82–3. Irmscher writes in a Marxist context.

124 Nadia Maria El Cheikh, *Byzantium Viewed by the Arabs*, p. 126. The date of his sources in this matter is unknown.

125 Michael Psellus, *Fourteen Byzantine Rulers*, p. 108.

126 Flemming, '*Quae corpore quaestum facit*,' pp. 41–3.

127 Bullough, 'The prostitute in the early Middle Ages,' p. 36.

128 James Brundage, 'Prostitution in the medieval canon law,' p. 151.

129 Ibid., p. 154. In 1335 the Greek Orthodox monk Matthew Blastares composed a manual of Byzantine church and civil laws, the *Syntagma alphabeticum*, which was a synthesis of earlier materials. One provision was that clerics who ran bordellos were to be punished twice as hard as laypeople (Irmscher, 'Die Bewertung der Prostitution im byzantinischen Recht,' p. 85).

130 Despite such turmoil, Palestine—and probably other regions of the Eastern Mediterranean world—was generally prosperous in Late Antiquity. See Alan Walmsley, 'Byzantine Palestine and Arabia: urban prosperity in Late Antiquity,' pp. 126–58.

Chapter 2: Public Women in Medieval Arabia

1 Robert Hoyland, *Arabia and the Arabs: From the Bronze Age to the Coming of Islam*, p. 169. Hoyland collects the most important literary sources on Arabia before Islam.

2 Muḥammad ibn Ḥabīb, *Kitāb al-Muḥabbar*, pp. 265–6; Patricia Crone, *Meccan Trade and the Rise of Islam*, pp. 48–9; Hoyland, *Arabia and the Arabs*, pp. 50–7; John Haldon, 'The resources of Late Antiquity,' pp. 57–8; Fred Donner, *Muhammad and the Believers*, pp. 30–3.

3 For an exhaustive account of the political, military, ecclesiastical, economic, social, and cultural history of Byzantium and the Arabs in particular at this time, see Irfan Shahîd, *Byzantium and the Arabs in the Sixth Century*.

4 Michael Lecker, 'Pre-Islamic Arabia,' p. 161; idem., *Muslims, Jews and Pagans: Studies on Early Islamic Medina*.

5 Irfan Shahîd, *The Martyrs of Najrân*, p. 7. The accounts of the many female Christian martyrs of Najrān do not specifically include any "holy harlots." However, one of them, a handmaiden named Mâḥyâ, is described as a woman "who had led a wicked life [...] throughout her life she was masculine in all her deeds," ibid., p. 55. Cf. Walter Dostal, '"Sexual Hospitality" and the problem of matrilinearity in Southern Arabia,' pp. 17–30.

6 Hoyland, *Arabia and the Arabs*, p. 44.

7 Ibid., p. 47.

8 On Chinese, cf. George Fadlo Hourani, *Arab Seafaring in the Indian Ocean in Ancient and Early Medieval Times*, pp. 46–50.

9 *The History of al-Ṭabarī*, vol. 5, p. 291.

10 Ibn Ḥabīb, *Kitāb al-Muḥabbar*, p. 264; Crone, *Meccan Trade*, p. 106 n. 95.

11 Crone, *Meccan Trade*, p. 106; also al-Thaʿālibī, *Laṭāʾif al-maʿārif*, trans. Clifford E. Bosworth as *The Book of Curious and Entertaining Information*, p. 102.

12 *The Fihrist of al-Nadīm*, vol. 1, p. 218.

13 Al-Masʿūdī, *Murūj al-dhahab*, vol. 3, p. 6. For more on banners, see al-Bukhārī below, n. 61.

14 Uri Rubin, '"Al-Walad li-l-Firāsh," on the Islamic campaign against "Zinā",' p. 13; *EI²*, *Supplement*, 'al-Ḥārith b. Kalada' (Ch. Pellat).

15 Al-Masʿūdī, *Murūj al-dhahab*, vol. 3, p. 7.

16 Later, however, the enemies of the Umayyads used such descent against them. Those who wished to insult Caliph Marwān ibn al-Ḥakam (r. 64–5/684–5) alleged that he was descended from a woman named al-Zarqāʾ (Blue Eyes) in Arabia, who "was among those who possessed the banners which indicated houses of prostitution," William Robertson Smith, *Kinship and Marriage in Early Arabia*, p. 171, citing Ibn al-Athīr, *al-Kāmil*; see the Carolus J. Tornberg-edited version, vol. 4, p. 194. It is curious that ʿUbayd, the husband of Sumayya, was also called Blue Eyes (al-Azraq) (*EI²*, s.v. "al-Azraḳī" (Johann W. Fück)). Marwān was a contemporary of Muʿāwiya and a distant cousin from the other of the two branches of the Umayyad family. We no doubt have here a deliberate allusion by anti-Umayyad polemicists to the account of Ziyād's descent in order to disparage the Marwānid branch of the family, which became the main branch of the Umayyad caliphs. Ibn al-Tiqṭaqā states in his history, *al-Fakhrī*, written in 701/1302, "Those who wished to disparage Marwān and reprove him said to him 'O, son of al-Zarqāʾ!' They said al-Zarqāʾ was their [the Marwānids'] grandmother. She was one of those possessing the flags which indicated the houses of the prostitutes

(*al-baghāyā)* during the time of paganism" (published under the title *Ta'rīkh al-Duwal al-islāmiyya*, p. 119). In his translation of this work as *Al Fakhri: On the Systems of Government and the Moslem Dynasties,* Charles J. Whitting is confused about this passage, saying "Whoever wished to blame and find fault with Marwan used to say to him, 'Child of the woman in blue.' [Zarqa, or 'the blue-eyed'] (the brackets are Whitting's). Zarqa, their grandmother, was, they said, one of the women with blue flags, with which they used to indicate whoreshops in the age of ignorance" (p. 116). Shirley Guthrie, *Arab Social Life in the Middle Ages*, p. 129, follows Whitting in saying the flags were blue, but this was the color of her eyes. The theologian Ibn Qayyim al-Jawziyya (d. 751/1350), who lived in Damascus, records on p. 29 of his *Akhbār al-nisā'* an anecdote related by the belletrist al-Zubayr ibn al-Bakkār (d. 256/870) about a singing girl named Salāmat al-Zuraqā' (Salāma of the blue-eyed ones) in Mecca, who was prostituted by her owner.

17 In Hoyland, *Arabia and the Arabs*, p. 138, citing R. A. Nicholson's translation.

18 Ibid., p. 134, citing A. J. Arberry's translation.

19 On the staging posts in Western Arabia, see Ṣāliḥ Aḥmad 'Alī, *al-Ḥijāz fī ṣadr al-Islām*, pp. 223–78.

20 Crone, *Meccan Trade*, p. 170 n. 11, with references to other versions of the number of such fairs; and see especially Sa'īd al-Afghānī, *Aswāq al-'Arab fī 'l-Jāhiliyya wa 'l-Islām.*

21 Muḥammad ibn Ḥabīb, *Kitāb al-Muḥabbar*, pp. 266–7; Crone, *Meccan Trade*, pp. 170–1.

22 Al-Afghānī, *Aswāq al-'Arab*, p. 295. The author does not give a source. It may have been Abū 'l-Faraj al-Iṣbahānī's (d. 356/967) *Kitāb al-Aghānī.*

23 Ibid., p. 323. Again no source is cited.

24 *EI*[2], s.v. ''Ukāẓ.'

25 Speros Vryonis, Jr., 'The panēgyris of the Byzantine saint: a study in the nature of a medieval institution, its origins and fate,' p. 263.

26 Evliya Chelebi, *Evliyâ Çelebi Seyahatnâmesi*, vol 7, p. 188.

27 Robert Dankoff and Sooyong Kim, *An Ottoman Traveller: Selections from the* Book of Travels *of Evliya Çelebi*, p. 299. Also cited in Vryonis, 'The panēgyris of the Byzantine saint,' p. 273.

28 Stephanie Budin, *The Myth of Sacred Prostitution in Antiquity*, p. 3.

29 Ibid.

30 Robertson Smith, *Kinship and Marriage in Early Arabia*, p. 165 n. 1.

31 *EI*[2], s.v. 'al-Azraḳī' (Johann W. Fück): his name means the "Blue-eyed One."

32 Maurice Gaudefroy-Demombynes, *Le pélerinage à la Mekka: étude d'histoire religieuse*, pp. 99, 185.

33 Idem, *Mahomet*, p. 48.

34 *The History of al-Ṭabarī*, vol. 6, p. 52.

35 Ed. and trans. Wahib Atallah as *Les idoles de Hicham ibn al-Kalbī*, p. 6.

36 *EI*[2], s.v. 'Isāf wā-Nā'ila' (Toufic Fahd), where it is also noted that al-Azraqī places the stones at the foot of the "hills" of al-Ṣafā and al-Marwa outside the shrine of the Kaaba. Fahd considers this legend to be edifying in nature, with the "intention of putting pilgrims on guard against sacred prostitution as it was

practiced in the Syrian temples" (Toufic Fahd, *Le panthéon de l'Arabie Centrale a la veille de l'hégire*, p. 104).

37 On sacrifices at the stones, see *The History of al-Ṭabarī*, vol. 6, p. 4.

38 Joseph Henninger, 'Menschenopfer bei den Arabern,' pp. 793–6.

39 S.v. 'Woman' in James Hastings (ed.), *A Dictionary of the Bible*, 993b. Cf. Robertson Smith, *Kinship and Marriage*, note E, 'Mother and Son as Associated Deities,' pp. 298–306. As late as the twelfth century, the famed Byzantine princess Anna Comnena asserted that Muslims indulged in every kind of sexual license and worshipped Aphrodite. See *The Alexiad of Anna Comnena* (trans. Edgar R. A. Sewter), p. 310.

40 *EI*[2], s.v. 'al-'Uzzā' (Michael C. A. Macdonald and Laila Nehmé).

41 Herodotus, *The Landmark Herodotus, The Histories*, p. 107.

42 Budin, *The Myth of Sacred Prostitution in Antiquity*; see the chapter 'Herodotos' [*sic*], pp. 58–92. Herodotus' account "is an almost poetic description of the current, conquered state of Babylon that pulls together a number of important themes running throughout the histories" (p. 87).

43 Carl Rathjens, *Die Pilgerfahrt nach Mekka*, pp. 64–5.

44 *EI*[2], s.v. ''Umra' (Rudi Paret-[Eric Chaumont]). A Muslim can do the *'umra* in conjunction with the pilgrimage to Mecca, or separately.

45 Joseph Chelhod, *Le sacrifice chez les Arabes*, p. 82.

46 Al-Bukhārī, *Ṣaḥīḥ*, 1206 and 2483. Sunnah.com/bukhari/21/10 and Sunnah.com/bukhari/46/43.

47 Clifford Edmund Bosworth, *The Mediaeval Islamic Underworld*, vol. 1, p. 20; the topic is discussed at length in Josef Horovitz, *Spuren griechischer Mimen im Orient*, in the chapter '"Mimus" im Arabischen,' pp. 76–88; cf. p. 27.

48 Chelhod, *Le sacrifice chez les Arabes*, p. 144.

49 Ibid., pp. 156–8.

50 Ibid., p. 165.

51 Julius Wellhausen, *Reste arabischen Heidentums*, pp. 110, 195.

52 William Robertson Smith, *The Religion of the Semites*, pp. 451–2.

53 Henninger, 'Menschenopfer bei den Arabern,' p. 794, where he says "Ihr Vorhandensein in der südarabischen Hochkultur ist sicher obwohl nicht alle Belege..."

54 Alfred F. L. Beeston, 'The so-called harlots of Ḥaḍramaut,' pp. 16–22.

55 Inscriptions have survived from the pre-Islamic people of Qatabān in the southwest corner of Arabia showing that women dedicated their daughters to the temples. See for example Albert Jamme, 'Some Qatabanian inscriptions dedicating "Daughters of God",' pp. 39–47.

56 Nevertheless, some later scholars persisted in claiming its presence. Maxime Rodinson, for instance, declared that at the time of Muhammad "[r]eligious rites seem to have involved occasional ritual copulation," and implied that this occurred in Mecca, *Muhammad*, p. 55. Perhaps this was a Western male fantasy.

57 Supplemented by Julius Wellhausen, 'Die Ehe bei den Arabern,' pp. 431–81. For more recent comments on the state of the subject, see Joseph Chelhod, 'Du nouveau à propos du "matriarcat" arabe,' pp. 76–106.

58 See for example *EI*[2], s.v. 'al-Mar'a,' part 2 (Joseph Chelhod), p. 472.

59 Robertson Smith, *Kinship and Marriage*, pp. 205–6.

60 See ibid., p. 206 n. 1, where Ignaz Goldziher has pointed out a reference to this in a satirical poem by Ḥassān ibn Thābit (d. ca. 40/659), the "poet laureate of the Prophet," found in Ibn Hishām's (d. 213/828 or 218/833) *Sīra* (Life of Muhammad).

61 Al-Bukhārī, *Ṣaḥīḥ*, vol. 6, pp. 132–3; trans. Octave Houdas and William Marçais as *Les traditions islamiques*, vol. 3, pp. 565–6.

62 *EI*², s.v. 'Ḳiyāfa' (Toufic Fahd).

63 The modern study of Ḥadīth and its reliability as a historical source is a rather vast field. The great majority of these traditions are considered apocryphal. For a recent overview of the state of the art, see A. Kevin Reinhart, 'Juynbolliana, Gradualism, the Big Bang, and Ḥadīth Study in the Twenty-First Century,' pp. 413–44.

64 Robertson Smith, *Kinship and Marriage*, pp. 139–40. Robinson Smith cites Ibn al-Mujāwir (d. 690/1291), who traveled extensively in Arabia in the seventh/thirteenth century, on sexual hospitality. This writer says that "east of these regions" (i.e. southeast of Mecca) lived a people called the Bahmiyya, among whom there was the following custom: "When [the guest] has eaten dinner, the host will say to his wife, 'Go and honour the guest.' So the wife comes and sleeps in the guest's arms until morning without fear or caution. In the morning each one rises and goes about his business" (*Ta'rīkh al-Mustabṣir*, trans. Gerald Rex Smith as *A Traveller in Thirteenth-Century Arabia*, p. 80). As we will see in Chapter 5, there is evidence that in the Middle Ages the Turks in Anatolia also offered their wives and daughters to guests as sexual hospitality. Ibn al-Mujāwir also says of a people called al-Sarw, who were composed of Arab tribes near al-Ṭā'if, "When one of them goes on a journey, his wife approaches her replacement husband, i.e. the wife's lover, who sleeps with her until her husband returns" (ibid., p. 55).

65 Robertson Smith, *Kinship and Marriage*, p. 152.

66 Ibn al-Mujāwir gives an example of a man who purchased a slave girl, had sex with her, and then took the vendor to court in an attempt to get his money back because she had a defect. He also mentions a group of seven men in Qalhāt on the coast of Oman who together bought a slave girl for sex (see his *Ta'rīkh al-Mustabṣir*, trans. Smith, *A Traveller in Thirteenth-Century Arabia*, pp. 162, 279). In *A Mirror for Princes*, composed in 475/1082, Kai Kā'ūs ibn Iskandar ibn Qābūs of the Ziyārid dynasty, which held sway south of the Caspian Sea in Iran, advised his son and destined successor to marry a woman to run the household and not for sexual pleasure. For the latter purpose he should purchase slave girls in the bazaar, "[w]hich involves neither so much expense [for a ruler] nor so much trouble" (Reuben Levy, trans., *A Mirror for Princes: The Qābūs Nāma*, p. 118).

67 Wellhausen, 'Die Ehe bei den Arabern,' pp. 464–5. See also Robertson Smith, *Kinship and Marriage*, pp. 82–4; *EI*², s.v. 'Mut'a' (Willi Heffening); *Encyclopaedia of the Qur'ān*, s.v. 'Temporary marriage' (Shahla Haeri). Maurice Gaudefroy-Demombynes, while agreeing that it could easily be confused with prostitution, also asserted that it could have originated from a rite of desacralization carried out at the completion of a pilgrimage (*Mahomet*, p. 549).

68 This is according to certain hadith: see Gautier H. A. Juynboll, *Encyclopedia of Canonical Ḥadīth*, p. 538, cf. 729. In *The History of al-Ṭabarī*, vol. 9, p. 138, it is stated that Muhammad married al-'Aliyya and then gave her gifts and left her. Were the gifts compensation for divorce or *mut'a?*

69 Harald Motzki, *The Origins of Islamic Jurisprudence: Meccan Fiqh before the Classical Schools*, pp. 142–5.

70 Ibid., p. 190.

71 Ibid., p. 283.

72 Ibid.

73 Ibid., p. 143.

74 Al-Jāḥiẓ, *Risālat al-Jāḥiẓ*, pp. 301–2; trans. Charles Pellat, *The Life and Works of Jāḥiẓ*, p. 57. What is meant by the latter is unclear. Was there a special category of temporary marriage, i.e. prostitution, for pilgrims? Cf. Ibn Kathīr, *Tafsīr al-Qur'ān al-'aẓīm*, 4:24, on hadith forbidding *mut'a*. See pp. 72–3 of this chapter at http://www.quran4u.com/Tafsir%20Ibn%20Kathir/Index.htm.

75 Motzki, *The Origins of Islamic Jurisprudence*, pp. 142–4. Ibn Qayyim al-Jawziyya (d. 751/1350) records in his *Akhbār al-nisā'* (p. 7) that the Umayyad caliph 'Abd al-Malik ibn Marwān (r. 65–86/685–705) said that if one wanted a *mut'a* relationship with a woman, she should be a Berber (*barbariyya*); if he wanted a woman for children, she should be a Persian (*fārisiyya*); and if he wanted a woman for service, she should be a Greek (*rūmiyya*). Lists of the attributes of women from various places and ethnicities had long been in circulation. The Christian physician Ibn Buṭlān (d. 458/1066) of Baghdad states, for example, in a treatise on how to buy slaves, that Indian women were meek and mild, women from Media were suave, coquettish, and good singers, Berber women were for pleasure, Greek women were good housekeepers and economical, Persian women were good mothers, and so forth. See Adam Mez, *The Renaissance of Islam*, trans. Salahuddin Khuda Bukhsh and David S. Margoliouth, pp. 160–2; and Aḥmad 'Abd ar-Rāziq, *La Femme au temps des Mamlouks en Égypte*, p. 53, who cites Ibn Buṭlān as Ibn 'Abdūn.

76 Robertson Smith, *Kinship and Marriage*, p. 84.

77 Joseph Henninger, 'La société bédouine ancienne,' p. 92 n. 86. In the early nineteenth century the Reverend Horatio Southgate traveled through Persia, where he encountered the institution of *mut'a*. He says it was practiced to a considerable extent by foreigners in the country, and that the females were almost always Armenians. He made further investigations, but the disclosures, he says, would be "shocking beyond description and prove the almost universal prevalence of the most abandoned profligacy." It was best to "draw a veil" over such details (Horatio Southgate, *Narrative of a Tour through Armenia, Kurdistan, Persia and Mesopotamia*, vol. 2, p. 38). Charles Bélanger traveled to Persia about the same time. He reports that Armenian priests, following the example of Persian *mollas*, contracted under the sanction of a temporary marriage the hire (*louée*) of a woman by the month, day, or hour (*Voyage aux Indes-orientales*, vol. 2, p. 207). Writing in the early twentieth century, Francis A. C. Forbes-Leith recorded that hundreds of women in every city and town in Persia earned a living by engaging in *mut'a*

arrangements with travelers and visitors (*Checkmate: Fighting Tradition in Central Persia*, p. 181).

78 *Ammianus Marcellinus*, vol. 1, p. 27.

79 *Ṣaḥīḥ*, vol. 7, book 62, number 52, available at sunnah.com, no pagination. See also Alfred F. L. Beeston, 'Temporary marriage in pre-Islamic South Arabia,' pp. 21–5.

80 See for example Robertson Smith, *Kinship and Marriage*, pp. 291–6.

81 In a political marriage, Muhammad contracted to marry his third wife 'Ā'isha when she was six years old. He consummated the marriage when she was around nine, according to *EI*², s.v. ''Ā'isha' (W. Montgomery Watt).

82 One wonders the extent to which the sale of slave girls affected the ratio between the sexes. Could their sale have functioned to help keep this ratio in balance?

83 This verse has the advantage of clearly defining the word *bighā'* as the sale of sexual favors. It is noteworthy that the religion of the slave girls is not mentioned. Seemingly this revelation applied to slave girls of any kind.

84 Book 43, nr. 7181 in the *Ṣaḥīḥ* of Muslim, available at sunnah.com. Cf. Abū Dā'ūd al-Sijistānī (d. 275/889), a slightly later traditionist whose compilation, *Kitāb al-Sunan*, was regarded as the third most authoritative, book 12, nr. 2304, available at sunnah.com. For a slightly different version, see Ibn Kathīr, *Tafsīr al-Qur'ān al-'aẓīm*, commentary on 24:33, pp. 85–6, which is available at http://www.quran4u.com/Tafsir%20Ibn%20Kathir/Index.htm.

85 Norman Daniel, *Islam, Europe and Empire*, p. 308.

86 Curiously, al-Ṭabarī records Muhammad as equivocating somewhat in this regard. He quotes him as saying "Now then, O people, you have a right over your wives and they have a right over you. You have [the right] that they should not cause any one of whom you dislike to tread your beds; and that they should not commit any open indecency (*fāḥisha*)." In other words, adultery should not be done openly. See *The History of al-Ṭabarī*, vol. 9, p. 113 and n. 772.

87 The various words in the Qur'ān which contain the same root as *bighā'* (*b-gh-y*) have nothing to do with prostitution. Nor is the root of *fāḥisha* (*f-ḥ-sh*) linked to it. See s.v. respectively in *Mu'jam alfāẓ al-Qur'ān al-karīm*. Edward W. Lane collected from the classical Arabic dictionaries all the meanings of the words derived from these roots in *An Arabic-English Lexicon*; cf. *Encyclopaedia of the Qur'ān*, s.v. 'Sex and Sexuality' (Devin Stewart), where *fāḥisha* is interpreted as illicit sex or prostitution. Al-Qurtubi, for example, the great exegete of the Qur'ān in the seventh/thirteenth century, cites Muqātil ibn Sulaymān (d. 150/767), who wrote the earliest surviving commentary on the Qur'ān, as saying that almost everywhere the Qur'an mentions "indecency" it implies fornication, *Tafsir al-Qurtubi*, vol. 1, p. 423.

88 For Christian theologians of medieval Europe, fornication covered a wide range of circumstances and relationships, of which prostitution was one (Jacques Rossiaud, *Medieval Prostitution*, p. 77).

89 The words *musāfiḥīn* and *musāfiḥāt* appear in the Qur'ān (4:24, 5:5, and 4:25 respectively) as synonyms for *zinā'*, (fornicating, or fornication). But their meaning is equally vague. W. Montgomery Watt associates these words with polyandry and suggests that the noun *sāfaḥa* in the dictionaries—derived from

the stem *s-f-ḥ*, which is found in these words—may be the same practice as *bighā'*, *Muhammad at Medina*, pp. 390–1. This is speculation.

90 *EI*[1], s.v. 'Zinā'' (Joseph Schacht); *EI*[2], s.v. 'Zinā'' (Rudolph Peters); *Encyclopaedia of the Qur'ān*, s.v. 'Adultery and Fornication' (Nadia Abu-Zahra). For Qur'ānic references to *zinā*, which elsewhere is also spelled *zinā'*, and its derivatives, see s.v. *z-n-y* in *Mu'jam alfāẓ al-Qur'ān al-karīm*, and Lane, *An Arabic-English Lexicon*.

91 E.g. *EI*[1], s.v. "Zinā'" (Joseph Schacht). Shelomo D. Goitein even translates *zinā'* in one place as "prostitution" ('The sexual mores of the common people,' p. 53).

92 Juynboll, *Encyclopedia of Canonical Ḥadīth*, pp. 324, 495, 684 and index.

93 Or was this requirement tantamount to abrogation of the verses forbidding or denouncing *zinā'* (17:32, 25:68, 60:12)—or at least equivocation in this respect? Noel Coulson holds that the proof for fornication was so rigorous and the punishment was so severe because the offense was so serious. It could result in the production of illegitimate children, which would threaten one's lineage. It was actually the issue of *zinā'*, not *zinā'* itself, that was illegitimate. See his 'Regulation of sexual behavior under traditional Islamic law,' pp. 66–8. It appears that in Coulson's view, fornication—in which he would include prostitution—was acceptable as long as no children were produced. In any case, if the proof of this act was well-nigh impossible to provide, and, as we have seen, the children born of liaisons with public women could be legally acknowledged, then the matter would seem to be moot.

94 It is curious that in the anonymous Persian mirror for princes, *Baḥr al-favā'id*, written in Aleppo between 1159 and 1162, our aforesaid 'Abd Allāh ibn al-'Abbās is cited as saying that God mentioned in His Book that there were 15 things that were absolutely unlawful, one of which was "the price of a prostitute" (trans. Julie Scott Meisami as *The Sea of Precious Virtues*, p. 138). As we have seen, however, this is not what God says. He speaks only of pimping slave girls. The same work then describes unlawful trades, one of which is the use of contraceptive measures for the purposes of the prostitution of male and female slaves (ibid., p. 139). In light of the previous claim, however, this is obviously a non sequitur.

95 Noel Coulson, *A History of Islamic Law*, p. 111.

96 *Ṣaḥīḥ*, vol. 3, book 34, nr. 439; vol. 3, book 34, nr. 440; vol. 3, book 36, nr. 483; vol. 7, book 63, nr 258; vol. 7, book 63, nr. 259, vol. 7, book 63, nr. 260; vol. 7, book 71, nr. 656. Available at sunnah.com.

97 Ibid., vol. 4, book 54, nr. 538; vol. 4, book 56, nr. 673.

98 *Ṣaḥīḥ*, book 10, nrs. 3803, 3805, 3806. Available at sunnah.com.

99 Ibid., book 26, nrs. 5578, 5579.

100 *Kitāb al-Sunan*, book 23, nrs. 3414, 3421, 3477. Available at sunnah.com.

101 Her name could also be 'Anāq, which was the name the Arabs gave to the daughter of Adam, the twin sister of Seth, and the wife of Cain. In zoology it meant a kind of lynx. Perhaps this was a generic name for prostitute.

102 *Kitāb al-Sunan*, book 11, nr. 2046.

103 Ibid., book 12, nr. 2257.
104 *Sunan*, 2523. Sunnah.com/nasai/23.
105 Meisami, *The Sea of Precious Virtues*, p. 102. The Prophet's servant Anas ibn Mālik (d. ca. 91–3/709–11) reports a similar edifying story from his own time (ibid.). Such stories are reminiscent of the tales of a few Christian saints.
106 The study of *tafsīr*, like that of Ḥadīth, is a broad subject. See *EI*², s.v. 'Tafsīr' (Andrew Rippin).
107 *Jāmiʿ al-bayān*, pt. 6, pp. 493–4, and pt. 14, p. 581 respectively.
108 Ibid., pt. 6, pp. 585–6.
109 Ibid., pt. 17, p. 293.
110 Ibid., pt. 13, p. 596.
111 Al-Qurṭubī, *al-Jāmiʿ li-aḥkām*, trans. Aisha Bewley (London, 2003), is available at https://archive.org/details/TafseerEQurtubiArabicalJameAlAhkamAlQuran. Note: These Ḥadīth works are arranged according to the chapters and verses in the Qur'an, so one can find the relevant commentary by Qur'anic chapter and verse and page numbers are not necessary.
112 Ibn Kathīr, *Tafsīr al-Qur'ān al-ʿaẓīm*. See in the respective chapters on pp. 44, 96, and 34, which are available at http://www.qtafsir.com/index.php?option=com_content&task=view&id=3137.
113 Ibid., see relevant chapter and verse at http://www.qtafsir.com/index.php?option=com_content&task=view&id=3137.
114 Ibid., see relevant chapter and verse at http://www.qtafsir.com/index.php?option=com_content&task=view&id=3137.
115 See the first three chapters of Coulson, *A History of Islamic Law*.
116 It is curious that a different term is used for each of these transactions. *Mahr* was also the term for dower, or bride price.
117 Mālik ibn Anas, *al-Muwaṭṭa'*, vol. 2, pp. 656–7; trans. Aisha Abdurrahman Bewley as *al-Muwatta of Imam Malik ibn Anas*, p. 267. *Al-Muwatta'* was "a manual of the doctrine currently endorsed by the 'Establishment' in Medina" (Coulson, *A History of Islamic Law*, p. 47).
118 *Ṣaḥīḥ*, vol. 3, book, 34, nr. 440.
119 Muḥammad ibn Ismāʿīl Ṣanʿānī, *Subul al-salām*, vol. 3, p. 14.
120 Some medieval canon lawyers in Europe also came to this conclusion about free-will alms from public women. See James Brundage, 'Prostitution in the medieval canon law,' p. 155.
121 Under the heading of wrongful sales (*al-bayʿ al-fāsid*), we read *lā yajūzu al-bayʿu bi-ilqā'i 'l-ḥajar wa 'l-mulāmasa. Mulāmasa* can mean "sexual intercourse," but here it means "touching." The entire phrase reads "Sale by casting dice or touching [the commodity] is not permitted" (Al-Qudūrī, *Mukhtaṣar*, p. 36.)
122 In medieval Europe, the neighborhood also held authority over mores (Rossiaud, *Medieval Prostitution*, pp. 61, 116).
123 Joseph Schacht, *The Origins of Muhammadan Jurisprudence*, p. 209. Banishment did not prevail among the Ḥanafīs. Nevertheless, they did use it. See Christian Lange, *Justice, Punishment and the Medieval Muslim Imagination*, p. 97.
124 Coulson, *A History of Islamic Law*, p. 19.
125 Pellat, *The Life and Works of Jāḥiẓ*, p. 261.

126 Ibn Qayyim al-Jawziyya records the following anecdote in his *Akhbār al-nisā'*, p. 147, without giving a time and place: "It was said to Abū 'l-Ṭumān al-'Utbī [unidentified], 'Tell us your most reprehensible deed.' He replied, 'The night of the convent [laylat al-dayr].' They said, 'What is the night of the convent?' He answered, 'I lodged with a Christian woman. I ate ṭafshalan [?] with pork. I drank some of her wine. I fornicated with her. I stole her dress and made off.'" Was the "convent" a brothel or inn?

127 See. *EI*², s.v. 'Shāhid' (Rudolph Peters).

128 Coulson, 'Regulation of sexual behavior under traditional Islamic law,' p. 63.

129 Also during the Middle Ages, many Muslim religious scholars and others were preoccupied with making lists of major sins based on the Qur'ān and Ḥadīth. There was no consensus. The number ran from four to 70. Sometimes fornication was included, and sometimes only the false accusation of fornication was included. Prostitution was never mentioned. See Ralph Stehly, 'Un problème de théologie islamique: la définition des fautes graves (*kabā'ir*),' pp. 165–81. It must also be said that Muslim literary sources from various later periods categorized many legitimate professions as disreputable or despised, but they were not necessarily immoral. Ranked below prostitutes, professional mourners and entertainers were butchers and tanners (Ira Lapidus, *Muslim Cities in the Later Middle Ages*, p. 82).

130 See the magisterial study of Michael Cook, *Commanding Right and Forbidding Wrong in Islamic Thought*, p. 67.

131 Ibid., p. 368.

132 See for instance ibid., p. 367.

133 James Bellamy, 'Sex and society in Islamic popular literature,' p. 27.

134 Ibid., p. 29.

135 Bellamy proposed that one reason for the change in moral view might be that Muslims felt they could not be less strict in sexual matters than were the adherents of the religions that they supplanted in Southwest Asia and North Africa (ibid., p. 40). This attitude would thus be a sign of the genuineness of the faith. This is, of course, another way of suggesting that Christianity, which in any case was less well disposed to sex than Islam, might have influenced the change in view.

136 Donner, *Muhammad and the Believers*, especially ch. 5, 'The emergence of Islam.'

137 See Motzki, *The Origins of Islamic Jurisprudence*, ch. 1, 'The beginnings of Islamic jurisprudence in the research of the nineteenth and twentieth centuries,' pp. 1–50.

138 Ignaz Goldziher, *Muhammedanischen Studien*, trans. Christa R. Barber and Samuel M. Stern as *Muslim Studies* (London, 1966–71), vol. 2, p. 39.

139 Donner, *Muhammad and the Believers*, p. 107. This may echo the report of the fourth-century Roman historian Ammianus Marcellinus on the Scenitic Arabs, or Saracens, who says, "it is unbelievable with what ardour both sexes give themselves up to passion" (*Ammianus Marcellinus*, trans. Rolfe, vol. 1, p. 29). Earlier, the Talmudic scholar Rabbi Nathan, who lived in Palestine in the second century, declared that, of all peoples, the Arabs had the greatest propensity toward fornication (Rodinson, *Muhammad*, p. 54).

140 Al-Thaʿālibī, *Laṭā'if al-ma'ārif*, trans. Bosworth, p. 91.

141 *EI*², s.v. 'al-Mar'a' (Joseph Chelhod), 477b; ibid., s.v. ''Umar b. Abī Rabī'a' (James E. Montgomery).

142 For an overview of the history of Mecca, see *EI*², s.v. 'Makka' (William Montgomery Watt et al.).

143 Holidays, including Sundays, were also good for public women in medieval Europe (Rossiaud, *Medieval Prostitution*, p. 63).

144 This holday originated in Fāṭimid Egypt in the early fifth/eleventh century (Nico J. G. Kaptein, *Muḥammad's Birthday Festival*, p. 23).

145 Some pilgrims did not have the most pious motives for the journey. The great historian Ibn al-Athīr (d. 630/1233) records, for example, that in 583/1188 the company of pilgrims from Iraq included an assemblage of riffraff, idlers, and troublemakers. At 'Arafa, outside Mecca, they picked a fight with company of pilgrims from Syria (*al-Kāmil*; trans. Donald S. Richards as *The Chronicle of Ibn al-Athir for the Crusading Period*, pt 2, p. 340).

146 Abū 'l-Faraj al-Iṣbahānī, *Kitāb al-Aghānī*, vol. 19, p. 6780. See also pp. 6781–2; Wellhausen, 'Die Ehe bei den Arabern,' p. 470 n. 2. *Kharqā'* was a nickname. It could mean "clumsy," or even "illicit" (Hans Wehr, *A Dictionary of Modern Written Arabic*). However, among poets it was a term for pure wine, which was compared to a virgin who was intact and without experience. See Reinhart Dozy, *Supplément aux dictionnaires arabes*. Obviously, the poet is having fun with wordplay.

147 Al-Muqaddasī, *Aḥsān al-taqāsīm fī ma'rifat al-aqālīm*, p. 36; trans. Basil Collins as *The Best Divisions for Knowledge of the Regions*, p. 32.

148 Despite the centrality of Mecca, for example, to the history of Muslim Arabia, it had no tradition of history writing from the end of the third/ninth to the beginning of the ninth/fifteenth century. See John Meloy, *Imperial Power and Maritime Trade: Mecca and Cairo in the Later Middle Ages*, pp. 24–5.

149 Ibn al-Mujāwir, *Ta'rīkh al-Mustabṣir*, p. 151. Harold R. P. Dickson records that in the early twentieth century public women were abundant in Jidda on the Red Sea and in the ports of Kuwait, Bahrain and Masqat on the Persian Gulf (*The Arab of the Desert: A Glimpse into Badawin Life in Kuwait and Sau'di Arabia*, p. 244). He also mentions that, when men in Kuwait would leave for pearling in the Gulf, some "amateur" prostitution was practiced by the divers' womenfolk in their absence. This resulted from the need to supplement the family income (ibid., p. 204). Presumably some "professional" women were available for the divers. Pearl fishing in the Gulf was probably well established before the rise of Islam. The earliest Muslim account of it is in al-Mas'ūdī's *Murūj al-dhahab* from the fourth/tenth century. See *EI*², s.v. 'al-Durr' (Julius Ruska).

150 Ibn al-Mujāwir, *Ta'rīkh al-Mustabṣir*, p. 255. Ibn Mājid (fl. second half of fifteenth century), the great Arab navigator of the Indian Ocean and pilot for Vasco da Gama, writes that the people of Socotra offered their women to strangers and their ruler was a woman. See his *Kitāb al-Fawā'id fī uṣūl 'ilm al-baḥr*, facsimile ed. published by Gabriel Ferrand as vol. 1 of *Instructions nautiques et routiers arabes et portugais des xv*ᵉ *et xvi*ᵉ *siècles*, fol. 70b.

151 Al-Mas'ūdī, *Murūj al-dhahab*, vol. 4, pp. 58–9; trans. Paul Lunde and Caroline Stone as *The Meadows of Gold*, pp. 279–80. Here, this event supposedly took place during the caliphate of al-Muntaṣir (r. 247–8/861–2), although al-Mas'ūdī cites al-Madā'inī. For a "Medina" version dating from the fourth-fifth/tenth-eleventh century, see Giorgio Levi Della Vida, *Arabic Papyri in the University Museum in Philadelphia (Pennsylvania)*, pp. 201–2 and n. v on p. 206. This story should be placed perhaps in the context of the rivalry between the Mālikī and Ḥanafī law schools of Medina (Arabia) and Kufa (Iraq) respectively.

152 Ibn al-Mujāwir, *Ta'rīkh al-Mustabṣir*, pp. 34–5. According to Dickson, writing between 1929 and 1936, the Bedouin considered Mecca to be one of the most immoral towns in Arabia. Both Mecca and Medina had prostitute quarters (Dickson, *The Arab of the Desert*, pp. 202–3). In Night 681 of the *Arabian Nights*, the protagonist makes the pilgrimage to Mecca and then visits Muhammad's tomb in Medina. At the place called al-Rawḍa, right next to the tomb, a band of women pass him and one of them propositions him. See Malcolm and Ursula Lyons, trans., *The Arabian Nights: Tales of 1001 Nights*, vol. 2, p. 759. More will be said about the *Nights* in the next chapter.

153 Dankoff and Kim, *An Ottoman Traveller*, p. 360. George Curzon reported on *mut'a* as a form of prostitution at the Shī'ī shrine of Mashhad in Persia in 1889 in his book *Persia and the Persian Question*, vol. 1, p. 165. Indeed, it seems that this practice is found even today at the pilgrimage centers of Iran (*Encyclopaedia of the Qur'ān*, s.v. 'Temporary marriage' (Shahla Haeri)).

154 Ibn al-Mujāwir, *Ta'rīkh al-Mustabṣir*, p.79.

155 Ibid., p. 117.

156 Ibid., p. 152; Guy Ducatez, 'Aden aux xiie et xiiie siècles selon Ibn al-Muǧāwir,' p. 197. One cannot tell for sure from the text if the author is referring to women in caravanserais in Iran, Arabia, or both. He probably means the Persians used this expression for public women in caravanserais in general.

157 Untitled work of el-Dimeşkî appended to Katib Chelebî's *Kitâb-ı Cihânnümâ*, facsimile reprint, pp. 488, 494, and 523, respectively. An English translation is in preparation under the editorship of Gottfried Hagen.

158 Ibid., pp. 492, 519, 523. See also al-Afghānī, *Aswāq al-'Arab*, p. 393.

159 Charles M. Doughty, *Travels in Arabia Deserta*, vol. 1, p. 151.

160 Ibid., vol. 2, p. 151.

161 Dickson, *The Arab of the Desert*, p. 176.

162 Ibid., p. 225.

163 Ibid., p. 244.

164 Ibid., pp. 245–6. Dickson also says here that public women were called *banāt al-hāwa* (daughters of love), *fa'innāt* (the avaricious ones), *fawāhish* (prostitutes), *banāt al-ḥarām* (daughters of sin), and *qiḥāb* (whores).

165 This seems to be true of all later Muslim literature as well, with the possible exception of a certain story told about the renowned mystic Jalāl al-Dīn al-Rūmī and his encounter with a prostitute in the seventh/thirteenth century. It will be described below in Chapter 5.

166 There is a hadith according to which a pregnant woman confessed to the Prophet that she had committed fornication and asked for the required divine

punishment. After the child was born, he ordered her to be stoned. Given such circumstances, there would have been no choice in his decision. See Juynboll, *Encyclopedia of Canonical Ḥadīth*, p. 658.

Chapter 3: Public Women in Medieval Egypt

1 For the history of Egypt from the Arab conquest to the Ottoman conquest, see vol. 1 of *The Cambridge History of Egypt*. For Alexandria in particular, see *EI*[3], s.v. 'Alexandria: early period' (Gary Leiser).

2 See Hugh Kennedy, 'Egypt as a province in the Islamic Caliphate, 641–868,' pp. 62–85.

3 *EI*[2], s.v. 'al-Shāfiʿī' (Eric Chaumont).

4 Thierry Bianquis, 'Autonomous Egypt from Ibn Ṭūlūn to Kāfūr, 868–969,' p. 106.

5 Ibid., pp. 87–8.

6 Ibid., pp. 117–18.

7 See Paul Walker, 'The Ismāʿīlī daʿwa and the Fāṭimid caliphate.'

8 This is described in amazing detail in Shelomo D. Goitein, *A Mediterranean Society: The Jewish Communities of the Arab World as Portrayed in the Documents of the Cairo Geniza.*

9 See Paula Sanders, 'The Fāṭimid State, 969–1171.'

10 On places of pilgrimage in Egypt, see al-Harawī (d. 611/1215), *Kitāb al-Ziyārāt*; trans. Janine Sourdel-Thomine as *Guide des lieux de pèlerinage*, pp. 78–120.

11 For an eyewitness account in 439/1047, see Nāṣir-i Khusraw, *Safarnāma*; trans. Wheeler Thackston as *Book of Travels*, pp. 48–51.

12 Paula Sanders, *Ritual, Politics, and the City in Fatimid Cairo*, p. 81.

13 Adam Mez, *The Renaissance of Islam*, trans. Salahuddin Khuda Bukhsh and David S. Margoliouth, reprint (Beirut, 1973), pp. 422–3. The Muslim historian al-Masʿūdī himself participated in it in 330/941 (*Murūj al-dhahab*, vol. 1, pp. 379–80).

14 Sanders, 'The Fāṭimid State,' p. 170.

15 Gary Leiser, 'The Crusader raid in the Red Sea in 578/1182–83.'

16 For an overview of Ayyūbid Egypt, see Michael Chamberlain, 'The crusader era and the Ayyūbid dynasty.'

17 Ibid., pp. 218–27.

18 For overviews of Mamlūk Egypt, see *EI*[2], s.v. 'Miṣr,' 5. *The Mamlūk Period 1250–1517* (Ulrich Haarmann); Robert Irwin, *The Middle East in the Middle Ages: The Early Mamluk Sultanate 1250–1389*; Linda Northrup, 'The Baḥrī Mamlūk Sultanate, 1250–1390'; and Jean-Claude Garcin, 'The regime of the Circassian Mamlūks.'

19 See the works in the previous note.

20 Northrup, 'The Baḥrī Mamlūk Sultanate,' pp. 273–86; Jonathan Berkey, 'Culture and society during the late Middle Ages,' pp. 391–9.

21 Garcin, 'The regime of the Circassian Mamlūks,' pp. 313–16; R. Stephen Humphreys, 'Egypt in the world system of the later Middle Ages,' pp. 458–60; *EI*[2], s.v. 'ʿAydhāb' (Hamilton A. R. Gibb).

22 In a fatwa that he wrote sometime between 871/1467 and 891/1486 on the permissibility of celebrating the birthday of the Prophet, the Egyptian polymath al-Suyūṭī (d. 911/1505) warned that this celebration provided an opportunity for men to mix with attractive women, which was tantamount to "wallowing in lust." See Nico J. G. Kaptein, *Muḥammad's Birthday Festival*, p. 53.

23 Boaz Shoshan, *Popular Culture in Medieval Cairo*, pp. 16–17, 70–2, 74. This was also true of the send-off of troops to battle. See for example the spectacle of the departure of the army from Cairo to conquer Cyprus in 829/1426 in Ibn Taghrībirdī, *al-Nujūm al-ẓāhira*; trans. William Popper as *History of Egypt, 1382–1469 A.D.*, pt. 4 in vol. 18 of *University of California Publications in Semitic Philology*, p. 34.

24 Ibid., p. 17; *EI*², s.v. 'Aḥmad al-Badawī' (Karl Vollers–Enno Littmann).

25 The Muslim rulers of al-Andalus were taxing prostitution before the fifth/eleventh century. Prostitutes paid a tax to the treasury, as a result of which they were called *kharājiyyāt* in Hispanic Arabic, meaning that they were compelled to pay the *kharāj* (which in the Muslim East was a land or poll tax). There were also—at least in some towns, especially in Cordoba—brothels that were called *dār al-kharāj* in a similar manner (Evariste Lévi-Provençal, *Histoire de l'Espagne musulmane*, vol. 3, pp. 445–6).

26 The economic and social life of the different non-Muslim peoples in the early years of Muslim rule in the Eastern Mediterranean littoral has been little studied. See the excellent article by Arietta Papaconstantinou, 'Between umma and dhimma: the Christians of the Middle East under the Umayyads,' notably p. 130.

27 Mez, *The Renaissance of Islam*, p. 163.

28 Sāwīrus ibn al-Muqaffa', *History of the Patriarchs of the Egyptian Church*, which is the most important source for the history for the Coptic Church of Egypt (vol. 4, pt. 2, p. 177) (English).

29 It is worthy of note that after the Christians conquered Valencia in al-Andalus from the Muslims, they encouraged the prostitution of Muslim women, which they taxed. The Christian king did not concern himself with the morality of Muslim women, who, in any case, were damned because of their religion and thus exploitable; see Mark D. Meyerson, 'Prostitution of Muslim women in the Kingdom of Valencia: religious and sexual discrimination in a medieval plural society,' p. 88.

30 This may actually mean that warriors from all around gathered at Damietta for the annual season of launching raids against Christian vessels and ports.

31 Al-Muqaddasī, *Aḥsān al-taqāsīm, fī ma'rifat al-aqālīm*, pp. 193, 196–202); trans. Basil Collins as *The Best Divisions for Knowledge of the Regions* (Reading, UK, 2001), pp. 163, 166–70.

32 Ibid., p. 36; trans. p. 32.

33 Michael Cook, *Commanding Right and Forbidding Wrong in Islamic Thought*, p. 302.

34 *Da'ā'im al-Islām* has been translated by Asaf Fyzee and Ismail Poonawala as *The Pillars of Islam*. On *mut'a* see vol. 2, pp. 214–16 and especially n. 222 on p. 214.

35 Majid Khadduri, *Islamic Jurisprudence, Shāf'ī's Risāla*, pp. 169–70, 175.

36 See Yaacov Lev, 'The suppression of crime, the supervision of markets, and urban society in the Egyptian capital during the tenth and eleventh centuries,' pp. 84–7.

37 Aḥmad 'Abd ar-Rāziq, 'La *ḥisba* et le *muḥtasib* en Égypte au temps des Mamlūks,' pp. 115–18; Jonathan P. Berkey, 'The *muḥtasibs* of Cairo under the Mamluks: toward an understanding of an Islamic institution,' pp. 251–3; Yaacov Lev, *State and Society in Fatimid Egypt*, pp. 160–1.

38 Note the places of its appearance and the medieval works describing it in *EI*², s.v. 'Ḥisba' (Claude Cahen and Mohamed Talbi). By the fifth/eleventh century, however, under the Great Seljuks the office of the *muḥtasib* had fallen into disrepute in much of the Muslim East. The great Persian poet Sa'dī (d. 691/1292) denounced the holders of this post for "walking around bare-assed while telling prostitutes to veil their faces" (see Christian Lange, 'Changes in the office of Ḥisba under the Seljuqs,' p. 162). Meanwhile, contemporaneously with the Fāṭimids, Sunni jurists in Baghdad, above all the ultra-conservative Ḥanbalīs, periodically campaigned—if not rampaged—against immorality. In 323/934 they attacked female singers and forbade men to walk in the streets with women (see Mez, *The Renaissance of Islam*, p. 362). In 464/1071–2, and from time to time thereafter, they attempted to ban prostitution in Baghdad (see George Makdisi, *Ibn 'Aqīl et la résurgence de l'islam traditionaliste au xi*ᵉ *siècle*, pp. 152–3). The brothels that zealous Ḥanbalīs destroyed around 464/1071–2 were back in operation within a few years. They netted the agent of the Grand Vizier Niẓām al-Mulk the sum of 1,800 gold dinars annually. The *'ulamā'* were outraged that the government was profiting from prostitution. Consequently, in order to placate them, the caliph offered to buy off the agent for 1,000 dinars, but he refused the offer. The caliph then pleaded with Niẓām al-Mulk, who agreed to pay the difference of 800 dinars to his agent and put a stop to the practice (idem, *The Rise of Humanism in Classical Islam and the Christian West*, p. 182).

39 Al-Maqrīzī, *Itti'āẓ al-ḥunafā'*, vol. 1, p. 272. On Banī Wā'il, see p. 276 n. 1.

40 Ibid., vol. 1, p. 283. On this vizier, see Muḥammad Ḥamdī al-Manāwī, *al-Wizāra wa'l-wuzarā' fī al-'aṣr al-fāṭimī*, pp. 244–5.

41 It is worthy of note that in a handbook for *muḥtasibs* composed in Muslim Seville by a certain Ibn 'Abdūn at the end of the fifth/eleventh or beginning of the sixth/twelfth century, prostitutes (*nisā' dūr al-kharāj*) were forbidden to stick their heads uncovered outside the brothel (*funduq*) (Lévi-Provençal, *Séville musulmane au début du xii*ᵉ *siècle: le traité d'Ibn 'Abdun sur la vie urbaine et les corps de métiers*, p. 113; Arabic text ed. Lévi-Provençal as *Trois traités hispaniques de ḥisba*, p. 50). In a similar treatise, also from al-Andalus, written perhaps a bit later by one Aḥmad ibn 'Abd Allāh ibn 'Abd al-Ra'ūf, "women are forbidden to stand at the doors of houses because those inside might be unveiled" (ibid., p. 113). This might be interpreted as a reference to prostitution. The same writer says that men are forbidden to employ women lest that result in what is forbidden (ibid., p. 114). Perhaps this would include pimping or managing a brothel.

42 In Ibn 'Abdūn's aforesaid handbook for *muḥtasibs*, ferrymen are forbidden to transport women who had the look of those of a dissolute life (*al-fujūr*) (Lévi-Provençal, *Séville musulmane au début du xii*[e] *siècle*, p. 127; Arabic text pp. 56–7).

43 In Ibn 'Abdūn's aforesaid handbook for *muḥtasibs*, women are forbidden to sit next to river banks in the summer if men appear there, Lévi-Provençal, *Séville musulmane au début du xii*[e] *siècle*, p. 103, Arabic text, p. 46.

44 Al-Maqrīzī, *Itti'āẓ al-ḥunafā*, vol. 2, pp. 38, 54, 76, 83, 87–9, 91, 95–6, 102–3, 110, 120; Heinz Halm, 'Der Treuhänder Gottes. Die Edikte des Kalifen al-Ḥākim,' especially pp. 21–4. Halm stresses the need to understand al-Ḥākim's decrees in light of a puritanical interpretation of Ismā'īlī law, that is, the caliph took it to an extreme in his role as God's trustee on earth (cf. Delia Cortese and Simonetta Calderini, *Women and the Fatimids in the World of Islam*, pp. 192–9).

45 Cortese and Calderini, *Women and the Fatimids*, p. 194. There is a drawing, apparently found in Fusṭāṭ and dated to the fifth/eleventh century, depicting a woman who, some guess, might be a "courtesan." She is completely nude and carries a lute in one hand and a cup of wine in the other. But because she is thickset, with short stocky legs and long heavy arms, she may actually be a dwarf. See David S. Rice, 'A drawing of the Fatimid period,' pp. 31–9.

46 Al-Musabbiḥī, *al-Juz' al-arba'ūn min Akhbār Miṣr*, eds Ayman Fu'ād Sayyid and Thierry Bianquis, p. 12.

47 Ibid., p. 68.

48 Ibn al-Ma'mūn al-Baṭā'ḥī, *Nuṣūṣ min akhbār miṣr*; ed. Ayman Fu'ād Sayyid as *Passages de la Chronique d'Egypte d'Ibn al-Ma'mūn*, p. 104.

49 *EI*[2], s.v. 'Radjab' (Meir J. Kister).

50 Goitein, *A Mediterranean Society*, vol. 1, p. 350, and vol. 2, p. 279, where a Jewish notable from Alexandria is falsely accused of having had an affair with a girl in a caravanserai.

51 Ibid., vol. 1, p. 350.

52 Ibid., vol. 5, p. 322.

53 Shelomo D. Goitein, 'The sexual mores of the common people,' pp. 45, 55.

54 Mez, *The Renaissance of Islam*, p. 362.

55 Al-Muqaddasī, *Aḥsān al-taqāsīm*, p. 441 (trans. Collins, pp. 355–6).

56 Al-Bīrūnī, *Ta'rīkh al-Hind*; trans. Edward C. Sachau as *Alberuni's India* (London, 1910), vol. 2, p. 157.

57 Al-Maqrīzī, *al-Mawā'iẓ wa 'l-i'tibār bi-dhikr al-khiṭaṭ wa 'l-āthār* (Cairo, 1853–4), vol. 1, p. 89. Hereinafter cited as *al-Khiṭaṭ*. Al-Maqrīzī gives a slightly different version of this information in his *Kitāb al-Sulūk li-ma'rifat duwal al-mulūk*, vol. 2, p. 151. Hereinafter cited as *al-Sulūk*.

58 This assertion, including the reference to al-Maqrīzī, has been accepted as fact in subsequent literature including *EI*[2], s.v. 'Bighā',' *Supplement* (Ed.).

59 Thackston, *Book of Travels*, p. 45.

60 Ibid., p. 52.

61 Al-Maqrīzī, *al-Sulūk*, vol. 1, p. 43. The first part of this work, which covers the Ayyūbids, has been translated by Roland J. C. Broadhurst as *A History of the Ayyūbid Sultans of Egypt* (see p. 37).

62 This is the conclusion of Ramazan Şeşen in *Salâhaddîn devrinde Eyyûbîler devleti*, p. 178.

63 Al-Maqrīzī, *al-Sulūk*, vol. 1, p. 45 (trans. p. 38); Andrew S. Ehrenkreutz, *Saladin*, p. 105.

64 Gary Leiser, 'The restoration of Sunnism in Egypt: Madrasas and Mudarrisūn 495–647/1101–1249,' pp. 239–40.

65 Ehrenkreutz, *Saladin*, p. 103.

66 The letter is found in 'Imād al-Dīn al-Iṣfahānī's (d. 597/1201) *al-Barq al-shāmī*, part 3, p. 103; cf. the abridgement by al-Bundārī as *Sanā al-Barq al-shāmī*, pp. 152–3.

67 Al-Maqrīzī, *al-Sulūk*, vol. 1, p. 73 (trans. p. 64).

68 Ibid., vol. 1, p. 86 (trans. p. 76).

69 Ibid., vol. 1, p. 119 (trans. p. 106); Hassanein Rabie, *The Financial System of Egypt*, pp. 119–20. The Abū 'l-Munajā canal was a short distance north of Cairo. See al-Maqrīzī, *al-Sulūk*, vol. 1, p. 119 n. 2. Gold was rather scarce in Egypt in the Ayyūbid period. A daily tax of 16 dinars—a dinar being the standard gold coin—would have been enormous (see Paul Balog, *The Coinage of the Ayyūbids*, pp. 35–6). Much of the gold in Egypt was drained off to finance Saladin's wars against the Crusaders in Syria. It was replenished to some degree by the European merchants in Alexandria.

70 Al-Maqrīzī, *al-Sulūk*, vol. 1, p. 134 (trans. p. 118). On p. 136 of the same work, he says the tax that the sultan accrued from his monopoly on winemaking was 17,000 dinars, which seems low compared to the amount of tax imposed. Perhaps this was net income after the tax farmer took his cut. The translation mistakenly gives 7,000 dinars (p. 120). See Rabie, *The Financial System of Egypt*, p. 120.

71 Al-Maqrīzī, *al-Sulūk*, vol. 1, p. 136 (trans. p. 120).

72 Ibid., vol. 1, p. 136 (trans. pp. 120–1).

73 Ibid., vol. 1, p. 142 (trans. p. 125).

74 Ibid.

75 Al-Maqrīzī, *al-Khiṭaṭ*, vol. 2, p. 373; especially idem, *Kitāb al-Muqaffā al-kabīr*, vol. 4, pp. 596–600; and Hans Gottschalk, *al-Malik al-Kāmil von Ägypten und seine Zeit*, pp. 82, 105.

76 Leiser, 'The restoration of Sunnism,' pp. 239–40.

77 Ibn Ḥajar al-'Asqalānī, *Raf' al-iṣr 'an quḍāt Miṣr*, vol. 2, p. 352; and Leiser, 'The restoration of Sunnism,' pp. 355–7.

78 Al-Maghribī, *Kitāb al-Mughrib*, section on Cairo ed. Ḥusayn Naṣār as *al-Nujūm al-zāhira fī ḥulā ḥaḍrat al-Qāhira*, pp. 29–32. Al-Maqrīzī included Ibn Sa'īd's description, with a few changes, in his *Khiṭaṭ*, vol. 1, pp. 367–8. The section of the *Khiṭaṭ* in which it is found was translated by Paul Casanova as vol. 4 of the Mémoires of the Institut Français d'Archéologie Oriental du Caire under the title *Description historique et topographique de l'Égypte*, part 4, pp. 57–9.

79 *EI*[2], *Supplement*, s.v. 'al-Djawbarī' (Stefan Wild); idem, 'Jugglers and fraudulent Sufis,' pp. 58–63.

80 The verb *qala'a* means "to take off one's clothes," but in this case she probably only took off her outer garments.

81 Al-Jawbarī, *al-Mukhtār fī kashf al-asrār*; ed. Manuela Höglmeier as *al-Ǧawbarī und*

sein Kašf al-asrār—ein Sittenbild des Gauners im arabisch-islamischen Mittelalter (7./13. Jahrhundert), pp. 373–6. The Arabic in this work can be somewhat problematic because of jargon, dialectical expressions, and unclear antecedents for pronouns.

82 Ibid., pp. 377–80.

83 On the course of this crusade, see Thomas C. Van Cleve, 'The Fifth Crusade.'

84 Jacques de Vitry, *Lettres de la Cinquième Croisade*, Latin texts ed. Robert B. C. Huygens and French trans. Gaston Duchet-Suchaux, p. 57.

85 Ibid., p. 123. The *History of the Patriarchs of the Egyptian Church* contains a contemporary—or at least near-contemporary—account of the Damietta campaign by a certain bishop named Yūṣāb. He makes the curious statement that among the Frankish troops were many Muslim women from al-Ghawr, the Jordan valley, in addition to the Frankish women from the Syrian coast. All these women were "to grind for them the wheat and serve them." See vol. 3, pt. 2, p. 218 (English) and p. 129 (Arabic) of the *History*, which is ascribed as a whole to Sāwīrus ibn al-Muqaffaʿ.

86 Oliver of Paderborn, 'The capture of Damietta,' p. 106.

87 Steven Runciman, *A History of the Crusades*, vol. 3, pp. 256–73; Joseph R. Strayer, 'The Crusades of Louis IX,' pp. 493–504.

88 Joinville & Villehardouin, *Chronicles of the Crusades*, trans. Margaret R. B. Shaw, p. 207.

89 Al-Maqrīzī, *al-Khiṭaṭ*, vol. 2, p. 90.

90 Abdul-Aziz Khowaiter, *Baibars the First: His Endeavours and Achievements*, pp. 10–16; Peter Thorau, *The Lion of Egypt: Sultan Baybars I and the Near East in the Thirteenth Century*, pp. 43–50.

91 Khowaiter, *Baibars the First*, pp. 16–27; Thorau, *The Lion of Egypt*, pp. 79–88.

92 For an encomium on his high ethical standards and hatred of indecent behavior (*al-fāḥish*), see al-ʿAynī, *al-Rawḍ al-zāhir fī sīrat al-Malik al-Zāhir "Ṭaṭar"*, pp. 22–3.

93 Ibn ʿAbd al-Ẓāhir, *Sīrat al-Sulṭān al-Malik al-Ẓāhir Baybars*, partial ed. and trans. Syedah Fatima Sadeque as *Baybars I of Egypt*, p. 325 of text, p. 193 of translation; Khowaiter ed. as *al-Rawḍ al-zāhir fī sīrat al-Malik al-Ẓāhir* (Riyad, 1396/1976), p. 176. In his book *La Femme au temps des Mamlouks en Égypte* (p. 47), ʿAbd ar-Rāziq says Sultan Quṭuz was the first to purge foreign prostitutes from the port and he cites al-Maqrīzī's *al-Sulūk*. But on the page cited this matter is not mentioned. ʿAbd ar-Rāziq's brief account of prostitution under the Mamlūks in the aforesaid work (pp. 45–8) is to be used with caution because the notes do not always match the text.

94 Olivia Remie Constable, *Housing the Stranger in the Mediterranean World: Lodging, Trade, and Travel in Late Antiquity and the Middle Ages*, p. 145. She also notes that in agreements between Mamlūk officials and Aragonese consuls in Alexandria in 1381 and 1386, the latter had to agree not to allow women of dubious character to live in their *fondaco* (p. 277).

95 Ibn ʿAbd al-Ẓāhir, *Sīrat*, p. 325 text (p. 199 trans.).

96 Ibn Baṭṭūṭa, *al-Riḥla*, trans. Hamilton A. R. Gibb as *The Travels of Ibn Baṭṭūṭa*, vol. 2, p. 425.

97 Al-Maqrīzī, *al-Sulūk*, vol. 1, p. 553. Cf. *al-Khiṭaṭ*, vol. 1, p. 106, where he says this occurred in 665; al-ʿAynī, *ʿIqd al-jumān*, vol. 1, p. 426. Ibn ʿAbd al-Zāhir only says he abolished the tax farming of hashish and ordered punishment for its consumption (*al-Rawḍ al-zāhir*, ed. Khowaiter, p. 266).

98 Al-Maqrīzī, *al-Sulūk*, vol. 1, p. 578; cf. idem, *al-Khiṭaṭ*, vol. 1, p. 106, where he says this occurred in 666/1268. Ibn ʿAbd al-Zāhir only mentions the banning of women sinners. He says they were imprisoned and forced [*sic*] to marry and the order to this effect was sent to all countries (*bilād*), which may have included Syria (*al-Rawḍ al-zāhir*, p. 350).

99 Al-Maqrīzī, *al-Sulūk*, vol. 1, p. 578.

100 Rabie, *The Financial System of Egypt*, pp. 26–32.

101 In *al-Khiṭaṭ*, vol. 1, p. 106, al-Maqrīzī simply says that the state lost revenue when the tax on prostitution was abolished.

102 Norman Daniel, *Islam and the West: The Making of an Image*, pp. 226–7.

103 On William, see Thomas O'Meara, 'The theology and times of William of Tripoli, O.P.: a different view of Islam.'

104 Al-Maqrīzī, *al-Sulūk*, vol. 1, pp. 595, 597; idem, *al-Khiṭaṭ*, vol. 1, p. 106; Ibn Kathīr, *al-Bidāya wa 'l-nihāya*, vol. 13, p. 260.

105 Li Guo, 'Paradise lost: Ibn Dāniyāl's response to Baybars' campaign against vice in Cairo,' p. 233. "The geomancy game" was apparently a reference to a trick used by beggars (ibid., p. 235). Guo states that Ibn Dāniyāl composed this poem in response to Baybars' attack on vice in 665/1267 rather than 667/1269. The sources, including al-Maqrīzī, are inconsistent on the date of both these attacks. Guo cites a late source, Ibn Iyās (d. ca. 930/1524), who says Baybars banned the tax farming of hashish, destroyed houses of forbidden activities and the wine therein, and forbade brothels (*al-khānāt min al-khawāṭi'*) throughout Egypt and Syria (Ibn Iyas, *Badā'iʿ al-zuhūr*, vol. 1, pt. 1, p. 326). Al-ʿAynī does not mention any such incident in 665 or 667 in vol. 2 of his *ʿIqd al-jumān*. Ibn ʿAbd al-Zāhir mentions only the incident of 667 (see p. 350 of the Khowaiter ed. of al-Rawd al-zahir).

106 Guo, 'Paradise lost,' p. 226.

107 Ibid., p. 231.

108 Mustafa Badawi, 'Medieval Arabic drama: Ibn Dāniyāl,' p. 18.

109 Ibid.

110 Ibid., p. 21. See also *EI*^{2}, s.v. 'Ibn Dāniyāl' (Jacob M. Landau). A literature devoted to scabrous themes, and which appealed to certain men and women of various classes, must have been in fairly wide circulation in the major cities of the heartlands of the Muslim world. Ibn al-Nadīm mentions works called 'Women used for unnatural sexual intercourse and whores' and 'Rare anecdotes about pimps (or procuresses)' by Abū al-ʿAnbas al-Ṣaymarī, a boon companion of the ʿAbbāsid caliph al-Mutawakkil. He died after 256/870. Ibn al-Nadīm also reports a number of anonymous titles about sexual intercourse, which included 'Jaded harlots and male prostitutes (*al-baghā'iyūn*).' See *al-Fihrist* (ed. and trans. Bayard Dodge as *The Fihrist of al-Nadīm*, vol. 1, pp. 332–3, and vol. 2, p. 736, respectively). None of these works is extant.

111 Li Guo, 'The devil's advocate: Ibn Dāniyāl's art of parody in his *Qaṣīdah* no. 71,' p. 180; idem, 'Reading *Adab* in historical light: factuality and ambiguity in Ibn Dāniyāl's "Occasional Verses" on Mamluk society and politics,' pp. 385, 397–400.

112 Rabie, *The Financial System of Egypt*, pp. 53–6, index; Robert Irwin, *The Middle East in the Middle Ages*, pp. 109–11.

113 Al-Maqrīzī records this in both his *al-Khiṭat*, vol. 1, p. 89, and *al-Sulūk*, vol. 2, p. 151. The two accounts differ slightly in detail. The translation is a composite.

114 Idem, *al-Khiṭat*, vol. 1, p. 89, and idem, *al-Sulūk*, vol. 2, p. 152. Again this is a composite translation. The functions of the various officials in the Mamlūk sultanate are discussed in Maurice Gaudefroy-Demombynes, *La Syrie à l'époque des Mamelouks*, pp. xix–cxix.

115 Al-Maqrīzī, *al-Sulūk*, vol. 2, p. 152 n. 1. The Tujayb are mentioned in idem, *al-Khiṭaṭ*, vol. 2, p. 297.

116 Edward G. Browne, *A Literary History of Persia*, vol. 3, p. 53; Irwin, *The Middle East in the Middle Ages*, pp. 118–19.

117 Al-Maqrīzī, *al-Sulūk*, vol. 2, p. 640. *Awlād* might be a reference here specifically to the children of *mamlūks*.

118 Ibid., vol. 2, p. 188; see also Carl Petry, 'Al-Maqrīzī's discussion of imprisonment and description of jails in the *Khiṭaṭ*,' p. 141.

119 Irwin, *The Middle East in the Middle Ages*, p. 120; Angus Donal Stewart, *The Armenian Kingdom and the Mamluks: War and Diplomacy during the Reigns of Het'um II (1289–1307)*, pp. 153–70.

120 Seta B. Dadoyan, *The Fatimid Armenians: Cultural & Political Interaction in the Near East*, pp. 144–53.

121 On the duties of the chief of police, or prefect, see Donald S. Richards, 'The office of Wilāyat al-Qāhira in Mamluk times,' pp. 441–7. He was in charge of security as well as suppressing the usual vices when called upon to do so. He could be the enforcement arm of the *muḥtasib*. In Night 343 of the *Arabian Nights*, the *wālī* of Cairo is in contact with all the brothel owners in the city. He goes in disguise in pursuit of two notaries who were at a house on a back street used for prostitution. The notaries and the brothel owner recognize him and then bribe him. See Malcolm and Ursula Lyons (trans.), *The Arabian Nights: Tales of 1001 Nights*, vol. 2, pp. 105–6. More will be said about the *Nights* below.

122 Al-Maqrīzī, *al-Sulūk*, vol. 2, pp. 640–1.

123 Ibid., pp. 641–2.

124 Ibid., p. 642.

125 See *EI*², s.v. 'Rawḍa' (Otfried Weintritt).

126 *Nuqra* being a kind of disk on which the inscription was stamped. On these dirhams, which were silver coins, see Paul Balog, *The Coinage of the Mamlūk Sultans of Egypt and Syria*, p. 55.

127 Al-Maqrīzī, *al-Khiṭaṭ*, vol. 2, p. 186; William Popper, *Egypt and Syria under the Circassian Sultans 1382–1468 A.D.: Systematic Notes to Ibn Taghrî Birdî's Chronicles of Egypt*, vol. 15 of *University of California Publications in Semitic Philology*, p. 35 on the location of the islands. On the venal Arghūn, see Irwin, *The Middle East in the Middle Ages*, pp. 130, 133–4.

128 Ile de la Jatte in the Seine in Paris had the same reputation in the late nineteenth century. I have not come across a specific reference to the practice of prostitution in small boats (feluccas) on the Nile, but this must have commonly occurred. We shall see hints of it later. When I was in Cairo in 1965 I was told that boats used by public women could be found at certain places. There were obvious advantages to plying the sex trade on the Nile and away from prying eyes. In the early twentieth century, one of the last houses of prostitution in Portland, Oregon was anchored in the Willamette River, which ran through the city (Gordon B. Dodds, *Oregon*, p.172).

129 Al-Maqrīzī, *al-Sulūk*, vol. 2, pp. 642, 647.

130 Ibid., p. 646.

131 On the importation of wine to Alexandria by European merchants, see Constable, *Housing the Stranger in the Mediterranean World*, pp. 276–8.

132 Al-Maqrīzī, *al-Sulūk*, vol. 2, p. 647; Irwin, *The Middle East in the Middle Ages*, p. 130.

133 Al-Maqrīzī, *al-Sulūk*, vol. 2, pp. 677, 723.

134 Al-Maqrīzī provides a long description of this plague in *al-Sulūk*, vol. 2, pp. 770, 772–87. See also Michael Dols, *The Black Death in the Middle East*, passim.

135 Described in the long poem by Guillaume de Machaut, *La prise d'Alixandre*. See Kenneth M. Setton, *The Papacy and the Levant*, vol. 2, pp. 258–86; al-Maqrīzī, *al-Sulūk*, vol. 3, pp. 105–8; Ibn Iyās, *Badā'i' al-zuhūr*, vol. 1, pt. 2, pp. 21–8 ff.

136 Al-Maqrīzī, *al-Khiṭaṭ*, vol. 1, p. 106. On a similar practice in ancient Greece, see Sarah Pomeroy, *Goddesses, Whores, Wives, and Slaves: Women in Classical Antiquity*, p. 89, and in Rome, Aline Rousselle, *Porneia: On Desire and the Body in Antiquity*, p. 94.

137 Ibn Iyās, *Badā'i' al-zuhūr*, vol. 1, pt. 1, p. 486.

138 Singing girls performed at the wedding of al-Kāmil Sha'bān in 746/1345 and the *ḍāmina*'s take was considerable (al-Maqrīzī, *al-Sulūk*, vol. 2, pp. 690–1). Thus this tax must have been reimposed shortly after al-Nāṣir's death.

139 Al-Maqrīzī, *al-Sulūk*, vol. 3, p. 266; cf. Ibn Iyās, *Badā'i' al-zuhūr*, vol. 1, pt. 2, pp. 166–7, who gives essentially the same report. He says the chief Shāfi'ī qadi banned all these activities.

140 In the later sixth/twelfth century, the 'Abbāsid caliph al-Nāṣir (d. 620/1223) reformed a somewhat inchoate movement called the *futuwwa*, which had consisted of young men, mystics, and guilds, into a kind of courtly brotherhood of the elite. By the eighth/fourteenth century it had devolved (again) into a more disreputable popular organization with lodges throughout much of the Middle East, including Cairo. One criticism leveled against its members in the eighth/fourteenth century was that they could force their wives into prostitution in order to help a brother who had fallen on hard times. Perhaps this occurred in Egypt during times of plague or famine. Certainly the ease of registering to work as a prostitute would have facilitated such a practice. See Robert Irwin, *The Arabian Nights: A Companion*, pp. 147–8.

141 On the female profession of *ḍāminat al-maghānī*, see 'Abd ar-Rāziq, *La Femme au temps des Mamlouks en Égypte*, pp. 78–80.

142 Al-Maqrīzī, *al-Sulūk*, vol. 3, p. 267; Ibn Iyās, *Badā'i' al-zuhūr*, vol. 1, pt. 2, p. 168.

143 Al-Maqrīzī, *al-Sulūk*, vol. 4, p. 486; Berkey, 'The *muḥtasibs* of Cairo under the Mamluks,' p. 264.

144 Ibid., p. 614; ibid.

145 John Meloy, 'Celebrating the *Maḥmal*: the Rajab Festival in fifteenth-century Cairo,' pp. 416–23.

146 Al-Maqrīzī, *al-Sulūk*, vol. 4, p. 666. 'Abd ar-Rāziq, *La femme au temps des Mamlouks en Égypte*, p. 47, seems to confuse Baybars with Barsbay in this matter.

147 Al-Maqrīzī, *al-Khiṭaṭ*, vol. 2, p. 78.

148 Al-'Asqalānī, *Raf' al-iṣr 'an quḍāt Miṣr*, vol. 2, p. 299.

149 Al-Maqrīzī, *al-Khiṭaṭ*, vol. 2, p. 162; Popper, *Egypt and Syria*, p. 34, on the Pool of al-Raṭlī.

150 I have translated *za'īrāt*, an unusual term, as "wanton women." It seems to have the connotation of "debauched." Reinhart Dozy translated it as "Bohemians." See his explication of this word in his *Dictionnaire détaillé des noms des vêtements chez les Arabes*, p. 259 n. 3. André Raymond and Gaston Wiet, *Les marchés du Caire: traduction annotée du texte de Maqrīzī*, p. 155, translate it as "ribaudes."

151 Dozy, *Dictionnaire détaillé*, p. 258, reads, correctly, *al-sāliqīn* (which can mean to throw someone on his back) for *al-mushāliqīn*, which is found in the Būlāq edition of *al-Khiṭaṭ* but is meaningless and must be a mistake.

152 Al-Maqrīzī, *al-Khiṭaṭ*, vol. 2, p. 96; Dozy, *Dictionnaire détaillé*, pp. 258–60; Raymond and Wiet, *Les marchés du Caire*, pp. 155–6.

153 Around the same time in Europe, prostitutes had to wear a visible sign of their profession, such as a knotted cord which fell from the shoulder and was in a color that contrasted with their dress (Jacques Rossiaud, *Medieval Prostitution*, p. 57). Writing about a century earlier, Ibn Dānyāl says in an ode that public women applied rouge to their cheeks (Guo, 'The devil's advocate,' p. 180). The Andalusian poet Ibn Bassām (d. 543/1147) records in his *al-Dhakhīra fī maḥāsin ahl al-Jazīra*, which he compiled in Seville, that the public women of the brothels (*kharājiyyāt al-khānāt*) used the husks of walnuts to color their lips (vol. 1, p. 242).

154 Al-Ṣafadī (d. 764/1363), who lived in Damascus and Cairo, says in his biographical dictionary *A'yān al-'aṣr*, which concentrates on his own time, that the coat of arms of the Mamlūk *amīr* Aqūsh was so stylish that all women, even prostitutes, were happy to have it tattooed on their wrists (cited by 'Abd ar-Rāziq, *La femme au temps des Mamlouks en Égypte*, p. 48). This had nothing to do, of course, with the business of prostitution.

155 Cited in Dozy, *Dictionnaire détaillé*, p. 409.

156 Edward Lane, *The Manners and Customs of the Modern Egyptians*, p. 49; Dozy, *Dictionnaire détaillé*, p. 410.

157 Cited in Dozy, *Dictionnaire détaillé*, p. 257.

158 Lane, *The Manners and Customs of the Modern Egyptians*, p. 44; Dozy, *Dictionnaire détaillé*, pp. 260–2.

159 Dozy, *Dictionnaire détaillé*, pp. 203–9; Yedida Stillman, *Arab Dress from the Dawn of Islam to Modern Times*, pp. 75–6.

160 As do Raymond and Wiet, *Les marchés du Caire*, p. 156 n. 2. Mez, *The Renaissance of Islam*, p. 423, accepts pantaloons.

161 Mounira Chapoutot-Remadi, 'Femmes dans la ville mamlūke,' pp. 149–50. While describing the reign of Barqūq, al-Maqrīzī makes one other apparent reference to the apparel of prostitutes. Blaming this sultan for introducing sodomy to Egypt because of his notorious attraction to handsome mamlūks, our author says under the year 791/1389 that, as a result, even prostitutes imitated young boys in their (the prostitutes') *bawār* (a fashion of dressing?) in order to increase business opportunities (*al-Sulūk*, vol. 3, p. 618). Perhaps this was a kind of headgear. Cf. Stillman, *Arab Dress*, p. 80.

162 Dozy, *Dictionnaire détaillé*, p. 260 n. 7.

163 Raymond and Wiet, *Les Marchés du Caire*, p. 156 n. 7. Club might be an alternative for dagger.

164 On white magic see *EI*^{2}, s.v. 'Nīrandj' (Toufic Fahd), for which various objects could be used. With respect to Egypt, the "Babylon of the magicians," see Ibn al-Nadīm, *al-Fihrist*, vol. 2, p. 726.

165 Dozy, *Dictionnaire détaillé*, p. 260 n. 7. See Lane, *The Manners and Customs of the Modern Egyptians*, pp. 393–4.

166 Chapoutot-Remadi, 'Femmes dans la ville mamlūke,' p. 160.

167 Al-Ḥājj, *al-Madkhal*, vol. 4, pp. 22–3. One wonders how a woman could make herself attractive only to her husband! Ibn 'Abdūn says in his handbook for *muḥtasibs* that women embroiderers (*ṭarrāzāt*) should be forbidden from access to the market because they are all whores (*qiḥāb*) (Lévi-Provençal, *Séville musulmane au début du xii*^{e} *siècle*, p. 105; Arabic trans., p. 47).

168 Al-Ḥājj, *al-Madkhal*, vol. 4, p. 21, see also vol. 1, pp. 234–8; Chapoutot-Remadi, 'Femmes dans la ville mamlūke,' pp. 149–50. Ibn 'Abdūn says in his handbook for *muḥtasibs* that respectable women should not dress to look like prostitutes or be flirtatious (Lévi-Provençal, *Séville musulmane au début du xii*^{e} *siècle*, p. 113; Arabic trans., p. 51). Furthermore, women's skirts and overcoats should be ample enough to cover everything, and no bare legs (p. 135; Arabic trans. p. 60).

169 Ibn 'Abdūn says in his aforementioned handbook that the *mutaqabbil* (the person who assessed the tax called the *qabāla*, the guarantee or contract) for *funduqs* for merchants and foreigners should not be a woman because that is a source of fornication (Lévi-Provençal, *Séville musulmane au début du xii*^{e} *siècle*, p. 110; Arabic trans., p. 49).

170 On the caravanserais near the candle-makers' market, see Plan II in Raymond and Wiet, *Les Marchés du Caire*.

171 *Al-Nujūm*, Popper trans. as *History of Egypt, 1382–1469 A.D.*, pt. 4, p. 147; Dols, *The Black Death in the Middle East*, pp. 114–15; Aḥmad Darrāǧ, *L'Égypte sous le règne de Barsbay, 825–841/1422–1438*, pp. 429–30.

172 *The Bondage and Travels of Johann Schiltberger*, p. 52. See also ibid., xxv–xxvi.

173 Translated from al-Ṣayrafī's *Inbā' al-haṣr* by Carl F. Petry in his 'Disruptive "Others" as depicted in chronicles of the late Mamlūk period,' pp. 184–5.

174 Ibid., p. 185.

175 Al-Maqrīzī, *al-Khiṭaṭ*, vol. 2, pp. 2, 93.

176 For a description of a *rab'*, see Jean-Claude Garcin et al., *Palais et maisons du Caire*, vol. 1. *Époque mamelouke*, pp. 137–40.

177 Bernadette Martel-Thoumian, 'Plaisirs illicites et châtiments dans les sources mamloukes fin ixe/xve–début x^e/xvie siècle,' p. 287, citing al-Sakhāwī's *Wajīz al-kalām*. Al-Sakhāwī also states that in 896/1491 20 prostitutes were caught in the Khan al-Khalīlī and fined. See Carl Petry, *The Criminal Underworld in a Medieval Islamic Society: Narratives from Cairo and Damascus under the Mamluks*, p. 152 n. 57.

178 Martel-Thoumian, 'Plaisirs illicites,' citing 'Abd al-Bāsiṭ's *Nayl al-amal*. On the location of the Ṣāliḥiyya between these markets, see Raymond and Wiet, *Les marchés du Caire*, pp. 187–9.

179 Martel-Thoumian, 'Plaisirs illicites,' p. 288.

180 Ibid., p. 289.

181 Ibn Iyās, *Badā'i' al-zuhūr*, trans. Gaston Wiet as *Journal d'un bourgeois du Caire: chronique d'Ibn Iyâs*, vol. 1, pp. 144–5; Petry, '"Quis Custodiet Custodes?" revisited: the prosecution of crime in the late Mamluk Sultanate,' p. 25; Martel-Thoumian, 'Plaisirs illicites,' p. 287.

182 Martel-Thoumian, 'Plaisirs illicites,' p. 288.

183 Garcin et al., *Palais et maisons du Caire*, vol. 1. *Époque mamelouke*, p. 165.

184 Carl F. Petry, 'The military institution and innovation in the late Mamlūk period,' pp. 64–5.

185 See for example Carl Petry, 'The estate of al-Khuwānd Fāṭima al-Khaṣṣbakiyya: royal spouse, autonomous investor,' pp. 182–5.

186 Aḥmad Darrāǧ, *L'Act de waqf de Barsbay*, pp. 18–20.

187 As Darrāǧ states concerning the administration of *waqfs*, "The sources are often content to condemn the religious as the sole malefactors. The sources say that, either by carelessness or dishonesty, they ignore the task to which they were appointed" (ibid., p. 20). It must be said that venality was a driving force among the Mamlūk elite. During a time of economic crisis in 808/1405–6, al-Maqrīzī states that government officials who got their jobs through bribery had difficulty meeting their own expenses and so connived to acquire wealth by any means, not caring if it led to "the enslaving of free women." See Adel Allouche, *Mamluk Economics: A Study and Translation of al-Maqrīzī's* Ighāthah, p. 52.

188 Writing in the fourth/tenth century, the geographer al-Muqaddasī reported an intriguing, albeit vague, kind of *waqf* for prostitution (*zinā'*) in the region of Sind, the lower Indus. Sind was under Muslim rule but had a large Hindu as well as a small Buddhist population. Our author says there were two idols in Habrawā, which is not further identified. The idols apparently had servants (*khuddām*) who lived from the income from prostitution, and for this purpose there were many *waqfs* established from prostitution. Anyone who wished to honor his daughter made her a *waqf* for this purpose. It is difficult to know what al-Muqaddasī was talking about (*Aḥsān al-taqāsīm*, p. 483; trans. Collins as *The Best Divisions*, p. 390).

189 Speaking of the holy and venerated town of Kairouan in Tunisia in the early twentieth century, Abdelwahab Bouhdiba states that all the neighborhoods were near the tombs of saints or *zāwiyas*, and that more than half the houses of prostitution in town were established in support of *waqfs*. The founders of

these *waqfs* did not hesitate to dedicate the revenue from the houses to the maintenance of sacred sites such as *zāwiyas* (*La sexualité en Islam*, p. 232). It would be difficult to imagine more absolute confirmation of the legality of prostitution in Islam. Religious institutions also received funding from prostitution in medieval Europe, such as a tax paid to a convent (Rossiaud, *Medieval Prostitution*, p. 123).

190 Darrāǧ, *L'Act de waqf de Barsbay*, p. 79–80.

191 Ibid., p. 80.

192 Ibid., p. 52.

193 Ibid., p. 81.

194 Ibid., p. 74. Open fornication in Cairo's bathhouses was reported in 746/1345 and 1346 (Petry, *The Criminal Underworld*, pp. 136, 152 n. 57). In the latter case a sinful woman had her hand cut off, although the justification for this is not clear.

195 Darrāǧ, *L'Act de waqf de Barsbay*, p. 8. The inscription can be found in Max van Berchem, *Matériaux pour un Corpus Inscriptionum Arabicarum, Égypte*, vol. 1, pp. 369–74. On the Bāb al-Lūq quarter, see Doris Behrens-Abouseif, *Azbakiyya and its Environs from Azbak to Ismā'īl, 1476–1879*, pp. 6–7.

196 Ibn Iyās, *Badā'i' al-zuhūr*, trans. Wiet as *Journal d'un bourgeois du Caire*, vol. 1, p. 25.

197 Ibid., vol. 1, p. 158.

198 Behrens-Abouseif, *Azbakiyya and its Environs*, pp. 19–35.

199 Petry, *Twilight of Majesty: The Reigns of the Mamlūk Sultans al-Ashraf Qāytbāy and Qānṣūh al-Ghawrī in Egypt*, pp. 138–9, 157.

200 Ibn Iyās, *Badā'i' al-zuhūr*, trans. Wiet as *Journal d'un bourgeois du Caire*, vol. 2, pp. 292–3. It is possible, but highly unlikely, that this was another woman named Anas.

201 Ibid., vol. 2, p. 294.

202 Ibid., vol. 2, p. 428.

203 Martel-Thoumian, 'Plaisirs illicites,' p. 286.

204 Ibn Iyās, *Badā'i' al-zuhūr*, trans. Wiet as *Journal d'un bourgeois du Caire*, vol. 1, p. 217.

205 Ibid., vol. 1, p. 260.

206 Ibid., vol. 1, pp. 58–9; Martel-Thoumian, 'Plaisirs illicites,' p. 286. In Ibn 'Abdūn's treatise for *muḥtasibs* in Muslim Seville, women were forbidden to wash their linens in gardens because they were nests (*awkār*) for fornication (Lévi-Provençal, *Séville musulmane au début du xii*[e] *siècle*, p. 101; Arabic text, p. 45).

207 In nights 863–8 of the *Arabian Nights*, a garden in Cairo is the setting for a sexual liaison. See Malcolm and Ursula Lyons, trans., *The Arabian Nights*, vol. 3, pp. 338–60. In Night 36, a garden in Baghdad is mentioned as a place of pleasure-seekers who were accompanied by prostitutes. See ibid., vol. 1, p. 260.

208 Ibn Iyās, *Badā'i' al-zuhūr*, trans. Wiet as *Journal d'un bourgeois du Caire*, vol. 1, p. 57.

209 Ibid., vol. 1, p. 375.

210 Ibid., vol. 2, pp. 281, 287, 330, 310, 317, 367. These assaults occurred between 924/1519 and 927/1521.

211 Ibid., vol. 2, p. 201.

212 Ibid., vol. 2, pp. 222–3.

213 Ibid., vol. 2, pp. 443–4.

214 Ibid., vol. 2, p. 451.

215 *EI*[3], s.v. 'Arabian Nights' (Ulrich Marzolph); Ulrich Marzolph and Richard van Leeuwen (eds), *The Arabian Nights Encyclopedia*, vol. 2, s.v. 'Baghdad' and 'Cairo.'

216 On this matter, see Boaz Shoshan, 'Social life and popular culture in the Arabian Nights,' pp. 50–4; Irmeli Perho, 'The *Arabian Nights* as a source for daily life in the Mamluk period,' pp. 139–62; Irwin, *The Arabian Nights: A Companion*, pp. 120–58.

217 It appears that some brothels could, in fact, be quite opulent. When Sultan al-Mu'ayyad Shaykh decided to build his mosque in Cairo in 819/1416, he ordered marble to be stripped for this purpose from "dwellings, courts, and the places which were [known] as 'houses of joy'" (see Ibn Taghrībirdī, *al-Nujūm*; trans. Popper as *History of Egypt*, pt. 3 in vol. 17 of *University of California Publications in Semitic Philology*, p. 41).

218 Karkh was a commercial district on the west side of Baghdad on the right bank of the Tigris (*EI*[2], s.v. 'al-Karkh' (Maximilian Streck [Jacob Lassner])). It was also an area of entertainment where public women were available (see Fuad Matthew Caswell, *The Slave Girls of Baghdad: the Qiyān in the Early Abbasid Era*, pp. 29–30). Ibn al-Ḥajjāj (ca. 330–91/941–1001), who became *muḥtasib* of Baghdad, wrote poetry about his visits to prostitutes in Karkh. See Lange, 'Changes in the office of *Ḥisba* under the Seljuqs,' p. 159.

219 The "standard" English translation of the *Nights* has long been Richard F. Burton's *A Plain and Literal Translation of the Arabian Nights Entertainments, Now Entitled the Book of the Thousand Nights and a Night*, which, despite the claim of the title, is in unidiomatic and painful English. It has now been mercifully replaced by the translation of Malcolm and Ursula Lyons as *The Arabian Nights*. For this story see vol. 3, pp. 561–76.

220 This word can refer either to myrtle or basil. See Henri-Paul-Joseph Renaud and Georges S. Colin (trans.), *Tuḥfat al-aḥbāb (Glossaire de la matière médicale marocaine)*, p. 11.

221 In Burton's *Supplemental Nights to the Book of the Thousand Nights and a Night*, vol. 2, pp. 12–16; Night 933 in Christian Maximilian Habicht's Arabic text, *Tausend und Eine Nacht*, vol. 11, pp. 345–8. Irwin has pointed out that this story is very close to one included in 'Alī al-Baghdādī's work on the wiles of women entitled *Kitāb al-Zahr al-'anīq*. The author was at the Mamlūk court in the early eighth/fourteenth century. In his version of the story, the man who loses his clothes is a deputy governor of al-Bahnasā, a city some 200 kilometers south of Cairo in Middle Egypt. See Irwin, *The Arabian Nights: A Companion*, p. 165.

222 As the poet says in Night 171 of the *Arabian Nights*,

"Whoever is tricked by harlots can find no escape.
He may construct a thousand forts of lead,
But this will do no good, nor will his castles help.

Women show treachery to all, both near or far,
With their dyed fingers and their plaited hair.
Their eyelids may be dark with kohl,
But men choke on the draughts they pour"
(Malcolm and Ursula Lyons (trans.), *The Arabian Nights,* vol. 1, p. 696).

223 Leo Africanus, *The History and Description of Africa*, vol. 3, p. 874. He also says there were filthy swarms of vagabonds in Cairo, by which he meant certain Sufis. He claims that he saw one of them "deflower a most beautiful woman" as she was leaving the bath at the market of Bayn al-Qaṣrayn in the heart of Cairo. Afterward, people flocked to touch her garment as if it were holy and regarded the Sufi as a man of great sanctity (vol. 2, p. 466).

224 George Bull (trans.), *The Pilgrim: The Travels of Pietro Della Valle,* p. 64.

225 Robert Dankoff and Sooyong Kim, *An Ottoman Traveller: Selections from the* Book of Travels *of Evliya Çelebi*, pp. 393–4; Yücel Dağlı et al. (eds), *Seyahatnâme,* vol. 10, pp. 106, 204–5. We can play a bit with Evliya's figures, assuming that they were fairly accurate. At the end of the eighteenth century Cairo had a population of 263,000 after declining from perhaps 300,000 around the middle of that century (see Daniel Crecelius, 'Egypt in the eighteenth century,' p. 77). During Evliya's time, some 75 years earlier, around 1675, we could reasonably guess that its population was close to 200,000. If half the population were female, and half of them were younger than 15, older than 40, or from the upper class of the rich and powerful who had no need to work, then about 6 percent of the women between the ages of 15 and 40 worked as prostitutes. This did not include the large number of public women who served the army, those who worked outside Bāb al-Lūq, or those who were unregistered. Thus perhaps close to 10 percent of the women between the ages of 15 and 40 participated in the trade. This strikes me as a large—but not impossible—number.

226 Carsten Niebuhr, *Reisebeschreibung von Arabien und anderen umliegenden Ländern*; trans. Robert Heron as *Travels through Arabia and other Countries in the East*, vol. 1, p. 84.

227 Curiously, Irwin states that among the well-off, "Wives in medieval Egypt were accustomed to demand money for coming to their husbands' beds and granting them sex—the *ḥaqq al-firāsh*, or bed fee" (*The Arabian Nights: A Companion,* p. 175). This would suggest considerable latitude on the part of respectable women to dispense their sexual favors as they wished and their ability to have an "open marriage."

228 Dağlı et al. (eds), *Seyahatnâme*, vol. 10, p. 205. Evliya states that when the brothels were torn down the women were banished. How long Cairo remained "cleansed" is not clear.

229 Ibid., vol. 10, p. 389.

230 Ibid., vol. 10, p. 274.

231 Ibid., vol. 10, p. 188 (both columns).

232 Africanus, *The History and Description of Africa*, vol. 3, p. 860. Syphilis had apparently reached Egypt—and presumably other regions of the Eastern Mediterranean—by the late fifteenth century. It was discussed in the Islamic medical literature of the sixteenth century. See Gary Leiser and Michael Dols, 'Evliyā Chelebi's description of medicine in seventeenth-century Egypt,' p. 205 n. 73, to which add Robert B. Serjeant, 'Notices on the "Frankish Chancre" (Syphilis) in Yemen, Egypt, and Persia.'

233 *Description de l'Égypte*, vol. 1, pp. 510, 518.

234 Dağlı et al. (eds), *Seyahatnâme*, vol. 10, p. 190.

235 Dankoff and Kim, *An Ottoman Traveller*, p. 402.

236 *EI*[2], s.v. 'Aḥmad al-Badawī' (Karl Vollers–Enno Littmann).

237 Dankoff and Kim, *An Ottoman Traveller*, p. 425. Cf. Annemarie Schimmel, 'Eros—heavenly and not so heavenly—in Sufi literature and life,' p. 120. The openly lascivious behavior at the site of al-Badawī's tomb may be a vestige of pagan customs associated with Ṭanṭā. See Ignaz Goldziher, *Muslim Studies*, vol. 2, p. 309.

238 For references to comments subsequent to those of Evliya on the presence of prostitutes at shrines in Egypt, see Hamilton A. R. Gibb and Harold Bowen, *Islamic Society and the West*, vol. 1, pt. 1, p. 290 n. 3. Africanus mentions the throngs of visitors to the shrine of al-Sayyida Nafīsa south of Cairo, but he says nothing about the presence of public women (*The History and Description of Africa*, vol. 3, pp. 877–8).

239 Petry, *The Criminal Underworld*, pp. 134–5.

240 One wonders if the great social historian Ibn Khaldūn was not influenced by the conspicuous prostitution in Cairo while formulating his theory of the rise and fall of civilizations in his famous *Muqaddimah*. He arrived in Egypt from Tunis in 784/1382 and spent most of the rest of his life in Cairo, where he died in 808/1406. He brought a draft of the *Muqaddimah* with him to Egypt, but rewrote it there. No doubt influenced by the easy availability of many pleasures in the Mamlūk capital, he wrote, "Among the things that corrupt sedentary culture, there is the disposition toward pleasures and indulgence in them, because of the great luxury (that prevails). It leads to diversification of the desires of the belly for pleasurable food and drink. This is followed by diversification of the pleasures of sex through various ways of sexual intercourse, such as adultery (*zinā'*) and homosexuality. This leads to destruction of the (human) species. It may come about indirectly, through the confusion concerning one's descent caused by adultery" (*The Muqaddimah*, trans. Franz Rosenthal, vol. 2, p. 295, Arabic text *Ta'rīkh Ibn Khaldūn*, vol. 1, p. 312).

241 As Martel-Thoumian, 'Plaisirs illicites,' p. 287.

242 The fact that working women were rarely imprisoned is again evidence that their trade was not a crime. Note Martel-Thoumian, 'De l'équité à l'arbitraire: état des prisons et des prisonniers sous les derniers Mamlouks (872–923/1468–1517),' pp. 211–12.

243 The legal and social acceptance of prostitutes by the highest level of authority in the early centuries of Islam was epitomized by the great 'Abd al-Raḥmān III, the Umayyad caliph of al-Andalus (r. 300–50/912–61). He did not hesitate to have a prostitute from the brothel (*dār al-kharāj*) with whom he was smitten appear in his cortege on a certain festival day when he set out from Cordoba to Madīnat al-Zahrā,' going through the western part of the city and leaving

via the Gate of the Perfume Sellers. This woman named Rasīs proceeded on this day on the back of a mule right between the caliph and his children, with face unveiled, coiffed with a cap (*qalansuwa*) and with a sword hanging from her belt, Lévi-Provençal, *Histoire de l'Espagne musulmane*, vol. 3, pp. 445–6, and p. 446 n. 2.

Chapter 4: Public Women in Medieval Syria

1 For overviews of Syrian history see Paul Cobb, 'The Empire in Syria, 705–763'; Stephen Humphreys, 'Syria'; Anne-Marie Eddé, 'Bilād al-Shām, from the Fāṭimid conquest to the fall of the Ayyūbids (359–658/970–1260)'; and, to some degree, Amalia Levanoni, 'The Mamlūks in Egypt and Syria: the Turkish Mamlūk Sultanate (648–784/1250–1382) and the Circassian Mamlūk Sultanate (784–923/1382–1517).' To these works can be added *EI²*, 'Shām,' *History to 1918* (Clifford E. Bosworth). For the Seljuk period see in particular Ali Sevim, *Suriye ve Filistin Selçukluları tarihi*, and Jean-Michel Mouton, *Damas et sa principauté sous les Saljoukides et les Bourides (468–549/1076–1154)*.

2 On Syria as a place of pilgrimage, see al-Harawī (d. 611/1215), *Kitāb al-Ziyārāt*, trans. Janine Sourdel-Thomine, pp. 3–78. Sacred and historical places are scattered throughout el-Dimeşkî's description of Syria included in his geography appended to Katib Chelebî's *Kitâb-ı Cihânnümâ* (pp. 552–610). See also the recent work of Josef W. Meri, *The Cult of Saints among Muslims and Jews in Medieval Syria*.

3 See plates VI, VIII, and XXVII in Martin Almagro et al., *Qusayr 'Amra: Residencia y Baños Omeyas en el desierto de Jordania*. For studies of them, see for example Janine Sourdel-Thomine and Bertold Spuler, *Die Kunst des Islam*, pp. 158–9; Robert Hillenbrand, '*La dolce vita* in early Islamic Syria: the evidence of later Umayyad palaces,' pp. 1–35; and Garth Fowden, *Quṣayr 'Amra: Art and the Umayyad Elite in Late Antique Syria*, pp. 57–84.

4 See for example Fuad Matthew Caswell, *The Slave Girls of Baghdad*, pp. 54–5.

5 Al-Muqaddasī, *Aḥsān al-taqāsīm*, p. 7 (trans. Collins, p. 6).

6 Ibid., p. 36 (trans. Collins, p. 32).

7 Ibn al-'Adīm, *Zubdat al-ḥalab min ta'rīkh Ḥalab*, vol. 1, pp. 202–3; *EI²*, 'al-Ma'arrī' (Pieter Smoor), especially p. 929.

8 Ibn al-Qifṭī, *Ta'rīkh al-Ḥukamā'*, p. 296. This was a somewhat standard Muslim description of life among the Byzantines and especially the Franks (see below, n. 33).

9 The Arabic here for "they are taken" is *yu'khadhna*, which is feminine third person plural ("the women are taken").

10 The Arabic here for "after each one of them takes a stamp" is *ba'da an ya'khudha kullu wāḥidin minhunna khāṭiman*, which is grammatically incorrect. The verb and the word "one" are masculine, while "them" is feminine!

11 Ibn al-Qifṭī, *Ta'rīkh al-Ḥukamā'*, p. 298. Cf. Guy Le Strange, *Palestine under the Moslems*, p. 491, and Adam Mez, *The Renaissance of Islam*, p. 362.

12 I have not managed to identify al-Ma'arrī the Bookbinder.

13 Clearly an error for Ibn Buṭlān. The writer Ibn Faḍlān was known to Yāqūt, but he died in the early fourth/tenth century. He is renowned for his report on the Bulgars of the Volga.

14 *'alā kullī wāḥid minhum.*

15 *yuzāyidūna 'alayhā.*

16 *ya'khudhūnahum.* Here "them" is masculine.

17 *kullu wāḥid minhum.*

18 Yāqūt, *Mu'jam al-buldān*, ed. Ferdinand Wüstenfeld as *Jacut's geographisches Wörterbuch*, vol 4, p. 339. Yāqūt also records a curious tale in which the women from two places in the neighborhood of Aleppo would seek to commit fornication whenever a tall stone, like a boundary marker between the two places, was pushed over in a quarrel between the people from each side. The men would then rush to the stone and raise it again, so it was "standing erect and firm." Then the women would return to their homes and regain their senses. Yāqūt does not give the source of this story, but he says that he found no one in Aleppo who had heard it (ibid., vol. 3, p. 760; Le Strange, *Palestine*, p. 295).

19 Aly Mazahéri believes the "auction" was the means by which the *muḥtasib* taxed and set the prices for the favors of each public woman according to her age, charm, and beauty. In this way the visitor would know, upon entry to her chamber, what the charge would be (*La vie quotidienne des musulmans au moyen âge, x*[e] *au xiii*[e] *siècle*, pp. 64–5).

20 Alan V. Murray's assertion that "assumptions about the presence of prostitutes on crusade have been misconceived and exaggerated" and are based on a too literal reading of the European sources is untenable as well as unrealistic ('Sex, death and the problem of single women in the armies of the First Crusade,' p. 268). Moreover, the ordinary knight, as one medievalist has stated, was "savage, brutal, and lustful" and was used to having concubines in addition to a wife; see Sidney Painter, 'Western Europe on the eve of the Crusades,' p. 15. For the Crusade of 1101, William IX, the duke of Aquitaine and count of Poitou, left his wife at home and traveled with a bevy of damsels; see James Lea Cate, 'The Crusade of 1101,' p. 348.

21 Edward Peters (ed.), *The First Crusade: The Chronicle of Fulcher of Chartres and Other Source Materials*, p. 54.

22 Rosalind Hill, 'Crusading warfare: a camp-follower's view 1097–1120,' p. 79.

23 Steven Runciman, *A History of the Crusades*, vol. 1, pp. 243–4.

24 Peters, *The First Crusade: The Chronicle of Fulcher of Chartres*, p. 64. It seems to have been common for soldiers to rape the women they seized as a consequence of war or pillage; too common in fact for this behavior to be mentioned very often in the sources. We will see a further instance below following the Muslim capture of Jerusalem from the Crusaders. It didn't matter if the female victim was a coreligionist. For example, Ibn al-Azraq (d. after 572/1176–7), in his chronicle *Ta'rīkh Mayyāfāriqīn wa Āmid*, says that Amīr Dā'ūd ibn Suqmān, the Artuqid ruler of Ḥisn Kayfā, plundered the outskirts of nearby Ṭanzī on the Upper Tigris in 528/1133–4 and raped the women "more disgracefully than even the Franks would have done" (trans. Carole Hillenbrand as *A Muslim Principality in Crusader Times: The Early Artuqid State*, p. 85; cf. p. 96). Ibn

al-Athīr reports that a few years earlier, in 496/1102, the Turkoman troops of Dā'ūd's father and uncle had pillaged the area of Dujayl near Baghdad where they "raped virgins" (*al-Kāmil*, trans. Donald S. Richards, pt. 1, p. 68). The same historian notes that in 517/1123, when Dubays ibn Ṣadaqa of the Mazyadid dynasty, which was centered on al-Ḥilla south of Baghdad, faced the 'Abbāsid caliph in battle, he promised his men the sack of Baghdad and the capture of women (ibid., p. 243; cf. pt. 2, p. 215). Al-Maqrīzī records that when the Khwārazmians, who had been driven into Southwest Asia from Central Asia by the Mongols, ravaged Manbij near Aleppo in 638/1241, "they ravished women publicly in the mosque," and he claimed their depredations were done in the service of the Ayyūbid ruler of Egypt (*al-Sulūk*, vol. 1, p. 303; trans. Roland J. C. Broadhurst, p. 262). Ibn Iyās tells us that when the Mamlūk sultan sent troops to Aleppo in 920/1515, they maltreated the people, breaking into their homes, stealing their textiles, and raping their women (*Badā'i' al-zuhūr*, trans. Gaston Wiet, vol. 1, p. 398). He says the Ottomans did the same when they pillaged Cairo in 922/1516 (ibid., vol. 2, p. 140).

25 James Brundage, 'Prostitution, miscegenation and sexual purity in the First Crusade,' p. 58.

26 Cate, 'The Crusade of 1101,' pp. 351, 366.

27 One might suppose that prostitutes were a greater feature of armies composed chiefly of foot soldiers than of armies composed mostly of cavalry. If so, this might help account for the lack of mention of their presence in Muslim armies, in which mounted archers customarily predominated. It might even help explain the savagery of Mongol troops toward captured women, as we will see below. On the other hand, when Saladin defeated the ruler of Mosul, Sayf al-Dīn Ghāzī, and his allies at Tall al-Sulṭān near Aleppo in 571/1176, he discovered that their camp was "more like a tavern, with all its wines, guitars, lutes, bands, singers, and singing girls" (Hamilton A. R. Gibb, 'The Rise of Saladin,' p. 570). See Abū Shāma (d. 665/1268), *Kitāb al-Rawḍatayn*, pt. 1, p. 355.

28 Brundage, 'Prostitution in the medieval canon law,' pp. 155–6.

29 Vern Bullough, 'The prostitute in the later Middle Ages,' p. 176.

30 Ibid., p. 177.

31 On papal incentives, especially indulgences, for going on crusade, see Norman Daniel, 'The legal and political theory of the crusade,' pp. 8–16.

32 Julie Scott Meisami (trans. and ed.), *The Sea of Precious Virtues*, p. 232.

33 On Muslim stereotypical views of sexual laxity among the Franks, see Carole Hillenbrand, *The Crusades: Islamic Perspectives*, pp. 274–82.

34 'Imād al-Dīn al-Iṣfahānī, *al-Fatḥ al-qussī*, p. 61; this excerpt has been included in Francesco Gabrieli's *Arab Historians of the Crusades*, p. 163.

35 The touching of anklet to earring is a favorite description of making love in Arabic literature. See e.g. Malcolm and Ursula Lyons (trans.), *The Arabian Nights: Tales of 1001 Nights*, vol. 1, p. 505, Night 118, and p. 725, Night 192.

36 Gabrieli adds a note here, saying "This is a hint of the true nature of these camp-followers, represented in the rest of the passage as fanatical hierodules of the Christian faith; but even this metaphor from the market, the request

with the eye (or the coin) of sin, could be understood in other than a literally venial sense" (*Arab Historians of the Crusades*, p. 206).

37 Al-Iṣfahānī, *al-Fatḥ al-qussī*, pp. 228–30; Gabrieli, *Arab Historians of the Crusades*, pp. 205–6.

38 Ibn Shaddād, *al-Nawādir al-sulṭāniyya*, trans. Donald S. Richards as *The Rare and Excellent History of Saladin*, pp. 37, 147, 155.

39 Edgar N. Johnson, 'The Crusades of Frederick Barbarossa and Henry VI,' p. 93.

40 Jean Richard, *The Crusades, c.1071–c.1291*, p. 283.

41 *The Chronicle of Richard of Devizes of the Time of King Richard the First*, ed. John T. Appleby, pp. 47–8.

42 In *The Crusades, c.1071—c.1291*, p. 283, Richard says Ibn al-Athīr noted prostitutes among the Franks at Saladin's siege of Acre and marveled at their devotion, which seemed an act of piety. I have not been able to confirm this. In *al-Kāmil*, trans. Richards, pt. 2, p. 368, Ibn al-Athīr only says that three Frankish women, who had been fighting in armor on horseback, were captured during the siege. He does not mention any public women. Historical reports of Frankish women in armor fighting on horseback against Muslims are reflected in the *Arabian Nights* (see the tale of 'King 'Umar ibn al-Nu'mān and his family' [Night 50] in Lyons and Lyons [trans.], *The Arabian Nights*, vol. 1, pp. 334–5).

43 Sidney Painter, 'The Third Crusade: Richard the Lionhearted and Philip Augustus,' pp. 77, 82.

44 Jacques de Vitry, *Lettres de la Cinquième Croisade*, pp. 49, 51, 53.

45 Ibid., p. 55.

46 Ibid., p. 53.

47 Albert Lecoy de la March, *La Chaire française au moyen âge, spécialement au xiiie siècle*, p. 415; Brundage, 'Prostitution, miscegenation and sexual purity in the First Crusade,' p. 63 n. 16.

48 Oleg Grabar, *The Illustrations of the Maqamat*, p. 115. Grabar refers to Paris MS 3929. He does not clearly specify which scene in the MS he has in mind. His method of matching *maqāmas* with the images in the accompanying microfiches is cumbersome. The one in question seems to be F7 on microfiche 2. The woman is playing a lute. But see also F12 where we find women dancers in a tavern posing like the woman on the aforesaid Fāṭmid bowl. (Cf. David S. Rice, 'Deacon or drink: some paintings from Samarra re-examined,' pp. 29–31. Rice discusses the tavern scene in F7, which corresponds to folio 34v in the Paris MS, and provides a clear plate.) It must be admitted that it is not always easy to distinguish men from women in these miniatures, even by attire. The dress which might have been characteristic of singer/prostitute is problematic. The actual text of the twelfth *maqāma* is rather vague about the women who may be present (cf. for example Amina Shah, *The Assemblies of Al-Hariri*, pp. 51–3).

49 Ibn al-Athīr, *al-Kāmil*, trans. Richards, pt. 1, p. 383; Gabrieli, *Historians of the Crusades*, p. 55.

50 Ibn al-'Adīm, *Zubdat al-ḥalab*, vol. 2, p. 491.

51 Ibid.; Nikita Elisséeff, *Nūr ad-Dīn, un grand prince musulman de Syrie au temps des croisades*, vol. 2, p. 577; Meisami (trans.), *The Sea of Precious Virtues*, p. xi.

52 Ibn al-'Adīm, *Zubdat al-ḥalab*, vol. 2, p. 505.

53 Meisami (trans.), *The Sea of Precious Virtues*, pp. 101–2.
54 Ibid., p. 139.
55 Exactly what the author means by contraception is somewhat problematic. See Meisami's comment (ibid., p. 351 n. 8).
56 Al-Maqrīzī, *al-Sulūk*, vol. 1, p. 58 (trans. Broadhurst, p. 51).
57 'Abd al-Raḥmān ibn Naṣr al-Shayzarī, *Nihāyat al-rutba fī ṭalab al-ḥisba*, trans. Ronald P. Buckley as *The Book of the Islamic Market Inspector*, p. 127.
58 Sibṭ ibn al-Jawzī, *Mir'āt al-zamān*, vol. 8, pt. 2, pp. 594–5. Cited by Abū Shāma, with slight variation, in his *al-Dhayl 'alā 'l-Rawḍatayn*, p. 111.
59 Al-Jawzī, *Mir'āt al-zamān*, vol. 8, pt. 2, pp. 594–5; Abū Shāma, *al-Dhayl 'alā 'l-Rawḍatayn*, p. 111.
60 Ibid., p. 597; ibid., p. 113.
61 Al-Dhahabī, *Ta'rīkh al-Islām*, vol. 44, p. 21. The silver dirham was the basic currency in Syria. A gold dinar was equal to 13½ dirhams. See Hassanein Rabie, *The Financial System of Egypt*, p. 174; Paul Balog, *The Coinage of the Ayyūbids*, p. 36. The reason for the rather significant difference between the amount of revenue generated from the tax on vice at the time of al-'Ādil and that at the time of al-Mu'aẓẓam is unclear.
62 Sibṭ, *Mir'āt al-zamān*, vol. 8, pt. 2, p. 597; Abū Shāma, *al-Dhayl 'alā 'l-Rawḍatayn*, p. 113. Sibṭ protested this action while saying that Sayf al-Dīn Ghāzī II (d. 576/1180), the Zangid ruler of Mosul, had done the same after the death of his uncle Nūr al-Dīn.
63 Sibṭ, *Mir'āt al-zamān*, vol. 8, pt. 2, p. 693; cf. Abū Shāma, *al-Dhayl 'alā 'l-Rawḍatayn*, p. 163.
64 Ibn Khallikān, *Wafayāt al-a'yān*, vol. 5, p. 334; cf. trans. William MacGuckin de Slane as *Ibn Khallikan's Biographical Dictionary*, vol. 5, p. 412.
65 Al-Maqrīzī, *al-Sulūk*, vol. 1, p. 553; cf. idem, *al-Khiṭaṭ*, vol. 1, p. 106, where he says this occurred in 665/1266–7.
66 Al-Dhahabī, *Ta'rīkh al-Islām*, vol. 49, pp. 50–1. It was unusual for al-Dhahabī to mention such events. They must have been exceptional.
67 Maurice Gaudefroy-Demombynes, *La Syrie à l'époque des Mamelouks*, p. 155. The author goes into detail on how Syria was governed.
68 Al-Dhahabī, *Ta'rīkh al-Islām*, vol. 51, p. 55. Women were also forbidden to go out to cemeteries "and so forth." In addition, smoking hashish and drinking wine were forbidden to everyone. Al-Shujā'ī's policy was strictly enforced. Again, it was exceptional policy for al-Dhahabī to have mentioned it.
69 Carl Petry, *The Criminal Underworld*, pp. 151–2.
70 Ibn Taghrībirdī, *al-Nujūm*, trans. Popper as *History of Egypt, 1382–1469 A.D.*, pt. 3 in vol. 14 of *University of California Publications in Semitic Philology*, p. 38.
71 Ibid., p. 50.
72 Al-Maqrīzī, *al-Sulūk*, vol. 4, pp. 1027–8.
73 Bernadette Martel-Thoumian, 'Plaisirs illicites et châtiments dans les sources mamloukes fin ixe/xve–début x^{e}/xvie siècle,' pp. 275–323.
74 Ibid., pp. 280, 322.
75 Described as early as Ibn Jubayr in 580/1184 as a beautiful spot (*Riḥla*, trans. Roland J. C. Broadhurst as *The Travels of Ibn Jubayr*, p. 288).

76 Martel-Thoumian, 'Plaisirs illicites,' pp. 286–7, 322. Here "foreign" woman may simply be a woman to whom the men were not related.
77 Al-Nu'aymī, *al-Dāris fī ta'rīkh al-madāris*, vol. 1, p. 205.
78 Martel-Thoumian, 'Plaisirs illicites,' pp. 291–2, 322.
79 Ibid., pp. 283, 322.
80 Ira Lapidus, *Muslim Cities in the Later Middle Ages*, pp. 88, 154–88, 160, 165–6, map p. 47.
81 Lyons and Lyons (trans.), *The Arabian Nights*, vol. 1, pp. 200, 204.
82 Martel-Thoumian, 'Plaisirs illicites,' p. 286.
83 Ibid., p. 288.
84 See the map on p. 196 of Mouton, *Damas et sa principauté.*
85 Al-Nu'aymī, *al-Dāris,* vol. 2, p. 244.
86 A *sharabdār* was literally a kind of wine steward or butler. In this instance, he may have been a personal assistant to the governor of the city or perhaps was an official charged with supervising taverns.
87 Apparently al-Zāwiya al-Yūnusiyya; see al-Nu'aymī, *al-Dāris*, vol. 2, p. 213.
88 Lapidus, *Muslim Cities*, pp. 62, 88, map p. 47. Mentioned in various places in al-Nu'aymī, *al-Dāris* (see index). On its relationship to the hippodrome see vol. 1, p. 590.
89 Martel-Thoumian, 'Plaisirs illicites,' p. 288.
90 Ibid., p. 286.
91 Ibid., pp. 289, 304, 323.
92 Ibid., pp. 284, 305, 323.
93 An outbreak of plague is reported in Syria in 903/1497–8 (Michael Dols, *The Black Death in the Middle East*, p. 314). It is unlikely, however, that her execution was intended to help mollify God who had, by means of this disaster, decided to punish the people because of their moral laxity. Jān Suwār's case does not seem to parallel that of Anas in Cairo.
94 Martel-Thoumian, 'Plaisirs illicites,' p. 314.
95 Ibid., p. 290.
96 In his geography appended to Katib Chelebî's *Kitâb-ı Cihânnümâ*, p. 567.
97 Ibid., p. 604.
98 Ibid., p. 562.
99 Ibid., p. 563.
100 Ibid., p. 564.
101 Gary Leiser, 'The endowment of the al-Zahiriyya in Damascus,' p. 47.
102 Jean-Baptiste Tavernier, *Les six voyages de Turquie et de Perse*, vol. 1, p. 202. It is worth noting here that Tavernier says that in Persia one could distinguish a courtesan from an honest woman by the fact that a courtesan always put her foot in the stirrup while riding a horse, but an honest woman would only put her foot in the straps attached to the stirrup (vol. 1, p. 300). Was this a sign of empowerment? He also says that in Persia men never danced. The only dancers were daughters of joy who were invited to festivals, and they performed countless gestures to entertain the audience (vol. 2, p. 265).
103 Yücel Dağlı et al. (eds), *Seyahatnâme*, vol. 9, p. 197.
104 This is on p. 474 of Henry Maundrell's 'A journey from Aleppo to Jerusalem

at Easter, AD 1697,' which is included in full in Thomas Wright (ed.), *Early Travels in Palestine*.

105 That is, the pasha's *tüfekci başı*. The pasha was the governor of the province of Aleppo and had his residence in the city. The *tüfekci başı* was the captain of his foot guard.

106 Alexander Russell, *The Natural History of Aleppo*, vol. 1, p. 262–3. The Osmanlis (Osmanlıs) were the Turkish-speaking officials in the retinue of the pasha. The Russells say the Janizaries (Janissaries) were mostly men who lived in a domestic manner in the exercise of various trades and were called to duty in wartime. The city guard was formed from them (vol. 1, p. 324).

107 Ibid., vol. 1, p. 220.

108 Ibid., vol. 2, p. 56.

109 Ibid., p. 84.

110 Ibid., vol. 1, p. 109.

111 Elyse Semerdjian, 'Sinful professions: illegal occupations of women in Ottoman Aleppo, Syria,' pp. 75–6; Eugene Rogan, *The Arabs: A History*, pp. 41–3. Semerdjian also gives examples of court cases concerning brothels in Aleppo in 1660, 1687, and 1776 (pp. 73–5), but these cases concerned procuring rather than prostitution as such. She notes that prostitutes sometimes appeared in court, but this was because the neighbors complained about them, not because they had committed a crime (pp. 70–2). Prostitution was not illegal. It was not a crime in Ottoman secular law (*qānūn*); see Colin Imber, 'Zinā in Ottoman Law,' p. 188. More will be said on this in the next chapter. As we have seen in the present work, the authorities allowed—with rare exception—prostitution to flourish as a legitimate but regulated trade. Furthermore, as we discussed in Chapter 2, what was illegal and what was immoral were not necessarily the same thing. Budayrī's chronicle is *Ḥawādith Dimashq al-yawmiyya*.

112 *Memoirs of Baron de Tott Containing the State of the Turkish Empire and the Crimea...*, vol. 2, pp. 127–8. The agent is described as the "*peseving-bachi* whose office is that of bailiff." *Pezevenk bashı* meant "chief pimp." On the etymology of *pezevenk*, which comes from the Armenian, see Robert Dankoff, *Armenian Loanwords in Turkish*, p. 29 nr. 63. I am grateful to him for bringing this to my attention.

113 The Nuṣayrīs, a Shi'i sect dispersed in Western Syria.

114 Constantin-François de Volney, *Travels through Egypt and Syria in the Years 1783, 1784 and 1785*, vol. 2, p. 100. Volney had read Baron de Tott. He says he had heard many entertaining anecdotes about the business of the women in these villages, but they were too indelicate to publish.

Chapter 5: Public Women in Medieval Anatolia

1 For an introduction to this period see Gary Leiser, 'The Turks in Anatolia before the Ottomans,' and Kate Fleet, 'The rise of the Ottomans.'

2 Ahmet Yaşar Ocak reviews the complex issues in this transformation in 'Social, cultural and intellectual life, 1071–1453.' See also the comments in Gary Leiser,

'Conclusion: research on the Seljuks of Anatolia: some comments on the state of the art.'

3 Ibn al-Athīr, *al-Kāmil*, trans. Donald S. Richards, pt. 2, pp. 271–2. The earliest account of this affair seems to be in 'Imād al-Dīn al-Iṣfahānī's *al-Barq al-shāmī*, written some three decades before *al-Kāmil*. As mentioned, 'Imād al-Dīn was Saladin's secretary and accompanied him on all of his campaigns. Most of *al-Barq* is lost, but an abridgement by al-Bundārī (d. ca. mid-seventh/thirteenth century) as *Sana al-Barq al-shāmī* has survived. In it we are told that Muhammad had a passion for singing girls and preferred an older singing girl to his young wife. Nothing else is said of the singing girl or how she figured in the negotiations among the parties. See Ramazan Şeşen, ''İmād al-Dīn al-Kātib al-İsfahānī'nin eserlerindeki Anadolu tarihiyle ilgili bahisler,' pp. 268–70.

4 Gerhard Väth, *Die Geschichte der artuqidischen Fürstentümer in Syrien und der Ǧazīra'l-Furātīya (496–812/1102–1409)*, pp. 113–15.

5 Ibn Bībī, *al-Awāmir al-'alā'iyya*, pp. 473–4. See Nejat Kaymaz, 'Anadolu Selçuklu sultanlarından II. Giyâsü'd-Dîn Keyhusrev ve devri,' pp. 49–51.

6 On the camp followers and pilgrims traveling with the Second Crusade, see Virginia G. Berry, 'The Second Crusade,' pp. 465, 467, 478, 483, 497, 502.

7 Translated in Edward Peters (ed.), *Christian Society and the Crusades, 1198–1229*, p. 17.

8 Steven Runciman, *A History of the Crusades*, vol. 3, p. 123. Pope Innocent III had commissioned the priest Fulk of Neuilly to preach the Fourth Crusade. Fulk had a reputation as a revivalist orator who had drawn great crowds of common people, including many usurers and prostitutes in the regions around Paris. See Edgar H. McNeal and Robert Lee Wolff, 'The Fourth Crusade,' pp. 157–8.

9 See for example Alexis Savvides, *Byzantium and the Near East: Its Relations with the Seljuk Sultanate of Rum in Asia Minor, the Armenians of Cilicia, and the Mongols A.D. c.1192–1237*, pp. 151–74. Savvides has translated John Lazaropoulos' description of the siege in full in 'The Trapezuntine sources of the Seljuk attack on Trebizond in A.D. 1222–1223,' pp. 103–20.

10 Rustam Shukurov, 'Trebizond and the Seljuks (1204–1299),' pp. 92–99, 108–112.

11 Savvides, *Byzantium and the Near East*, pp. 164–5, and idem, 'The Trapezuntine sources of the Seljuk attack on Trebizond,' p. 112.

12 Claude Cahen, *Pre-Ottoman Turkey*, p. 125.

13 Savvides, 'The Trapezuntine sources of the Seljuk attack on Trebizond,' p. 103.

14 Shukurov, 'Trebizond and the Seljuks,' p. 110.

15 Yāqūt, *Mu'jam al-buldān*, vol. 1, p. 206.

16 Al-Dhahabī, *Ta'rīkh al-Islām*, vol. 44, p. 21.

17 Also called *Kulliyyāt-i Shams-i Tabrīz*.

18 The abbreviated version of the *Dīwān* was published by Badī' al-Zamān Furūzānfar under the title *Dīwān-i kāmil-i Shams-i Tabrīzī*. The Turkish translation was by Abdülbakî Gölpınarlı as *Dîvân-ı Kebir*. See Erdoğan Merçil, *Türkiye Selçuklularında meslekler*, p. 7.

19 Furūzānfar (ed.), *Dīwān-i kāmil-i Shams-i Tabrīzī*, trans. Gölpınarlı as *Dîvân-ı Kebir*, vol. 4, p. 252, vol. 7, pp. 234, 368; Merçil, *Türkiye Selçuklularında meslekler*, p. 127.

20 Ibid., pp. 213, 258, 326, 491, 549, vol. 2, p. 266; ibid.

21 Shams al-Dīn Aflākī, *Manāqib al-'ārifīn*, Eng. trans. John O'Kane as *The Feats of the Knowers of God*, p. 259; noted by Speros Vryonis, Jr. in *The Decline of Medieval Hellenism in Asia Minor and the Process of Islamization from the Eleventh through the Fifteenth Century*, p. 310 n. 92.

22 Because Peacock played the harp, which was not a traditional Turkish instrument, Aydın Taneri, in his evaluation of Aflākī, believes she was not a Muslim (*Türkiye Selçukluları kültür hayatı*, p. 67). Elsewhere Aflākī mentions another woman harpist whose mother was named "Awriyā," which was not a Turkish or Muslim name (Aflākī, *Manāqib al-'ārifīn*, trans. O'Kane, p. 643).

23 For a catalogue of surviving Seljuk caravanserais, see İsmet İlter (ed.), *Tarihî Türk hanları*, pp. 14–59, 79–91, 117–20. For a good sense of the scale of some of them, see Can Binan, 'Kervansaraylar.'

24 Speros Vryonis, Jr. has pointed out that al-Rūmī gave high moral and mystical value to work and that mysticism justified both labor and financial profit ('The economic and social worlds of Anatolia in the writings of the Mawlawi (Mevlevi) dervish Eflaki,' pp. 190–2). Related to this, Vryonis has also suggested that al-Rūmī was "affected by the economic wealth of the mistresses of the centers of carnal commerce." See his 'Sexual relations of men and women as presented in the writings of the Mevlevi dervish Aflaki in Seljuk and Beylik Anatolia, thirteenth-fourteenth century,' p. 581.

25 Aflākī, *Manāqib al-'ārifīn*, trans. O'Kane, pp. 259–60.

26 Ibid., p. 384; noted by Vryonis, *The Decline of Medieval Hellenism*, p. 310 n. 92.

27 Al-Rūmī believed that women were important at every level of society. On his general attitude and behavior toward them, see Vryonis, 'Sexual relations of men and women,' pp. 577–89.

28 *EI*[2], s.v. 'Rābi'a al-'Adawiyya al-Ḳaysiyya' (Margaret Smith-[Ch. Pellat]).

29 As we have seen, most of the early Christian writings concerning the lives of the saints were in Greek. Many, if not most, of these stories continued to be in circulation among the Greek-speaking Christian population in Anatolia while under Seljuk rule. During the long process of the conversion of Greek speakers to Islam, there was considerable syncretism in all aspects of cultural life. It is not impossible that some of the elements in Aflākī's stories about al-Rūmī and prostitutes have their roots in these early Christian writings.

30 Aflākī, *Manāqib al-'ārifīn*, trans., O'Kane, p. 260.

31 Ayşıl Tükel Yavuz, 'The baths of Anatolian Seljuk caravanserais.' Scholarly attempts to describe the functions of the many rooms in surviving caravanserais, and the connections of these rooms to each other, have uniformly overlooked the role of these institutions as brothels.

32 Speros Vryonis, Jr., 'Man's immediate ambiance in the mystical world of Eflaki, the Mawlawi dervish, Qonya (1286–1291, d. 1360),' p. 369.

33 In Taneri's view, caravanserais were the entertainment centers of the Seljuk sultanate (*Türkiye Selçukluları kültür hayatı*, p. 67). Constable has briefly discussed caravanserais as brothels (*Housing the Stranger in the Mediterranean World*, pp. 100–2).

34 Ibn Baṭṭūṭa, *al-Riḥla*, trans. Hamilton A. R. Gibb as *The Travels of Ibn Baṭṭūṭa*, vol. 2, pp. 425–6.

35 *Masālik al-abṣār fī mamālik al-amṣār*, partial trans. Étienne Quatremère as 'Notice de l'ouvrage qui a pour titre *Mesalek al-Absar fi Memalek Alamsar, Voyages des yeux dans les royaumes des différentes contrées*,' p. 358. Near the town of Denizli were the renowned and well-developed hot springs of ancient Hierapolis, which perhaps contributed to local hedonism.

36 Friedrich Giese (trans.), *Die altosmanischen anonymen Chroniken (Tevārīkh-i āl-i Osmān)*, pp. 35–36.

37 Vryonis, *The Decline of Medieval Hellenism in Asia Minor*, p. 350 n. 83.

38 Mehmed Fuad Köprülü pointed out Qāḍī Aḥmad's reference to Taptuk as early as 1935 in *Les origines de l'Empire Ottoman*, trans. of Turkish version, *Osmanlı devleti'nin kuruluşu*, by Gary Leiser as *The Origins of the Ottoman Empire*, p. 106. On sexual hospitality among the Turks, see especially Osman Turan, 'Selçuk devri vakfiyeleri: I. Şemseddin Altun-Aba vakfiyesi ve hayatı,' pp. 216–20. The Arab traveler Abū Dulaf, who composed a treatise in the fourth/tenth century recounting his journey across Central Asia from Bukhara to Kan-čou, the capital of the Western Uyghurs, comments on the sexual hospitality of the Turkish tribe of the Qarluqs. He says that when caravans arrive in their country, the daughters, wives, and sisters of the chiefs and their subordinates offer themselves to the caravanners. If a man is pleased with a woman, she takes him to her home. See Gabriel Ferrand, *Relations de voyages et textes géographiques arabes, persans et turks relatifs a l'Extrême-Orient du viiie au xviiie siècles*, vol. 1, pp. 215–16.

39 On some of these sites, see al-Harawī (d. 611/1215), *Kitāb al-Ziyārāt*, trans. Janine Sourdel-Thomine, pp. 131–6.

40 On this fair, see Faruk Sümer, *Yabanlu Pazarı: Selçuklular devrinde milletlerarası büyük bir fuar*.

41 *EI*², s.v. 'Tamgha' (G. Leiser). When the Il-Khānid state began to disintegrate, one of the self-governing entities that arose in its territory was that of the Sarbadārids in western Khurāsān (eastern Iran). When the ill-natured and bloodthirsty 'Alī ibn Shams al-Dīn became their ruler (r. 748–52/1347–51), he banned wine and hemp for a while and supposedly had 500 prostitutes thrown in a well (Köprülü, *Islam in Anatolia after the Turkish Invasion (Prolegomena)*, trans. Gary Leiser, p. 35). This may have been part of a backlash against the Mongols or, more likely, another example of a new dynasty attempting to justify its authority by taking the "moral high ground."

42 When Baybars came to Kayseri, the townspeople set up a sultanal tent for him in the garden of the palace where the Seljuk sultans often resided. There they attempted to entertain him with a band, singers, and individual musicians. However, as the self-proclaimed leader of the Muslim world, he decided that such entertainment was improper and had them removed (Nejat Kaymaz, *Pervâne Mu'înü'd-dîn Süleyman*, pp. 163–4). This may have been only a propaganda gesture or, as Taneri suggests, he was taken aback by the lively and colorful spectacle of the pleasures found in Seljuk Anatolia (*Türkiye Selçukluları kültür hayatı*, pp. 66–7).

43 Gary Leiser, 'The *waqf* as an instrument of cultural transformation in Seljuk Anatolia,' p. 73.

44 Ibid. The nature of the "shops" among the endowment properties of Ibn Jājā is specified to some degree, for example a painter's shop, a shop in the butcher's market, and three shops in the shoe market (p. 75). Still, almost all endowments included shops whose functions are unknown. Fariba Zarinebaf has mentioned an incident in 1825 in the Zeyrek Başı quarter of Istanbul where a religious figure, a sheikh, and another person rented a shop which they turned into a brothel with more than 200 women (*Crime and Punishment in Istanbul: 1700–1800*, p. 98). We don't know if the shop was included in a *waqf*, but this is at least evidence that shops were rented for the sex trade.

45 Leiser, 'The *waqf* as an instrument of cultural transformation,' p. 67 for example.

46 It is curious that *bāhnāmes*, "medical" works devoted to sexual issues, began to appear in Anatolia in the fifteenth century. Usually translated into Turkish from Arabic or Persian, they contain many folk ideas about sexual relations. They describe, for example, the kinds of herbs one should ingest in order to cause or prevent pregnancy. One wonders if this lore was common knowledge among public women. Research on these works has just begun. They may tell us much about sex and contemporary society. See for instance Şaban Doğan, 'Anadolu Türk tıbbında bahnameler ve Musa Bin Mesud'un Bahname tercümesi.'

47 For the period 1700–1800, see Zarinebaf, *Crime and Punishment in Istanbul*, ch. 5, 'Prostitution and the vice trade.' Sema Nilgün Erdoğan's *Sexual Life in Ottoman Society* is to be used with great caution. It presents a hodgepodge of material, mostly late, with little documentation and no critical analysis. It is noteworthy that prostitutes are features, if not major characters, in several of the earliest Turkish novels that appeared at the end of the nineteenth century. They are used as symbols of the ills of society and—in one case—of European imperialism. Yet they are sympathetic women and are not vilified. See Robert Finn, *The Early Turkish Novel, 1872–1900*, pp. 14–15, 29, 81, 93.

48 Colin Imber, 'Zinā in Ottoman law,' p. 188.

49 Ibid., pp. 188–9.

50 Leslie Peirce, *The Imperial Harem: Women and Sovereignty in the Ottoman Empire*, pp. 201–2; Evliya Chelebi also reports this affair (Yücel Dağlı et al. (eds), *Seyahatnâme*, vol. 1, p. 76); and see *EI*², s.v. 'Luṭfī Pasha' (Colin Imber).

51 In Peirce, *The Imperial Harem*, p. 202. Sanderson also reported that there were no less than 1,000 whores in Istanbul; see *The Travels of John Sanderson in the Levant 1584–1602*, p. 82.

52 It seems that by then prostitutes commonly entertained clients in boats on the Bosphorus. Perhaps the commotion resulted in part from rounding up such boats. According to Erdoğan in *Sexual Life in Ottoman Society* (p. 35), boatmen were forbidden to rent boats to young couples in 1580.

53 Clarence Dana Rouillard, *The Turk in French History, Thought, and Literature (1520–1660)*, p. 249 and n. 4.

54 Dağlı et al. (eds), *Seyahatnâme*, vol. 1, p. 213.

55 Sieur Du Loir, a French traveler who arrived in Istanbul in 1639 and remained there for 17 months, reported that there were no brothels in the city except at

Galata for sailors (Rouillard, *The Turk in French History*, p. 268). He also claimed that Turkish women could engage in extramarital affairs without difficulty.

56 On Galata, see *İstanbul Ansiklopedisi*, s.v. 'Galata' (Halil İnalcık).

57 Dağlı et al. (eds), *Seyahatnâme*, vol. 1, p. 213.

58 Ibid., pp. 159, 223.

59 *İstanbul Ansiklopedisi*, s.v. 'Ortaköy Hamamı' (Tarkan Okçuoğlu).

60 Yücel Dağlı et al. (eds), *Seyahatnâme*, vol. 1, p. 155, and index under *bekârhâne*.

61 See Jean-Louis Bacqué-Grammont, 'The charms and dangers of the Meadow of Kağıthane. An example of a fragmented report in Evliya Çelebi's narrative of his travels.'

62 Şule Pfeiffer-Taş, 'The markets of Bursa, Kayseri and Urfa,' trans. Gary Leiser, p. 197.

63 Dağlı et al. (eds), *Seyahatnâme*, vol. 5, p. 121. On Evliya's travels in Anatolia, see Feridun M. Emecen, 'Notes on Evliyâ Çelebi's travels in Anatolia,' trans. Gary Leiser, pp. 100–7.

64 Robert Dankoff, *The Intimate Life of an Ottoman Statesman: Melek Ahmed Pasha (1588–1662), as Portrayed in Evliya Çelebi's* Book of Travels, p. 98; retold in Dankoff and Kim, *An Ottoman Traveller*, p. 109.

65 Ibid.

66 Ibid., pp. 99 and 110 respectively.

67 Dağlı et al. (eds), *Seyahatnâme*, vol. 3, p. 226, *niçe bin zenâne ve zâniye kirlenüp*. *Zâniye*, or, in the original Arabic pronunciation *zāniyya*, was, of course, the word for whore or adulteress.

68 Dankoff and Kim, *An Ottoman Traveller*, pp. 104–5. Cf. Erdoğan, *Sexual Life in Ottoman Society*, pp. 34–5, who says that prostitutes worked as laundresses in Istanbul in the late sixteenth century.

69 Dağlı et al. (eds), *Seyahatnâme*, vol. 5, p. 115.

70 Ibid., p. 185. In 1660 Evliya accompanied Melek Ahmed Pasha on a campaign along the Dalmatian coast against the Venetians. He says that in the taverns of Split, which was a port on the Adriatic that belonged to the Venetians, there were very attractive prostitutes. They wore clothes of black mohair, just like men. On their heads they wore a black hat that he calls a *tartur-ı eflâtûniyye*, which was apparently some kind of high bonnet (ibid., p. 262). Again public women were clearly distinguished by their clothing.

71 Ibid., vol. 7, p. 183.

72 Ibid., p. 190.

73 Ibid., vol. 8, p. 48.

74 Ibid., p. 238.

Excursus: Prostitution as an Incentive to Long-Distance Trade

1 George Fadlo Hourani, *Arab Seafaring in the Indian Ocean in Ancient and Early Medieval Times*, pp. 103–5.

2 On the dangers of sailing in the Red Sea itself, see John Meloy, *Imperial Power and Maritime Trade: Mecca and Cairo in the Later Middle Ages*, pp. 51–66.

3 On the sea route to Canton, see ibid., pp. 69–74.

4 In the early first century, Strabo claimed that the large number of prostitutes in Corinth was a great attraction for sailors and travelers, and the money they spent on the girls helped make the city rich (see *The Geography of Strabo*, vol. 8, p. 378).

5 On these two works See *EI*[2], *Supplement*, s.v. 'Akhbār al-Ṣīn wa 'l-Hind' (Ch. Pellat).

6 Gabriel Ferrand (trans.), *Voyage du marchand arabe Sulaymân en Inde et en Chine, rédigé en 851, suivi de remarques par Abû Zayd Ḥasan (vers 916)*, p. 122; Arabic text ed. 'Abd Allāh al-Ḥabashī as *Riḥlat al-Sīrāfī*, p. 83.

7 Buzurg ibn Shahriyār, *Livre des Merveilles de l'Inde*, edition of Arabic text and trans. Pieter A. van der Lith and L. Marcel Devic, pp. 27–30. This island appears in a number of later Muslim sources (see Gabriel Ferrand, *Relations de voyages et textes géographiques arabes, persans et turks relatifs a l'Extrême-Orient du viii*[e] *au xviii*[e] *siècles,* index under "femmes").

8 In nights 803–6 of the *Arabian Nights*, the protagonist sails on a merchantman for the Island of Waq, somewhere between India and China. Upon the arrival of the ship, a band of women crowd around the merchants' goods and then, at nightfall, "a huge number of women arrived like a locust swarm, walking with naked swords in their hands, enveloped in coats of mail." The entire army consisted of virgin girls ruled by a woman. They too inspected the goods. Afterward, the protagonist goes off with them in military disguise to their camp. See Malcolm and Ursula Lyons (trans.), *The Arabian Nights,* vol. 3, pp. 205–15.

9 Ibn Baṭṭūṭa, *al-Riḥla*, vol. 4, trans. Hamilton A. R. Gibb and Charles F. Beckingham as *The Travels of Ibn Baṭṭūṭa*, p. 785.

10 Ibid., pp. 823–4.

11 Ibid., p. 826.

12 Ibid., p. 828.

13 Most of these sources have been collected and translated by Ferrand in *Relations de voyages et textes géographiques.*

14 Basim Musallam, *Sex and Society in Islam: Birth Control before the Nineteenth Century*, p. 94.

15 Ibn Khurradādhbih, *Kitāb al-Masālik wa 'l-mamālik*, pp. 66–7. Qumār was Khmer or Cambodia.

16 Al-Mas'ūdī, *Murūj al-dhahab*, vol. 1, p. 192. It is noteworthy, by the way, that al-Mas'ūdī says he met Abū Zayd in Basra (ibid., p. 164).

17 Trans. Guy Le Strange as *The Geographical Part of the Nuzhat-al-qulūb*, p. 223.

18 Ferrand (trans.), *Voyage du marchand arabe Sulaymân*..., p. 66.

19 Ibid., pp. 80–1; Arabic text p. 57.

20 This begs the question, of course, of how common the practice was whereby a host court provided female companionship to visiting diplomatic missions. Their journeys could be long and dangerous. If they did not take women with them, or acquire them along the way, these missions may have expected sexual hospitality to be provided at their destination by their hosts. I have come across no reference to such a practice in the medieval Muslim world, but this does not mean it did not occur. If it did, it would certainly add a new dimension to

the roles of public women or courtesans in society, giving them a noteworthy place in diplomacy.

21 *The Travels of Marco Polo*, p. 100.

22 Ibid., p. 187.

23 Ibn Baṭṭūṭa, *al-Riḥla*, vol. 4, trans. Gibb and Beckingham as *The Travels of Ibn Baṭṭūṭa*, p. 893.

24 Paul Kahle determined that the *Khiṭāynāma* was an authentic work quite independent of Marco Polo and needed to be studied seriously ('Eine islamische Quelle über China um 1500,' pp. 95–6). For a recent discussion of 'Alī Akbar Khiṭā'ī and his work, see Mevhibe Pınar Emiralioğlu, 'Cognizance of the Ottoman world: visual and textual representations in the sixteenth-century Ottoman Empire (1514–1596),' pp. 185–222. I am grateful to Gottfried Hagen for bringing this to my attention.

25 Gottfried Hagen, *Ein osmanischer Geograph bei der Arbeit: Entstehung und Gedankenwelt von Kātib Čelebis Ǧihānnümā*, p. 205.

26 Lit. "the Uncaused Giver" (*Vahhâb-ı bî-illet*).

27 Lit. "the Living One, the Helper" (*Hayy-ı Müsteân*).

28 *Kitâb-ı Cihânnümâ*, facsimile reprint, pp. 179–80. Translated by John Curry in the forthcoming English translation under the editorship of Gottfried Hagen.

29 Constable claims that "few Muslim traders visited Christian markets outside the Iberian Peninsula during the later middle ages," but she provides no evidence for this (*Housing the Stranger in the Mediterranean World*, p. 328). She holds that one reason would have been the lack of appropriate lodging (inns and hostelries) for them in most Christian ports. But profit, not lodging, was the motive for long-distance trade, as was the case for the Indies and China. Moreover, she seems to assume that Muslims would not have taken passage on European ships and does not mention the travel of native Christian and Jewish merchants from the Levant to Europe.

30 Paul Larivaille, *La vie quotidienne des courtisanes en Italie au temps de la renaissance (Rome et Venise, xve et xvie siècles)*, pp. 36–40, 186–93; Jacques Rossiaud, *Medieval Prostitution*, index under "Venice."

31 Larivaille, *La vie quotidienne des courtisans*, p. 39.

32 Ibid., p. 191.

33 *The Four Voyages of Christopher Columbus*, ed. and trans. John M. Cohen, pp. 17–19.

34 Ibid., p. 139. "So began the rape of the New World" in Laurence Bergreen, *Columbus: The Four Voyages*, p. 143; on the sexuality of the natives, see pp. 142–4.

35 Laurence Bergreen, *Over the Edge of the World: Magellan's Terrifying Circumnavigation of the Globe*, p. 101.

36 Ibid., p. 117.

37 Magellan also carried valuable goods, of course, which were to be used as gifts or in trade. Among them were garments of red and yellow cloth, violet silk robes, and green velvet robes, all "made in the Turkish style" (ibid., pp. 245, 262, 323).

38 Ibid., p. 260–2, 264. When James Cook reached Tahiti in 1769, his men also thought they had found an earthly paradise. Because the Tahitians lacked

metal, the women would eagerly offer themselves for a nail. Cook had difficulty getting his men to continue their voyage. See Nicholas Thomas, *Cook: the Extraordinary Voyages of Captain James Cook*, p. xxvi.

39 Shelomo D. Goitein, 'The sexual mores of the common people,' p. 44.

40 Ibid., p. 58.

41 Marco Polo reports on the people of Kūlam, saying, "They are all black-skinned and go stark naked, both males and females, except for gay loin-cloths. They regard no form of lechery or sensual indulgence as sin." See *The Travels of Marco Polo*, trans. Latham, p. 262. A century later, citing a sheikh from Multān in northwest India, Ibn Faḍl Allāh al-'Umarī rhapsodized about the beauty of Indian women (*Masālik al-abṣār*, partial trans. Quatremère, pp. 199–200), and Ibn Battuta said of the people on the Maldive Islands, "Their women folk do not cover their heads. [...] Most of them wear only one apron from the navel to the ground, the rest of their bodies being uncovered" (*al-Riḥla*, vol. 4, trans. Gibb and Beckingham as *The Travels of Ibn Baṭṭūṭa*, p. 827).

42 Goitein, 'The sexual mores of the common people,' p. 57 n. 41, and idem, *Letters of Medieval Jewish Traders*, pp. 335–8.

43 Ibn al-Ḥājj, *al-Madkhal*, vol. 4, pp. 39–76.

44 Ibid., p. 54.

45 Ibid., p. 74.

46 Lyons and Lyons (trans.), *The Arabian Nights*, Night 711, vol. 2, p. 832.

Bibliography

'Abd ar-Rāziq, Aḥmad, *La femme au temps des Mamlouks en Égypte* (Cairo, 1973).
——— 'La *ḥisba* et le *muḥtasib* en Égypte au temps des Mamlūks,' *AI* 13 (1977), pp. 115–78.
Abū 'l-Faraj al-Iṣbahānī, *Kitāb al-Aghānī*, 24 vols (Cairo, 1390/1970).
Abū Shāma, *Kitāb al-Rawḍatayn*, 2 vols in 1 (1875?), reprint (Beirut, 1974?).
——— *al-Dhayl 'alā 'l-Rawḍatayn*, ed. 'Izzat al-'Aṭṭār al-Ḥusaynī (1947), reprint (Beirut, 1974).
Abu-Zahra, Nadia, 'Adultery and fornication,' in Jane Dammen McAuliffe (ed.), *Encyclopaedia of the Qur'ān*, 6 vols (Leiden, 2001–6), vol. 1, pp. 28–30.
Al-Afghānī, Sa'īd, *Aswāq al-'Arab fī 'l-Jāhiliyya wa 'l-Islām* (Damascus, 379/1960).
Aflākī, Shams al-Dīn, *Manāqib al-'ārifīn*; trans. John O'Kane as *The Feats of the Knowers of God* (Leiden, 2002).
'Alī, Ṣāliḥ Aḥmad, *al-Ḥijāz fī ṣadr al-Islām* (Beirut, 1990).
Allouche, Adel, *Mamluk Economics: A Study and Translation of al-Maqrīzī's* Ighāthah (Salt Lake City, UT, 1994).
Almagro, Martin et al., *Qusayr 'Amra: Residencia y Baños Omeyas en el desierto de Jordania* (Madrid, 1975).
Ammianus Marcellinus, *Ammianus Marcellinus*, trans. John Rolfe, 3 vols (Cambridge, MA, 1982–6).
Anna Comnena, *The Alexiad of Anna Comnena*, trans. Edgar R. A. Sewter (Harmondsworth, Middlesex, 1969).
Apollonius of Rhodes, *The Voyage of Argo*, trans. E. V. Rieu (Harmondsworth, Middlesex, 1981).
Appleby, John T. (ed.), *The Chronicle of Richard of Devizes of the Time of King Richard the First* (London, 1963).
Al-'Aynī, *al-Rawḍ al-zāhir fī sīrat al-Malik al-Zāhir "Ṭaṭar"*, ed. Hans Ernst (Cairo, 1962).
——— *'Iqd al-jumān*, ed. Muḥammad Muḥammad Amīn, 4 vols (Cairo, 1987–92).
Bacqué-Grammont, Jean-Louis. 'The charms and dangers of the Meadow of Kağıthane: an example of a fragmented report in Evliya Çelebi's narrative of his travels,' in

Bill Hickman and Gary Leiser (eds), *Turkish Language, Literature, and History: Travelers' Tales, sultans, and scholars since the eighth century* (London, 2015), pp. 33–45.

Badawi, Mustafa, 'Medieval Arabic drama: Ibn Dāniyāl,' in Paul Kahle (ed.) with notes by Derek Hopwood, *Three Shadow Plays by Muḥammad Ibn Dāniyāl* (Cambridge, 1992).

Bagnall, Roger, 'A trick a day to keep the tax man at bay? The prostitute tax in Roman Egypt,' *Bulletin of the American Society of Papyrologists*, 28 (1991), 5–12.

Balog, Paul, *The Coinage of the Mamlūk Sultans of Egypt and Syria* (New York, NY, 1964).

——— *The Coinage of the Ayyūbids* (London, 1980).

Barchard, David, 'Sykeon rediscovered? A site at Kiliseler near Baypazarı,' *Anatolian Studies* 53 (2003), pp. 175–9.

Baron de Tott, François, *Memoirs of Baron de Tott: Containing the State of the Turkish Empire and the Crimea, During the Late War with Russia. With Numerous Anecdotes, Facts, and Observations, on the Manners and Customs of the Turks and Tartars*, trans. from the French (translator unknown). 2 vols (London, 1786).

Barrois, Georges A. (trans. and ed.), *The Fathers Speak: St Basil the Great, St Gregory Nazianzus, St Gregory of Nyssa* (Crestwood, NY, 1986).

Barthold, Vasily V., *La découverte de l'asie* (Paris, 1947).

Al-Baṭā'ḥī, Ibn al-Ma'mūn, *Nuṣūṣ min Akhbār Miṣr*; ed. Ayman Fu'ād Sayyid as *Passages de la chronique d'Egypte d'Ibn al-Ma'mūn* (Cairo, 1983).

Beard, Mary, and John Henderson, 'With this body I thee worship: sacred prostitution in Antiquity,' *Gender and History* 9 (1997), pp. 480–503.

Beeston, Alfred F. L., 'The so-called harlots of Ḥaḍramaut,' *Oriens* 5 (1952), pp. 16–22.

——— 'Temporary marriage in pre-Islamic South Arabia,' *Arabian Studies* 4 (1978), pp. 21–5.

Behrens-Abouseif, Doris, *Azbakiyya and its Environs from Azbak to Ismā'īl, 1476–1879* (Cairo, 1985).

——— 'Waḳf: in Egypt,' *EI*².

Bélanger, Charles, *Voyage aux Indes-orientales, pendant les années 1825–1829*, 4 vols (Paris, 1834–48).

Bellamy, James, 'Sex and society in Islamic popular literature,' in Afaf Lutfi al-Sayyid-Marsot (ed), *Society and the Sexes in Medieval Islam* (Malibu, CA, 1979), pp. 23–42.

Berchem, Max van, *Matériaux pour un Corpus Inscriptionum Arabicarum, Égypte*, 1 vol. in 4 fascicles (Paris, 1894–1903).

Bergreen, Laurence, *Over the Edge of the World: Magellan's Terrifying Circumnavigation of the Globe* (New York, NY, 2003).

——— *Columbus: The Four Voyages, 1492-1504* (New York, NY, 2011).

Berkey, Jonathan, 'Culture and society during the late Middle Ages,' in Carl F. Petry (ed.). *The Cambridge History of Egypt* (Cambridge, 1998), vol. 1, pp. 375–411.

——— 'The *muḥtasibs* of Cairo under the Mamluks: toward an understanding of an Islamic institution,' in Michael Winter and Amalia Levanoni (eds), *The Mamluks in Egyptian and Syrian Politics and Society* (Leiden, 2004), pp. 245–76.

Berry, Virginia G., 'The Second Crusade,' in Kenneth M. Setton (ed), *A History of the Crusades*, vol. 1, *The First Hundred Years*, ed. Marshall Baldwin, 2nd ed. (Madison, WI, 1969), pp. 463–512.

Bianquis, Thierry, 'Autonomous Egypt from Ibn Ṭūlūn to Kāfūr, 868–969,' in Carl F. Petry (ed). *The Cambridge History of Egypt* (Cambridge, 1998), pp. 86–119.
(Editor), 'Bighā',' *EI², Supplement.*
Binan, Can, 'Kervansaraylar,' in Doğan Kuban (ed.), *Selçuklu çağında Anadolu sanatı* (Istanbul, 2002), pp. 227–50.
Al-Bīrūnī, *Ta'rīkh al-Hind*; trans. Edward C. Sachau as *Alberuni's India*, 2nd ed., 2 vols (London, 1910).
Bosworth, Clifford E., *The Mediaeval Islamic Underworld*, 2 vols (Leiden, 1976).
——— 'Shām,' History to 1918. *EI²*.
Bouhdiba, Abdelwahab, *La sexualité en Islam*, 2nd ed. (Paris, 1979).
Brock, Sebastian P. and Susan Ashbrook Harvey (trans.), *Holy Women of the Syrian Orient* (Berkeley, CA, 1998).
Browne, Edward G., *A Literary History of Persia*, 4 vols (1902), reprint (Cambridge, 1984).
Brundage, James, 'Prostitution in the medieval canon law,' in Vern Bullough and James Brundage (eds), *Sexual Practices and the Medieval Church* (Buffalo, NY, 1982), pp.149–60.
——— 'Prostitution, miscegenation and sexual purity in the First Crusade,' in Peter W. Edbury (ed), *Crusade and Settlement* (Cardiff, 1985), pp. 57–65.
Budayrī, Aḥmad, *Ḥawādith Dimashq al-yawmiyya*, ed. Aḥmad 'Izzat 'Abd al-Karīm (Cairo, 1959).
Budin, Stephanie, *The Myth of Sacred Prostitution in Antiquity* (Cambridge, 2008).
Al-Bukhārī, *Ṣaḥīḥ*, Sunnah.com; trans. Octave Houdas and William Marçais as *Les traditions islamiques*, 4 vols (1903–14), reprint (Paris, 1977).
Bullough, Vern, 'The prostitute in the early Middle Ages,' in Vern Bullough and James Brundage (eds), *Sexual Practices and the Medieval Church* (Buffalo, NY, 1982), pp. 34–42.
Al-Bundārī, *Sanā al-Barq al-shāmī*, ed. Fatḥiyya al-Nabarāwī (Cairo, 1979).
Burton, Richard F., *A Plain and Literal Translation of the Arabian Nights Entertainments, Now Entitled the Book of the Thousand Nights and a Night*, 10 vols (Benares, i.e., London, 1885).
——— *Supplemental Nights to the Book of the Thousand Nights and a Night*, 6 vols (Benares, i.e., London, 1886–8).
Buzurg ibn Shahriyār, *Kitāb 'Ajā'ib al-Hind*; eds and trans. Pieter A. van der Lith and L. Marcel Devic as *Livre des Merveilles de l'Inde* (1883–6), reprint (Tehran, 1966).
Cahen, Claude, *Pre-Ottoman Turkey* (New York, NY, 1968).
Cahen, Claude and Mohamed Talbi, 'Ḥisba,' *EI²*.
Cameron, Averil, *Procopius and the Sixth Century* (Berkeley, CA, 1985).
——— *The Mediterranean World in Late Antiquity, AD 395–600* (London, 1993).
Casson, Lionel, *Travel in the Ancient World* (1974), reprint (Baltimore, MD, 1994).
Caswell, Fuad Matthew, *The Slave Girls of Baghdad: the Qiyān in the Early Abbasid Era* (London, 2011).
Cate, James Lea, 'The Crusade of 1101,' in Kenneth M. Setton (ed.), *A History of the Crusades*, vol. 1, *The First Hundred Years*, ed. Marshall Baldwin, 2nd ed. (Madison, WI, 1969), pp. 343–67.
Chamberlain, Michael, 'The crusader era and the Ayyūbid dynasty,' in Carl F. Petry (ed.), *The Cambridge History of Egypt* (Cambridge, 1998), vol. 1, pp. 211–41.

Chapoutot-Remadi, Mounira, 'Femmes dans la ville mamlūke,' *Journal of the Economic and Social History of the Orient* 38 (1995), pp. 145–64.
Chaumont, Eric, 'al-Shāfi'ī,' *EI²*.
Chelhod, Joseph, *Le sacrifice chez les Arabes: recherches zur l' l'évolution, la nature et la fonction des rites sacrificiels en Arabie occidentale* (Paris, 1955).
——— 'Du nouveau à propos du "matriarcat" arabe,' *Arabica* 28 (1981), pp. 76–106.
——— 'al-Mar'a,' part 2. *EI²*.
Cobb, Paul, 'The Empire in Syria, 705–763,' in Chase F. Robinson (ed.), *The New Cambridge History of Islam* (Cambridge, 2010), vol. 1, pp. 226–68.
Columbus, Christopher, *The Four Voyages of Christopher Columbus*, ed. and trans. John M. Cohen (London, 1969).
Constable, Olivia Remie, *Housing the Stranger in the Mediterranean World: Lodging, Trade, and Travel in Late Antiquity and the Middle Ages* (Cambridge, 2003).
Constantelos, Demetrios J., *Poverty, Society and Philanthropy in the Late Mediaeval Greek World* (New Rochelle, NY, 1992).
Cook, Michael, *Commanding Right and Forbidding Wrong in Islamic Thought* (Cambridge, 2000).
Cortese, Delia and Simonetta Calderini, *Women and the Fatimids in the World of Islam* (Edinburgh, 2006).
Coulson, Noel, *A History of Islamic Law* (Edinburgh, 1964).
——— 'Regulation of sexual behavior under traditional Islamic law,' in Afaf Lutfi al-Sayyid-Marsot (ed.), *Society and the Sexes in Medieval Islam* (Malibu, CA, 1979), pp. 63–8.
Crecelius, Daniel, 'Egypt in the eighteenth century,' in M. W. Daly (ed.), *The Cambridge History of Egypt* (Cambridge, 1998), vol. 2, pp. 59–86.
Crone, Patricia, *Meccan Trade and the Rise of Islam* (Princeton, NJ, 1987).
Curzon, George, *Persia and the Persian Question*, 2 vols (London, 1892).
Dadoyan, Seta B., *The Fatimid Armenians: Cultural & Political Interaction in the Near East* (Leiden, 1997).
Daniel, Norman, *Islam, Europe and Empire* (Edinburgh, 1966).
——— 'The legal and political theory of the crusade,' in Kenneth M. Setton (ed.), *A History of the Crusades*, vol. 6, *The Impact of the Crusades on Europe*, eds Harry Hazard and Norman Zacour (Madison, WI, 1989), pp. 3–38.
——— *Islam and the West: The Making of an Image* (1960), reprint (Oxford, 1993).
Dankoff, Robert, *The Intimate Life of an Ottoman Statesman: Melek Ahmed Pasha (1588–1662), as Portrayed in Evliya Çelebi's Book of Travels* (Albany, NY, 1991).
——— *Armenian Loanwords in Turkish* (Wiesbaden, 1995).
Dankoff, Robert and Sooyong Kim, *An Ottoman Traveller: Selections from the* Book of Travels *of Evliya Çelebi* (London, 2010).
Darrāğ, Aḥmad, *L'Égypte sous le règne de Barsbay, 825–841/1422–1438* (Damascus, 1961).
——— *L'Act de waqf de Barsbay* (Cairo, 1963).
Dauphin, Claudine, 'Brothels, baths and babes: prostitution in the Byzantine Holy Land,' *Classics Ireland* 3 (1996), available at http://www.ucd.ie/cai/classics-ireland/1996/Dauphin96.html, no pagination.

Dawes, Elizabeth and Norman H. Baynes, *Three Byzantine Saints: Contemporary Biographies Translated from the Greek* (1948), reprint (Crestwood, NY, 1996).
Dennis, George (ed. and trans.), *The Taktika of Leo VI* (Washington, 2010).
Description de l'Égypte, 9 vols text, 14 vols plates (Paris, 1809–28).
de Vitry, Jacques, *Lettres de la Cinquième Croisade*, Latin texts ed. Robert B. C. Huygens and trans. Gaston Duchet-Suchaux (N.p., Belgium, 1998).
Al-Dhahabī, *Ta'rīkh al-Islām*, ed. 'Umar 'Abd al-Salām Tadmurī, 52 vols (Beirut, 1987–2000).
Dickson, Harold R. P., *The Arab of the Desert: A Glimpse into Badawin Life in Kuwait and Sau'di Arabia* (1949), reprint (London, 1959).
Dio Chrystostom, *Dio Chrysostom* (Discourses), trans. James W. Cohoon and Henry Lamar Crosby, 5 vols (Cambridge, MA, 1932–51).
Dodds, Gordon B., *Oregon* (New York, NY, 1977).
Doğan, Şaban, 'Anadolu Türk tıbbında bahnameler ve Musa Bin Mesud'un Bahname tercümesi,' *Abant Izzet Baysal Üniversitesi Sosyal Bilimler Ensitütsü Dergisi* 13 (2013), pp. 123–36.
Dols, Michael, *The Black Death in the Middle East* (Princeton, NJ, 1977).
Donner, Fred, *Muhammad and the Believers: At the Origins of Islam* (Cambridge, MA, 2010).
Dostal, Walter, '"Sexual hospitality" and the problem of matrilinearity in southern Arabia,' *Proceedings of the Seminar for Arabian Studies* 20 (1990), pp. 17–30.
Doughty, Charles M., *Travels in Arabia Deserta* (1888), reprint (New York, NY, 1921).
Downey, Glanville, 'Libanius' oration in praise of Antioch (oration XI),' *Proceedings of the American Philosophical Society* vol. 103, no. 5 (October 15, 1959), pp. 652–86.
——— *Ancient Antioch* (Princeton, NJ, 1963).
Dozy, Reinhart, *Dictionnaire détaillé des noms des vêtements chez les Arabes* (1845), reprint (Beirut, n.d.).
——— *Supplément aux dictionnaires arabes*, 2 vols (1881), reprint (Beirut, 1981).
Drijvers, Jan Willem, *Helena Augusta: The Mother of Constantine the Great and her Finding of the True Cross* (Leiden, 1992).
Ducatez, Guy, 'Aden aux xiie et xiiie siècles selon Ibn al-Muğāwir,' *AI* 38 (2004), pp. 159–200.
Ebu Bekir el-Dimeşkî, Untitled work appended to Katib Chelebî's *Kitâb-ı Cihânnümâ*, facsimile reprint (Istanbul, 2008).
Eddé, Anne-Marie, 'Bilād al-Shām, from the Fāṭimid conquest to the fall of the Ayyūbids (359–658/970–1260),' in Maribel Fierro (ed.), *The New Cambridge History of Islam* (Cambridge, 2010), vol. 2, pp. 161–200.
Ehrenkreutz, Andrew S., *Saladin* (Albany, NY, 1972).
El Cheikh, Nadia Maria, *Byzantium Viewed by the Arabs* (Cambridge, MA, 2004).
Elisséeff, Nikita, *Nūr ad-Dīn, un grand prince musulman de Syrie au temps des croisades*, 3 vols (Damascus, 1967).
Emecen, Feridun M., 'Notes on Evliyâ Çelebi's travels in Anatolia,' trans. Gary Leiser in Nuran Tezcan et al. (eds), *Evliyâ Çelebi: Studies and Essays Commemorating the 400th Anniversary of his Birth* (Istanbul, 2012), pp. 100–7.

Emiralioğlu, Mevhibe Pınar, 'Cognizance of the Ottoman World: visual and textual representations in the sixteenth-century Ottoman Empire (1514–1596),' Ph.D. dissertation, University of Chicago, 2006.
Erdoğan, Sema Nilgün, *Sexual Life in Ottoman Society* (2000), reprint (Istanbul, 2007).
Eusebius, *The History of the Church: From Christ to Constantine*, trans. Geoffrey A. Williamson (1965), reprint (Harmondsworth, Middlesex, 1967).
Evliya Chelebi, *Evliyâ Çelebi Seyahatnâmesi*, eds Yücel Dağlı et al, 10 vols (Istanbul, 1999–2007).
Fahd, Toufic, *Le panthéon de l'Arabie centrale a la veille de l'hégire* (Paris, 1968).
——— 'Isāf wā-Nā'ila,' *EI*².
——— 'Ḳiyāfa,' *EI*².
——— 'Nīrandj,' *EI*².
Ferrand, Gabriel, *Relations de voyages et textes géographiques arabes, persans et turks relatifs a l'Extrême-Orient du viii*ᵉ *au xviii*ᵉ *siècles*, 2 vols (Paris, 1913–14).
——— (trans.), *Voyage du marchand arabe Sulaymân en Inde et en Chine, rédigé en 851, suivi de remarques par Abû Zayd Ḥasan* (vers 916) (Paris, 1922).
Finn, Robert, *The Early Turkish Novel, 1872–1900* (Istanbul, 1984).
Fleet, Kate, 'The rise of the Ottomans,' in Maribel Fierro (ed.), *The New Cambridge History of Islam* (Cambridge, 2010), vol. 2, pp. 313-31.
Flemming, Rebecca, '*Quae corpore quaestum facit*: the sexual economy of female prostitution in the Roman Empire,' *Journal of Roman Studies* 89 (1999), pp. 38–81.
Forbes-Leith, Francis A. C., *Checkmate: Fighting Tradition in Central Persia* (1927), reprint (New York, NY, 1973).
Foss, Clive, 'Late Antique Antioch,' in Christine Kondoleon (ed.), *Antioch: The Lost Ancient City* (Princeton, NJ, 2000), pp. 23–7.
Fowden, Garth, *Quṣayr 'Amra: Art and the Umayyad Elite in Late Antique Syria* (Berkeley, CA, 2004).
Fück, Johann W., 'al-Azraḳī,' *EI*².
Fyzee, Asaf and Ismail Poonawala, *The Pillars of Islam*, 2 vols (New Delhi, 2002–4).
Gabrieli, Francesco, *Arab Historians of the Crusades*, trans. from the Italian by E. J. Costello (Berkeley, CA, 1969).
Garcin, Jean-Claude, 'The regime of the Circassian Mamlūks,' in Carl F. Petry (ed.), *The Cambridge History of Egypt* (Cambridge, 1998), vol. 1, pp. 290–317.
——— et al., *Palais et maisons du Caire*, vol. 1, *Époque mamelouke* (Paris, 1982).
Garland, Lynda, *Byzantine Empresses: Woman and Power in Byzantium AD 527–1204* (London, 1999).
Gaudefroy-Demombynes, Maurice, *Le pèlerinage à la Mekka: étude d'histoire religieuse* (Paris, 1923).
——— *La Syrie à l'époque des Mamelouks* (Paris, 1923).
——— *Mahomet* (1957), reprint (Paris, 1969).
Gelzer, Heinrich, *Leontios' von Neapolis Leben des heiligen Johannes des Barmherzigen, Erzbischofs von Alexandrien* (Freiburg and Leipzig, 1893).
Gibb, Hamilton A. R., 'The rise of Saladin,' in Kenneth M. Setton (ed.), *A History of the Crusades*, vol. 1: *The First Hundred Years*, ed. Marshall Baldwin, 2nd ed. (Madison, WI, 1969), pp. 563–89.
——— ''Aydhāb,' *EI*².

Gibb, Hamilton A. R. and Harold Bowen, *Islamic Society and the West: A Study of the Impact of Western Civilization on Moslem Culture in the Near East*, 1 vol. in 2 parts (1950–7), reprint (London, 1965–9).

Giese, Friedrich (trans.), *Die altosmanischen anonymen Chroniken (Tevārīkh-i āl-i Osmān)*. In *Abhandlungen für die Kunde des Morgenlandes*, vol. 17, pt. 1 (Leipzig, 1925).

Goitein, Shelomo D., *A Mediterranean Society: The Jewish Communities of the Arab World as Portrayed in the Documents of the Cairo Geniza*, 6 vols (Berkeley, CA, 1967–93).

——— *Letters of Medieval Jewish Traders* (Princeton, NJ, 1973).

——— 'The sexual mores of the common people,' in Afaf Lutfi al-Sayyid-Marsot (ed.), *Society and the Sexes in Medieval Islam* (Malibu, CA, 1979), pp. 43–61.

Goldziher, Ignaz, *Muhammedanischen Studien*; trans. Christa R. Barber and Samuel M. Stern as *Muslim Studies*, 2 vols (London, 1966–71).

Gottschalk, Hans, *Al-Malik al-Kāmil von Ägypten und seine Zeit* (Wiesbaden, 1958).

Grabar, Oleg, *The Illustrations of the Maqamat* (Chicago, IL, 1984).

Guo, Li, 'Paradise lost: Ibn Dāniyāl's response to Baybars' campaign against vice in Cairo,' *Journal of the American Oriental Society* 121 (2001), pp. 219–25.

——— 'The devil's advocate: Ibn Dāniyāl's art of parody in his Qaṣīdah No. 71,' *Mamluk Studies Review* 7 (2003), pp. 177–209.

——— 'Reading *Adab* in historical light: factuality and ambiguity in Ibn Dāniyāl's "Occasional Verses" on Mamluk society and politics,' in Judith Pfeiffer and Sholeh A. Quinn (eds), *History and Historiography of Post-Mongol Central Asia and the Middle East: Studies in Honor of John E. Woods* (Wiesbaden, 2006), pp. 383–403.

Guthrie, Shirley, *Arab Social Life in the Middle Ages* (London, 1995).

Haarmann, Ulrich, 'Miṣr: 5. The Mamlūk Period 1250–1517,' *EI²*.

Haas, Christopher, *Alexandria in Late Antiquity: Topography and Social Conflict* (Baltimore, MD, 1997).

Habicht, Christian Maximilian (ed.), *Tausend und Eine Nacht*, Arabic text, 12 vols (Breslau, 1825–43).

Haeri, Shahla, 'Temporary marriage,' in Jane Dammen McAuliffe (ed.), *Encyclopaedia of the Qur'ān*, 6 vols (Leiden, 2001–6).

Hagen, Gottfried, *Ein osmanischer Geograph bei der Arbeit: Entstehung und Gedankenwelt von Kātib Čelebis Ğihānnümā* (Berlin, 2003).

Haldon, John, 'The resources of Late Antiquity,' in Chase F. Robinson (ed.), *The New Cambridge History of Islam* (Cambridge, 2010), vol. 1, pp. 19–71.

Halm, Heinz, 'Der Treuhänder Gottes. Die Edikte des Kalifen al-Ḥākim,' *Der Islam* 63 (1986), pp. 11–72.

Ḥamd Allāh al-Mustawfī al-Qazwīnī, *Nuzhat-al-qulūb*; partially trans. Guy Le Strange as *The Geographical Part of the Nuzhat-al-qulūb* (Leiden, 1919).

Al-Harawī, *Kitāb al-Ziyārāt*; trans. Janine Sourdel-Thomine as *Guide des lieux de pèlerinage* (Damascus, 1957).

Hastings, James (ed.), *A Dictionary of the Bible*, 4 vols (Edinburgh, 1898–1902).

Heffening, Willi, 'Mut'a,' *EI²*.

Henninger, Joseph, 'Menschenopfer bei den Arabern,' *Anthropos* 53 (1958), pp. 721–805.

——— 'La société bédouine ancienne,' in Francesco Gabrieli (ed.), *L'Antica Società Beduina* (Rome, 1959), pp. 69–93.
Herodotus, *The Landmark Herodotus: The Histories*, ed. Robert B. Strassler and trans. Andrea L. Purvis (New York, NY, 2007).
Hill, Rosalind, 'Crusading warfare: a camp-follower's view 1097–1120,' in R. Allen Brown (ed.), *Proceedings of the Battle Conference on Anglo-Norman Studies*, 1 (1978), (Ipswich, 1979), pp. 75–83.
Hillenbrand, Carole, *The Crusades: Islamic Perspectives* (Edinburgh, 1999).
Hillenbrand, Robert, '*La dolce vita* in early Islamic Syria: the evidence of later Umayyad palaces,' *Art History* 5 (1982), pp. 1–35.
Horovitz, Josef, *Spuren griechischer Mimen im Orient* (Berlin, 1905).
Hourani, George Fadlo, *Arab Seafaring in the Indian Ocean in Ancient and Early Medieval Times* (1951), reprint (Beirut, 1963).
Hoyland, Robert, *Arabia and the Arabs: From the Bronze Age to the Coming of Islam* (London, 2001).
Humphreys, R. Stephen, 'Egypt in the world system of the later Middle Ages,' in Carl F. Petry (ed.), *The Cambridge History of Egypt* (Cambridge, 1998), vol. 1, pp. 445–61.
——— 'Syria,' in Chase F. Robinson (ed.), *The New Cambridge History of Islam* (Cambridge, 2010), vol. 1, pp. 506–40.
Ibn 'Abd al-Ẓāhir, *Sīrat al-Sulṭān al-Malik al-Ẓāhir Baybars*; partially ed. and trans. Syedah Fatima Sadeque as *Baybars I of Egypt* (Decca, Pakistan, 1956); ed. Abdul-Aziz Khowaiter as *al-Rawḍ al-zāhir fī sīrat al-Malik al-Ẓāhir* (Riyad, 1396/1976).
Ibn al-'Adīm, *Zubdat al-ḥalab min ta'rīkh Ḥalab*, ed. Suhayl Zakkār, 2 vols (Damascus, 1997).
Ibn al-Athīr, *al-Kāmil*, ed. Carolus J. Tornberg, 13 vols (1851–76), reprint (Beirut, 1965–7); partially trans. Donald S. Richards as *The Chronicle of Ibn al-Athir for the Crusading Period*, 3 vols (Farnham, Surrey, England, 2005–8).
Ibn al-Azraq, *Ta'rīkh Mayyāfāriqīn wa Āmid*; trans. and ed. Carole Hillenbrand as *A Muslim Principality in Crusader Times: The Early Artuqid State* (Istanbul, 1990).
Ibn Bassām, *al-Dhakhīra fī maḥāsin ahl al-Jazīra*, ed. Iḥsān 'Abbās, 4 vols (Beirut, 1978–9).
Ibn Baṭṭūṭa, *al-Riḥla*; trans. Hamilton A. R. Gibb as *The Travels of Ibn Baṭṭūṭa*, 3 vols in 2 (Cambridge, 1956–72).
——— *al-Riḥla*; vol. 4 trans. Hamilton A. R. Gibb and Charles F. Beckingham (London, 1994).
Ibn Bībī, *al-Awāmir al-'alā'iyya*, facsimile edition (Ankara, 1956).
Ibn Faḍl Allāh al-'Umarī, *Masālik al-abṣār fī mamālik al-amṣār*; partially trans. Étienne Quatremère as 'Notice de l'ouvrage qui a pour titre *Mesalek Alabsar fi Memalek Alamsar, Voyages des yeux dans les royaumes des différentes contrées'*. Notices et extraits des manuscrits de la Bibliothèque Nationale, vol. 13, pt. 1 (1838), pp. 151–384.
Ibn Ḥabīb, Muḥammad, *Kitāb al-Muḥabbar* (Hyderabad, Deccan, 1361/1942).
Ibn Ḥajar al-'Asqalānī, *Raf' al-iṣr 'an quḍāt Miṣr*, eds Ḥāmid 'Abd al-Majīd et al., 2 vols (Cairo, 1957–61).

Ibn al-Ḥājj, *al-Madkhal*, 4 vols in 2 (Cairo, 1380/1960).
Ibn Iyās, *Badā'i' al-zuhūr*, ed. Muḥammad Muṣṭafā, 6 vols (Cairo, 1302/1982); partially trans. Gaston Wiet as *Journal d'un bourgeois du Caire: chronique d'Ibn Iyâs*, 2 vols (Paris, 1955–60).
Ibn al-Jawzī, Sibṭ, *Mir'āt al-zamān*, vol. 8 in 2 pts (Hyderabad, Deccan, 1951–2).
Ibn Jubayr, *Riḥla*; trans. Roland J. C. Broadhurst as *The Travels of Ibn Jubayr* (1952), reprint (New Delhi, 2003).
Ibn Kathīr, *al-Bidāya wa 'l-nihāya*, 14 vols in 7 (Cairo, 1932–9).
——— *Tafsīr al-Qur'ān al-'aẓīm*. Online at http://www.quran4u.com/Tafsir%20 Ibn%20Kathir/ Index.htm.
Ibn Khaldūn, *The Muqaddimah*, trans. Franz Rosenthal, 2nd ed. (Princeton, NJ, 1967), original Arabic text version titled *Ta'rīkh Ibn Khaldūn* (1867), reprint, 7 vols (Beirut, 1971).
Ibn Khallikān, *Wafayāt al-a'yān*, ed. Iḥsān 'Abbās, 8 vols (Beirut, [1968]–72); trans. William MacGuckin de Slane as *Ibn Khallikan's Biographical Dictionary*, ed. Syed Moinul Haq, 7 vols (incomplete) (New Delhi, 1996).
Ibn Khurradādhbih, *Kitāb al-Masālik wa 'l-mamālik*, ed. Michael J. de Goeje (Leiden, 1889).
Ibn Mājid, *Kitāb al-Fawā'id fī uṣūl 'ilm al-baḥr*, facsimile edition pub. Gabriel Ferrand as vol. 1 of *Instructions nautiques et routiers arabes et portugais des xve et xvie siècles* (Paris, 1921–3).
Ibn al-Mujāwir, *Ta'rīkh al-Mustabṣir*; trans. Gerald Rex Smith as *A Traveller in Thirteenth-Century Arabia* (London, 2008).
Ibn al-Muqaffa', Sāwīrus, *History of the Patriarchs of the Egyptian Church*, eds and trans. Antoine Khater and Oswald H. E. Khs-Burmester, vol. 2, pt. 2–vol. 4, pt. 2 (Cairo, 1948–74).
Ibn al-Nadīm, *al-Fihrist*; ed. and trans. Bayard Dodge as *The Fihrist of al-Nadim: A Tenth-Century Survey of Muslim Culture*, 2 vols (New York, NY, 1970).
Ibn Qayyim al-Jawziyya, *Akhbār al-nisā'* (Beirut, n.d.).
Ibn al-Qifṭī, *Ta'rīkh al-Ḥukamā'*, ed. Julius Lippert (Leipzig, 1903).
Ibn Sa'īd al-Maghribī, *Kitāb al-Mughrib*. Section on Cairo ed. Ḥusayn Naṣār as *Al-Nujūm al-zāhira fī ḥulā ḥaḍrat al-Qāhira* (Cairo, 1970).
Ibn Shaddād, *al-Nawādir al-sulṭāniyya*; trans. Donald S. Richards as *The Rare and Excellent History of Saladin* (Aldershot, Hampshire, 2002).
Ibn Taghrībirdī, *al-Nujūm al-ẓāhira*; trans. William Popper as *History of Egypt, 1382–1469 A.D.*, 9 parts, *University of California Publications in Semitic Philology* (Berkeley, CA: University of California Publications, 1954–63).
Ibn al-Tiqṭaqā, *al-Fakhrī*, pub. as *Ta'rīkh al-Duwal al-islāmiyya* (Beirut, 1380/1960); trans. Charles J. Whitting as *Al Fakhri: On the Systems of Government and the Moslem Dynasties* (London, 1947).
İlter, İsmet (ed.), *Tarihî Türk hanları* (Ankara, 1969).
'Imād al-Dīn al-Iṣfahānī, *al-Fatḥ al-qussī*, ed. Carlo Landberg (Leiden, 1888).
——— *al-Barq al-shāmī*, pt. 3, ed. Muṣṭafā al-Ḥayyārī (Amman, Jordan, 1987).
Imber, Colin, 'Zinā' in Ottoman law,' in Colin Imber, *Studies in Ottoman History and Law* (Istanbul, 1996), pp. 175–206.
——— 'Luṭfī Pasha,' *EI*^{2}.

İnalcık, Halil, 'Galata,' *İstanbul Ansiklopedisi*, 8 vols (Istanbul, 1993).
Irmscher, Johannes, 'Die Bewertung der Prostitution im byzantinischen Recht,' in Mihail Andreev et al. (eds), *Gesellschaft und Recht im griechischen-römischen Altertum*, part 2 (Berlin, 1969), pp. 77–94.
Irwin, Robert, *The Middle East in the Middle Ages: The Early Mamluk Sultanate 1250–1389* (Carbondale, IL, 1986).
——— *The Arabian Nights: A Companion* (Harmondsworth, Middlesex, England, 1995).
Al-Jāḥiẓ, *Risālat al-Jāḥiẓ*, ed. Ḥasan al-Sandūbī (Cairo, 1352/1933).
Jamme, Albert, 'Some Qatabanian inscriptions dedicating "Daughters of God",' *Bulletin of the American Schools of Oriental Research* nr. 138 (1955), pp. 39–47.
Al-Jawbarī, *al-Mukhtār fī kashf al-asrār*; ed. Manuela Höglmeier as *al-Ǧawbarī und sein Kašf al-asrār—ein Sittenbild des Gauners im arabisch-islamischen Mittelalter (7./13. Jahrhundert)* (Berlin, 2006).
Jenkins, Romilly J. H., 'Social life in the Byzantine Empire,' in Joan M. Hussey (ed.), *The Cambridge Medieval History*, vol. 4, *The Byzantine Empire*, part 2, *Government, Church and Civilization* (Cambridge, 1967), pp. 78–103.
John Chrysostom, *The Homilies of St. John Chrysostom on the Epistles of St. Paul the Apostle to Timothy, Titus, and Philemon* (Oxford, 1843).
——— *The Homilies of John Chrysostom on the Gospel of St. Matthew*, 3 vols (Oxford, 1854–93).
Johnson, Edgar N., 'The crusades of Frederick Barbarossa and Henry VI,' in Kenneth M. Setton (ed.), *A History of the Crusades*, vol. 2, *The Later Crusades, 1189–1311*, eds Robert Lee Wolff and Harry Hazard, 2nd ed. (Madison, WI, 1969), pp. 87–122.
Joinville, Jean de and Villehardouin, Geffroy de, *Chronicles of the Crusades*, trans. Margaret R. B. Shaw (1963), reprint (Harmondsworth, Middlesex, 1983).
Juynboll, Gautier H. A., *Encyclopedia of Canonical Ḥadīth* (Leiden, 2007).
Kahle, Paul, 'Eine islamische Quelle über China um 1500,' *Acta Orientalia* 12 (1934), pp. 91–110.
Al-Kalbī, Hishām, *Kitāb al-Aṣnām*; ed. and trans. Wahib Atallah as *Les idoles de Hicham ibn al-Kalbī* (Paris, 1969).
Kaptein, Nico J. G., *Muḥammad's Birthday Festival* (Leiden, 1993).
Kaymaz, Nejat, 'Anadolu Selçuklu sultanlarından II. Giyâsü'd-dîn Keyhüsrev ve Devri,' Ph.D. dissertation (Ankara University, 1958).
——— *Pervâne Mu'înü'd-dîn Süleyman* (Ankara, 1970).
Kennedy, Hugh, 'Egypt as a province in the Islamic Caliphate, 641–868,' in Carl F. Petry (ed.), *The Cambridge History of Egypt* (Cambridge, 1998), vol. 1, pp. 62–85.
Khadduri, Majid, *Islamic Jurisprudence, Shāf'ī's Risāla* (Baltimore, 1961).
Khowaiter, Abdul-Aziz, *Baibars the First: His Endeavours and Achievements* (London, 1978).
Kister, Meir J., 'Radjab,' *EI*².
Kleberg, Tönnes, *Hôtels, restaurants et cabarets dans l'antiquité romaine* (Uppsala, 1957).
Köprülü, Mehmed Fuad, *Islam in Anatolia after the Turkish Invasion (Prolegomena)*, pub. as an article in Turkish (1922), trans. Gary Leiser (Salt Lake City, UT, 1993).
——— *Les origines de l'Empire Ottoman* (1935); trans. from the Turkish version, *Osmanlı devleti'nin kuruluşu* (1959), by Gary Leiser as *The Origins of the Ottoman Empire* (Albany, NY, 1992).

Krueger, Derek, *Symeon the Holy Fool: Leontius's Life and the Late Antique City* (Berkeley, CA, 1996).

Landau, Jacob M., 'Ibn Dāniyāl,' *EI*².

Lane, Edward, *The Manners and Customs of the Modern Egyptians* (London, 1908).

——— *An Arabic-English Lexicon* (1863–93), reprint (New York, NY, 1955–6).

Lange, Christian, *Justice, Punishment and the Medieval Muslim Imagination* (Cambridge, 2008).

——— 'Changes in the office of Ḥisba under the Seljuqs,' in Christian Lange and Songül Mecit (eds), *The Seljuqs: Politics, Society and Culture* (Edinburgh, 2011), pp. 157–81.

Lapidus, Ira, *Muslim Cities in the Later Middle Ages* (Cambridge, MA, 1967).

Larivaille, Paul, *La vie quotidienne des courtisanes en Italie au temps de la renaissance (Rome et Venise, xv*e *et xvi*e *siècles)*, (Paris, 1975).

Le Strange, Guy, *Palestine under the Moslems* (1890), reprint (Beirut, 1965).

Lecker, Michael, *Muslims, Jews and Pagans: Studies on Early Islamic Medina* (Leiden, 1995).

——— 'Pre-Islamic Arabia,' in Chase F. Robinson (ed.), *The New Cambridge History of Islam* (Cambridge, 2010), vol. 1, pp. 153–70.

Lecoy de la March, Albert, *La chaire française au moyen âge, spécialement au xiii*e *siècle*, 2nd ed. (Paris, 1886).

Leiser, Gary, 'The restoration of Sunnism in Egypt: madrasas and mudarrisūn 495–647/1101–1249,' Ph.D. dissertation (University of Pennsylvania, 1976).

——— 'The Crusader raid in the Red Sea in 578/1182–83,' *Journal of the American Research Center in Egypt* 14 (1977), pp. 87–100.

——— 'The endowment of the al-Zahiriyya in Damascus,' *Journal of the Economic and Social History of the Orient* 27 (1984), pp. 33–55.

——— 'The Turks in Anatolia before the Ottomans,' in Maribel Fierro (ed.), *The New Cambridge History of Islam* (Cambridge, 2010), vol. 2, pp. 301–12.

——— 'Conclusion: research on the Seljuks of Anatolia: some comments on the state of the art,' in Andrew C. S. Peacock and Sara Nur Yıldız (eds), *The Seljuks of Anatolia: Court and Society in the Medieval Middle East* (London, 2013), pp. 264–75.

——— 'The *waqf* as an instrument of cultural transformation in Seljuk Anatolia,' in Ismail Poonawala (ed.), *Turks in the Indian Subcontinent, Central and West Asia* (New Delhi, 2016), pp. 64–84.

——— 'Tamgha,' *EI*².

——— 'Alexandria: early period,' *EI*³.

Leiser, Gary and Michael Dols, 'Evliyā Chelebi's description of medicine in seventeenth-century Egypt,' *Sudhoffs Archiv, Zeitschrift für Wissenschaftsgeschichte* 71 (1987), pp. 197–216, 72 (1988), pp. 49–68.

Leo Africanus, *The History and Description of Africa*, ed. Robert Brown, 3 vols (London, 1896).

Leontsini, Stavroula, *Die Prostitution im frühen Byzanz*, Ph.D. dissertation (University of Vienna, 1988) (pub. Vienna, 1989).

Lev, Yaacov, 'The suppression of crime, the supervision of markets, and urban society in the Egyptian capital during the tenth and eleventh centuries,' *Mediterranean Historical Review* 3 (1988), pp. 71–95.

——— *State and Society in Fatimid Egypt* (Leiden, 1991).
Levanoni, Amalia, 'The Mamlūks in Egypt and Syria: the Turkish Mamlūk Sultanate (648–784/ 1250–1382) and the Circassian Mamlūk Sultanate (784–923/1382–1517),' in Maribel Fierro (ed.), *The New Cambridge History of Islam* (Cambridge, 2010), vol. 2, pp. 237–84.
Levi Della Vida, Giorgio, *Arabic Papyri in the University Museum in Philadelphia (Pennsylvania)* (Rome, 1981).
Lévi-Provençal, Evariste, *Séville musulmane au début du xiie siècle: le traité d'Ibn 'Abdun sur la vie urbaine et les corps de métiers* (1947), reprint (Paris, 2001).
——— *Trois traités hispaniques de ḥisba* (Cairo, 1955).
——— *Histoire de l'Espagne musulmane*, 3 vols (Paris, 1967).
Levy, Reuben (trans.), *A Mirror for Princes: The Qābūs Nāma* (New York, NY, 1951).
Lyons, Malcolm and Ursula Lyons (trans.). *The Arabian Nights: Tales of 1001 Nights*, 3 vols (London, 2008).
McAuliffe, Jane Dammen et al., *Encyclopaedia of the Qur'ān*, 5 vols (Leiden: Brill, 2001–6)
Macdonald, Michael C. A. and Laila Nehmé, 'al-'Uzzā,' *EI*[2].
Machaut, Guillaume de, *La prise d'Alixandre*, ed. and trans. R. Barton Palmer (New York, NY, 2002).
Magoulias, Harry, 'Bathhouse, inn, tavern, prostitution and the stage as seen in the lives of the saints of the sixth and seventh centuries,' *Epeteris Hetaireias Vyzantinōn Spoudon* 38 (1971), pp. 233–52.
Makdisi, George, *Ibn 'Aqīl et la résurgence de l'islam traditionaliste au xie siècle* (Damascus, 1963).
——— *The Rise of Humanism in Classical Islam and the Christian West* (Edinburgh, 1990).
Malalas, John, *The Chronicle of John Malalas*, trans. Elizabeth Jeffreys et al. (Melbourne, Australia, 1986).
Mālik ibn Anas, *al-Muwaṭṭa,'* ed. Muḥammad Fu'ād 'Abd al-Bāqī, 2 vols ([Cairo], 1370/1951); trans. Aisha Abdurrahman Bewley as *Al-Muwatta of Imam Malik ibn Anas* (London, 1989).
Al-Manāwī, Muḥammad Ḥamdī, *al-Wizāra wa'l-wuzarā' fī al-'aṣr al-fāṭimī* (Cairo, 1970).
Mango, Cyril, 'Daily life in Byzantium,' *Jahrbuch der Österreichischen Byzantinistik*, 31/1: XVI. *Internationaler Byzantinistenkongress*, Akten I/1 (1981), pp. 337–53.
Mango, Cyril and Roger Scott (trans.), *The Chronicle of Theophanes Confessor: Byzantine and Near Eastern History AD 284–813* (Oxford, 1997).
Al-Maqrīzī, *Itti'āẓ al-ḥunafā,'* eds Jamāl al-Dīn al-Shayyāl and Muḥammad Ḥilmī Muḥammad Aḥmad, 3 vols (Cairo, 1387–93/1967–73).
——— *al-Mawā'iẓ wa 'l-i'tibār bi-dhikr al-khiṭaṭ wa 'l-āthār*, 2 vols (Cairo, 1853–4); partially trans. Paul Casanova as *Description historique et topographique de l'Égypte*, 4 parts, pub. among the Mémoires of the Institut Français d'Archéologie Oriental du Caire (Cairo, 1900–20).
——— *Kitāb al-Muqaffā al-kabīr*, ed. Muḥammad al-Ya'lāwī, 8 vols (Beirut, 1991).
——— *Kitāb al-Sulūk li-ma'rifat duwal al-mulūk*, eds Muḥammad Muṣṭafā Ziyāda and Sa'īd 'Abd al-Fattāḥ 'Āshūr, 4 vols (Cairo, 1956–73); first part trans. Roland J. C. Broadhurst as *A History of the Ayyūbid Sultans of Egypt* (Boston, 1980).

Marco Polo, *The Travels of Marco Polo*, trans. Ronald Latham (Harmondsworth, Middlesex, England, 1958).
Martel-Thoumian, Bernadette, 'Plaisirs illicites et châtiments dans les sources mamloukes fin ixe/xve–début x[e]/xvie siècle,' *AI* 39 (2005), pp. 275–323.
——— 'De l'équité à l'arbitraire: état des prisons et des prisonniers sous les derniers Mamlouks (872–923/1468–1517),' *AI* 40 (2006), pp. 205–46.
Martin, Annick, 'Alexandrie à l'époque romaine tardive: l'impact du christianisme sur la topographie et les institutions,' in Christian Décobert and Jean-Yves Empereur (eds), *Alexandrie médiévale*, 2 vols (Cairo, 1998–2002), vol. 1, pp. 9–21.
Marzolph, Ulrich, 'Arabian Nights,' *EI*[3].
Marzolph, Ulrich and Richard van Leeuwen (eds), *The Arabian Nights Encyclopedia*, 2 vols (Santa Barbara, CA, 2004).
Al-Mas'ūdī, *Murūj al-dhahab*, ed. Yūsuf As'ad Dāghir, 4 vols (Beirut, 1965–6); partially trans. Paul Lunde and Caroline Stone as *The Meadows of Gold* (London, 1989).
Matthews, J. F., 'The tax law of Palmyra: evidence for economic history in a city of the Roman East,' *Journal of Roman Studies* 74 (1984), pp. 157–80.
Maundrell, Henry, 'A journey from Aleppo to Jerusalem at Easter, AD 1697,' in Thomas Wright (ed.), *Early Travels in Palestine* (1848), reprint (New York, NY, 1969), pp. 383–512.
Mazahéri, Aly, *La vie quotidienne des musulmans au moyen âge, x[e] au xiiie siècle* (Paris, 1951).
McGinn, Thomas, *Prostitution, Sexuality, and the Law in Ancient Rome* (Oxford, 1998).
——— *The Economy of Prostitution in the Roman World: A Study of Social History and the Brothel* (Ann Arbor, MI, 2004).
McNeal, Edgar H. and Robert Lee Wolff, 'The Fourth Crusade,' in Kenneth M. Setton (ed.), *A History of the Crusades*, vol. 2, *The Later Crusades, 1189–1311*, eds Robert Lee Wolff and Harry Hazard, 2nd ed. (Madison, WI, 1969), pp. 153–85.
Meloy, John, 'Celebrating the Maḥmal: the Rajab Festival in fifteenth-century Cairo,' in Judith Pfeiffer and Sholeh A. Quinn (eds), *History and Historiography of Post-Mongol Central Asia and the Middle East: Studies in Honor of John E. Woods* (Wiesbaden, 2006), pp. 404–27.
——— *Imperial Power and Maritime Trade: Mecca and Cairo in the Later Middle Ages* (Chicago, IL, 2010).
Meisami, Julie Scott (trans.), *Baḥr al-favā'id – The Sea of Precious Virtues* (Salt Lake City, UT, 1991).
Merçil, Erdoğan, *Türkiye Selçuklularında meslekler* (Ankara, 2000).
Meri, Josef W., *The Cult of Saints among Muslims and Jews in Medieval Syria* (Oxford, 2002).
Meyerson, Mark D., 'Prostitution of Muslim women in the Kingdom of Valencia: religious and sexual discrimination in a medieval plural society,' in Marilyn J. Chiat and Kathryn Reyerson (eds), *The Medieval Mediterranean: Cross-Cultural Contacts* (St. Cloud, MN, 1988), pp. 87–95.
Mez, Adam, *The Renaissance of Islam*, trans. Salahuddin Khuda Bukhsh and David S. Margoliouth (1937), reprint (Beirut, 1973).
Montgomery, James E., ''Umar b. Abī Rabī'a,' *EI*[2].
Moschos, John, *The Spiritual Meadow*, trans. John Wortley (Kalamazoo, MI, 1992).

Motzki, Harald, *The Origins of Islamic Jurisprudence: Meccan Fiqh before the Classical Schools* (Leiden, 2002).
Mouton, Jean-Michel, *Damas et sa principauté sous les Saljoukides et les Bourides (468–549/1076–1154)* (Cairo, 1994).
Muʿjam alfāẓ al-Qurʾān al-karīm, 2 vols (Cairo, 1390/1970).
Al-Muqaddasī, *Aḥsān al-taqāsīm fī maʿrifat al-aqālīm*, ed. Michael J. de Goeje (Leiden, 1906); trans. Basil Collins as *The Best Divisions for Knowledge of the Regions* (Reading, 2001).
Murray, Alan V., 'Sex, death and the problem of single women in the armies of the First Crusade,' in Ruthy Gertwagen and Elizabeth Jeffreys (eds), *Shipping, Trade and Crusade in the Medieval Mediterranean* (Farnham, Surrey, 2012), pp. 255–68.
Al-Musabbiḥī, *al-Juzʾ al-arbaʿūn min Akhbār Miṣr*, eds Ayman Fuʾād Sayyid and Thierry Bianquis (Cairo, 1978).
Musallam, Basim, *Sex and Society in Islam: Birth Control before the Nineteenth Century* (Cambridge, 1983).
Muslim ibn al-Ḥajjāj, *Ṣaḥīḥ*. Available at sunnah.com/bukhari.
Al-Nasāʾī, *Sunan*. Available at sunnah.com/nasai.
Nāṣir-i Khusraw, *Safarnāma*; trans. Wheeler Thackston as *Book of Travels* (Albany, NY, 1986).
Niebuhr, Carsten, *Reisebeschreibung von Arabien und anderen umliegenden Ländern*; trans. Robert Heron as *Travels through Arabia and other Countries in the East*, 2 vols (Edinburgh, 1792).
Nöldeke, Theodore, 'Some Syrian saints,' in Theodore Nöldeke, *Sketches from Eastern History* (1892), reprint (Beirut, 1963), pp. 207–35.
Northrup, Linda, 'The Baḥrī Mamlūk Sultanate, 1250–1390,' in Carl F. Petry (ed.), *The Cambridge History of Egypt* (Cambridge, 1998), vol. 1, pp. 242–89.
Al-Nuʿaymī, *al-Dāris fī taʾrīkh al-madāris*, ed. Jaʿfar al-Ḥusnī, 2 vols in 4 parts (Damascus, 1948–51).
Ocak, Ahmet Yaşar, 'Social, cultural and intellectual life, 1071–1453,' in Kate Fleet (ed.), *The Cambridge History of Turkey* (Cambridge, 2009), vol. 1, pp. 353–422.
Okçuoğlu, Tarkan, 'Ortaköy Hamamı,' *İstanbul Ansiklopedisi*, 8 vols (Istanbul, 1993–5).
Oliver of Paderborn, 'The capture of Damietta,' trans. John J. Gavigan. In Edward Peters (ed.), *Christian Society and the Crusades 1198–1229* (Philadelphia, PA, 1971), pp. 49–139.
O'Meara, Thomas, 'The theology and times of William of Tripoli, O. P.: a different view of Islam,' *Theological Studies* 69 (2008), online edition.
Oxford Classical Dictionary, eds Simon Hornblower and Antony Spawforth, s.v. "collatio lustralis," 3rd ed. (Oxford, 1999).
Painter, Sidney, 'Western Europe on the eve of the Crusades,' in Kenneth M. Setton (ed.), *A History of the Crusades*, vol. 1, *The First Hundred Years*, ed. Marshall Baldwin, 2nd ed. (Madison, WI, 1969), pp. 3–29.
——— 'The Third Crusade: Richard the Lionhearted and Philip Augustus,' in Kenneth M. Setton (ed.), *A History of the Crusades*, vol. 2, *The Later Crusades, 1189–1311*, eds Robert Lee Wolff and Harry Hazard (Madison, WI, 1969), pp. 45–85.
Palladius, *The Lausiac History of Palladius*, trans. William K. Lowther Clarke (London, 1918).

Papaconstantinou, Arietta, 'Between umma and dhimma: the Christians of the Middle East under the Umayyads,' *AI* 42 (2008), pp. 127–56.
Paret, Rudi and Eric Chaumont, ''Umra,' *EI*².
Peirce, Leslie, *The Imperial Harem: Women and Sovereignty in the Ottoman Empire* (Oxford, 1993).
Pellat, Charles, *The Life and Works of Jāḥiẓ* (Berkeley, CA, 1969).
——— 'Akhbār al-Ṣīn wa 'l-Hind,' *EI², Supplement.*
——— 'al-Ḥārith b. Kalada,' *EI², Supplement.*
Peters, Edward (ed.), *The First Crusade: The Chronicle of Fulcher of Chartres and Other Source Materials* (Philadelphia, PA, 1971).
——— (ed.), *Christian Society and the Crusades, 1198–1229* (Philadelphia, PA, 1971).
Peters, Rudolph, 'Shāhid,' *EI*².
——— 'Zinā',' *EI*².
Petry, Carl F., *Twilight of Majesty: The Reigns of the Mamlūk Sultans al-Ashraf Qāytbāy and Qānṣūh al-Ghawrī in Egypt* (Seattle, WA, 1993).
——— (ed.), *The Cambridge History of Egypt*, vol. 1 (Cambridge, 1998).
——— 'The military institution and innovation in the late Mamlūk period,' in Carl F. Petry (ed.), *The Cambridge History of Egypt* (Cambridge, 1998), vol. 1, pp. 462–89.
——— '"Quis custodiet custodes?" Revisited: the prosecution of crime in the late Mamluk Sultanate,' *Mamlūk Studies Review* 3 (1999), pp. 13–30.
——— 'Disruptive "Others" as depicted in chronicles of the late Mamlūk period,' in Hugh Kennedy (ed.), *The Historiography of Islamic Egypt (c. 950–1800)* (Leiden, 2001), pp. 167–94.
——— 'Al-Maqrīzī's discussion of imprisonment and description of jails in the Khiṭaṭ,' *Mamluk Studies Review* 7 (2001), pp. 137–43.
——— 'The estate of al-Khuwand Fāṭima al-Khaṣṣbakiyya: royal spouse, autonomous investor,' in Michael Winter and Amalia Levanoni (eds), *The Mamluks in Egyptian and Syrian Politics and Society* (Leiden, 2004), pp. 277–94.
——— *The Criminal Underworld in a Medieval Islamic Society: Narratives from Cairo and Damascus under the Mamluks* (Chicago, IL, 2012).
Perho, Irmeli, 'The *Arabian Nights* as a source for daily life in the Mamluk period,' *Studia Orientalia* 85 (1999), pp. 139–62.
Pfeiffer-Taş, Şule, 'The markets of Bursa, Kayseri and Urfa,' trans. Gary Leiser. In Nuran Tezcan et al. (eds), *Evliyâ Çelebi: Studies and Essays Commemorating the 400th Anniversary of his Birth* (Istanbul, 2012), pp. 195–207.
Pharr, Clyde (trans.), *The Theodosian Code and Novels* (1952), reprint (New York, NY, 1969).
Pilon, Mary, 'Jump in prostitution arrests in Super Bowl week,' *New York Times*, January 29, 2014. Available at http://www.nytimes.com/2014/01/30/sports/football/jump-in-prostitution-arrests-in-super-bowl-week.html?_r=0.
Pomeroy, Sarah, *Goddesses, Whores, Wives, and Slaves: Women in Classical Antiquity* (New York, NY, 1995).
Popper, William, *Egypt and Syria under the Circassian Sultans 1382–1468 A.D.: Systematic Notes to Ibn Taghrî Birdî's Chronicles of Egypt*, vol. 15 of *University of California Publications in Semitic Philology* (Berkeley, CA, 1995).

Procopius, *Secret History*, trans. Geoffrey A. Williamson (Harmondsworth, Middlesex, 1966).
——— *History of the Wars*. Books I and II (Persian Wars), trans. Henry Bronson Dewing (1914), reprint (London, 2007).
Psellus, Michael, *Fourteen Byzantine Rulers*, trans. Edgar R. A. Sewter (Harmondsworth, Middlesex, 1979).
Al-Qudūrī, *Mukhtaṣar* (Istanbul, 1319/1901).
Al-Qurtubi, *Tafsir al-Qurtubi: Classical Commentary of the Holy Qur'an*, trans. Aisha Bewley (London, 2003).
——— *al-Jāmiʿ li-aḥkām al-Qur'ān*, 20 vols (Cairo, 1952–67), reprint (Beirut, 1985).
Rabie, Hassanein, *The Financial System of Egypt* (Oxford, 1972).
Rathjens, Carl, *Die Pilgerfahrt nach Mekka* (Hamburg, 1948).
Raymond, André and Gaston Wiet, *Les marchés du Caire: traduction annotée du texte de Maqrīzī* (Cairo, 1979).
Reinhart, A. Kevin, 'Juynbolliana, gradualism, the Big Bang, and Ḥadīth study in the twenty-first century,' *Journal of the American Oriental Society* 130 (2010), pp. 413–44.
Renaud, Henri-Paul-Joseph and Georges S. Colin (trans.), *Tuḥfat al-aḥbāb (Glossaire de la matière médicale marocaine)* (Paris, 1934).
Rice, David S., 'Deacon or drink: some paintings from Samarra re-examined,' *Arabica* 5 (1958), pp. 15–33.
——— 'A drawing of the Fatimid period,' *Bulletin of the School of Oriental and African Studies* 21 (1958), pp. 31–9.
Richard of Devizes, *The Chronicle of Richard of Devizes of the Time of King Richard the First*, ed. John T. Appleby (London, 1963).
Richard, Jean, *The Crusades, c. 1071–c. 1291* (Cambridge, 1999).
Richards, Donald S., 'The office of *Wilāyat al-Qāhira* in Mamluk times,' in Urbain Vermeulen and Jo van Steenbergen (eds), *Egypt and Syria in the Fatimid, Ayyubid and Mamluk Eras IV* (Leuven, 2005), pp. 441–57.
Rippin, Andrew, 'Tafsīr,' *EI²*.
Rodinson, Maxime, *Muhammad* (1971), reprint (New York, NY, 1980).
Rogan, Eugene, *The Arabs: A History* (New York, NY, 2009).
Rossiaud, Jacques, *Medieval Prostitution* (Oxford, 1988).
Rostovtzeff, Michael I. et al., *The Excavations at Dura-Europos, Preliminary Report of the Ninth Season of Work, 1935–36, Part I, The Agora and Bazaar* (New Haven, CT, 1944).
Rouillard, Clarence Dana, *The Turk in French History, Thought, and Literature (1520–1660)* (Paris, 1938).
Rousselle, Aline, *Porneia: On Desire and the Body in Antiquity* (Oxford, 1988).
Rubin, Uri, '"Al-Walad li-l-Firāsh," on the Islamic campaign against "Zinā"',' *Studia Islamica* 78 (1993), pp. 5–26.
Al-Rūmī, Jalāl al-Dīn, *Kulliyyāt-i Shams-i Tabrīz*, ed. Badīʿ al-Zamān Furūzānfar, 3 vols in 1 (Tehran, 1977).
——— *Dīwān-i kāmil-i Shams-i Tabrīzī*, 3 vols in 1 (Tehran, 198?); Turkish trans. Abdülbakî Gölpınarlı as *Dîvân-ı Kebir*, 1st ed., 1957–60, 7 vols (Ankara, 1992).

Runciman, Steven, *The Emperor Romanus Lecapenus and his Reign: A Study of Tenth-Century Byzantium* (1929), reprint (Cambridge, 1995).
——— *Byzantine Civilization* (1933), reprint (Cleveland, OH, 1970).
——— *A History of the Crusades* (1954), reprint, 3 vols (Harmondsworth, Middlesex, 1965).
Ruska, Julius, 'al-Durr,' *EI*².
Russell, Alexander, *The Natural History of Aleppo*, 2nd rev. ed. Patrick Russell, 2 vols (London, 1794).
Russell, James, 'The Persian invasions of Syria/Palestine and Asia Minor in the reign of Heraclius: archaeological, numismatic and epigraphic evidence,' in *The Dark Centuries of Byzantium (7th–9th c.)* (Athens, 2001), pp. 41–71.
Ṣan'ānī, Muḥammad ibn Ismā'īl, *Subul al-salām*, 4 vols (Beirut, 1998).
Sanders, Paula, *Ritual, Politics, and the City in Fatimid Cairo* (Albany, NY, 1994).
——— 'The Fāṭimid state, 969–1171,' in Carl F. Petry (ed.), *The Cambridge History of Egypt* (Cambridge, 1998), vol. 1, pp. 151–74.
Sanderson, John, *The Travels of John Sanderson in the Levant 1584–1602*, ed. William Foster (London, 1931).
Savvides, Alexis, *Byzantium and the Near East: Its Relations with the Seljuk Sultanate of Rum in Asia Minor, the Armenians of Cilicia, and the Mongols A.D. c.1192–1237* (Thessaloniki, 1981).
——— 'The Trapezuntine sources of the Seljuk attack on Trebizond in A.D. 1222–1223,' *Ἀρχεῖον Πόντου (Pontic Archive)* 43 (1990–1), pp. 103–20.
Schacht, Joseph, *The Origins of Muhammadan Jurisprudence* (Oxford, 1967).
——— 'Zinā',' *EI*¹.
Schiltberger, Johann, *The Bondage and Travels of Johann Schiltberger*, trans. John Buchan Telfer (London, 1879).
Schimmel, Annemarie, 'Eros—heavenly and not so heavenly—in Sufi literature and life,' in Afaf Lutfi al-Sayyid-Marsot (ed.), *Society and the Sexes in Medieval Islam* (Malibu, CA, 1979), pp. 119–41.
Scott, Samuel Parsons (trans. and ed.), *The Civil Law*, 17 vols (Cincinnati, OH, 1932).
Semerdjian, Elyse, 'Sinful professions: illegal occupations of women in Ottoman Aleppo, Syria,' *Hawwa* 1 (2003), pp. 60–85.
Serjeant, Robert B., 'Notices on the "Frankish Chancre" (Syphilis) in Yemen, Egypt, and Persia,' *Journal of Semitic Studies* 10 (1965), pp. 241–52.
Şeşen, Ramazan, "İmād al-Dīn al-Kātib al-İsfahānī'nin eserlerindeki Anadolu tarihiyle ilgili bahisler,' *Selçuklu Araştırmaları Dergisi* 3 (1971), pp. 249–369.
——— *Salâhaddîn devrinde Eyyûbîler devleti* (Istanbul, 1983).
Setton, Kenneth M., *The Papacy and the Levant (1204 – 1571)*, 4 vols (Philadelphia, PA, 1976–84).
Sevim, Ali, *Suriye ve Filistin Selçuluları tarihi* (Ankara, 1983).
Shah, Amina, *The Assemblies of Al-Hariri* (London, 1981).
Shahîd, Irfan, *The Martyrs of Najrân* (Brussels, 1971).
——— *Byzantium and the Arabs in the Sixth Century* (Washington, 1995).
——— "Ukāẓ,' *EI*².
Al-Shayzarī, 'Abd al-Raḥmān ibn Naṣr, *Nihāyat al-rutba fī ṭalab al-ḥisba*; trans. Ronald P. Buckley as *The Book of the Islamic Market Inspector* (Oxford, 1999).

Shoshan, Boaz, *Popular Culture in Medieval Cairo* (Cambridge, 1993).
——— 'Social life and popular culture in the *Arabian Nights*,' in Ulrich Marzolph and Richard van Leeuwen (eds), *The Arabian Nights Encyclopedia* (Santa Barbara, CA, 2004), vol. 1, pp. 50–4.
Shukurov, Rustam, 'Trebizond and the Seljuks (1204–1299),' *Mésogeios* 25–6 (2005), pp. 71–136.
Al-Sijistānī, Abū Dā'ūd, *Kitāb al-Sunan*. Available at Sunnah.com.
Al-Sīrāfī, Abū Zayd Ḥasan, *Riḥlat al-Sīrāfī*, ed. 'Abd Allāh al-Ḥabashī (Abu Dhabi, 1999).
Smith, Margaret and Charles Pellat, 'Rābi'a al-'Adawiyya al-Ḳaysiyya,' *EI*².
Smith, William Robertson, *The Religion of the Semites* (1894), reprint (New York, NY, 1972).
——— *Kinship and Marriage in Early Arabia* (1903), reprint (Boston, MA, n.d.).
Smoor, Pieter, 'al-Ma'arrī,' *EI*².
Sourdel-Thomine, Janine and Bertold Spuler, *Die Kunst des Islam* (Berlin, 1973).
Southgate, Horatio, *Narrative of a Tour through Armenia, Kurdistan, Persia and Mesopotamia*, 2 vols (London, 1840).
Stehly, Ralph, 'Un problème de théologie islamique: la définition des fautes graves (*kabā'ir*),' *Revue des Études Islamiques* 65 (1977), pp. 165–81.
Stewart, Angus Donal, *The Armenian Kingdom and the Mamluks: War and Diplomacy during the Reigns of Het'um II (1289–1307)*, (Leiden, 2001).
Stewart, Devin, 'Sex and Sexuality,' in Jane Dammen McAuliffe (ed.), *Encyclopaedia of the Qur'ān*, 6 vols (Leiden, 2001–6).
Stillman, Yedida, *Arab Dress from the Dawn of Islam to Modern Times* (Leiden, 2003).
Strabo, *The Geography of Strabo*, trans. Horace Leonard Jones, 8 vols (1928), reprint (Cambridge, MA, 1960–9).
Strayer, Joseph R., 'The Crusades of Louis IX,' in Kenneth M. Setton (ed.), *A History of the Crusades*, vol. 2, *The Later Crusades, 1189–1311*, eds Robert Lee Wolff and Harry Hazard, 2nd ed. (Madison, WI, 1969), pp. 487–518.
Streck, Maximilian and Jacob Lassner, 'al-Karkh,' *EI*².
Sullivan, Amy, 'Cracking down on the Super Bowl sex trade,' *Time*, February 6, 2011. Available at http://content.time.com/time/nation/article/0,8599,2046568,00.html.
Sümer, Faruk, *Yabanlu Pazarı: Selçuklular devrinde milletlerarası büyük bir fuar* (Istanbul, 1985).
Al-Ṭabarī, *The History of al-Ṭabarī*; vol. 5 trans. Clifford E. Bosworth as *The Sāsānids, the Byzantines, the Lakhmids, and Yemen* (Albany, NY, 1999); vol. 6 trans. William Montgomery Watt and Michael V. McDonald as *Muhammad at Mecca* (Albany, NY, 1989); vol. 9 trans. Ismail Poonawala as *The Last Years of the Prophet: The Formation of the State A.D. 630–632/A.H. 8–11* (Albany, NY, 1990).
——— *Jāmi' al-bayān*, ed. 'Abd Allāh ibn 'Abd al-Muḥsin al-Turkī, 26 vols (Cairo, 1422/2001).
Taneri, Aydın, *Türkiye Selçukluları kültür hayatı* (Konya, 1978).
Tavernier, Jean-Baptiste, *Les six voyages de Turquie et de Perse*, ed. Stéphane Yerasimos, 2 vols (Paris, 1981).

Al-Thaʿālibī, *Laṭāʾif al-maʿārif*; trans. Clifford E. Bosworth as *The Book of Curious and Entertaining Information* (Edinburgh, 1968).

Thomas, Nicholas, *Cook: the Extraordinary Voyages of Captain James Cook* (New York, NY, 2003).

Thorau, Peter, *The Lion of Egypt: Sultan Baybars I and the Near East in the Thirteenth Century*, trans. Peter M. Holt (London, 1992).

Turan, Osman, 'Selçuk devri vakfiyeleri: I. Şemseddin Altun-Aba vakfiyesi ve Hayatı,' *Belleten* 11 (1947), pp. 197–235.

Valle, Pietro Della, *The Pilgrim: The Travels of Pietro Della Valle*, trans., abridged, and introduced by George Bull (London, 1989).

Van Cleve, Thomas C., 'The Fifth Crusade,' in Kenneth M. Setton (ed.), *A History of the Crusades*, vol. 2, *The Later Crusades, 1189–1311*, eds Robert Lee Wolff and Harry Hazard, 2nd ed. (Madison, WI, 1969), pp. 377–428.

Väth, Gerhard, *Die Geschichte der artuqidischen Fürstentümer in Syrien und der Ǧazīra'l-Furātīya (496–812/1102–1409)* (Berlin, 1987).

Vollers, Karl and Enno Littmann, 'Aḥmad al-Badawī,' *EI*².

Volney, Constantin-François de, *Travels through Egypt and Syria in the Years 1783, 1784 and 1785*, trans. from the French, 2 vols (New York, NY, 1798).

Vryonis, Speros, Jr., *The Decline of Medieval Hellenism in Asia Minor and the Process of Islamization from the Eleventh through the Fifteenth Century* (1971), 2nd rev. ed. (New York, NY, 2011).

——— 'Man's immediate ambiance in the mystical world of Eflaki, the Mawlawi Dervish, Qonya (1286–1291, d. 1360),' *Σύμμειχτα (Symmeikta)* 9 (1994), pp. 365–77.

——— 'The panēgyris of the Byzantine saint: a study in the nature of a medieval institution, its origins and fate,' in idem, *Byzantine Institutions, Society and Culture*, vol. 1, *The Imperial Institution and Society* (New York, NY, 1997), pp. 251–92.

——— 'The economic and social worlds of Anatolia in the writings of the Mawlawi (Mevlevi) Dervish Eflaki,' in Jayne Warner (ed.), *Cultural Horizons: a Festschrift in Honor of Talat S. Halman* (Syracuse, NY, 2001), pp. 188–97.

——— 'Sexual relations of men and women as presented in the writings of the Mevlevi dervish Aflaki in Seljuk and Beylik Anatolia, thirteenth-fourteenth century,' in *Polyptychon: Homenaje a Ioannis Hassiotis* (Granada, 2008), pp. 577–89.

Walker, Paul, 'The Ismāʿīlī daʿwa and the Fāṭimid caliphate,' in Carl F. Petry (ed.), *The Cambridge History of Egypt* (Cambridge, 1998), vol. 1, pp. 120–50.

Walmsley, Alan, 'Byzantine Palestine and Arabia: urban prosperity in late Antiquity,' in Neil Christie and Simon Loseby (eds), *Towns in Transition: Urban Evolution in Late Antiquity and the Early Middle Ages* (London, 1996), pp. 126–58.

Ward, Benedicta (trans.), *The Sayings of the Desert Fathers: The Alphabetical Collection* (Kalamazoo, MI, 1984).

——— *Harlots of the Desert* (London, 1987).

Watt, William Montgomery, *Muhammad at Medina* (Oxford, 1956).

——— ''Ā'isha,' *EI*².

——— et al., 'Makka,' *EI*².

Wehr, Hans, *A Dictionary of Modern Written Arabic* (Ithaca, NY, 1966).

Weintritt, Otfried, 'Rawḍa,' *EI*².

Wellhausen, Julius, 'Die Ehe bei den Arabern,' *Nachrichten von der Königlichen Gesellschaft der Wissenschaften und der Georg-Augustus-Universität zu Göttingen*, nr. 11 (1893), pp. 431–81.

——— *Reste arabischen Heidentums*, 2nd ed. (Berlin, 1897).

Whittow, Mark, 'The late Roman/early Byzantine Near East,' in Chase F. Robinson (ed.), *The New Cambridge History of Islam* (Cambridge, 2010), vol. 1, pp. 72–97.

Wild, Stefan, 'Jugglers and fraudulent Sufis,' in *Proceedings of the VIth Congress of Arabic and Islamic Studies* (Stockholm, 1972), pp. 58–63.

——— 'al-Djawbarī,' *EI*², *Supplement*.

Wilkinson, John, 'Jerusalem under Rome and Byzantium 63 BC–637 AD,' in Kamil J. Asali (ed.), *Jerusalem in History* (New York, NY, 2000), pp. 75–104.

Xenophon, *The Persian Expedition*, trans. Rex Warner (Harmondsworth, Middlesex, 1979).

Yāqūt, *Muʿjam al-buldān*; ed. Ferdinand Wüstenfeld as *Jacut's Geographisches Wörterbuch*, 6 vols (Leipzig, 1866–73).

Yavuz, Ayşıl Tükel, 'The baths of Anatolian Seljuk caravanserais,' in Nina Ergin (ed.), *Bathing Culture of Anatolian Civilizations: Architecture, History, and Imagination* (Leuven, 2011), pp. 77–141.

Zarinebaf, Fariba, *Crime and Punishment in Istanbul: 1700–1800* (Berkeley, CA, 2010).

Index

Venice
  prostitution in 246–7
Vitalios, monk 14–15, 258 *n.* 18

wakāla 142
wālī 105, 127, 129, 132, 140, 146–8, 150, 173–4, 198, 282 *n.* 121
wālī 'l-shurṭa 122, 194
William of Tripoli, Dominican friar 119–20

Zangī, Muslim ruler in Syria 188
zinā' 68, 76, 270 *n.* 90–1, 270 *n.* 93, 286 *n.* 188, 290 *n.* 240
Ziyād ibn Abīhi, governor of Iraq under Mu'āwiya 52–3, 57, 264 *n.* 16
Zosimas, St. 13